PEOPLE, MARKETS, GOODS:
ECONOMIES AND SOCIETIES IN HISTORY

Volume 4

The First Century of Welfare

PEOPLE, MARKETS, GOODS:
ECONOMIES AND SOCIETIES IN HISTORY

ISSN: 2051–7467

Series editors
Barry Doyle – University of Huddersfield
Nigel R. Goose – University of Hertfordshire
Steve Hindle – The Huntington Library
Jane Humphries – University of Oxford
Kevin O'Rourke – University of Oxford

The interactions of economy and society, people and goods, transactions and actions are at the root of most human behaviours. Economic and social historians are participants in the same conversation about how markets have developed historically and how they have been constituted by economic actors and agencies in various social, institutional and geographical contexts. New debates now underpin much research in economic and social, cultural, demographic, urban and political history. Their themes have enduring resonance – financial stability and instability, the costs of health and welfare, the implications of poverty and riches, flows of trade and the centrality of communications. This new paperback series aims to attract historians interested in economics and economists with an interest in history by publishing high quality, cutting edge academic research in the broad field of economic and social history from the late medieval/early modern period to the present day. It encourages the interaction of qualitative and quantitative methods through both excellent monographs and collections offering path-breaking overviews of key research concerns. Taking as its benchmark international relevance and excellence it is open to scholars and subjects of any geographical areas from the case study to the multi-nation comparison.

PREVIOUS TITLES

1. *Landlords and Tenants in Britain, 1440–1660: Tawney's* Agrarian Problem *Revisited*, edited by Jane Whittle, 2013

2. *Child Workers and Industrial Health in Britain, 1780–1850*, Peter Kirby, 2013

3. *Publishing Business in Eighteenth-Century England*, James Raven, 2014

The First Century of Welfare

Poverty and Poor Relief in Lancashire, 1620–1730

Jonathan Healey

THE BOYDELL PRESS

© Jonathan Healey 2014

All Rights Reserved. Except as permitted under current legislation
no part of this work may be photocopied, stored in a retrieval system,
published, performed in public, adapted, broadcast,
transmitted, recorded or reproduced in any form or by any means,
without the prior permission of the copyright owner

The right of Jonathan Healey to be identified as
the author of this work has been asserted in accordance with
sections 77 and 78 of the Copyright, Designs and Patents Act 1988

First published 2014
The Boydell Press, Woodbridge

ISBN 978 1 84383 956 9

The Boydell Press is an imprint of Boydell & Brewer Ltd
PO Box 9, Woodbridge, Suffolk IP12 3DF, UK
and of Boydell & Brewer Inc.
668 Mt Hope Avenue, Rochester, NY 14620-2731, USA
website: www.boydellandbrewer.com

A catalogue record for this book is available
from the British Library

The publisher has no responsibility for the continued existence or accuracy of URLs for
external or third-party internet websites referred to in this book, and does not guarantee
that any content on such websites is, or will remain, accurate or appropriate.

This publication is printed on acid-free paper

Typeset by BBR, Sheffield

For my family

Contents

List of Figures   ix
List of Tables   xi
Preface   xii
List of Abbreviations   xvi

Prologue: Becoming Poor   1

Introduction: The First Century of Welfare   4
   Marginality and misfortune: poverty in the first century of
     welfare   12
   Historians and the poor   15
   Conclusion: 'deserving' poverty   25

PART I: CONTEXTS

1. Lancashire, 1600–1730: A Developing Society   29
   Landscape and people   34
   Population and demography   37
   Agriculture   41
   Industry and trade   45
   Social structure   50
   Conclusion: a developing society   54

2. The Arrival and Growth of Poor Relief   55
   The sixteenth-century background   56
   The response to '39 Elizabeth'   58
   The Civil War and after   66
   Parish and township   71
   Obtaining relief: meeting needs to resources   77
   Conclusion   81

3. Pauper Tales   82
    Records of relief: the accounts of overseers of the poor   83
    Censuses of the poor   86
    Voices of the poor? Pauper petitions   87
    The politics of petitioning   97
    Understanding poverty and poor relief   106

PART II: MARGINALITY

4. Marginal People: Descending into Poverty?   113
    Decayed households? Social mobility in pauper petitions,
    1626–1710   116
    Conclusion   125

5. Resourceful People: Survival Strategies of the Lancashire Poor   127
    Self-sufficiency: land, property and labour   129
    Dependence on others: kin, neighbours and charity   146
    Conclusion   168

PART III: MISFORTUNE

6. Dependent People: Endemic Poverty   171
    Multiple hardships   173
    Old age   174
    Ill health   179
    The nuclear household: formation and breakdown   189
    Economic risk   204
    Environmental risk   207
    Conclusion   211

7. Crisis Poverty   212
    Poverty crises in Lancashire, 1630–1715: a chronology   213
    Crises, 1630–70   215
    Dearth and depression: the crisis of 1674–75   224
    Crises, 1680–1715   234
    'Never so sickley a time known': the crisis of 1727–30   240
    Conclusion   253

Conclusion: Worldly Crosses   255

Bibliography   258
Index   299

Figures

1. Lancashire Hundred boundaries   32

2. Pauper apprentices in Whalley parish, 1631–36   64

3. Poor relief expenditure by Prescot churchwardens,
   1635–50   67

4. Poor relief expenditure in Prestwich, Heaton, Heaton
   Fallowfield, Alkrington and Tonge, 1646–83   69

5. Mean number of named recipients of poor relief in
   Prestwich, 1646–83   69

6. Annual mean dole per named recipient in Prestwich,
   1646–83   70

7. Composite of poor expenditure in Lancashire townships,
   1690–1750   79

8. *The Cunning Northerne Begger*   162

9. Desertions, imprisonments and enlistments by
   half-decade, from Lancashire pauper petitions, 1625–1709   198

10. Seasonal distribution of first petitions for poor relief,
    1626–1709   206

11. First petitions for poor relief in records of Lancashire
    Quarter Sessions, 1626–1710   214

12. First petitions and barley prices, 1640–1710   214

13. First petitions for poor relief, 1628–40   216

14. *A True Representation of the Present Sad and Lamentable
    Condition of the County of Lancaster* (1649)   219

15. First petitions for poor relief, 1646–54   221

16. First petitions for poor relief, 1653–66   223

17. Grain prices at Swarthmoor, 1673–78   226

18. Monthly burial totals in fifty Lancashire parishes, 1668–79   229

19.   First petitions for poor relief, 1668–80   230

20.   Poor expenditure in Prestwich, Heaton, Redditch Heaton,
      Alkrington and Tonge, 1647–81   230

21.   First petitions for poor relief, 1692–1705   237

22.   Poor law expenditure in Bury township, 1692–1713   237

23.   Prices of barley and wheat at Lytham, 1724–30   243

24.   Prices of potatoes and oats at Lytham, 1724–30   243

25.   Monthly burial totals in forty-two Lancashire registers,
      1720–35   244

26.   Composite mean of poor account expenditures, 1710–39   244

27.   Monthly burials in Leigh parish, 1720–35   247

28.   Poor expenditure in Atherton, 1710–32   247

29.   Explicitly medical expenditure in Atherton (i), 1710–32   248

30.   Explicitly medical expenditure in Atherton (ii), 1710–32   248

31.   Paupers in receipt of medical relief, 1710–32   250

Tables

1.	Estimates of the Lancashire population, 1563–1750	39
2.	Recorded occupations of first-time petitioners, 1626–1710	117
3.	Household poverty by occupation (male-headed households) in Bolton, 1686 and 1699	137
4.	Household poverty by occupation (female-headed households) in Bolton, 1686 and 1699	137
5.	Poor relief in Bolton, 1674–99	231
6.	Percentage of households by circumstance in Bolton, 1674–99	232
7.	Characteristics of pauper households in Bolton, 1674	233
8.	Paupers of Atherton, 1710–32	251
9.	Dole expenditure in Atherton, 1710–32	251
10.	Atherton pensioners, 1710–32	252

Preface

This is a book about poverty. It is a book about why some people in seventeenth and early-eighteenth-century England ended up so destitute that they called upon formal poor relief for support. It uses a uniquely fascinating archive – the collection of pauper petitions contained in the papers of the Lancashire magistracy – to try and understand what kinds of circumstances brought people so low.

Those who like their history heavily theorized will probably not like this book. I have generally tried to eschew grand narratives and all-encompassing theses and to let the documents speak for themselves. I use 'documents' here carefully, because whilst I do believe the petitions contain the echoes of the voices of the poor, these voices have only reached us through documents written – for the most part – by their wealthier neighbours. They are hybrid voices. But although the book is short on the grand narrative, it does have an underlying argument that the new system of social welfare created by the Tudors and fully implemented under the Stuarts provided an important function in early modern society. This function was to mitigate the hardships that came from the challenges and misfortunes of life in the underdeveloped society that was early modern England. Old age, sickness, family breakdown, poor harvests, fires and floods, all constituted terrifying 'risks', particularly in a society in which most people, most of the time, lived in small nuclear households. And vulnerability to such risks was partly determined by the social environment. You were more likely to end up poor if you were landless, or lived away from your relatives, or simply by dint of being female. By the end of the period, the Poor Law was providing some security, at least for the most marginal, what one of the Lancashire paupers called, in 1689, the 'crosses and losses in this world' (in his case, the most obvious misfortune was that his wife had suffered 'a cancer in her brest these four yeares'). Meanwhile, by providing some social security in the face of harvest failures, the Poor Law was a major weapon in the war against famine even if – as it happens – it remained of little use in the face of epidemic disease.

Some readers, indeed, may find this view rather optimistic, especially when it is based upon a county which spent relatively little per capita on its poor. I am not entirely convinced that 'optimism' and 'pessimism' are useful concepts when dealing with early modern history, as they presuppose the kind of value judgements that fog our views of the past. But if we see the broadly successful support of a basic standard of subsistence for the most vulnerable members of a fundamentally fairly poor society as a 'good', then – yes – this is in some ways an optimistic book.

In Lancashire, the development of this system of support took place in the seventeenth century. And although the county was perhaps unusual in its backwardness in social policy in 1600, the seventeenth century more generally in England was the century which this formalized, tax-funded poor relief became truly national and regular in scope. As countless historians have shown, even in 1700 there were regional variations, and tax-funded relief through parishes and townships was only one element in the way English society supported its poor (and they supported themselves). But it is not 'Whiggish', nor does it preclude the acknowledgement of medieval poor relief *or* the failings of the Old Poor Law, to see this century as involving a pivotal shift. For in the seventeenth century, in England, the public purse became *the* major guarantor of the survival of the poor. By any token this was a major change, and hence the book's title.

The research behind this started some years ago, and in the process of bringing it to completion I've accrued many, many debts. Martin Ingram did most to nurture the project, and such was his influence that whenever I write I still imagine his careful, questioning, but ultimately supportive voice telling me what he thinks of it, cautioning me against the most egregious errors. I've also enjoyed countless discussions with colleagues in Oxford, Cambridge and elsewhere about the work. Amongst many supportive scholars, the input of Paul Slack, Steve Hindle, Joanna Innes, Leigh Shaw-Taylor, Richard Hoyle, Steve Gunn, Clive Holmes, Nigel Goose and Laurence Brockliss has – at various moments – been hugely valuable. The first person to notice my love of English social history was not me, but my first tutor at Magdalen, Emily Cockayne. That was fourteen years ago now, but in a sense the seed for the book was planted all the way back then.

I would also like to thank Magdalen College, Oxford, and the Arts and Humanities Research Council, who funded the research in its earliest stages. Thanks are also due to the Economic History Society, who elected me to a Tawney Fellowship in 2007–08, the Economic and Social Research Council, who provided a Postdoctoral Fellowship in 2009, to St Hilda's College, Oxford, who employed me in 2009–10 as a Departmental Lecturer, to the Master and Fellows of St Catherine's College, Oxford who elected me to a Fellowship in 2010, and to the President and Fellows of Kellogg College, Oxford, who elected me to a Fellowship there in 2012. Smaller, but very valuable, funding was also provided, at various stages, by Lancaster Royal Grammar School and by the Oxford University Department for Continuing Education.

My debts to colleagues are huge, but I particularly wanted to mention those at St Catz and my current colleagues at the Department for Continuing Education as especially supportive. I'm convinced that those who teach make the best writers, and I've learnt plenty over the years about my own work, and the period and its complexities, from discussions with my undergraduate students, most especially the St Catz 2009 History matriculands, and the students to whom I've taught Local History at OUDCE. Thanks are also due to the efficiency and expertise of the staff of the many archives of the North West, but especially those at the Lancashire Archives at Preston.

But even more crucial has been the encouragement of some brilliant and inspirational friends. From Magdalen and (later) London, huge thanks to Phil Abraham, Rachel Antony-Roberts, James Barber, Anna Dominey, Paul Dudley-Ward, Adrian Fradd, Eleanor Green (and Tom and now William), Jo Harston, Matthew Holdcroft, Liz and Vach Kashyap (and now Cate and James), Katy Pullen, Kath Radice (and Brendan and the boys), Paz Tayal, and Daisy Thornton. And from my days in Oxford as a postgraduate and an early career academic I wanted especially to thank Annette Walton, Miranda Kaufmann, Gemma Allen, Tiffany Shumaker, Gabriel Glickman, Elizabeth Scott-Baumann, Shreya Sarawgi, Si Hackett, and Patty Sachamitr. You've not just inspired me, but most importantly you've all distracted me from work and from the project. Those distractions have made it a better book.

My family have been behind the book from the beginning: my parents, my brother Alex, and my grandparents all supported the project very keenly. I hope they find the finished product interesting. If nothing else, the research gave me a great excuse to spend long periods of the last nine years at home in the North West. My parents-in-law, John and Christine, have shown great interest and support for the project too.

Finally, my wife Sophie has been brilliant from day one – supportive, generous, and always treating the book and its difficult author with time and a great sense of humour. It simply would never have been completed without her. You were the best of all distractions.

Abbreviations

AgHR	*The Agricultural History Review*
AHEW	J. Thirsk and H. P. R. Finberg (eds), *The Agrarian History of England and Wales*, 8 vols (Cambridge, 1967–2000).
BALS	Bolton Archives and Local Studies
CRO (B)	Cumbria Record Office, Barrow Branch
CRO (C)	Cumbria Record Office, Carlisle Headquarters
CRO (K)	Cumbria Record Office, Kendal Branch
CS	Chetham's Society
CW1, CW2, CW3	*Transactions of the Cumberland and Westmorland Antiquarian and Archaeological Society*, First, Second and Third Series
EcHR	*The Economic History Review*
HMC	Historical Manuscripts Commission
LA	Lancashire Archives
LPRS	Lancashire Parish Register Society
LPS	*Local Population Studies*
MALS	Manchester Archives and Local Studies
PP	*Past & Present*
RSEH	Records of Social and Economic History
RSLC	The Record Society of Lancashire and Cheshire
THSLC	*Transactions of the Historic Society of Lancashire and Cheshire*
TNA	The National Archives
TRHS	*Transactions of the Royal Historical Society*
VCH Lancs	W. Farrer and J. Brownbill (eds), *The Victoria History of the County of Lancaster*, 8 vols (London, 1906–14).
WA	Wigan Archives

Prologue: Becoming Poor

To William Banke & his son Abraham, 11s 10d.

Accounts of the Overseers of the Poor of
Hawkshead Quarter (1709/10)[1]

A story lies behind every entry in an account book. The story behind the series of doles given to William Bank and his son Abraham by the township of Hawkshead, however, is mostly obscure. William had been baptized in Hawkshead in 1639, his father an apparently well-off farmer who – when he composed his will in 1681 – styled himself a yeoman.[2] The family farm, Esthwaite Waterside, was a good one, and still stands today at the northern end of Esthwaite Water: an unremarkable but attractive whitewashed homestead, very much in the local style. We know from the parish register that William lived at Waterside for the first thirteen years of his marriage, having wed one Agnes Wilson in 1660, the year of the Restoration. He had seven children by Agnes in the 1660s and early 1670s, and at least four of these survived their infancy.

However, between the birth of their last children (the twins Matthew and Lucy) in 1673, and William's death in 1717, the family suffered a dramatic collapse in fortune. Sometime between 1673 and 1676, William and Agnes moved across the parish, to Low Wray on the north-western banks of Lake Windermere. Here, in February 1674, they took up a freehold of arable and wood called Wadbarrow, but in 1676 Agnes died and was buried that September.[3] Around the following February, William got another woman pregnant, this time one Dorothy Dodgson, whose

---

1 CRO (K), WPR/83/7/3, Hawkshead Overseers' Accounts, 1690–1750.
2 *The Oldest Register Book of the Parish of Hawkshead, 1568–1704*, ed. H. S. Cowper (London, 1897); LA, WRW/William Banke, 1681; *The Second Register Book of the Parish of Hawkshead in the Diocese of Carlisle and the County of Lancaster, 1705–1797*, ed. K. Leonard and G. O. G. Leonard (Hawkshead, 1968).
3 CRO (C), D/NT/38, Bargain and Sale, 1679.

previous life in Hawkshead is obscure save when she gave birth to a son in 1674, the product of an illicit liaison with a Scotsman. Despite this previous impropriety, and perhaps because of the couple's more recent one, William and Dorothy wed in July 1677 and their child was born legitimate. But shortly afterwards William was heavily in debt, and in 1679 Wadbarrow was sold to a Kendal tanner for £55 10s.[4] In 1680 William, still styled a 'yeoman', was hired by Thomas Rawlinson to 'hedge fence mow worke and dry the hay growing in the fields' for the quarterly sum of £2 15s. By 1681, William was simply recorded as Rawlinson's servant.[5]

A year later, Dorothy gave birth to the couple's penultimate child, Abraham, at Hawkshead Hill, and it was he who apparently completed William's descent into poverty. We know little about the boy save what we can glean from the parish registers and the overseers' accounts, the latter of which begin to survive from 1690.[6] We can see that William was in receipt of a pension as early as 1704, and that he was allocated 2s 1d in 1706 when Dorothy was buried. We can also tell that – despite being in his late twenties – Abraham was relieved as part of his father's household in 1709/10, and was recorded in the burial register at his death in 1711 as 'Abraham, son of William Bank'. It seems likely that Abraham was in some way incapacitated, forcing him to live at home with his father. It appears, then, that the combination of a long-term collapse of economic fortune, the loss of two wives, the (permanent?) incapacity of a son, and – by this stage – creeping old age, had left William poor, and claiming relief.

Around the same time, Thomas Gerrard, who lived in Little Hilton,[7] far to the south, asked his neighbour for help. Gerrard was sick, and had a young family: his eldest child was six years old, his youngest but sixteen days. It was not an especially long journey, but given his family commitments and the incapacity from his illness, Gerrard felt unable to travel to Wigan to make his case to justices there, so in 1699 he called upon Richard Tyldesley – a labourer – for help. The petition that survives in the papers of Lancashire's Quarter Sessions contains, it would seem, Tyldesley's own words. He describes the plight of his neighbour with an extraordinary vividness.[8]

'Thomas Gerrard', he wrote, 'is now and hath lain sick in bed this

4   Ibid.
5   CRO (B), BD/HJ/90/Bundle 24/6, Bond, 1680; BD/HJ/89/Bundle 10/2, Affidavit, 1681.
6   CRO (K), WPR/83/7/3, Hawkshead Overseers' Accounts, 1690–1750.
7   Now Little Hulton.
8   LA, QSP/823/53.

five weekes, his wife is now in child bed was allmost recovered but now relapsed. The husband and new borne child lye in one poor bed the 3 children scarce recovered of sicknes. There is neither meat nor fire in the house.' All they had received in poor relief was six shillings, 'which will not pay and maintaine a person to looke after them', and had not their neighbours offered their charity, 'they had been all starved & miserably perished in the house before this'. But charity had its limits, especially – though this was unsaid – at a time of high prices such as 1699, so 'now their charity begins to slacken so that tis impossible they should any one of 'em subsist 3 dayes longer but will miserably perish for want of releefe'. The justices who heard the petition were moved enough to order the family's relief. The parish of Tyldesley, in which they were legally settled, was to give them twenty shillings for present necessity, and 3s 4d per month.

The stories of the Banks of Hawkshead and the Gerrards of Little Hilton have only come down to us through the accidents of documentary survival. We know little about the real lives of those who lived in poverty in past times. There are no social surveys, such as the great ones of Joseph Rowntree and Henry Mayhew; literary sources are scanty; official records of poor relief laconic, spotty, and difficult to interpret. But they illustrate much about why people became poor, how they tried to get by, and why so many eventually called upon England's unique Poor Law. These are the themes of this book.

Introduction: The First Century of Welfare

So long as there is any naturall or necessarie meanes left to live, none must depend upon the helpe of the lawe.

An Ease for Overseers of the Poore (1601)[1]

The English 'Old Poor Law' was unique. Lasting from the twilight years of the Tudor dynasty until 1834, it provided for a regular compulsory tax in every English (and Welsh) parish, the proceeds of which were to be spent on that parish's neediest poor. Its uniqueness, at least in its earlier years, lay in the fact it was a *national* system, as applicable – in theory – to the wilds of Northumberland as it was in the dense lanes of the City of London. Indeed, though many stimuli to its appearance were pan-European, such as population growth, rising prices, humanism, and 'reformation', and though England was just one of many states attempting major innovations in its policies towards the poor, it was only England that successfully constructed such a nationwide safety net. While formal poor relief on the Continent remained largely urban and often Church-administered, the English Poor Law was run by institutions of the state (primarily the civic parish), and it covered rural as well as urban areas.[2]

The real origins of the system lay in the sixteenth century. There had been important developments before then, such as the emergence of the parish as a unit of civil administration, and a growing willingness of late medieval parliaments to legislate on social matters. Indeed, consideration for the poor was an age-old concern, and there seems to have been a powerful charitable impulse in the late medieval countryside.[3] Nevertheless, the Tudor century still stands out. Rising population and inflation rapidly

---

1 *An Ease for Overseers of the Poore* (Cambridge, 1601), p. 23.
2 For the wider European picture: R. Jütte, *Poverty and Deviance in Early Modern Europe* (Cambridge, 1994).
3 C. Dyer, 'Poverty and its Relief in Late Medieval England', *PP*, 216 (2012), 41–78.

altered the nature of poverty, both rural and urban, both in reality and in the eyes of legislators. Growing numbers of 'structural poor' – men and women who were able to work but who were still underemployed – provided a challenge to neat distinctions between 'undeserving' and 'impotent' poor.[4] Religious and political changes, meanwhile, combined to shatter much of the medieval landscape of charity.[5] Monasteries, which had provided relief for the poor, were dissolved and abolished in 1536 and 1540; chantries, the source of much charity, felt the swing of the legislative axe in 1547. Hospitals and almshouses, major bedrocks of medieval social welfare, suffered too. It has recently been estimated that nearly half of them closed between 1530 and 1559.[6]

At around the same time, however, the intellectual movement we know of as 'humanism', with its desire to improve the social health of the commonwealth, was feeding into a growth in power and ambition of the Tudor state; together these created a new optimism about what the government could and should achieve.[7] And so, lawmakers in Westminster turned their attention to the problem of poverty while governors (especially urban governors) in localities up and down the kingdom tried to erect the administrative structures that might relieve and discipline the swelling ranks of the poor. Their problem, common to European states, was essentially threefold: how to relieve the 'deserving', how to punish the 'undeserving', and how to get the able-bodied back to work. The focus of this book is on the first of these.

Tudor legislative attempts to organize the relief of the deserving poor saw the growing acceptance of the need to regularize and bureaucratize charitable giving on the part of wealthier householders. This was not a straightforward process, nor did central government either monopolize the policy-making initiative or trample over existing structures. Historians have repeatedly, and rightly, emphasized how the development of the English Poor Law in the Tudor century was a two-way process in which local communities often acted in advance of statute. Towns like London, York, and Norwich were instigating complex rate-based systems of poor relief before Parliament declared it compulsory, as were some rural

4   P. Slack, *Poverty and Policy in Tudor and Stuart England* (London, 1988), pp. 2–8.
5   P. A. Fideler, *Social Welfare in Pre-Industrial England: The Old Poor Law Tradition* (Basingstoke, 2005), pp. 8–102.
6   M. K. McIntosh, *Poor Relief in England, 1350–1600* (Cambridge, 2012), p. 125.
7   P. Slack, *From Reformation to Improvement: Public Welfare in Early-Modern England* (Oxford, 1999), pp. 5–28; Fideler, *Social Welfare*, pp. 37–102.

communities in the south and east of the country.[8] But what distinguished England from her neighbours was the *national* scope of her
poor relief system. By the early 1690s, when France – the most powerful
state in Europe – was experiencing wartime famine and trying desperately to implement an effective poor rate, England's system was already
well established, and probably capable of feeding around 5 per cent of
its population every year.[9] And for a patchwork of local experiments to
become a national system of social welfare, action was required in the
form of legislation from Parliament, established as it was as the supreme
lawmaking body in the kingdom.[10]

A statute in 1531 had ordered Justices of the Peace (JPs) to keep registers
of the deserving poor who were to be allowed to beg, but the key legislation was in 1552, 1563 and 1572, followed by the more famous statutes
of 1598 and 1601.[11] The 1552 statute ordered the registering of the poor
and those able to support them in every parish, as well as the creation of a
parish officer dedicated to the relief of the poor – 'collectors for the poor'
– of which there were to be two or more in each parish. There was to be
a semi-voluntary collection for the poor amongst those listed as having
the ability to pay, and anyone unwilling to contribute (theoretically at
least) could be reported to a bishop for admonishment. The 1552 statute
lapsed in 1555, but that year was effectively replaced in its entirety and
with only slight modifications to the process of appointing collectors. But
this new act again lasted only a few years, and was technically replaced in
its entirety by a new poor law of 1563. This latter act stipulated that those
who refused to give money to the collectors would be hauled before a JP
and could be sent to gaol; thus Parliament was laying the foundations of
the compulsory rate.

What happened next is not quite clear. The traditional picture, as
described by Paul Slack, is that a statute of 1572 introduced compulsory
rates, but that because these were entirely managed by JPs they proved

---

8   Slack, *Poverty and Policy*, pp. 123–9; M. K. McIntosh, 'Poor Relief in Elizabethan
English Communities: an Analysis of Collectors' Accounts', *EcHR*, forthcoming.
9   P. Berger, 'French Administration in the Famine of 1693', *European Studies Review*, 8
(1978), 101–27; Slack, *Poverty and Policy*, pp. 170–3.
10   G. R. Elton, 'Parliament', in *The Reign of Elizabeth I*, ed. C. Haigh (Basingstoke,
1984), pp. 79–100 (p. 84).
11   22 Henry VIII, c. 12; 5 & 6 Edw. VI, c. 2; 2 & 3 Philip & Mary, c. 5; 5 Eliz. I, c. 3; 14
Eliz. I, c. 5; 39 Eliz. I, c. 3; 43 Eliz. I, c. 2; Slack, *Poverty and Policy*, pp. 124–31.

unworkable.[12] Marjorie McIntosh, however, has argued that the 1572 statute *did not* fully dismantle older legislation, but merely 'erected additional institutions above the level of parish support'.[13] Its compulsory rating was actually not for the support of the poor in their homes, but was for the provision of 'abiding houses' for those poor who were not housed in their home parish. The older system of collectors was left in place and the new overseers' role was to look after the poor in the 'abiding houses'.[14]

McIntosh's work also shows that poor relief systems were developing quietly in some rural and urban communities, particularly in southern and central England often in only partial regard to statute law.[15] It is, indeed, plausible that the 1552 and 1563 legislation had the most influence 'on the ground', rather than that of 1572 (or indeed the Act of 1576, which established stocks of goods for the unemployed poor to work on). But McIntosh's reading of statute law does not quite carry conviction. The 1552 and 1555 statutes clearly no longer had force of law after 1563 for the simple reason that they had been given a time limit and that Parliament had stopped renewing them. As to the statute of 1563, she points out a slight discrepancy in the 1572 statute, in that while the text refers to the repeal of *all* previous statutes, the marginal heading refers only to laws about beggars and vagabonds. And yet, the text of the statute could not be clearer: the statutes of 1531, 1550 (an Act for the punishment of vagabonds and idle persons) and 1563 were to be repealed, 'and every braunche article clause and sentence in them & every of them conteyned, shal bee from and after the Feast of Saincte Bartholomewe Th'apostell next commynge utterly void frustrate and of none effect'.[16] In any case, the 1563 statute had a time limit set to the end of the first session of the next Parliament, and so lapsed unless Parliament renewed it, which they apparently failed to do in 1566. Moreover, the wording of the clause relating to the compulsory rate is actually rather hard to unpick: on my reading it could refer to rates to support either the homeless poor in 'abiding places' *or* the impotent poor in their parishes, or perhaps most likely both or either. Perhaps the main lesson is a more basic one, that statute law after 1572 was simply too ambiguous to work properly.

The key development, then, came in 1598. The statute of this year, part

---

12   Slack, *Poverty and Policy*, pp. 124–5.
13   McIntosh, *Poor Relief*, pp. 228–9.
14   Ibid., p. 168.
15   Esp. ibid., pp. 127–38, 225–69.
16   14 Eliz. I, c. 5.

of a larger group of social policy legislation, created the fundamental basis of the English and Welsh system of poor relief that lasted to 1834. It was, of course, heavily based on earlier laws, but – as Slack pointed out some time ago – it was this Act which created the effective administrative systems to ensure local compliance. Four overseers of the poor were to be appointed in each parish, they were to tax 'every inhabitant and occupier of lands', and were to spend the money raised on relieving the impotent poor. In addition, they were to maintain stocks for the able-bodied unemployed to work on, to bind out poor children as parish apprentices. Begging was forbidden, except by those given permission to ask for food in their own parish. Three years later, in 1601, a new version of the act was passed, which freed small parishes to appoint just two overseers if they chose, and – strikingly – removed the clause allowing limited begging. Indeed, combined with an act against vagrancy in 1598, the legislation of the last years of Elizabeth should have eradicated begging from the English landscape.[17] The system was then subject to further reform in the late seventeenth century, with statutes of 1662 and 1692 clarifying settlement law, which determined which paupers were the responsibility of which parish.[18] In addition, the 1662 act told large northern parishes to treat administrative subdivisions, notably townships, as effectively equivalent to parishes for Poor Law purposes.

So legislators gradually put in place the statutory backing behind an effective welfare system, but there was still a crucial problem: it was all very well for Parliament to set laws, but those laws needed translation into action on the ground. There had, of course, been statutes that proved completely ineffective in the face of local opposition and indifference, such as the infamous slavery clause of the 1547 Vagrancy Act.[19] So there had to be a process by which the Poor Law became embedded in local society, and developed from abstract entries on the statute book to a critical day-to-day reality. This process was already, it seems, under way in some parts before 1598, and McIntosh has argued that collectors for the poor and poor rates were already present in 'many' southern and central

---

17   39 Eliz. I, c. 4.
18   13 & 14 Charles II, c. 12; 3 William & Mary, c. 11; There was a little-known attempt at reform in 1626 which fell victim to the dissolution of Parliament: Slack, *From Reformation to Improvement*, pp. 43–4; for details of the suggested new statute: *Proceedings in Parliament, 1626*, ed. W. B. Bidwell and M. Jansson, 4 vols (London, 1991–96), vol. 4, pp. 118–26, 200–2.
19   C. S. L. Davies, 'Slavery and Protector Somerset: the Vagrancy Act of 1547', *EcHR*, 2nd Ser., 19 (1966), 533–49.

parishes before the Act. She found collectors and/or fixed assessments for
the poor in some 208 parishes in total between 1552 and 1598.[20] But there
is clear evidence, nonetheless, that the late-Elizabethan statutes marked a
major watershed, particularly in the North. In Chester, a 'general meeting'
of churchwardens and overseers was immediately called to study the new
law, which had been brought up by a returning justice.[21] Parishioners in
part of Yorkshire's West Riding also met immediately to discuss the new
legislation, though they protested at the imposition of rates as 'many are
able to give relief which are not able to give money'.[22] As will be seen, there
is evidence that formal poor relief in south Lancashire effectively dated
from this moment. Even McIntosh herself, who argues for significant
formal relief before 1598, points out that costs immediately shot up in a
number of parishes after the statute of that year.[23] Indeed, in 1601 their
importance received perhaps its most powerful endorsement, for in that
year someone in the publishing trade felt it worth their while to produce a
printed guide to the office of overseer of the poor.[24]

The late Elizabethan statutes' success probably came down to two
factors. First, they greatly clarified earlier legislation. The 1572 statute
is unclear as to what its compulsory rates were for (hence the divergent
understandings of Slack and McIntosh), and created a confusing array
of officers (collectors of the rates seem to have been added to the old
collectors for the poor, and there were the new 'overseers', probably
managers for the 'abiding places').[25] The 1598 statute was, by contrast, a
model of clarity: the rates were parochial, they were managed by parish
officers, and there was only to be one type of dedicated officer charged
with the care of the poor, the parochial overseer (though churchwardens
were to share the burden). Secondly, enforcement was now shared effectively between parish officers and justices of the peace. Whereas the 1552
collections had been overseen by bishops (who were few in number and
often distant), and those of 1563 backed by the enforcement of justices
(but still only after 'exhortation' by a bishop), the 1598 statute placed
initial oversight in the hands of JPs, of whom there were many. The 1572

20 McIntosh, *Poor Relief*, pp. 252–69; see also, M. K. McIntosh, *Poor Relief and Community in Hadleigh, Suffolk 1547–1600* (Hatfield, 2013).
21 Slack, *From Reformation to Improvement*, pp. 41–2.
22 Quoted in Slack, *Poverty and Policy*, p. 127.
23 McIntosh, *Poor Relief*, pp. 282–3.
24 *An Ease for Overseers*.
25 McIntosh, *Poor Relief*, pp. 228–9.

statute, meanwhile, had charged JPs with keeping registers of the poor in their divisions, an unrealistically burdensome task (remember, of course, that the poor tended to be old and sick, so there was likely to be plenty of 'turnover' in their numbers). By contrast, that of 1598 allowed parish officers to do the legwork and to make the majority of the decisions, while JPs oversaw the process, hearing appeals. The genius of the 1598 and 1601 statutes lay not in what they said about poor relief, for their ideas were nothing new, but in the way they balanced the resources of parish and magistracy to ensure compliance.[26]

From this moment, then, the direction of the tide was set, it was just a question of which rocks would hold out longest. It used to be thought that the process of implementation was slow: W. K. Jordan believed that as late as 1660 only 7 per cent of the money expended on the care of the poor derived from taxation; Slack, while rightly criticizing Jordan, was still relatively conservative, suggesting that only about a third of parishes were 'accustomed to raising taxes for the poor' by 1660. By 1700, though, he thought the practice was 'well-nigh universal'.[27] But this view is changing. McIntosh's research showing the existence of formal poor relief before 1598 is part of this shift. Steve Hindle, meanwhile, has produced evidence for a much wider implementation before the Civil War than previously thought, and shown how quickly the system was rekindled after it.[28] There is still much local work to be done on this issue, but it would appear from recent studies that the crucial phase in the spread of rate-based poor relief was the early seventeenth century rather than the post-Civil War decades.

Even within the process of implementation, however, there was another story of rising expenditure of which there has been surprisingly little told. Put simply, Tudor and early Stuart historians have focused on the spread of formal mechanisms of poor relief, in particular rating, rather than on how much money was actually spent on the poor. This is more understandable than working the other way around, but the rise of costs is clearly critical. If the spread of poor rates is a key gauge of the *appearance* of the Poor Law, then its increasing costs are testament to its developing *maturity*. Put

26 Slack, *Poverty and Policy*, p. 126.
27 W. K. Jordan, *Philanthropy in England, 1480–1660: A Study of the Changing Pattern of English Social Aspirations* (London, 1959), p. 140; Slack, *Poverty and Policy*, pp. 169–70.
28 McIntosh, *Poor Relief*, pp. 252–69; S. Hindle, *On the Parish? The Micro-Politics of Poor Relief in Rural England, c.1550–1750* (Oxford, 2004), pp. 229–56; S. Hindle, 'Dearth and the English Revolution: the Harvest Crisis of 1647–50', *EcHR*, 2nd Ser., 61, Supplement 1 (2008), 64–98.

another way, we can only credit the Old Poor Law as an effective system of social welfare if we can see that it was meeting the basic needs of a significant proportion of the poor themselves. Here, the seventeenth century emerges as decisive, for there is little doubt that – once rates were established – costs rose and, essentially, kept rising. Richard Gough of Myddle (Shropshire) remembered in 1702 that in 'the first yeare that hee was marryed, (which was about the yeare 1633) hee payd onely four pence to the poore, and now [i.e. 1702] I pay almost twenty shillings per annum'.[29] In Lacock in Wiltshire, around £10 was spent each year in the 1590s, and this had risen to some £113 4s per annum for the seven years between 1666 and 1674.[30] Slack, and Joan Kent and Steve King have shown a general swelling of poor relief costs in many parishes up to the early decades of the eighteenth century, while work in progress on poor accounts across rural England backs up their findings.[31] Projected reform of the Poor Law by statute in 1626 focused not on compliance with rates, but with issues such as settlement (which parish was responsible for which pauper), the number of overseers per parish, the formalities of their office, and what to do with men who abandoned their wives.[32] By 1662, when the next critical piece of legislation was passed, it dealt primarily with the issue of settlement. That Parliament had moved on to such matters suggests that the basic tenets of the 1598 and 1601 system were functioning relatively well. Indeed, the scope of the system by the later Stuart years was paid the ultimate compliment when commentators started to argue against it, chafing at high expenditures, and Parliament started trying to reduce costs.[33] In 1692, a statute demanded a signature from a JP before anyone was added to the relief lists; this was followed in 1697 with legislation ordering that recipients of parish doles were to wear badges; then, in 1723, Parliament stipulated that no additions were to be made to the relief lists without JPs taking evidence on oath.[34] Potentially more drastically, parishes under the 1723 act were allowed to set up workhouses and to

29   R. Gough, *The History of Myddle*, ed. D. Hey (Harmondsworth, 1981), p. 146.
30   F. H. Hinton, 'Notes on the Administration of the Relief of the Poor of Lacock, 1583–1834', *Wiltshire Archaeological Magazine*, 49 (1940–42), 166–218 (pp. 166–71).
31   Slack, *Poverty and Policy*, pp. 162–87; J. Kent and S. King, 'Changing Patterns of Poor Relief in Some English Rural Parishes, *circa* 1650–1750', *Rural History*, 14 (2003), 119–56. I intend to publish on this soon.
32   *Proceedings in Parliament, 1626*, vol. 4, pp. 118–26.
33   Slack, *Poverty and Policy*, pp. 192–5.
34   3 William & Mary, c. 11; 8 & 9 William III, c. 30; 9 Geo. I, c. 7.

apply a 'workhouse test', stopping relief to any pauper who refused to reside in one. The legislative pendulum had swung.

Let us just take stock. In telling the story of the initial appearance of the English Old Poor Law, we have seen that the 1598 and 1601 statutes present a critical juncture, that the key period in the implementation of formal relief structures was probably the early seventeenth century, and that the Stuart age as a whole saw the Poor Law maturing into a high-spending and wide-ranging welfare system. The seventeenth century, then, was a major turning point. It saw the English state, from Parliament down to the parishes, take on the subsistence needs of its poorest members. It saw the acceptance, either out of charity, duty or just obedience, by middling households up and down the country that they should be taxed to support their poor neighbours. If, as one historian has argued, there were two strands to English welfare history, voluntary and customary *societas* and mandatory *civitas*, then the seventeenth century saw a major victory for the latter.[35] It was the century when the 'overseer of the poor' became a ubiquitous feature of the English parish, when village notables got used to meeting at least once a year to discuss matters of poverty, and when every English man, woman and child grew to know which parish had responsibility for their relief. If historians have recently pointed out that this was the culmination of a long process, and that there were medieval antecedents to much of the 'Elizabethan' poor law, then it was still only in the seventeenth century that everything came together in a viable system of poverty relief, capable of providing a robust safety net when all other ways of making do had failed.[36] The seventeenth century was, then, the first century of welfare.

Marginality and misfortune: poverty in the first century of welfare

The main purpose of this book is not to discuss the implementation and form of poor relief in seventeenth-century England. Although such issues will inevitably come in to what follows, this is field of historical enquiry that has been well ploughed. Instead, the book will look at poverty from – so far as is possible – the eyes of the poor themselves. The main question

---

35   Fideler, *Social Welfare*.
36   E.g. Dyer, 'Poverty and its Relief'.

is, what led people to depend on formal poor relief for their subsistence? What personal catastrophes, what individual experiences, what family contingencies forced people to go to their township officers and to ask for a pension or a dole? What kinds of people were likely to fall into such dependency, what might they be able to do to stop their descent into destitution?

On the face of it, the questions seem simple enough. According to the 'Act for the Relief of the Poor' of 43 Elizabeth I, c. 2, overseers in each parish were to set to work 'all such persons, maried or unmaried, havinge no means to maintaine them, use no ordinarie and dailie trade of lief to get their living by', and relieve with cash 'the lame impotente olde blinde and suche other amonge them beinge poore and not able to work'. Poor children, meanwhile, were to be apprenticed.[37] Legal provision for the deserving poor, then, revolved around a two-pronged system of work for the unemployed and cash doles for the incapacitated. But the terminology of the statute was vague and – crucially – there was ample room for discretion on the part of the churchwardens, overseers, vestrymen, and justices of the peace who were charged with carrying the system into operation.[38]

As it happens, although we have an increasingly detailed knowledge of the operation of the Poor Laws at the local level, our understanding of the nature of 'deserving' poverty and its relief is incomplete. There has been work on this in recent years, notably on the relationship between hardship and the life cycle, and on the ability of the social and economic environment to provide a buffer against total destitution. Yet it has tended to rely upon the complex and potentially distorting processes of family reconstitution and nominal record linkage, and it has focused on the eighteenth century and beyond. Much of the best research on the sixteenth and seventeenth centuries has lent heavily on the great urban censuses of the poor, while the most important recent major book on rural poor relief has concentrated on the *politics* of poverty, only touching briefly on questions of who needed relief and why.

The aim of this book is gain a better understanding of poverty in the seventeenth century – the first century of welfare – and as such it is a book as much about poverty as it is about poor relief. It will use a new set of

37   43 Eliz. I, c. 2.
38   Cf. M. Goldie, 'The Unacknowledged Republic: Officeholding in Early Modern England', in *The Politics of the Excluded, 1500–1850*, ed. T. Harris (Basingstoke, 2001), pp. 153–94.

sources which allow a refocusing away from family reconstitutions, away from urban censuses, and away from the eighteenth century. Its focus will be the ancient county of Lancashire. Part of an isolated and relatively backward region, areas within Lancashire were nonetheless undergoing significant and dynamic economic growth in our period, with textile industries (notably cotton) developing in the east, and metalworking in the south-west. These subregional industrial zones not only saw economic growth, including incorporation into wider national and international market zones, but they also experienced related changes to local social and employment structures. The market-sensitive portion of the workforce was expanding, while at the same time both the degree of sensitivity to, and the character of, that market were changing.

But the main reason that Lancashire is so fascinating is not economic; it is archival. Lancashire has a very small number of surviving accounts from its overseers of the poor, the usual bedrock of studies of the Poor Law. There are some listings of the poor, including three wonderfully detailed censuses of the poor for the small town of Bolton from 1674, 1686 and 1699. But even this is not the most important set of sources in the county, for contained in the papers of the Lancashire Quarter Sessions can be found several thousand petitions. These cover appeals for adjudication over all kinds of matters of local politics, from bridge maintenance to social disorder; but one of the major components, from the 1620s to the early years of the eighteenth century, is petitions for poor relief. The number of these petitions is so great that one historian in one book cannot hope to exploit them fully, or even truly comprehend their scope. I have counted over three thousand first petitions for poor relief (i.e. those which were not simply restating a case made at an earlier date) in the Lancashire archive between the 1620s and 1700s; and even this total does not include the very large number of petitions asking not for a pension but for the parish to provide housing. They each contain a brief appeal for support by an individual pauper, often also on behalf of their family; the appeal was usually framed as a description of the causes of the petitioner's poverty together (sometimes) with some discussion of their attempts to stave off dependence on the parish by 'making shift'. The petitions, which I will discuss in greater detail in chapter 3, constitute one of the most vivid and detailed sources for pre-modern poverty anywhere in the world, let alone England. They form the heart of this book. But before we look at them and the county itself in more detail, we need to consider previous work on early modern English poverty.

Historians and the poor

For many years, the interests of Poor Law historians lay with legislative and administrative developments. The earliest histories focused squarely on the statute book and relevant case law.[39] Statute law also lay at the heart of Beatrice and Sidney Webb's classic account of the history of the Old Poor Law, written in the early twentieth century, though here the recounting of legal disputes had given way to a more generalized narrative of implementation.[40] In the half century or so following, local case studies were undertaken, some more useful than others, and the intimate parochial detail allowed by these was employed to flesh out the bare bones of the law.[41] Nonetheless, studies remained resolutely top-down in their

---

39   E.g. R. Burn, *History of the Poor Laws: With Observations* (London, 1764); G. Nicholls, *A History of the English Poor Law*, 2 vols (London, 1904).

40   B. Webb and S. Webb, *English Local Government, Vol. VII: English Poor Law History, Part One: The Old Poor Law* (London, 1927).

41   E.g. E. H. Rideout, 'Poor Law Administration in North Meols in the Eighteenth Century', *THSLC*, 81 (1930), 62–109; F. G. Emmison, 'The Relief of the Poor at Eaton Socon, 1706–1834', *Publications of the Bedfordshire Historical Record Society*, 15 (1933), 1–98; Hinton, 'Notes'; M. F. Bond, 'Windsor's Experiment in Poor-relief, 1621–1829', *Berkshire Archaeological Journal*, 48 (1945), 31–42; C. M. L. Bouch, 'Poor Law Documents of the Parish of Great Salkeld', CW2, 49 (1949), 142–7; M. Hopkirk, 'The Administration of Poor Relief, 1604–1832, Illustrated from the Parochial Records of Danbury', *Essex Review*, 58 (1949), 113–21; I. Fitzroy Jones, 'Aspects of Poor Law Administration, Seventeenth to Nineteenth Centuries, from Trull Overseers' Accounts', *Proceedings of the Somersetshire Archaeological and Natural History Society*, 95 (1950), 72–105; A. Fessler, 'The Official Attitude towards the Sick Poor in Seventeenth-century Lancashire', *THSLC*, 102 (1950), 85–113; H. R. Evans, 'Poor-Law Administration at Ashburton from 1598–1612', *Devon and Cornwall Notes and Queries*, 25, no. 2 (1952), 41–7; P. H. Goodman, 'Eighteenth Century Poor Law Administration in the Parish of Oswestry', *Transactions of the Shropshire Archaeological Society*, 56 (1960), 328–42; A. W. Coats, 'Economic Thought and Poor Law Policy in the Eighteenth Century', *EcHR*, 2nd Ser., 13 (1961), 34–78; J. F. Pound, 'An Elizabethan Census of the Poor: the Treatment of Vagrancy in Norwich, 1570–1580', *University of Birmingham Historical Journal*, 8 (1962), 135–51; F. D. Price, 'A North Oxfordshire Parish and its Poor: Wigginton, 1730–1830', *Cake and Cockhorse*, 2 (1962), 1–6; R. V. H. Burne, 'The Treatment of the Poor in the Eighteenth Century in Chester', *Journal of the Chester and North Wales Architectural, Archaeological and Historic Society*, 52 (1965), 33–48; C. E. Mullineux, *Pauper and Poorhouse: A Study of the Administration of the Poor Laws in a Lancashire Parish* (Pendlebury, 1966); *Poor Relief in Elizabethan Ipswich*, ed. J. Webb (Suffolk Records Society, ix, Ipswich, 1966); G. W. Oxley, 'The Permanent Poor in South-west Lancashire under the Old Poor Law', in *Liverpool and Merseyside: Essays in the Economic and Social History of the Port and its Hinterland*, ed. J. R. Harris (London, 1969), pp. 16–49; *The Norwich Census of the*

approach, seeking to chart the implementation of social policy rather than reconstruct peoples' experience of it. Particularly influential were detailed monographs by E. M. Leonard (published before the Webbs' volume), Dorothy Marshall and Ethel Hampson, the last a county-level study of Poor Law administration in Cambridgeshire covering the whole period from 1597 to 1834.[42] Specific policy initiatives, such as Puritan projects for the poor in the Interregnum and Bristol's experiment with a 'Corporation for the Poor' in the 1690s, were also subjected to special scrutiny.[43] A. L. Beier, meanwhile, made the important finding that – in Warwickshire at least – the mechanisms of poor relief remained fully operational through the late 1640s and the 1650s.[44] Thus, when George Oxley published his brief synthesis of work on the Old Poor Law in 1974, historians had a good idea of the kinds of relief offered, the development of indoor relief, and the late-eighteenth-century recourse to expedients such as Speenhamland and the 'Roundsman' system.[45]

This top-down approach – focusing on policy and implementation – has continued to flourish, and indeed has arguably reached its apogee in the last thirty years.[46] Joanna Innes' work, for example, has located

Poor, 1570, ed. J. F. Pound (Norfolk Record Society, xl, Norwich, 1971); W. A. Cassell, 'The Parish and the Poor in New Brentford, 1720–1834', *Transactions of the London and Middlesex Archaeological Society*, 23 (1972), 174–93; S. R. Broadbridge, 'The Old Poor Law in the Parish of Stone', *North Staffordshire Journal of Field Studies*, 13 (1973), 11–25; *Poverty in Early Stuart Salisbury*, ed. P. Slack (Wiltshire Record Society, xxxi, Devizes, 1975); A. W. Coats, 'The Relief of Poverty, Attitudes to Labour and Economic Change in England, 1660–1782', *International Review of Social History*, 21 (1978), 98–121.

42   E. M. Leonard, *The Early History of English Poor Relief* (Cambridge, 1900); D. Marshall, *The English Poor in the Eighteenth Century: A Study in Social and Administrative History* (London, 1926); E. M. Hampson, *The Treatment of Poverty in Cambridgeshire, 1597–1834* (Cambridge, 1934).

43   V. Pearl, 'Puritans and Poor Relief: the London Workhouse, 1649–1660', in *Puritans and Revolutionaries: Essays in Seventeenth-Century History Presented to Christopher Hill*, ed. D. H. Pennington and K. Thomas (Oxford, 1978), pp. 206–32; *Bristol Corporation of the Poor: Selected Records, 1696–1898*, ed. E. E. Butcher (Bristol Record Society, iii, Bristol, 1932).

44   A. L. Beier, 'Poor Relief in Warwickshire, 1630–60', *PP*, 35 (1966), 77–100.

45   G. W. Oxley, *Poor Relief in England and Wales, 1601–1834* (Newton Abbot, 1974).

46   See: A. L. Beier, *The Problem of the Poor in Tudor and Early Stuart England* (London, 1983); A. L. Beier, *Masterless Men: The Vagrancy Problem in England, 1560–1640* (London, 1985); A. Fletcher, *Reform in the Provinces: The Government of Stuart England* (London, 1986), pp. 183–93; J. F. Pound, *Poverty and Vagrancy in Tudor England*, 2nd edn (London, 1986), pp. 1–36; see also: S. Hindle, *The Birthpangs of Welfare: Poor Relief and Parish Governance in Seventeenth-Century Warwickshire* (Dugdale Society Occasional

social policy developments in the 'long' eighteenth century firmly within their political and cultural context.[47] Steve King, meanwhile, has explored regional variations in approaches to the poor from the beginning of the eighteenth century to the middle of the nineteenth, and has undertaken the most wide-ranging quantitative work on overseers' accounts yet seen, arguing that geographical variations reflected specifically regional welfare cultures and implementation policies.[48] This was then complemented by an article he co-authored with Joan Kent, also heavily based on overseers' accounts, showing gradually rising costs between 1650 and 1750.[49] There has, meanwhile, been a continual flow of local studies.[50] More recently,

Papers, xl, Stratford-upon-Avon, 2000); S. Hindle, *The State and Social Change in Early Modern England, 1550–1640* (Basingstoke, 2000), pp. 153–62; S. Hindle, 'Dearth, Fasting and Alms: the Campaign for General Hospitality in Late Elizabethan England', *PP*, 172 (2001), 44–86; S. Hindle, *On the Parish?*, pp. 229–56.

47   J. Innes, 'Parliament and the Shaping of Eighteenth-Century English Social Policy', *TRHS*, 5th Ser., 40 (1990), 63–92; J. Innes, 'The "Mixed Economy of Welfare" in Early Modern England: Assessments of the Options from Hale to Malthus (c.1683–1803)', in *Charity, Self-interest and Welfare in the English Past*, ed. M. Daunton (London, 1996), pp. 139–80; J. Innes, 'The State and the Poor: Eighteenth-century England in European Perspective', in *Rethinking Leviathan: the Eighteenth-Century State in Britain and Germany*, ed. J. Brewer and E. Hellmuth (Oxford, 1999), pp. 225–80.

48   S. King, 'Reconstructing Lives: the Poor, the Poor Law and Welfare in Calverley, 1650–1820', *Social History*, 22 (1997), 318–38; S. King, *Poverty and Welfare in England, 1700–1850: A Regional Perspective* (Manchester, 2000); S. King, 'Locating and Characterizing Poor Households in Late-Seventeenth Century Bolton: Sources and Interpretations', *LPS*, 68 (2002), 42–62.

49   Kent and King, 'Changing Patterns'.

50   V. Pearl, 'Social Policy in Early Modern London', in *History and Imagination: Essays in Honour of H. R. Trevor-Roper*, ed. H. Lloyd-Jones, V. Pearl and B. Worden (London, 1981), pp. 115–31; P. Rushton, 'The Poor Law, the Parish and the Community in North-east England, 1600–1800', *Northern History*, 25 (1989), 135–52; J. Boulton, 'Going on the Parish: the Parish Pension and its Meaning in the London Suburbs, 1640–1724', in *Chronicling Poverty: the Voices and Strategies of the English Poor, 1640–1840*, ed. T. Hitchcock, P. King and P. Sharpe (London, 1997), pp. 19–46; J. Broad, 'Parish Economies of Welfare, 1650–1834', *Historical Journal*, 42 (1999), 985–1006; S. King, 'Reclothing the English Poor, 1750–1840', *Textile History*, 33 (2002), 37–47; S. A. Williams, 'Malthus, Marriage and Poor Law Allowances Revisited: a Bedfordshire Case Study, 1770–1834', *AgHR*, 52 (2004), 56–82; J. Healey, 'The Development of Poor Relief in Lancashire, c.1598–1680', *Historical Journal*, 53 (2010), 551–72; J. Healey, 'Poverty in an Industrializing Town: Deserving Hardship in Bolton, 1674–99', *Social History*, 35 (2010), 125–47; S. A. Williams, *Poverty, Gender and Life-cycle under the English Poor Law* (Woodbridge, 2011). Also: J. A. Johnston, 'The Parish Registers and Poor Law records of Powick, 1663–1841', *Transactions of the Worcestershire Archaeological Society*, 9 (1984), 55–66; S. MacFarlane,

Paul Fideler's lively synthesis has looked at pre-industrial welfare practices from a largely cultural-historical standpoint.[51] Marjorie McIntosh, meanwhile, has discussed late medieval and Tudor-period poor relief and, in an important argument, has shown that poor rates predated the 1598 statute in many rural parishes.[52]

Finally, in a highly original and heavily legalistic argument, Lorie Charlesworth has made a forceful case that the Poor Law created a common-law *right* to relief for the destitute poor, ultimately underpinned by the law of settlement (about which, she argues – correctly – historians have exaggerated the negatives).[53] Despite some distinctly idiosyncratic historiography, Charlesworth's book clarifies an important point about the doctrinal aspects of the Poor Law. Indeed, the idea that a right to relief had become entrenched as a *cultural* expectation by the later eighteenth century would find plenty of support from social historians. But Charlesworth has made the crucial contention that this, in a technical sense, was also a common-law right. Her argument, however, is weak on the critical issues of interpretation and discretion, particularly over time. It may well be that by the eighteenth century it was widely accepted that the destitute had a right to relief in their place of settlement; but was this also true of the seventeenth century? Despite a useful argument about the legal importance of the New Poor Law, when it comes to treatment of the operation of the law pre-1834, Charlesworth's work is curiously ahistorical. Indeed, she has little evidence that anyone in the seventeenth

---

'Social Policy and the Poor in the Later Seventeenth Century', in *The Making of the Metropolis: London, 1500–1700*, ed. A. L. Beier and R. Finlay (London, 1986), pp. 252–77; I. Nelson, 'Providing for the Poor, 1600–1834', in *Wivelsfield: the History of a Wealden Parish*, ed. H. Warne (Wivelsfield, 1994), pp. 123–43; N. C. Webb, 'Poverty and the Poor Law in Formby, 1701–1900', *Lancashire Local Historian*, 9 (1994), 12–19; M. A. Parsons, 'Poor Relief in Troutbeck, 1640–1836', CW2, 95 (1995), 169–86; P. Jones, *Making Ends Meet (Poor Relief in 18th Century Mangotsfield)* (Downend, 1998); R. L. Brown, *The Parish Pauper and the Poor Law: The Poor Law in Welshpool* (Welshpool, 2002); A. Poole, 'Welfare Provision in Seventeenth-century Kent: a Look at Biddenden and Neighbouring Parishes', *Archaeologia Cantiana*, 126 (2006), 257–77; H. Vaux, 'The Poor of Otham and Nearby Parishes: the Coxheath Poor House', *Archaeologia Cantiana*, 126 (2006), 49–70.

51   Fideler, *Social Welfare*; other textbooks with a later focus include: J. D. Marshall, *The Old Poor Law, 1795–1834*, 2nd edn (Basingstoke, 1985); L. H. Lees, *The Solidarities of Strangers: the English Poor Laws and the People, 1700–1948* (Cambridge, 1998); A. Brundage, *The English Poor Laws, 1700–1930* (Basingstoke, 2002).

52   McIntosh, *Poor Relief*.

53   L. Charlesworth, *Welfare's Forgotten Past: A Socio-Legal History of the Poor Law* (Abingdon, 2010), esp. pp. 50–2.

century interpreted the Poor Law as conferring a common-law right to relief, even if technically it might have done. Meanwhile, fundamental to her argument is that a right to relief existed for the 'destitute' poor; but destitution is a culturally determined concept, susceptible to shifts over time and across space. One man's destitution might be another man's austerity. Impotency, another central concept to the operation of the Poor Law, and particularly to the decision as to whether a pauper should be relieved in cash or in work, is again something that does not submit to the precise definitions demanded by law. At what precise moment of an old widow's descent into aged decrepitude did she become impotent? Was it when her hands failed? Her eyesight? Was it when she could no longer dress herself? This critical aspect of discretion was effectively written into the Poor Law statutes, and it gave crucial breathing space for officers to interpret the law in differing ways, something that Charlesworth largely ignores.

And yet, as much as destitution and impotence were partly subjective, if we distil Charlesworth's argument to a more straightforward point that the Poor Law conferred a right upon Englishmen *not to starve* (so long as they were willing to work), then it does become very useful. There was a powerful natural-law belief in the right to basic subsistence, and this had existed since the Middle Ages (at least).[54] What the Poor Law did was give this the backing of common-law doctrine. Indeed, the 1662 Act 'For the Better Relief of the Poor', which Charlesworth sees as critical through its settlement provisions, implies that this was central purpose of the law as it then stood, for it laments that defective settlement law and poor implementation of relief provisions 'doth enforce many to turn incorrigible rogues and others to perish for want'. In fact, many of the historians Charlesworth castigates for ignoring the right to relief would indeed accept – and celebrate – the fact that the Poor Law conferred a right not to starve to death, albeit one dependent on a willingness to work. What is really helpful about her book, though, is to show to historians that this was not just a hangover from older theological and philosophical traditions, but it was something that came to have the force of law.

Most influential within the top-down tradition, however, has been the work of Paul Slack. In addition to contributing a short textbook on

---

54   S. G. Swanson, 'The Medieval Foundations of John Locke's Theory of Natural Rights: Rights of Subsistence and the Principle of Extreme Necessity', *History of Political Thought*, 18 (1997), 399–459.

the early modern Poor Law,[55] Slack has also produced two crucial works of historical scholarship on the nature and cultural underpinnings of pre-industrial poor relief.[56] The more recent of these, based on his Ford Lectures, recounts and reflects on the changing theoretical, intellectual, and practical approaches to poverty and the poor from the Reformation to the so-called era of 'Improvement'. The earlier book, *Poverty and Policy in Tudor and Stuart England*, takes a broader approach, sketching the cultural and central-political background to developing relief strategies, but also going into considerable detail about the contours of local implementation, particularly in small towns. In fact, it also reflected a major shift in the historiography of poverty that was gathering pace when *Poverty and Policy* was published in 1988. This was pushing the focus away from policy-making and towards questions relating to the lived experience of paupers. Reflecting a broader change in the focus of social historians away from institutions and politics, and led by scholars writing in the 1960s and early 1970s, this stemmed from an increasing willingness of social historians to quantify and to apply social theory to the past. Most fundamentally, however, it emerged from a desire to write 'history from below'.

The impact of this scholarship, often referred to as the 'New Social History', has been the great enrichment of our knowledge of pre-industrial life, including the place of the Poor Law within that life.[57] In particular, three critical developments in our understanding of pre-industrial poverty have stemmed directly from this. First, it has become clear that official rate-funded relief was only one part of the domestic economy of the poor, or – as one historian has evocatively put it – just one part of the wider 'welfare patchwork'.[58] Thus, historians have been increasingly interested in the so-called 'economy of makeshifts' by which paupers scratched together enough income, or made enough savings, to survive,

---

55   P. Slack, *The English Poor Law, 1531–1782* (Basingstoke, 1990); also: P. Slack, 'Poverty and Politics in Salisbury, 1597–1666', in *Crisis and Order in English Towns, 1500–1700: Essays in Urban History*, ed. P. Clark and P. Slack (London, 1972), pp. 164–203; P. Slack, 'Books of Orders: the Making of English Social Policy, 1577–1631', *TRHS*, 5th Ser., 30 (1980), 1–22.

56   Slack, *Poverty and Policy*; Slack, *From Reformation to Improvement*.

57   Many of the original questions were posed in P. Laslett, *The World We Have Lost* (London, 1965); also: P. Laslett, *The World We Have Lost – Further Explored* (London, 1983). For a defence of the associated methodologies, see: K. Wrightson, 'The Enclosure of English Social History', *Rural History*, 1 (1990), 73–81.

58   King, *Poverty and Welfare*, p. 58.

often without calling upon their parish. Secondly, there has been a welcome focus on the 'micro-politics' of the Poor Law, emphasizing that the implementation of social policies was never a simple question of one group imposing their will on another, whether the Government imposing its will on the localities, or officers imposing their will on the poor. Rather, local practice was *negotiated*, with the poor themselves constituting active agents. Finally, attempts to interrogate the question of just who the poor *were* in sociological and economic terms have led historians to highlight the importance of so-called 'life-cycle poverty'. Those in need are thus discovered to have been the sufferers of certain disabilities relating to the progression through life, notably youth, old age, and those moments in which families were overburdened with dependants. Let us take these historiographical developments in turn.

The term 'economy of makeshifts' was originally coined by Olwen Hufton in her work on the poor of late *Ancien Régime* France, and refers to the diverse strategies of income-generation and expenditure-saving undertaken by marginal individuals and households.[59] Thus, historians of the English poor have argued that those facing destitution might take income from wages, communal resources, loans, neighbourly and kin support, local endowed charities and of course poor relief, in order to get by.[60] Moreover, work on this 'economy' has served to re-emphasize the importance of the paid labour of women and children within families,

---

59   O. Hufton, *The Poor of Eighteenth-Century France, 1750–1789* (Oxford, 1974); for another early approach to the same issue see: R. Smith, 'The Relief of Urban Poverty Outside the Poor Law, 1800–1850: a Study of Nottingham', *Midland History*, 11 (1974), 215–24.

60   M. H. D. van Leeuwen, 'The Logic of Charity: Poor Relief in Preindustrial Europe', *Journal of Interdisciplinary History*, 24 (1994), 589–613 (pp. 600–6); I. K. Ben-Amos, 'Gifts and Favors: Informal Support in Early Modern England', *Journal of Modern History*, 72 (2000), 295–338; J. Boulton, '"It is extreme necessity that makes me do this": Some "Survival Strategies" of Pauper Households in London's West End during the Early Eighteenth Century', *International Review of Social History*, Supplement 8 (2000), 47–70; S. King and A. Tomkins (eds), *The Poor in England, 1700–1850: An Economy of Makeshifts* (Manchester, 2003); C. Muldrew and S. King, 'Cash, Wages and the Economy of Makeshifts in England, 1650–1800', in *Experiencing Wages: Social and Cultural Aspects of Wage Forms in Europe since 1500*, ed. P. Scholliers and L. D. Schwarz (Oxford, 2003), pp. 155–82; Hindle, *On the Parish?*, pp. 15–95; I. K. Ben-Amos, *The Culture of Giving: Informal Support and Gift-Exchange in Early Modern England* (Cambridge, 2008). For treatment of an earlier period: M. K. McIntosh, 'Local Responses to the Poor in Late Medieval and Tudor England', *Continuity and Change*, 3 (1988), 209–45. For an emphasis of *institutional* variety of provision, see: Innes, 'Mixed Economy'.

and to show some of the ways that poor families made the savings necessary to balance their budgets. This makeshift economy stood as an important buffer zone between marginality and total destitution, and to some extent poverty as relieved by the Poor Law was a result of the *failure* of this economy to ensure sufficient support. The implications of this strand of historical research have not yet been fully explored, especially regarding such important concepts as proletarianization and the 'domestic' economy. If nothing else, makeshift economies served to take the sting out of increased dependency on wages, especially if the immiseration of the supposed male 'breadwinner' is overemphasized. This latter point, indeed, deserves particular emphasis in the light of recent work by Craig Muldrew, who has argued (separately) that many labourers had small garden plots, and that spinning provided a major source of income for women.[61] At the same time, the evident willingness of marginal kin groups to pool resources obviously complicates the established picture in which the nuclear household was the prime form of both social and economic organization.[62] For the study of poor relief, however, one of the most important points to arise is that the support provided by the Poor Law was, as Lynn Hollen Lees points out, *residual*.[63] Formal relief was intended to step in at the last moment, when all other legitimate avenues of making do had been exhausted. It was needs driven rather than contingency driven.

Micro-politics is a rather newer concept in terms of its applicability to

---

61   C. Muldrew, *Food, Energy and the Creation of Industriousness: Work and Material Culture in Agrarian England, 1550–1780* (Cambridge, 2011), pp. 106–11; C. Muldrew, '"Th'ancient Distaff" and "Whirling Spindle": Measuring the Contribution of Spinning to Household Earnings and the National Economy in England, 1550–1770', *EcHR*, 2nd Ser., 65 (2012), 498–526.

62   Laslett, *World We Have Lost*, pp. 90–9; cf. N. Tadmor, 'The Concept of the Household Family in Eighteenth-Century England', *PP*, 151 (1996), 111–40; N. Tadmor, 'Early Modern English Kinship in the Long Run: Reflections on Continuity and Change', *Continuity and Change*, 25 (2010), 15–48.

63   Lees, *Solidarities of Strangers*, pp. 19–111. Lees writes of the era of 1700–1834 as one in which 'residualism' was 'taken for granted'. Note, however, that Ottaway dissents from this view, pointing to the apparently generous 'care packages' given to elderly paupers in the eighteenth century. To a point, of course, such judgements are subjective, but the evidence presented in this book does suggest a *generalized* assumption that poor relief only stepped in when other avenues were failing to provide an acceptable standard of living. What that 'acceptable' standard was, and how conceptions of it changed over time, remains an intractable issue. S. Ottaway, 'Providing for the Elderly in Eighteenth-Century England', *Continuity and Change*, 13 (1998), 391–418 (p. 411).

the Poor Laws. Studies of the related ideas of micro-politics and 'negotiation' have been influenced by the school of historians – notably Keith
Wrightson – who have highlighted the 'political' aspects of everyday life
in the past.[64] The key essay was that of Wrightson on the 'Politics of the
Parish', but the work of the anthropologist James C. Scott, particularly
on 'weapons of the weak', has also been hugely influential.[65] Additionally,
many questions were posed in the important collection of essays edited
by Tim Hitchcock, Peter King and Pamela Sharpe, published in 1997,
on the 'voices and strategies' of the English poor in the (very) long
eighteenth century.[66] In particular, the latter volume explored the possibilities presented by underexploited sources on the actual experiences of
the poor, such as pauper letters, petitions and inventories, as well as more
established social historical evidence such as overseers' accounts and court
depositions. But the most detailed work has been that of Steve Hindle,
culminating in his 2004 book, *On the Parish? The Micro-Politics of Poor
Relief in Rural England, 1550–1750.*[67] Conceived partly to complement
Slack's urban-focused *Poverty and Policy*, Hindle's book provided a
thoughtful exploration of the miniature power struggles behind the

64   See, in particular, the essays in P. Griffiths, A. Fox and S. Hindle (eds), *The Experience
of Authority in Early Modern England* (Basingstoke, 1996); M. J. Braddick and J. Walter
(eds), *Negotiating Power in Early Modern Society: Order, Hierarchy, and Subordination in
Britain and Ireland* (Cambridge, 2001).
65   K. Wrightson, 'The Politics of the Parish in Early Modern England', in Griffiths, Fox
and Hindle (eds), *Experience of Authority*, pp. 10–46. Also: J. C. Scott, *Weapons of the
Weak: Everyday Forms of Peasant Resistance* (London, 1985); J. C. Scott, *Domination and
the Arts of Resistance: Hidden Transcripts* (London, 1990).
66   Hitchcock, King and Sharpe, *Chronicling Poverty*; also: R. W. Hoyle and C. J.
Spencer, 'The Slaidburn Poor Pasture: Changing Configurations of Popular Politics in the
Eighteenth- and Early Nineteenth-Century Village', *Social History*, 31 (2006), 182–205;
J. Healey, 'Poverty, Deservingness and Popular Politics: the Contested Relief of Agnes
Braithwaite, 1701–06', *THSLC*, 145 (2007), 131–56.
67   S. Hindle, 'Exclusion Crises: Poverty, Migration and Parochial Responsibility in
English Rural Communities, c.1560–1660', *Rural History*, 7 (1996), 125–49; S. Hindle,
'The Problem of Pauper Marriage in Seventeenth-Century England', *TRHS*, 6th Ser., 8
(1998), 71–89; S. Hindle, 'Power, Poor Relief and Social Relations in Holland Fen, c.1600–
1800', *Historical Journal*, 41 (1998), 67–98; S. Hindle, 'Exhortation and Entitlement:
Negotiating Inequality in English rural communities, 1550–1650', in Braddick and Walter
(eds), *Negotiating Power*, pp. 102–22; S. Hindle, '"Not by bread only"? Common Right,
Parish Relief and Endowed Charity in a Forest Economy, c.1600–1800', in King and
Tomkins (eds), *Poor in England*, pp. 39–75; S. Hindle, 'Dependency, Shame and Belonging:
Badging the Deserving Poor, c.1550–1750', *Cultural and Social History*, 1 (2004), 29–58;
S. Hindle, *On the Parish?*

overall formulation of Poor Law policy across two centuries, showing that relief policies were not simply dictated 'from above'.[68] Rather they were negotiated between often competing loci of power, including central government, county elites, local officeholders, and the poor themselves. The distribution of poor relief, moreover, served as an arena for the more general contestation of social relations.[69] Indeed, Hindle's work has done much to qualify – though never completely overturn – the notion that the Poor Law acted as a form of social control.

Through Scott, much of this work has been profoundly influenced by anthropology; by contrast, scholarship on life-cycle poverty has taken its cue from another branch of the social sciences – demography, and notably the historical demography undertaken by members of the Cambridge Group for the History of Population and Social Structure. Critical here has been Tim Wales's important essay, published in 1984, on the social and family circumstance of paupers in seventeenth-century Norfolk.[70] Thus childhood, old age, and the problems of being 'overcharged with children' have become established as the best-known causes of need in pre-industrial England, with the importance of these factors being amply demonstrated by a body of work, including that of Wales, W. Newman-Brown, Richard Smith, Steve King, and most recently, Samantha Williams.[71] Similarly important has been the notion of 'nuclear hardship', elucidated most effectively in an article by Peter Laslett in 1988.[72] This held that, in a

---

68   Hindle, *On the Parish?*, pp. 361–449.
69   Cf. Goldie, 'Unacknowledged Republic'.
70   T. Wales, 'Poverty, Poor Relief and the Life-cycle: Some Evidence from Seventeenth-Century Norfolk', in *Land, Kinship and Life-cycle*, ed. R. M. Smith (Cambridge, 1984), pp. 351–404.
71   E.g. W. Newman-Brown, 'The Receipt of Poor Relief and Family Situation: Aldenham, Hertfordshire, 1630–90', in Smith (ed.), *Land, Kinship and Life-cycle*, pp. 405–22; M. Pelling, 'Old Age, Poverty, and Disability in Early Modern Norwich: Work, Remarriage, and other Expedients', in *Life, Death and the Elderly*, ed. M. Pelling and R. M. Smith (London, 1991), pp. 74–101; T. Sokoll, 'Old Age in Poverty: the Record of Essex Pauper Letters, 1780–1834', in Hitchcock, King and Sharpe (eds), *Chronicling Poverty*, pp. 127–54; R. M. Smith, 'Ageing and Well-being in Early-Modern England: Pension Trends and Gender Preferences under the English Old Poor Law, c.1650–1800', in *Old Age from Antiquity to Post-Modernity*, ed. P. Johnson and P. Thane (London, 1998), pp. 64–95; King, 'Reconstructing Lives'; King, *Poverty and Welfare*; L. A. Botelho, *Old Age and the English Poor Law, 1500–1700* (Woodbridge, 2004); S. R. Ottaway, *The Decline of Life: Old Age in Eighteenth-Century England* (Cambridge, 2004), pp. 173–276; Williams, *Poverty*.
72   P. Laslett, 'Family, Kinship and the Collectivity as Systems of Support in Pre-industrial

society in which the nuclear household was a fairly strictly observed social norm, and in which both kin densities were low and inter-kin economic interactions infrequent, any kind of misfortune that disrupted the self-supporting capacity of the household was likely to be disastrous. There was no safety net in the form of extended household groupings, as there was in many non-nuclear household societies. Thus societies based on a nuclear family structure are, it is contended, more likely to place the onus for support for the needy on the 'collectivity' in the form of public sector institutions such as the English Poor Law.

To a considerable extent, and partly reflecting its institutional relationship with the Cambridge Group, work on life-cycle poverty relies on the linkage of family reconstitution data to the accounts of overseers of the poor, but such techniques (as the best work is well aware) leave significant blind spots. Youth, old age, and parenthood, for example, are relatively easy to identify through family reconstitution, household breakdown perhaps less so, and the identification of sickness is especially difficult. Those who moved between parishes are often invisible, and there are particular difficulties with applying these methods to large parishes, especially northern ones, where the unit of administration for poor relief (the township) was usually different from that which registered vital events (the parish). Thus, the concept of 'life-cycle poverty' works as a useful explanation as to why so many of the poor seem to be old or overburdened with children, but it cannot be stretched into becoming a full model for why people ended 'up on the parish'.

Conclusion: 'deserving' poverty

This book sits squarely in this tradition of history from below. It uses a unique archive of pauper petitions to ask why people became poor in pre-industrial England. The central argument is that poverty for most households came when two forces intersected. On the one hand, the character of *marginality* was determined by the socio-economic structure, marginal households and individuals being those who were broadly at risk of indigence. These were – in other words – poor in the wider sense of having few material possessions, persistently low incomes, and little

Europe: a Consideration of the "Nuclear Hardship" Hypothesis', *Continuity and Change*, 3 (1988), 153–75.

chance of saving enough money to cushion themselves against temporary difficulties. The marginal population was not necessarily a proletariat.[73] Rather, the marginal population was an amorphous group within society that was broadly 'at risk' of destitution. On the other hand, destitution itself (i.e. the experience of poverty so total that individuals and households felt they needed to apply for poor relief) was usually set off most immediately by some form of contingency or *misfortune*, such as sickness, an accident, family breakdown, the onset of old age, or a wider economic crisis.

The book is divided into three sections. Part 1 introduces the economic history of Lancashire, and the process by which the Poor Law became established there. It concludes with a discussion of the main sources used, and of what they tell us about the politics of poverty and poor relief in the period. Part 2 will explore the lives of paupers on the margins of society: the extent to which 'the poor' formed a distinctive class in early modern Lancashire, and the survival strategies they used in order to 'make shift' and to stay off relief. Finally, part 3 will peer into the causes of poverty, asking just what personal characteristics and catastrophes might push people from marginal lives into dependence on formal poor relief. It will describe and explore the main kinds of 'deserving poverty'. Essentially, it argues that most of the poor were either old, sick, or single, or some combination of the three; many also were in families that had too many children, and a smaller number were suffering from able-bodied unemployment or from other 'environmental' misfortunes, such as fire. In the final chapter, the book will look in more detail at the relationship between the fluctuating economic environment and the world of the poor. As with more personal contingencies, the Poor Law provided support for large numbers of the marginal in times of trade depression, epidemics, and – most especially – dearth. It was, then, a safety net against the varied misfortunes of pre-industrial life: the 'crosses and losses in this world', as one petitioner put it, vividly, in the year of the Glorious Revolution.[74]

73   L. Shaw-Taylor, 'Parliamentary Enclosure and the Emergence of an English Agricultural Proletariat', *Journal of Economic History*, 61 (2001), 640–62, esp. pp. 641–3.
74   LA, QSP/667/7.

PART I:
CONTEXTS

I

Lancashire, 1600–1730: A Developing Society

> But a man may judge of the goodnesse of the soile, partly by the consti-
> tution and complexion of the inhabitants, who are to see to, passing
> faire and beautifull, and in part, if you please, by the cattaile. For, in
> their kine and oxen, which have goodly heads and faire spread hornes,
> and in body are well proportionate withall, you shall find in maner no
> one point wanting, that *Mago* the Carthaginian doth require …
>
> William Camden (trns. Philemon Holland), *Britannia* (1610)[1]

In the summer of 1701, Agnes Braithwaite – a septuagenarian widow from
Hawkshead – travelled to Lancaster Quarter Sessions.[2] We do not know
whether she went on foot, as would have befitted her poverty, or whether
she got a lift, perhaps with a friend or neighbour on horseback. She was,
she claimed, 'a very poore impotent person aged very neare eighty years',
so the latter seems most likely. On the other hand, one of Hawkshead's
overseers later complained of how she was not so incapacitated that she
could not 'travel to do mishcheef', as Justices could themselves see, so
perhaps she walked after all.

Of course, no trace has been left to us of Agnes's route south, from the
county's northernmost parish to its traditional administrative hub. Most
likely she went east first, either crossing Windermere by ferry or passing
down its western shore, crossing the Leven at Newby Bridge. If she took
the latter route, she would have had the option of crossing Morecambe
Bay at low tide, coming ashore at Hest Bank. If she wanted to avoid the
treacherous sands, she would have swung east – from the ferry via the
Lyth Valley, to Newby Bridge and along the sheer southern limestone face
of Whitbarrow Scar. Where she reached the River Kent, in the shadow
of the imposing Levens Hall and its medieval pele tower, she would have
turned sharply south, down the old Kendal to Lancaster road – turnpiked

---

1   W. Camden, *Britannia*, trans. P. Holland (London, 1610), p. 745.
2   For Braithwaite's story, see: Healey, 'Poverty, Deservingness, and Popular Politics'.

in the late eighteenth century and now the A6. This she would have followed south on a dreary trudge, through miles of green pasture fields, past numberless isolated farmhouses, occasionally stopping off in one of the small, dark-stoned villages that dotted the way: Milnthorpe, Beetham, Warton-in-Lonsdale. On her left, rolling green drumlins grazed by cattle and sheep, and perhaps the occasional small field of barley, reaching its fullest height as she travelled, for the harvest was approaching; on her right the commons, woods, and limestone outcrops of the Yealands and Warton Crag. Once she passed south of the great mass of the crag, a new vista opened up on her right-hand side. She would have watched Morecambe Bay go through its daily motions: tides will have disappeared out as far as the eye could see, to the distant strip of Walney Island far on the western horizon. As they receded, local people – perhaps most commonly women and children – followed, picking the fresh fruits of the sea: the cockles and shrimps for which the Bay is still renowned today.

Her journey was a rural one, and it is one that her mother would have recognized – if she herself had made it – when Agnes was born in the 1620s. The roads were the same; the landscape of small pasture farms, woodlands and stone-built houses would have been similarly recognizable. The large common fells of her home parish of Hawkshead were still unenclosed, and the sands of the Bay were still a livelihood to many; north Lancashire remained one of England's poorest regions. Had Agnes's mother followed her daughter's journey, though, she would have noticed some small changes. There were probably fewer fields of barley around 1700 compared with the 1620s, which would have surprised her, given that the people she saw would have been better fed. The people that Agnes's mother would have met in the 1620s would have remembered the famine year of 1623, where one out of every twenty had died; those whom Agnes met remembered the hard years of the 1690s, but as a time of high prices and low wages, not of death. A large number of the houses were new too, a sign of the relative prosperity of pasture farming in the second half of the seventeenth century. Agnes will have seen the door-lintels with their dates that still exist in abundance today (though she might not have understood them). If she came by the sands, she would – as she approached the coast – have looked to the shore at the farms at Bolton Holmes and Red Bank, both of which had seen some rebuilding in the previous decades. If she came by land, she will have passed a series of dark stone houses in the middle of the long, strung-out village of Bolton-le-Sands, many of which had recently been rebuilt and which survive to this day bearing date-stones from within her lifetime. Indeed, where the two routes converged at Slyne, there survives a wonderful cobble and sandstone, two-and-a-half storey house, with a clear date-stone above the roadside entrance, bearing the date 1681, when it was apparently substantially rebuilt by Cornelius and Mary Green.

A little way to the south of Slyne, Agnes would have started to sense that she was approaching her destination. Lancaster is not really visible from the northern approach road, so perhaps it was a general thickening of the population as she entered the township of Skerton that first alerted her; perhaps it was an increase in the volume of traffic – men on horseback, women going to market, farmers' servants with their animals – or perhaps it was the smell, for towns at the time were heaving masses of people and animals, and of their respective wastes. But sooner or later, the town itself will have come into view, with its sandstone buildings, its Priory church, and above all its foreboding and ancient castle, sat on the west side of the town, watching and menacing it: a prison as much as a fortress, and a feared destination for the county's debtors and felons.

In Lancaster, Agnes will have experienced something quite different. A quickening of life: there were shops, markets, hawkers; a grammar school and some wonderfully ornate lodgings, used by the assize judges. Perhaps she walked past the shop of William Stout, probably in Market Street. If she had come via the sands, she had already passed William's birthplace at Red Bank in Bolton-le-Sands, but by 1701, William had set up his small shop in the county town. His autobiography, one of the great treasures of the age's social history, tells of an increasingly commercial town, benefiting from growing coastal and Atlantic trade. It was a place whose quiet confidence pointed to a rather different future from the slow change that was creeping over its rural hinterlands. It looked outwards to the rest of the country, and increasingly to the rest of the world.

Most descriptions of the County Palatine of Lancaster – the Lancashire that was effectively dismembered in local government reforms of 1974 – came from people who entered it from the south, however (Figure 1). These southerners would have been presented with a very different world in 1701 compared with the one that Agnes Braithwaite walked through from the north. The pasture fields were still there, as was the landscape dotted with stone houses and farms; but they would have seen people not just tending sheep and milking cattle, but many more of them would have been working at looms, or – in the south-west of the county – scraping away at opencast coalmines. Far from the sleepy villages of Warton and Bolton-le-Sands, their routes will have taken them through

Figure 1: Lancashire Hundred boundaries

teeming, growing towns like Liverpool – 'London in miniature', said Celia
Fiennes in 1698 – Wigan, or Manchester.[3] To the east, they would still
have seen great unenclosed moors of the Pennines, then as now, forming a
formidable barrier between Lancashire and the West Riding of Yorkshire.
They could still look down to the west upon the vast, undrained mosses of
the county's seaboard. But they will have sensed a new quickness about the
economy: traders walking in and out of Manchester with bundles of white
cloth, merchants negotiating with manufacturers over bales of raw cotton,
shipped from Turkey to be worked on the looms of Bolton and Blackburn.
Woollen clothes carried on horseback down from the Pennine towns of
Bury and Rochdale; linen-websters busy weaving sailcloths, all ready to
fit out the ships that were gathering in the expanding port of Liverpool.
In a few years that port was to take a leap into the unknown, constructing
the dry dock that would allow it to occupy the leading position amongst
English slaving ports within fifty years. Around Wigan, they will have seen
how nature's boon of coal was literally fuelling a metalworking industry
of growing sophistication. If they stopped in Wigan for any length of
time, they will have watched its potato market, England's first. Some of
the vegetables had come from Ireland, but others were grown locally. A
curious visitor might have followed a potato-trading farmer back to his
estate on the Fylde, in the middle of the county, where they will have seen
a developed and profitable agrarian economy, founded on arable farming,
which was in turn helping to feed the growing towns of the county, not
just in the south but further north at Preston.

It was this economic landscape against which our story of poverty
played out. Pauper lives were economic lives. The region's economy
mattered. It helped determine the social structure of which they were a
part, and the opportunities they had for productive labour to support
themselves. There was, indeed, a genuine and general dynamism within
the Lancashire economy, with new industries being undertaken, new
markets tapped, and new wealth being created. This was particularly the
case by the end of the period. When Daniel Defoe came to describe the
Manchester region in his famous *Tour Through the Whole Island of Great
Britain* (1727), he presented a prospering town and hinterland, complete
with a growing population. 'The Manchester trade we all know', he
enthused, 'and all that are concerned in it know that it is, as all our other

---

3   Quoted in D. E. Ascott, F. Lewis and M. Power, *Liverpool, 1660–1750: People,
Prosperity and Power* (Liverpool, 2006), p. 14.

manufactures are, very much encreased within these thirty or forty years'. And 'as the manufacture is encreased, the people must be encreased of course'.[4] But there was also significant local and regional variety: the south-east, south-west and north of the county comprising distinctive (if interconnected) economic and social 'zones', each with certain common characteristics. Finally, the period was also one of integration within national and international networks of exchange, culture and politics. We need, then, to consider this economic world in which our paupers lived.

Landscape and people

Our place of study was, and to some extent still is, a harsh landscape.[5] Suffering from one of the wettest climates amongst English counties, Lancashire must have seemed a strange place to southern travellers at the beginning of our period. Bounded in the east by the Pennines, the land sweeps down towards the sea in the west, the harsh millstone grit of the hills with its vast open commons, scattered stony farmhouses and occasional solitary churches giving way to the flatter lands of the Manchester basin, the Fylde, and the Lancashire plain. Here, plusher pastures mixed with cornfields and more nucleated and prosperous settlements. Yet, even in these parts, semi-wilderness was never far away, for here were the massive wetlands of Martin Mere and Chat Moss, and the sand dunes and salt marshes of the immediate coast. Here also were the great rivers, which cut the county into horizontal segments. The Mersey separated Lancashire from the more prosperous Cheshire plain to the south and beyond that the English Midlands; further north, the Irwell, Ribble and Lune all carved their own paths through the county, each one presenting a major obstacle to travellers wishing to journey north or south. Even more treacherous were the sands of Morecambe Bay, passable at low tide but only with an experienced guide, which served to separate Furness from the rest of the county. This latter region, Furness, was closer in character to Cumberland and Westmorland than it was to the rest of Lancashire, and in places it exceeded even the Pennines in ruggedness, giving the county its highest

---

4 D. Defoe, *A Tour Through the Whole Island of Great Britain*, ed. G. D. H. Cole and D. C. Browning, 2 vols (London, 1962), vol. 2, pp. 261–2.
5 See: R. Millward, *Lancashire: An Illustrated Essay on the History of the Landscape* (London, 1955); N. J. Higham, *A Frontier Landscape: The North West in the Middle Ages* (Macclesfield, 2004).

point (801 metres above sea level) and its two major lakes, Coniston and Windermere, the latter shared with Westmorland.[6]

Not surprisingly, this difficult landscape helped to leave the county one of the least developed in England. In the 1515 Lay Subsidy, Lancashire had been the poorest assessed county (Cumberland, Westmorland, Durham and Northumberland, which were exempted, were probably poorer).[7] The region's medieval poverty is attested even today by a lack of pre-sixteenth-century buildings, and by the great distances from one original parish church to the next.[8] In the 1660s, according to its Hearth Tax returns, Lancashire had one of the lowest densities of larger houses in the whole country.[9] Hardly helpful was the proximity of the Scottish border, and the scatter of pele towers – fortified buildings of the middling and lower gentry – is a reminder of the ferocity of cross-border conflict before 1603.[10] By our period, this warfare had theoretically ceased, though Lancashire still had to face four more invasions from the north, in 1648, 1651, 1715 and 1745.

To an extent this was still a society characterized by isolation and backwardness. Over two-thirds of marriages amongst the county's gentry were between two individuals from within the county, while literacy appears to have been low.[11] According to a sample of early-seventeenth-century court depositions from Salford, West Derby and Leyland hundreds, 9 per cent of gentlemen, 43 per cent of yeomen, 64 per cent of tradesmen, 86 per cent of husbandmen, 94 per cent of labourers and male servants, and 98 per cent of women were unable to sign their names.[12] Other

6   J. D. Marshall, 'Communities, Societies, Regions and Local History: Perceptions of Locality in High and Low Furness', *Local Historian*, 26 (1996), 36–47.

7   R. S. Schofield, 'The Geographical Distribution of Wealth in England, 1334–1649', *EcHR*, 2nd Ser., 18 (1965), 483–510 (p. 508); also, E. J. Buckatzsch, 'The Geographical Distribution of Wealth in England, 1086–1843: an Experimental Survey of Certain Tax Assessments', *EcHR*, 2nd Ser., 3 (1950), 180–202.

8   See for example: Higham, *Frontier Landscape*; C. Hartwell, M. Hyde and N. Pevsner, *Lancashire: Manchester and the South-East* (London, 2004), pp. 19–31; R. Pollard and N. Pevsner, *Lancashire: Liverpool and the South-West* (London, 2006), pp. 18–25, 29–32.

9   T. Arkell, 'Identifying Regional Variations from the Hearth Tax', *Local Historian*, 33 (2003), 148–74 (p. 156).

10   Higham, *Frontier Landscape*, pp. 17, 38, 153; A. White, *Pele Towers of the Morecambe Bay Area: A Survey* (Lancaster, 1972).

11   B. G. Blackwood, *The Lancashire Gentry and the Great Rebellion, 1640–60* (CS, 3rd Ser., xxv, Manchester, 1973), p. 26.

12   K. Wrightson, 'The Puritan Reformation of Manners, with special reference to the

pointers suggest a low level of education even amongst the county's elite: between 1590 and 1640, for example, fewer than 30 per cent of Lancashire magistrates had been to university, a lower level than either Yorkshire or Somerset. By the early eighteenth century there is evidence that this situation was improving. As W. K. Jordan pointed out, Lancastrians made significant bequests to educational causes in the sixteenth and early seventeenth centuries, and this benevolence continued into the eighteenth when the county saw considerable investment in charity schools.[13]

The established church was weak. A population of around 200,000 in 1650 was supposed to find its way into just 64 parish churches and 128 chapels of ease and even within these the quality of provision was hardly high.[14] In 1622 it was reported that at least 52 places of worship in Lancashire had no Book of Homilies, while in 1633 the ministers of 19 churches and 32 chapels were supposed to have been grossly negligent in their duties.[15] It is also clear that many livings were desperately poor. Even as late as 1778, most Lancashire curates were paid between £40 and £50 a year, while in Furness the going rate was, according to one historian, 'no more than the annual wage of a ploughman or a shepherd'.[16] Given these factors, Lancashire unsurprisingly developed into a centre for nonconformity, and the county was simultaneously England's most Catholic, while also including the second strongest concentration of Protestant dissent, behind Essex.[17] It has been calculated that in 1715 some 35 per cent of the county's land was owned by Catholics, although their numbers and wealth were heavily concentrated in the western lowlands.[18] By contrast, the south-east of the county contained an impressive knot of Puritan preachers and congregations, notably around Manchester and Bolton.[19] The apex of this latter movement came during the 1640s and 1650s, when Presbyterian church government was introduced to the

Counties of Lancashire and Essex' (Cambridge Univ. PhD thesis, 1974), pp. 119–20; J. K. Walton, *Lancashire: A Social History, 1558–1939* (Manchester, 1987), pp. 32–3.

13   W. K. Jordan, *The Social Institutions of Lancashire: A Study of the Changing Patterns of Aspirations in Lancashire, 1480–1660* (CS, 3rd Ser., xi, Manchester, 1962), pp. 29–75.

14   Ibid., p. 37; see also: C. Haigh, *Reformation and Resistance in Tudor Lancashire* (London, 1975), pp. 1–97, 225–46.

15   Wrightson, 'Puritan Reformation', pp. 273–4.

16   J. Addy, 'Bishop Porteus' Visitation of the Diocese of Chester, 1778', *Northern History*, 13 (1977), 175–98 (pp. 180, 183); Walton, *Lancashire*, p. 95.

17   Walton, *Lancashire*, pp. 92–3.

18   Ibid., p. 46.

19   Haigh, *Reformation and Resistance*, pp. 295–315; R. C. Richardson, *Puritanism in*

county and aggressive policies aimed at the 'reformation of manners' were launched by the ascendant Puritans, but this of course proved to be only temporary.[20] The Restoration effectively brought the downfall of Lancashire Puritanism, but Protestant nonconformity lived on through the proliferation of Dissenting sects in the later seventeenth century. Presbyterians, Independents, Baptists and Quakers formed new congregations, again concentrated in the south-east of the county but with outposts in the culturally isolated uplands.[21]

While the established church struggled, older forms of popular culture seem to have maintained their vitality. The county suffered two major witch crazes in the first half of the seventeenth century.[22] More tangible than this was the survival of wakes as a form of popular festivity, greater in northern parts than elsewhere, into the eighteenth century and beyond.[23] Marital practices were in some ways also distinctive, at least at the beginning of our period. Child marriage had been relatively common amongst the county's gentry in the sixteenth century, while it has been argued that the process of marriage itself was less formalized amongst the wider population than was the case in the southern and eastern lowlands.[24] Largely as a result of this, it seems, the ratio of illegitimate to legitimate births was exceptionally high in the North West up to the 1650s.[25] After this, the illegitimacy ratio tailed off, though it remained roughly double the national average.

Population and demography

However backward and conservative the county was, it began in our period to experience an important process of industrialization and economic development. Of course, Lancashire was still some way from its place in

North-West England: A Regional Study of the Diocese of Chester to 1642 (Manchester, 1972), pp. 1–22.

20   Wrightson, 'Puritan Reformation'.

21   Walton, *Lancashire*, pp. 92–5.

22   R. Poole (ed.), *The Lancashire Witches: Histories and Stories* (Manchester, 2002).

23   R. Poole, 'Lancashire Wakes Week', *History Today*, 34, no. 8 (1984), 22–9; F. Heal, *Hospitality in Early Modern England* (Oxford, 1990), pp. 363–5.

24   Haigh, *Reformation and Resistance*, pp. 87–97; R. Adair, *Courtship, Illegitimacy and Marriage in Early Modern England* (Manchester, 1996), pp. 148–87.

25   Wrightson, 'Puritan Reformation', p. 54; Adair, *Courtship, Illegitimacy and Marriage*, p. 63.

the economic sun, but by the 1760s at the latest, the southern part around Liverpool and Manchester formed one of the most advanced economic regions in England and perhaps elsewhere.[26] One of the most important changes was the growth in population. The demography of the county has not been subjected to systematic study, despite the widespread publication of parish registers, and so we are forced to generalize from spotty data. Nonetheless, enough research has been done to suggest a broadly convincing picture of the major changes.[27] The period was one of growth, though not necessarily at a uniform pace or with an equal geographical spread. Neither did this growth proceed without major setbacks.

It is worth dividing the period into three, with the decades before 1660 seeing the last stutters of the great sixteenth-century population growth and – arguably – some signs of a Malthusian crisis.[28] Birth rates were high, but so was mortality, with recurrent peaks in response to plague and, in 1623, famine.[29] Following this was a period of stagnation in which a more 'low-pressure' demographic regime pertained, characterized by low death rates, even lower birth rates, and an easing of the regularity and severity of mortality crises, thanks in part to the disappearance of both

26   This is the impression to be gained from J. C. Stobart, *The First Industrial Region: North-west England, c.1700–60* (Manchester, 2004). The suggestion, made by the editors of a 2004 collection of essays on the cotton industry, that Lancashire remained in the 1780s 'a barren and isolated locality' is not sustainable: D. A. Farnie and D. J. Jeremy (ed.), *The Fibre that Changed the World: the Cotton Industry in International Perspective, 1600–1990s* (Oxford, 2004), preface.

27   E.g. W. G. Howson, 'Plague, Poverty and Population in Parts of North-west England, 1580–1720', *THSLC*, 112 (1960), 29–55; R. Speake, 'The Historical Demography of Warton Parish before 1801', *THSLC*, 122 (1970), 43–65; J. T. Swain, *Industry before the Industrial Revolution: North-east Lancashire, c.1500–1640* (CS, 3rd Ser., xxxii, Manchester, 1986), pp. 16–32; Walton, *Lancashire*, pp. 24–6; C. B. Phillips and J. H. Smith, *Lancashire and Cheshire from AD 1540* (London, 1994), pp. 5–12, 66–70.

28   Walton, *Lancashire*, p. 30.

29   E.g. R. S. France, 'A History of Plague in Lancashire', *THSLC*, 90 (1938), 1–175. It should be noted that many of the identifications of cases of 'plague' are extremely unsafe, although some, like that in Preston in 1630–31, are well established. It is perhaps best read in conjunction with: A. B. Appleby, *Famine in Tudor and Stuart England* (Liverpool, 1978), pp. 99–101; see also: Howson, 'Plague, Poverty and Population'; T. S. Willan, 'Plague in Perspective: the Case of Manchester in 1605', *THSLC*, 132 (1983), 29–40. On famine in the region: Laslett, *World We Have Lost*, pp. 130–2; C. D. Rogers, *The Lancashire Population Crisis of 1623* (Manchester, 1975); Swain, *Industry*, pp. 22–5; R. W. Hoyle, 'Famine as Agricultural Catastrophe: the Crisis of 1622–4 in East Lancashire', *EcHR*, 2nd Ser., 63 (2010), 974–1002; J. Healey, 'Land, Population, and Famine in the English Uplands: A Westmorland Case Study', *AgHR*, 59 (2011), 151–75.

Table 1: Estimates of the Lancashire population, 1563–1750

Date	Source	Estimate (nearest 10,000)
1563	Diocesan population returns	90,000
1664	Hearth tax assessments	160,000
1690	Hearth tax assessments	190,000
1700	Dr John Kay (1835)	170,000
1750	Dr John Kay (1835)	300,000

plague and famine, although not yet epidemic disease.[30] Finally, starting at different times in different areas, the county began from around 1700 to embark on a long period of demographic growth, the available evidence suggesting that by the 1750s sustained and strong expansion was under way.[31] These broad trends are suggested by Table 1.[32]

As with most of the country then, the period from the middle of the sixteenth century to the Civil War saw significant growth in the Lancashire population.[33] Figures derived from the 1563 diocesan population returns and the 1664 hearth tax assessments suggest a total increase from around 90,000 to 160,000 in that century. However, this growth was disproportionately strong in the deaneries of Manchester, Warrington and Amounderness, and to a lesser extent Blackburn (roughly equivalent to Salford, West Derby, Amounderness and Blackburn hundreds). It was much weaker in the hundreds of Leyland and Lonsdale, with population in some parts hardly growing at all.[34] With growth came limited urbanization, leaving around one out of every nine Lancastrians living in towns of a thousand or more inhabitants by 1664.[35] By that date there were nine or ten such settlements, with Manchester at the top of the county's urban hierarchy with a population of around four thousand. Preston and Wigan

30   Phillips and Smith, *Lancashire and Cheshire*, pp. 5–12, 66–70; Speake, 'Historical Demography', pp. 52–60.
31   Walton, *Lancashire*, pp. 77–9; Phillips and Smith, *Lancashire and Cheshire*, pp. 66–70.
32   *Annual Report of the Poor Law Commissioners for England and Wales*, 13 vols (London, 1835–47), vol. 1, p. 302; Walton, *Lancashire*, p. 25; Phillips and Smith, *Lancashire and Cheshire*, p. 67.
33   Cf. E. A. Wrigley and R. Schofield, *The Population History of England, 1541–1871: A Reconstruction* (London, 1981), p. 495.
34   Walton, *Lancashire*, pp. 24–5; Phillips and Smith, *Lancashire and Cheshire*, pp. 5–9.
35   Walton, *Lancashire*, p. 25.

had around two thousand inhabitants each, while Warrington, Bolton and Bury were not much smaller.[36]

This growth took place despite a series of mortality crises in the region, with that of 1623 the most serious, killing around 5 per cent of the county's population.[37] Other periods of high mortality occurred during the Civil War and the later 1650s, and although these were the product of war and disease (including plague) rather than directly from hunger, the regularity of major crises has led to the suggestion that the county was suffering a Malthusian crisis from the 1620s to the 1660s.[38] The fact that the most favoured explanation for the massive mortality in 1623 is famine lends support to this assertion, as – arguably – does the severe dearth of 1647–50.[39] Nonetheless, we should be cautious before accepting this too readily. To blame the disease and hunger that came with war on overpopulation would seem to miss the point,[40] and it is clear from the chronology of outbreaks of plague that no easy correlation existed with food shortage.[41] Moreover, there is evidence of starvation in the region in the 1590s, well before much of the major population increase.[42] In reality, something rather more complex was probably at play, with the population growth of the 'long' sixteenth century leading to imbalances within the agrarian economy and a degree of overspecialization in non-arable farming and in industry.[43] There may also have been a proliferation of cottagers and subtenants in the countryside.[44] In the post-Civil War period – by contrast – stronger industrial and commercial-agricultural development allowed Lancashire to tap into the more prosperous national

36   Ibid.; Stobart, First Industrial Region, p. 37.

37   Rogers, Lancashire Population Crisis, p. 10.

38   Walton, Lancashire, pp. 29–30.

39   For a dissenting view see: J. Perkins, 'Deaths in Stuart Lancashire: Some New Interpretations', Lancashire Local Historian, 8 (1993), 18–32; also, see: C. J. Duncan and S. Scott, 'The Mortality Crisis of 1623 in North-west England', LPS, 58 (1997), 14–25; the later dearth has not received much attention, but see: Hindle, 'Dearth and the English Revolution'.

40   Unless, that is, one sees the Civil Wars as symptoms of overpopulation, on which see: J. A. Goldstone, Revolution and Rebellion in the Early Modern World (Oxford, 1991), pp. 63–169, esp. pp. 83–92.

41   P. Slack, The Impact of Plague in Tudor and Stuart England (Oxford, 1985), pp. 53–78.

42   Appleby, Famine, pp. 109–21; Phillips and Smith, Lancashire and Cheshire, pp. 66–70.

43   Appleby, Famine, pp. 17–94; Swain, Industry, esp. pp. 77–107.

44   Healey, 'Land, Population, and Famine', pp. 172–4.

economy, which was at the same time benefiting from both greater market integration and higher real wages.[45]

After the middle of the seventeenth century a rather different set of conditions arose, involving a lower pressure demographic regime as both birth rates and death rates fell.[46] There were also fewer detectable mortality crises, although high burial totals hit the north of the county around 1670, and most areas suffered occasional epidemics.[47] Most notably, however, the county was able to ride out seriously deficient harvests in 1659–62, 1674–75 and 1698–99 without any detectable rise in mortality, an achievement which contrasts strikingly with Scotland, which suffered localized mortality crises in 1674–75 and a serious famine in the 1690s.[48] The final phase of growth then began at different times in different places. In Furness in the north, it only began in earnest in the 1730s.[49] Further south, in the more industrialized and developed areas, growth began earlier, with Rossendale's expansion beginning around the 1710s, though in Whalley and Great Harwood it had to wait until the 1730s.[50] The most impressive early increases took place in West Derby Hundred, where population apparently rose by some 60 per cent between 1664 and 1720.[51] Mortality crises remained, and there was a serious demographic setback in 1727–30, but overall these did not stem the tide of growth.

Agriculture

Lancashire remained one of the most agriculturally backward corners of England. Poor soils and a wet climate combined with factors such as low investment and remoteness from the main produce markets in London and the South East to ensure that the county's farmers achieved only modest

---

45 Appleby, *Famine*, pp. 155–93.

46 This and the following section is based on a survey of published parish registers.

47 Cf. A. J. Gritt, 'Mortality Crisis and Household Structure: An Analysis of Parish Registers and the Compton Census, Broughton, Lancashire, 1667–1676', *LPS*, 79 (2008), 38–65.

48 K. J. Cullen, *Famine in Scotland: the 'Ill Years' of the 1690s* (Edinburgh, 2010), pp. 10–11 and *passim*.

49 J. D. Marshall, *Furness and the Industrial Revolution* (Barrow-in-Furness, 1958), p. 101; Speake, 'Historical Demography', p. 53.

50 Walton, *Lancashire*, p. 77; S. Schwarz, 'Economic Change in North-east Lancashire, c.1660–1760', *THSLC*, 144 (1994), 47–93 (pp. 57–8).

51 Phillips and Smith, *Lancashire and Cheshire*, pp. 66–7.

productivity and prosperity.[52] This said, there were signs of development, partly as the county became drawn into national marketing networks and partly as its own non-farming population grew.

There was a broad division between the eastern uplands and the lowland seaboard regions. In the Pennines, as well as in the mountainous parts of Furness, low-intensity pasture farming was the norm, with rough summer grazing on the common moor or fell combined with wintering on plusher, more improved valley fields held in severalty.[53] Only limited arable culti-vation took place, and then only of poor grains (mostly barley and oats) for simple subsistence. A petition by Pendle Forest copyholders from 1607 (albeit likely exaggerated) complained that their lands were 'extremely barren and unprofitable and as yet capable of no other use but only oats – and that but only in dry years and not without continued charge of every third year's manuring'.[54] The main form of pasture farming was the rearing of cattle, especially after the Irish Cattle Act of 1667 wiped out much of the region's competition, but there were nonetheless pockets in which sheep-rearing played a greater role.[55] Hill farms were generally poor even by contemporary standards; yet the century after 1650 was undoubtedly one of relative prosperity in the North West, with rising levels of inventoried wealth and (more lastingly) a significant level of rebuilding.[56]

Lower-lying parts enjoyed greater prosperity. Successful dairy farms circled the major towns, while cattle-rearing brought wealth to farmers in West Derby and Leyland hundreds. A great arc of mixed farms ran from the Manchester region in the south-east to Preston in the north, taking

52   D. Hey, 'Yorkshire and Lancashire', in *AHEW*, vol. 5, pp. 59–86.
53   A. J. L. Winchester, *The Harvest of the Hills: Rural Life in Northern England and the Scottish Borders, 1450–1700* (Edinburgh, 2000), pp. 5–122.
54   Swain, *Industry*, p. 41.
55   G. H. Tupling, *The Economic History of Rossendale* (CS, New Ser., lxxxvi, Manchester, 1927), pp. 165–6; Marshall, *Furness*, p. xxi; Walton, *Lancashire*, pp. 23–4, 74–6; Phillips and Smith, *Lancashire and Cheshire*, pp. 25–30, 78–81; Swain, *Industry*, pp. 34–55; Winchester, *Harvest of the Hills*, pp. 5–25.
56   M. Overton, *Agricultural Revolution in England: the Transformation of the Agrarian Economy, 1500–1850* (Cambridge, 1996), p. 93; K. Wrightson, *Earthly Necessities: Economic Lives in Early Modern Britain* (London, 2000), pp. 230–1; R. Machin, 'The Great Rebuilding: a Reassessment', *PP*, 77 (1977), 35–56; M. E. Garnett, 'The Great Rebuilding and Economic Change in South Lonsdale, 1600–1730', *THSLC*, 137 (1987), 55–75; R. W. Brunskill, *Traditional Buildings of Cumbria: the County of the Lakes* (London, 2002).

in the Fylde and parts of the Ribble valley.[57] Here, there were pockets of specialized arable cultivation, notably of barley and some wheat, and a degree of diversification was at least possible. In 1721, for example, Nicholas Blundell of Little Crosby was growing poppies, tulips, chives, radish, lettuce, Welsh onions, cabbage, spinach, wheat, apples, peas, and beans, as well as walnut, hornbeam, fir, mulberry, beech, and elm trees, and much more.[58] The county was also a pioneer in the adoption of the potato from the seventeenth century onwards.[59]

Nonetheless, there is much evidence of continued backwardness long into the eighteenth century. As late as 1795, the use of turnips was very limited even in west Lancashire, and neither vetches nor lucerne appear to have been widespread, though clover was more common (as a fodder crop for horses).[60] Classic enclosure of open fields was notable by its relative absence in the county, though this was undoubtedly a product of the fields' rarity, and those that did exist seem to have gradually disappeared with little protest.[61] More important were the larger schemes for taking in wide sections of manorial waste, although these were generally concentrated in the 'long' sixteenth century rather than the period after 1630.[62]

Land tenures proved relatively durable. Secure copyholds dominated the hills of the east, while tenants in Furness tended to hold their lands by the similar border 'tenant right'.[63] Although there were some attempts

57   Walton, *Lancashire*, pp. 74–5; Hey, 'Yorkshire and Lancashire', p. 61.
58   N. Blundell, *The Great Diurnal of Nicholas Blundell of Little Crosby, Lancs. transcribed by Frank Tyrer*, ed. J. J. Bagley, 3 vols (RSLC, cx, cxii, cxiv, Chester, 1966–72), vol. 3, pp. 52–63.
59   R. N. Salaman, *The History and Social Influence of the Potato* (Cambridge, 1949), pp. 451–2.
60   J. Holt, *A General View of the Agriculture of the County of Lancashire* (London, 1795), p. 61 and *passim*; Walton, *Lancashire*, p. 75.
61   Higham, *Frontier Landscape*, pp. 94–5; G. Youd, 'The Common Fields of Lancashire', *THSLC*, 113 (1961), 1–41; Winchester, *Harvest of the Hills*, p. 147. There was a cluster of protests in the south-east of the county between 1548 and 1552, and odd disturbances up to the 1640s, but the period after this appears to have been, in terms of enclosure-related incidents, completely calm: A. Charlesworth (ed.), *An Atlas of Rural Protest in Britain, 1548–1900* (London, 1983), pp. 31–49.
62   J. Porter, 'Waste Land Reclamation in the Sixteenth and Seventeenth Centuries: the Case of South-eastern Bowland, 1550–1630', *THSLC*, 127 (1977), 1–23; J. Porter, *The Making of the Central Pennines* (Ashbourne, 1980), pp. 30–4; J. Thirsk, 'The Crown as projector on its own estates, from Elizabeth I to Charles I', in *The Estates of the English Crown, 1558–1640*, ed. R. W. Hoyle (Cambridge, 1992), pp. 297–352 (pp. 309–10, 316–17).
63   Hey, 'Yorkshire and Lancashire', p. 68; E. Evans and J. V. Beckett, 'Cumberland,

by large landowners to convert these to market rents, especially after the union of the crowns under James VI and I, these were of limited success.[64] In the west, leasehold was of more importance, while the south-west of the county was often characterized by more complex tenures in the form of 'lifeleasehold'. This gave secure tenure for the lives of three nominated individuals, who paid a significant entry fine but then enjoyed low annual rents from then onwards.[65] In general however, leasehold does not appear to have become as established as it did elsewhere, though whether this was a cause or a symptom of backwardness is as yet unclear.[66] In addition, a recent study of the development of agrarian capitalism suggests that family farms dominated in the North West until the later eighteenth century at least.[67]

The weakness of the county's agriculture meant that it was to some extent dependent on external supplies for grain. Some evidence for the significance of imported food can be gained from William Stout's recording of grain shipments from Danzig and even America in 1729, but as this was an exceptionally bad year at home the circumstances were untypical.[68] Indeed, there is even evidence for exports of grain out of the region: Sarah Fell, for example, took part in a venture transporting and retailing oats by coast to Bristol in the 1670s, and recent work has suggested that northern farmers were supplying London with oats (for horses) in the later seventeenth century, though this trade collapsed in the 1690s.[69] Nonetheless, it seems safe to assume that Lancashire, with its rising population and generally poor agriculture, would have been a net importer of foodstuffs from quite early on. Furthermore, it seems that Lancastrians ate cheaply. Potatoes have already been highlighted as

---

Westmorland, and Furness', in *AHEW*, vol. 5, pp. 3–29 (p. 9); R. W. Hoyle, 'An Ancient and Laudable Custom: the Definition and Development of Tenant Right in North-western England in the Sixteenth Century', *PP*, 116 (1987), 24–55.

64   Appleby, *Famine*, pp. 67–83.

65   A. J. Gritt, 'The Operation of Lifeleasehold in South-west Lancashire, 1649–97', *AgHR*, 53 (2005), 1–23.

66   Cf. Overton, *Agricultural Revolution*, pp. 154–6.

67   L. Shaw-Taylor, 'The rise of agrarian capitalism and the decline of family farming in England', *EcHR*, 65 (2012), 26–60.

68   W. Stout, *The Autobiography of William Stout of Lancaster, 1665–1752*, ed. J. D. Marshall (CS, 3rd Ser., xiv, Manchester, 1967), p. 204.

69   S. Fell, *The Household Account Book of Sarah Fell of Swarthmoor Hall*, ed. N. Penney (Cambridge, 1920), *passim*; S. Hipkin, 'The Coastal Metropolitan Corn Trade in Later Seventeenth-century England', *EcHR*, 2nd Ser., 65 (2012), 220–55 (pp. 238–44).

a source of nourishment for ordinary families, but the staple foodstuffs probably remained oats and barley, even in the late eighteenth century.[70] This will have had implications for the cost of poor relief, for the living costs of the northern, oat- and barley-eating poor will have been low relative to those of wheat-eating southerners. Even so, surviving accounts clearly show that wheat was grown and retailed, even in Furness.[71]

Industry and trade

Broadly speaking, the county's industry divided into two regions, with the south-west engaging in metalworking and fuel-based industries, and the south-east heavily involved in the manufacture of textiles.[72] In the former, in an area roughly coterminous with West Derby Hundred, there developed an impressive array of mineral-based industries broadly situated on the most accessible parts of the coalfield.[73] The eastern parts of this were relatively lightly exploited, but the western regions were undergoing rapid development, at least after about 1690.[74] According to the best estimates, output on the south-western coalfield rose from around 13,500 tons per annum in 1590 to 22,000 in the 1690s.[75] This comparatively modest increase was then dramatically exceeded in the eighteenth century, with annual output rising to some 78,000 tons around 1740. Individual pits, however, remained relatively small, with few employing more than a dozen miners.

This quantitative expansion of coal production, together with the excellent quality of local seams of the low-sulphur 'cannel' or 'smith's coal', provided a fillip for the growth of a wide variety of industries. Metal-smelting, in particular, increased significantly in importance

---

70 J. D. Marshall, *Old Lakeland: Some Cumbrian Social History* (Newton Abbot, 1971), p. 46; Appleby, *Famine*, p. 6.

71 Fell, *Household Account Book*, *passim*.

72 Stobart, *First Industrial Region*, pp. 64–137; the distinction is inspired by E. A. Wrigley, *Continuity, Chance and Change: the Character of the Industrial Revolution in England* (Cambridge, 1988).

73 Stobart, *First Industrial Region*, pp. 104–8; J. G. Timmins, *Made in Lancashire: A History of Regional Industrialization* (Manchester, 1998), p. 20.

74 J. Langton, *Geographical Change and the Industrial Revolution: Coalmining in South West Lancashire, 1590–1799* (Cambridge, 1979), pp. 35–44, 83–93.

75 Ibid., p. 43.

across our period.[76] Iron was the main product, but there were additional outposts of copper- and lead-smelting too.[77] Metalworking also grew to complement this. In the seventeenth century the most important of these industries were the brass and pewter manufactures of the Wigan district, which achieved an impressive level of output.[78] With the eighteenth century, however, came the growth of the English pottery industry, ultimately superseding pewter as the main provider of tableware, and the glory days of the latter industry in Lancashire were well behind it by the second quarter of the eighteenth century.[79] By this time, bell-founding had developed in the town as an offshoot of the brass industry, and for a time in the late seventeenth and early eighteenth centuries Wigan supplied churches across the North, the Midlands and much of Wales.[80] There was also another important centre of gravity in the Atherton district, between Wigan and Bolton, where nail-making grew from medieval roots into a major local employer in the later eighteenth century.[81] In addition, more localized but nonetheless significant industries sprung up in the eighteenth century around Warrington (wires, pins, and tools), Ashton-in-Makerfield (locks and hinges), and Liverpool, Preston, Wigan, and Prescot (watches and clocks).[82]

There is no doubt that the rise of Liverpool was instrumental in the success of the south-western region. From a fishing community of fewer than a thousand inhabitants (albeit one with a borough corporation) at the start of our period, Lancashire's principal port grew to a size of around 22,000 in 1750.[83] By that time, the seven medieval streets had blossomed into some 222 streets, squares, alleys and lanes.[84] Its existence served the interests of the region in three main ways: as a gateway to wider national and international markets, as a market in itself, and as a source

76   Timmins, *Made in Lancashire*, pp. 23–5.

77   Ibid., pp. 23, 54–5.

78   R. J. A. Shelley, 'Wigan and Liverpool Pewterers', *THSLC*, 97 (1947), 2–16.

79   Timmins, *Made in Lancashire*, pp. 27–8; Shelley, 'Wigan and Liverpool', p. 16; Walton, *Lancashire*, p. 74.

80   Timmins, *Made in Lancashire*, pp. 24–5.

81   G. N. Tupling, 'The Early Metal Trade and the Beginnings of Engineering in Lancashire', *Transactions of the Lancashire and Cheshire Antiquarian Society*, 61 (1951), 1–34 (pp. 20–1).

82   Timmins, *Made in Lancashire*, p. 25; Tupling, 'Early Metal Trade', pp. 16–25.

83   Stobart, *First Industrial Region*, p. 37; P. G. E. Clemens, 'The Rise of Liverpool, 1665–1750', *EcHR*, 2nd Ser., 29 (1976), 211–25.

84   Ascott, Lewis and Power, *Liverpool*, pp. 8–15.

of investment in local industry and commerce.[85] In particular, the corporation of Liverpool invested in projects aimed at opening up the town and region to its markets overseas, spending some £50,000 on docks and warehouses between 1710 and 1750.[86] Meanwhile, between 1724 and 1736, work was completed on the Mersey and Irwell navigation, which was to remain the main sea route between Manchester and Liverpool until the opening of the Manchester Ship Canal in 1894.[87]

Simultaneously, textile manufactures around Manchester, and up the whole eastern side of the county as far north as Blackburn, Burnley and Colne, were beginning to take off.[88] Most impressive was the growing manufacture of cotton-based cloths from the early seventeenth century. To begin with, cotton was used for the making of fustians: coarse cloths comprising – in this context – a linen warp and cotton weft.[89] Lancashire was engaged in the manufacture of fustians possibly as early as the 1570s, and certainly by about 1600.[90] In the 1620s the industry was well established around Bolton, Manchester and Blackburn, and by mid-century it had made the vast fortune of Humphrey Chetham, dealer in cotton goods and one of the great educational philanthropists of the age.[91] In the later seventeenth century, cotton also began to be introduced to the Manchester linen manufactures to create 'cotton-linens'; meanwhile, a thriving smallware industry grew in the latter town, and by 1700 a variety of cotton-based fabrics were retailed at home, in Ireland and internationally.[92] It was, however, in the eighteenth century that these industries really took off. The 'calico acts' of 1700 and 1721, by taking no action

85   Timmins, *Made in Lancashire*, pp. 45–55; Stobart, *First Industrial Region*, p. 123.

86   Walton, *Lancashire*, p. 70.

87   A. Hayman, *Mersey and Irwell Navigation to Manchester Ship Canal, 1720–1887* (Manchester, 1981), pp. 8–13.

88   A. P. Wadsworth and J. De Lacy Mann, *The Cotton Trade and Industrial Lancashire, 1600–1780* (Manchester, 1931), pp. 52, 314; Schwarz, 'Economic Change', p. 69.

89   Wadsworth and Mann, *Cotton Trade*, p. 15.

90   N. Lowe, *The Lancashire Textile Industry in the Sixteenth Century* (CS, 3rd Ser., xx, Manchester, 1972), p. 99; D. Winterbotham, '"Sackclothes and fustyans and such like com'odyties". Early Linen Manufacture in the Manchester Region', in *A History of Linen in the North West*, ed. E. Roberts (Lancaster, 1998), pp. 22–43 (p. 26); *Lancashire Quarter Sessions Records*, ed. J. Tait (CS, New Ser., lxxvii, Manchester, 1917), pp. 121, 249.

91   Wadsworth and Mann, *Cotton Trade*, pp. 15–16; Timmins, *Made in Lancashire*, p. 15; S. J. Guscott, *Humphrey Chetham, 1580–1653: Fortune, Politics and Mercantile Culture in Seventeenth-Century England* (CS, 3rd Ser., xlv, Manchester, 2003).

92   Wadsworth and Mann, *Cotton Trade*, pp. 14, 111–16.

against linens or fustians (the latter being explicitly exempted by the 1736 'Manchester Act'), left the Lancashire industries unmolested while effectively cutting out much of the Indian competition for British if not yet international markets.[93] The stage had been set for one of the great success stories of economic history.

Woollens and linen, meanwhile, continued to be of major importance in many parts of the county.[94] Pure linen manufactures were originally concentrated around Manchester but the march of cotton led them to lose comparative importance.[95] Where they remained dominant was in the lowland districts in the west of the county in which local and Irish raw materials were spun and woven into coarse cloths. Woollens also remained strong, although they had undergone a major restructuring since the 1500s. By the first half of the seventeenth century, woollen and worsted yarns were combined in the production of 'bays' (i.e. baize) in the Rochdale, Bury and Rossendale districts, while pure worsted fabrics were beginning to replace older, carded woollens by 1700.[96] At the same time, cotton-based cloths superseded woollens in many areas, notably around Blackburn and Oldham and to some extent also Bury.[97] Indeed, the woollen industry appears comparatively languid when set against the advance of cotton, but this should not be exaggerated.[98]

Just as the south-western region was centred on Liverpool, the growing town of Manchester acted as the beating heart of the textile zone. The future Cottonopolis had been an economic hub for some time, but its influence had generally outstripped its actual size.[99] The town's population lay somewhere near two thousand around 1600, and was closer to four thousand by 1664.[100] This slow expansion was followed by steadily increasing growth into the eighteenth century, and a 1773 enumeration

93   Ibid., pp. 111–28; M. J. Daunton, *Poverty and Progress: An Economic and Social History of Britain, 1700–1850* (Oxford, 1995), pp. 544–5.

94   J. K. Walton, 'Proto-industrialisation and the First Industrial Revolution: the Case of Lancashire', in *Regions and Industries: A Perspective on the Industrial Revolution in Britain*, ed. P. Hudson (Cambridge, 1989), pp. 41–68 (pp. 47–59); Timmins, *Made in Lancashire*, pp. 11–16.

95   Wadsworth and Mann, *Cotton Trade*, pp. 24, 79, 218; Timmins, *Made in Lancashire*, pp. 14–16.

96   Walton, 'Proto-industrialisation', pp. 51–9; Timmins, *Made in Lancashire*, pp. 11–14.

97   Wadsworth and Mann, *Cotton Trade*, p. 79.

98   Walton, 'Proto-industrialisation', p. 56.

99   T. S. Willan, *Elizabethan Manchester* (CS, 3rd Ser., xxvii, Manchester, 1980).

100   Ibid., pp. 37–8; Stobart, *First Industrial Region*, p. 37.

shows a town that had swollen to a size of well over 22,000, so we can guess that it stood at around 10,000 or so by the end of our period.[101] Aside from being an organizational centre for much of the textile industries, Manchester was also involved in production. In particular, the finishing of cloth was carried out there, with a third of all recorded textile occupations in Manchester wills between 1701 and 1760 involving this branch of the trade.[102] The townspeople also busied themselves with the earlier processes, and a 1751 census of looms found 4,674 in the parish, or roughly one to every household.[103] This said, most of the manufacturing processes still took place in the countryside, as remained the norm in pre-industrial England.[104]

Aside from simple growth, the textile industries also saw technological and economic innovation and development. The heroic age of the spinning jenny and water frame lay in the future, but there was development nonetheless. Innovation in terms of the fabrics produced was one area, with the so-called 'new draperies' introduced to cloth manufacture between the late sixteenth and the later seventeenth centuries.[105] Moreover, one should be careful not to downplay the monumental importance of the growing use of cotton from 1600 onwards. This was the first widespread manufacturing of the fibre in Britain, and is a stunning and quite unexpected innovation for such an isolated region, particularly given how distant the source of the raw material was. Technology also changed, with the introduction of the 'Dutch' or 'Engine' loom to the Manchester smallwares industry in the reign of Charles II allowing the town to challenge and perhaps surpass London in that branch of textile manufacturing by the 1670s.[106] There was also organizational change. *Trading* in cotton wool had always been the preserve of large merchant capitalists, but by the 1680s the 'putting-out system', by which workers were linked to industrial capitalists in ties of debt closely resembling piecework wages, was centralizing the control of *manufacture* too.[107] Traditional woollens

---

101 Stobart, *First Industrial Region*, p. 37; Walton, *Lancashire*, p. 65.

102 Stobart, *First Industrial Region*, p. 77.

103 Wadsworth and Mann, *Cotton Trade*, p. 326.

104 Walton, 'Proto-industrialisation'; J. Thirsk, *The Rural Economy of England: Collected Essays* (London, 1984), pp. 217–33.

105 Wrightson, *Earthly Necessities*, pp. 166–8.

106 Wadsworth and Mann, *Cotton Trade*, pp. 98–106; R. M. Dunn, 'The London Weavers' Riot of 1675', *Guildhall Studies in London History*, 1 (1973), 13–23.

107 Wadsworth and Mann, *Cotton Trade*, pp. 78–91; Walton, 'Proto-industrialisation', p. 62.

remained dominated by older forms of organization, in which production was controlled by small, independent craftsmen-manufacturers, but putting-out was nonetheless associated with the growth of worsteds in the eighteenth century.[108] As we will see, textile manufactures were a major source of employment for the poor.

The picture that emerges is of two dynamic industrial regions in the south-west and south-east of the county which, although they interlocked in some measure, were nonetheless identifiably distinct. Further north the industrial picture is less impressive. North of the Ribble, there was only limited industrial production, mostly small-scale linen manufactures.[109] Lancaster's most prosperous period came later, though in Furness there was a tradition of small-scale industry using abundant local supplies of fuel-wood, as well as some mining in the hills around Coniston Water. Additionally, the area around Hawkshead formed part of the Kendal cloth-manufacturing zone, specializing in rough woollens for the national market, though this was in decline by the early 1600s.[110]

Social structure

The principal noble family in the county was the Stanleys, Earls of Derby since medieval times.[111] Their political power, which had seen them mediate between court and county under the Tudors, had by the late seventeenth century already peaked, and their troubles during the Civil War and Restoration (including the execution of the seventh earl at Bolton in 1651) led them to lose much of their grip on county affairs by the 1710s. Nonetheless, they remained the county's largest landowners, as

108   Walton, 'Proto-industrialisation', pp. 52, 55–6.
109   M. Robinson, 'The Linen Industry in North Lancashire and Cumbria, 1660–1830', in Roberts (ed.), *History of Linen*, pp. 44–65; B. Pidcock, 'Domestic Textile Production in the Sixteenth and Seventeenth Centuries', in *Rural Industries of the Lune Valley*, ed. M. Winstanley (Lancaster, 2000), pp. 20–40.
110   M. Elder, *The Slave Trade and the Economic Development of Eighteenth-Century Lancaster* (Halifax, 1992); M. Mullet, 'Reformation and Renewal, 1450–1690', in *A History of Lancaster, 1193–1993*, ed. A. White (Edinburgh, 2001), pp. 73–116 (pp. 102–7); N. Dalziel, 'Trade and Transition, 1690–1815', in ibid., pp. 117–72 (pp. 117–35); Appleby, *Famine*, pp. 85–7; R. K. Bingham, *Kendal: A Social History* (Milnthorpe, 1995), pp. 183–209.
111   Walton, *Lancashire*, pp. 12–13, 39–40, 84–5.

well as one of the richest families in England.[112] There were other major landholders in the county: the Walmsleys of Dunkenhalgh, for example, or the Molyneux family of Sefton; and the reigning monarch was a major owner through the Duchy of Lancaster. However, the most important social tier below the Stanleys were those gentry households (including those just mentioned) wealthy enough to serve as justices of the peace, and in this regard Lancashire was not well endowed. In 1640 there were just 39 lay gentry with JP status, fewer than one for every ten townships, and while the figure had risen to 95 in 1720 this was still below one to every four townships.[113] Moreover, Lancashire's gentry were generally poor, even when compared with those of Yorkshire. According to the detailed research of B. G. Blackwood, there were 774 gentry families in the county in 1642 (using a relatively wide definition).[114] Of these, 24 had landed incomes of above £1,000 a year, while 89 received between £250 and £999, making a total of 113 households with over £250 a year in land. This total, again around one to every four townships, represented just 15 per cent of all gentle households, compared with the equivalent figure of 47 per cent in Yorkshire.

What the county did have, however, was a growing class of entrepreneurs, particularly associated with the textile industries.[115] Some went on to amass considerable fortunes: Humphrey Chetham, for example, died with personal estate to the value of over £13,000.[116] Moreover, it was possible to do this even from fairly humble origins. Thomas Touchet began his career as a Warrington pin-maker, but through judicious marriage and entry into textiles he became Manchester's richest manufacturer and dealer of linen and cottons at his death in 1744.[117] There also existed a legion of small cloth dealers and self-employed manufacturers.[118] On the other hand, industries which required heavy investment in fixed capital, such as coalmining and metal-smelting, tended to be dominated more by gentry.[119]

---

112 Ibid., p. 85.
113 Ibid., p. 86.
114 Blackwood, *Lancashire Gentry*, pp. 11–18.
115 Wadsworth and Mann, *Cotton Trade*, pp. 29–35, 72–8.
116 Ibid., p. 34.
117 A. J. Kidd, 'Touchet, Samuel (c.1705–1773)', in *Oxford Dictionary of National Biography* (Oxford, 2004).
118 Wadsworth and Mann, *Cotton Trade*, pp. 74–82; Swain, *Industry*, pp. 113–15; also: S. Pearson, *Rural Houses of the Lancashire Pennines, 1560–1760* (London, 1985).
119 Walton, *Lancashire*, p. 73.

The extent to which a proletariat was developing is difficult to assess. Historians of the industrial regions have shown that workers often practised a 'dual economy' of farming and weaving or spinning in which earnings from industry made up for the smallness of the estate, while agricultural pursuits provided some security against slumps in trade.[120] Nonetheless, there is strong evidence for large marginal populations in some areas, notably in the textile zones. Though they were massively exaggerating the numbers, the petitioners to the council of state in 1654 claimed that 'no less' than '20,000 poor ... are employed in Lancashire by the great manufacture of fustians'.[121] In 1664, the Hearth Tax returns show extensive areas of south-east and central Lancashire having more than 40 per cent of assessed householders exempted on grounds of poverty.[122] In fact, it has recently been argued – albeit using data from the early eighteenth century and a relatively restrictive focus on the market-orientated activities of adult males – that by-employment in the region, including in the textile industries, was rare and usually the preserve of the relatively wealthy.[123]

The position in other industries is rather less certain. There were undoubtedly coalminers with very little in the way of other incomes, but the small size of most pits meant that they were probably few in number, while the situation in the nail-making and other metal industries is as yet unclear.[124] In agriculture, the evidence of proletarianization is very limited. In particular, Wrightson's belief that, by the Civil War, there was 'a very large agricultural proletariat of landless and virtually landless labourers' in Lancashire has been challenged by Andy Gritt.[125] The latter cites the

---

120   E.g. Wadsworth and Mann, *Cotton Trade*, pp. 25–8; M. Brigg, 'The Forest of Pendle in the Seventeenth Century, I', *THSLC*, 113 (1961), 65–96 (pp. 90–1); Swain, *Industry*, p. 121.
121   *Seventeenth-Century Economic Documents*, ed. J. Thirsk and J. P. Cooper (Oxford, 1972), p. 258.
122   Walton, *Lancashire*, p. 29; Phillips and Smith, *Lancashire and Cheshire*, pp. 126–7. This was also the case in Furness, but it seems likely that this was due to the general poverty of this region rather than the existence of a large proletariat.
123   S. A. J. Keibek and L. Shaw-Taylor, 'Early Modern Rural By-employments: a Re-examination of the Probate Inventory Evidence', *AgHR*, 61 (2013), 244–81.
124   Langton, *Geographical Change*, p. 43.
125   Wrightson, 'Puritan Reformation', p. 180. Elsewhere in his thesis, Wrightson suggested that a sample of unlicensed alehouse keepers, in which 45 per cent were husbandmen, 31 per cent artisans and 12 per cent widows, was 'a fair sample of the poor' (pp. 88–9); A. J. Gritt, 'The "Survival" of Service in the English Agricultural Labour Force: Lessons from Lancashire, c.1650–1851', *AgHR*, 50 (2002), 25–50 (pp. 34–8).

lists of those taking the Protestation Oaths in 1642 for four townships (Croston, Ulnes Walton, Goosnargh and Whittingham) in the agricultural heartlands in the west and centre of the county. Here, Gritt found, the ratio of hired workers to farmers was little more than 0.7, suggesting only a very small proletariat. Similarly, pointing to listings of plebeian Catholics in an earlier article by Blackwood, Gritt showed that even in Amounderness Hundred, where they were considerably more numerous than elsewhere in the county, labourers and servants accounted for just 16.7 per cent of all names.[126] Nonetheless, we should not be too optimistic. Evidence produced for Cheshire by the Cambridge Group for the History of Population and Social Structure suggests that labourers were much more common in the early-eighteenth-century North West than has been supposed.[127] A study of statements in English church courts, indeed, found that nearly a fifth of witnesses in the Diocese of Cheshire (1591–1675) self-identified as poor in some sense.[128] The upland parts of the region, meanwhile, appear to have been undergoing a steady structural transformation which tended towards an increase in the number of marginal households. In industrial parts of the Pennines this was represented by subdivision of holdings and piecemeal encroachment on manorial wastes by poor cottagers.[129] Where there was little industry, meanwhile, there seems to have been a general trend towards polarization of customary landholding in the hills, although most of the suggestive research is admittedly based on communities in Yorkshire and Westmorland.[130] Yet even with all this, upland communities were still remarked upon for their egalitarian social structures as late as the early nineteenth century.[131]

---

126   B. G. Blackwood, 'Plebeian Catholics in Later Stuart Lancashire', *Northern History*, 25 (1989), 153–73.

127   Keibek and Shaw-Taylor, 'Early Modern Rural By-employments', p. 260.

128   A. Shepard, 'Poverty, Labour and the Language of Social Description in Early Modern England', *PP*, 201 (2008), 51–95 (p. 73).

129   Tupling, *Economic History*, pp. 42–97, 161–8.

130   J. D. Marshall, 'Agrarian Wealth and Social Structure in Pre-industrial Cumbria', *EcHR*, 2nd Ser., 33 (1980), 503–21; A. H. Duxbury, 'The Decline of the Cumbrian Yeoman – Ravenstonedale: a Case Study', *CW2*, 94 (1994), 201–13; R. W. Hoyle and H. R. French, 'The Land Market of a Pennine Manor: Slaidburn, 1650–1780', *Continuity and Change*, 14 (1999), 349–83; J. Healey, 'Agrarian Social Structure in the Central Lake District: the Fall of the "Mountain Republic"?', *Northern History*, 44, no. 2 (2007), 73–91.

131   J. V. Beckett, 'The Decline of the Small Landowner in Eighteenth- and Nineteenth-century England: Some Regional Considerations', *AgHR*, 30 (1982), 97–111 (pp. 100–2); Healey, 'Agrarian Social Structure', pp. 73–7.

Conclusion: a developing society

Lancashire's poor lived within a regional economy that was shifting its balance from farming to industry and commerce, and which was at the same time dragging itself out of its medieval poverty and towards industrial revolution. The course of this economic development is critical to our understanding of the contours of poverty. The weak tax base and the small size of the agricultural proletariat must have been critical factors behind the relatively slow development of poor relief after 1598. The cultural and political isolation of the county allowed some of the major policy decisions to be taken at a regional level. Textile industries served to employ some of the most vulnerable members of society, reducing the dependence of the very young, the weak and the old on poor relief. Yet at the same time, the entering of the county into wider trading networks meant that shocks to global exchange could be felt keenly in the households of the poor. Even the county's topography, with its massive parishes and dispersed population, had a significant impact on the local politics of the Poor Laws in the seventeenth century, as will be seen in the next chapter.

2

The Arrival and Growth of Poor Relief

Constables of Hadocke and Goleborne came to have me write theire presentments for assizes, and when I had donne I writt: 'Poore is provided, highways repaired, these querys answered, and clarke unrewarded' att which they laughed most heartily.
Diary of Roger Lowe of Ashton-in-Makerfield (20 August 1664)[1]

Before going on to explore the lives of the Lancashire poor, we need to understand the process by which the Poor Laws became part of everyday life in the county.[2] This was a process in which the major steps were taken in the seventeenth century, and so this chapter will tell the story of how this dramatic development in social welfare came about. It is both a necessary backdrop to the 'pauper tales' to be told in the rest of the book, and a fascinating case study of how a piece of Parliamentary legislation gradually came to be accepted and enforced in one of the more isolated corners of the land.

Unfortunately, the normal bedrock of studies of the implementation of the Poor Law, overseers' accounts, do not survive for Lancashire in any great quantity until the 1690s, so historians must argue from impressionistic and difficult sources. Household accounts and family archives, which provide information about the payment of poor rates, give some insight. The papers of parochial churchwardens also provide a sidelight onto the administration of the Poor Laws, as – occasionally – do the records of manorial courts. The main set of source material, however, is that left by Quarter Sessions. There exists a large volume of documents (especially petitions) reporting about the specific circumstances relating to the poor in parishes and townships, and concentrated in the century from the 1620s to the 1720s. These almost always involved some kind of dispute about relief

---

1   R. Lowe, *The Diary of Roger Lowe of Ashton-in-Makerfield, Lancashire, 1663–74*, ed. W. L. Sachse (London, 1938), pp. 69–70.
2   This chapter is an extended version of: Healey, 'Development'.

practices, and thus are 'politically charged' documents. Nonetheless, they provide an invaluable window into the character of local practice. In addition to the papers of Quarter Sessions, we also have two other sets of governmental sources. First, the minutes and orders of the 'Sheriff's Table', which was an informal meeting of justices at Assize week for the purposes of local administration; and secondly, the returns made to the Privy Council in the 1630s.[3] The latter constitute a set of reports about local poor relief practices of variable detail. They almost certainly – in order to avoid censure by central government – exaggerate local conformity to the tenets of the Poor Laws, but they also provide the earliest systematic attempt to document local social policies on a countywide basis. Finally, come the eighteenth century, we can get a more detailed picture from the larger volume of overseers' accounts that survive, which can then be supplemented by the returns made to Parliament in the early nineteenth century of expenditure in 1748–50.

The sixteenth-century background

Although the Poor Laws of 1598 and 1601 are often taken to be a watershed in English social welfare history, they came on the back of many decades of legislation aimed at tackling the problem of poverty and the poor in Tudor England.[4] Indeed, in a recent revisionist account – discussed in the introduction – Marjorie McIntosh has argued that the importance of the statutes of 1552 and 1563 has been significantly undervalued. Unfortunately there is little primary source material with which to test this in Lancashire. No poor accounts survive from before the 1630s, so if there were pre-1598 attempts to instigate organized, rate-funded relief then we do not know about them, though there does exist a small census of the poor, compiled for the township of Crompton in 1597, the purpose of which remains obscure.[5] We can, however, bring together

3   *Proceedings of the Lancashire Justices of the Peace at the Sheriff's Table During Assize Week*, ed. B. W. Quintrell (RSLC, cxxi, Chester, 1981); Webb and Webb, *English Poor Law History, Part One*, pp. 92–5; B. W. Quintrell, 'Government in Perspective: Lancashire and the Privy Council, 1570–1640', *THSLC*, 131 (1981), 35–62 (pp. 53–7). Also: H. Langelüddecke, '"Patchy and Spasmodic"?: The Response of Justices of the Peace to Charles I's Book of Orders', *English Historical Review*, 113 (1998), 1231–48.
4   Slack, *English Poor Law*, pp. 3–13, 51–3; Slack, *Poverty and Policy*, pp. 113–37.
5   Oldham Local Studies and Archives, UDCr/18, Crompton Poor, 1597.

scattered and highly impressionistic evidence at least to suggest there was some – very rudimentary – provision. The churchwardens of Prescot, for example, received 14d from their poor box between 1549 and 1550, which hints that they were making the weekly collections for the impotent stipulated in Protector Somerset's statute of 1547.[6] In 1579, 'consideringe the greate inconveniences which doe dailie aryse to the inhabitants of this towne by reason of the multitude of idle and loytringe persons', the mayor of Liverpool ordered that a tax be collected under the terms of the 1576 statute 'towardes the provisyon of suche stockes and stores within this towne as by the said statute mente and intended'.[7] In order to better manage the stock, the town placed its administration into the hands of four men (two of whom were aldermen), thus creating an office akin to that of the overseer of the poor. A workhouse scheme, meanwhile, was suggested for the county in 1582 by Mr Robert Worsley, keeper of the gaol of Manchester, though nothing seems to have come of it.[8] Returning to Prescot, we find a tantalizing reference to 2d 'spent with staing aboute the poremans gathering' in 1589, although there is of course no guarantee that this had anything to do with poor *relief*.[9] Similarly obscure is the tax levied in 1593 in Sharples and recorded in the Shuttleworth accounts 'for the maintenance of the poore people in Ashton-under-Lyne'.[10] In fact, the magistrates of Lancashire and Cheshire were specifically criticized by the Lord Lieutenant for their 'remissness' in instigating formal relief for the poor in 1586.[11] Around 1590, moreover, an enquiry into the state of

6   *The Churchwardens' Accounts of Prescot, Lancashire, 1523–1607*, ed. F. A. Bailey (RSLC, civ, Preston, 1953), p. 29.
7   *Liverpool Town Books: Proceedings of Assemblies, Common Councils, Portmoot Courts, &c, 1550–1862*, ed. J. A. Twemlow, 2 vols (Liverpool, 1918–35), vol. 2, pp. 353–4.
8   *The Annals of Manchester: A Chronological Record from the Earliest Times to the End of 1885*, ed. W. E. A. Axon (Manchester, 1886), p. 39.
9   *Churchwardens' Accounts of Prescot*, p. 107.
10   *The House and Farm Accounts of the Shuttleworths of Gawthorpe Hall*, ed. J. Harland, 4 vols (CS, Old Ser., xxxv, xli, xliii, xlvi, Manchester, 1856–58), vol. 1, p. 83. Reginald Sharpe France, who was exceptionally ready to ascribe mortality crises to disease and especially plague, makes no mention of any epidemic at Ashton this year, but as the burial register only survives from 1595 one may have evaded notice thus far: France, 'History of Plague'. There was a serious plague in London in 1592–94, and around the same time in Staffordshire: D. M. Palliser, 'Dearth and Disease in Staffordshire, 1540–1670', in *Rural Change and Urban Growth: Essays in English Regional History in Honour of W. G. Hoskins*, ed. C. W. Chalklin and M. A. Havinden (London, 1974), pp. 54–75 (pp. 60–1).
11   Hindle, *State and Social Change*, p. 154.

the Church in the county reported that 'the provision for the poor by a common and certain collection according to statute in all churches' had been 'utterly neglected'.[12] If McIntosh has recently unearthed evidence of some provision for the poor in the South before the statute of 39 Elizabeth, it has to be said that in Lancashire the evidence points in entirely the opposite direction. Indeed, the published Quarter Sessions orders from 1590–92 contain no references to parochial poor relief, in clear contrast to those after 1601.[13] The chances are that if much formal provision did exist, it was *ad hoc*, contingent and locally specific.

The response to '39 Elizabeth'

There are clear signs of change after the two great statutes of 1598 and 1601. The papers of the Shuttleworth family, which held land around Bolton and Burnley, contain references to a number of poor rates in the immediate aftermath of the 1598 statute. In August and September that year, the family paid a shilling per month on their Sharples properties 'for the relieffe of the poore within the parishe of Boulton', as well as 2s 6d a month for their lands in Rivington.[14] Meanwhile, the neighbouring parish of Deane took a total of 13s 10d for a period of three months at the same time.[15] In 1600, the family paid a rate of ½d per acre on their lands at Gawthorpe 'to the power of Ightenhill'.[16] In these jurisdictions, it seems, the 1598 Poor Law was immediately implemented.[17] Indeed, the Justices of Bolton Division would later recall that 'the impotent poore they have beene provided for throughout our whole division ever since 39 Eliz: and the statute in that behalfe hath beene ever since more duly executed hereabout (as wee believe) then in any other place that wee know of'.[18] The fact these Justices highlighted their division's own precocity cautions us against extrapolating too much from the experience of the Bolton region. But the record of a poor rate in Ightenhill (Whalley parish) tells us

12   'The State, Civil and Ecclesiastical, of the County of Lancaster, about the year 1590', in *Chetham Miscellanies vol. 5* (CS, Old Ser., xcvi, Manchester, 1875), pp. 1–13 (p. 12).
13   *Lancashire Quarter Sessions Records*, pp. 1–68.
14   *House and Farm Accounts*, vol. 1, p. 113.
15   Ibid., vol. 1, pp. 114–15.
16   Ibid., vol. 1, pp. 128–9.
17   Appleby, *Famine*, pp. 109–21.
18   TNA, SP16/265/86, Report of the Justices of Bolton Division, 18 April 1634.

they were not as unusual as they said, and indeed their claim was mirrored by a similar one from Bury parish in 1638, stating that 'the statute for the reliefe of the poore' had been 'put in due execucion' since 1601.[19] The parish of Prescot, meanwhile, appointed its first overseers of the poor, one for each quarter, in 1606, and Childwall had followed by 1611.[20] For 1613, there is an oblique reference to overseers in the papers of the manor court of Cartmel, showing such offices were not unknown even in the remote northern reaches of the county.[21] The records of the courts of Quarter Sessions for the first decade of the seventeenth century also reveal some evidence of working poor relief. The court ordered in 1601 that Elizabeth Rymyngton was to have two shillings per month and a house from 'the inhabitants of Melling'.[22] In 1603, Peter Lathome of Eccleston was unable to find any grandfather or grandmother to care for Hugh Clayton and so the parish 'must pay 8d a week for Hugh's relief'.[23] Such references continue sporadically.[24]

Evidence from the next quarter century suggests that implementation remained slow, and could be contested. It may be telling that what is probably the first reference to a poor rate found in the Quarter Sessions order books, in 1600, refers to the occasion on which Thomas Bridge, a carpenter of Tottington, assaulted Matthew Brine when the latter demanded 9d from the defendant when 'collecting for the poor'.[25] In 1626, when attempting to collect a tax for the succour of John Leighe, the parish of Eccleston faced complaints from 'all the cottingers of the towne' that they 'had as much need as hee', suggesting there was no consensus about relief, though not necessarily fundamental opposition to rating as such.[26] In the parishes of Rochdale and Middleton, according to a report during Charles I's Personal Rule, it was only in 1626 that the poor 'were first restrained from wanderinge and provided for by laye'.[27] A similar report from Amounderness Hundred states that as late as 1636

---

19 TNA, SP16/395/46, Report of the Justices of Bury Division, 12? July 1638.

20 *Churchwardens' Accounts of Prescot*, p. 154; R. Stewart-Brown, *Notes on Childwall* (Liverpool, 1914), p. 89.

21 LA, DDCa/7/1/3.

22 *Lancashire Quarter Sessions Records*, p. 102.

23 Ibid., p. 167.

24 Ibid., *passim*.

25 Ibid., p. 85.

26 LA, QSB/1/6/46–8.

27 TNA, SP16/351/111, Report of the Justices of Rochdale Division, March 1637. See Healey, 'Development', p. 560n for further discussion of this; also D. J. Wilkinson, 'The

the officers of Lytham, Poulton and Bispham claimed that they 'have noe poore people within those three parishes but they are sett on worke & sufficiently provided for within themselves without begging'.[28]

Other communities adopted compromise measures between full systems of rating for the poor and older, less coercive approaches. Meeting on Monday 12 June 1598, the governors of Liverpool agreed to set up a house of correction, and that

> the poore impotente people and children, whose names are set downe in a catalogue to be releived within this said towne, shall have licence to goe abroad within the towne, in such sorte and to suche howses within the severall stretes of the same as hereafter shalbe limitted and appointed.[29]

A similar attempt to circumvent the need for regular poor rates by allowing regulated begging is evident from the Privy Sessions order made at Ormskirk in 1624.[30] This declared that the 'needy and impotent poore' were to 'aske and have reasonable relieffe within this parishe', so long as they did not beg more than once a week at the same house, or at all outside the parish, and so long as they were 'orderly'. Meanwhile, there were to be no more poor rates until further notice. Indeed, this order has been interpreted by one historian as a 'last ditch stand by opponents of the Poor Law' though it might equally have been an attempt to claw back the cost of relief after the famine of 1623.[31] Even in the 1630s, localized begging was tolerated in the Liberties of Cartmel and Furness, where a number of parishes reported in November 1637 that paupers were allowed to 'goe abroad' amongst their neighbours so long as they did not 'wander out'.[32] Indeed, many parishes in North Lonsdale were still in 1636 using a system of 'billeting', in which paupers were tabled in consenting households, in

Justices of the Peace and their Work in Lancashire, 1603–1642' (Univ. of Oxford M.Litt. thesis, 1982), p. 138.
28   TNA, SP16/330/64, Report of the Justices of Amounderness Hundred, 22 August 1636.
29   *Liverpool Town Books*, vol. 2, pp. 751–3.
30   LA, QSB/1/22/30.
31   G. W. Oxley, 'The Old Poor Law in West Derby Hundred, 1601–1837' (Univ. of Liverpool PhD thesis, 1966), p. 10.
32   TNA, SP16/382/10, Report of the Justices of Cartmel and Furness Liberties, 13 February 1638.

order to circumvent the need for regular taxation.[33] Thus voluntary but organized charity was used as a substitute for rates, a compromise akin to that found in 1600s Somerset in which paupers were assigned to individual households from which they would regularly beg alms.[34]

Whatever the state of poor relief in Lancashire at the start of the 1620s, the systems in place proved woefully inadequate in dealing with the economic and social crisis in the first half of that decade. According to the most detailed estimates, something like 5 per cent of the county's population died as a result of famine between 1622 and 1624.[35] The disaster seems to have prompted the Assize judges to enforce fortnightly divisional meetings in which JPs could direct the 'mayntaynaunce of the pore, and other matters concerninge the good of the countrie'.[36] It is certainly possible that subsequent memories of the famine goaded parishes into more regular use of redistributive taxation to fund poor relief, and there is an order in the Quarter Sessions rolls which suggests a new drive to enforce it in the vast parishes of Bury and Manchester at the time.[37]

It is, however, the reports from Lancashire JPs to the Privy Council in response to the Caroline Books of Orders, notably that of 1631, which provide us with our first truly wide-ranging evidence. Books of Orders were a regular feature of English social policy between 1577 and 1631, and were designed to mitigate the worst impact of dearth and plague.[38] They had been issued in periods of especial crisis, most recently in 1622. For our purposes, the key Book was the so-called *Orders and Directions*, issued in the first month of 1631, and which marked a quickening of central government's attempts to direct social policy.[39] Its provisions, that the poor should

33 TNA, SP16/330/99, Report of the Justices of North Lonsdale, 9 August 1636; Hindle, *On the Parish?*, pp. 65–6.
34 HMC, *Report on the Manuscripts of the Marquis of Lothian Preserved at Blickling Hall, Norfolk* (London, 1905), p. 78, 'Orders concerning the Statute for the Releif of the poore agreed at Ilmynster, the 11th of April [1601?]'. In Pittington (County Durham), a parish-owned flock of sheep was used to maintain the poor until it was replaced by a rate assessment in 1624: Rushton, 'Poor Law, the Parish and the Community', p. 137.
35 Rogers, *Lancashire Population Crisis*, p. 10.
36 HMC, *Fourteenth Report, Appendix, Part IV: The Manuscripts of Lord Kenyon* (London, 1894), p. 28, 'Orders by the Judges of Assize for the County of Lancaster, 1623'.
37 LA, QSR/23, Quarter Sessions Roll, 1623, 16 October.
38 Slack, 'Books of Orders'; B. W. Quintrell, 'The Making of Charles I's Book of Orders', *English Historical Review*, 95, no. 376 (1980), 553–72.
39 *Orders and Directions, together with a commission for the better administration of justice, and more perfect information of His Majestie* (London, 1631).

be relieved and regulated and that Justices should meet monthly within their 'divisions' to do the same, were to be enforced by a royal commission of all Privy Councillors, and it is the reports from the divisional JPs to this commission which give us our key material. Many returns are highly stereotyped and anodyne, yet when read carefully they provide valuable evidence of the state of poor relief in the 1630s. In Lancashire, the story told is essentially one of widespread compliance with the Poor Law statutes.[40]

In all the surviving returns, the overwhelming majority of reported parishes and townships were appointing overseers of the poor, collecting poor rates and making regular doles. The portion relating to the Poor Law of the return made by the Blackburnshire Justices on 18 August 1634 is typical:

> Wee have spent much labour and paines in execucion of the Statutes for the poore wherein the fruites of our labours have yeilded such satisfaction unto us as hath made our burthens seeme lesse heavie for within theise twoe yeares in this little hundred wee have bound 200: apprentises or thereaboutes poore boyes and girles which before begged and wee have taken course from tyme to tyme for the releife of the aged and impotente poore soe that wee have fewe that begg with us; unless yt bee forrenners which come out of other counties and those wee restraine as much as wee can by our privie searches[,] watch and ward &c.[41]

In Rochdale at the same time it was reported that 'there hath bene everie yeare … [since 1628] an annuall taxation of at least towe hundred pounds for reliefe of the impotent'.[42] Justices at Standish, sitting for Leyland Hundred in 1635, repeated much of the Blackburnshire report word for word, they having 'taken course from tyme to time for reliefe of the aged & impotent poore, so that wee have few or none that begg with us, unles it bee forrainers which come out of other countries'.[43] These examples could easily be multiplied.

Just occasionally, rather more detail is forthcoming. The August 1636 return from Poulton-le-Fylde Division lists those 'aged & impotent poore people' who were receiving weekly doles in the parish of Kirkham that

40   It has been plausibly argued that this was the case for the country as a whole: Langelüddecke, '"Patchy and Spasmodic"?'.
41   TNA, SP16/273/55, Report of the Justices of Blackburn Hundred, 18 August 1634.
42   TNA, SP16/273/56, Report of the Justices of Rochdale Division, 18 August 1634.
43   TNA, SP16/291/128, Report of the Justices of Leyland Hundred, June 1635.

year.[44] It records eight pensioners as well as 'Widdowe Hodgson & 2 young children not fitt to bee bound apprentice', who 'hath a house provided for her by the said overseers & churchwardens, & maneteineth her selfe by her worke without any weekly allowance', making nine pauper household heads. Of these, seven were women, all but one being widows, and two were men: Alexander Horneby of Rossacre, 'aged 80 yeares & impotent' and John Lancaster 'of Weeton a poor sickman'. Two pensioners received 12d per week, a sizeable allowance for the 1630s, three took home 10d per week, while the remaining three made do with 8d, giving a mean of 9¾d per week.

Even more impressive was the list compiled in 1638 apparently of all the pensioners in Lonsdale Hundred.[45] Recording the names and weekly doles of sixty-one individuals across the hundred, north and south of Morecambe Sands, the document represents an impressive feat of data compilation. The mean weekly amount received by the fifty-nine pensioners whose information is legible was, at 5.4d, significantly lower than that found in Kirkham, but it was probably still about enough to pay for a half to two-thirds of someone's living costs. The twenty-four pensioners in south Lonsdale received on average 6.1d per week and were 82 per cent male; the thirty-seven from north of the Sands took a weekly average of 4.9d and were 69 per cent *fe*male. The lower pensions in the northern part of the hundred can perhaps be explained by the weaker rate base in this very poor part of the county, and we might also be seeing the shadow of a later development of official relief. The gender difference is much harder to understand, and may simply have come about by chance. It is also worth mentioning that the pensions found in Lancashire are not drastically different from those found by Tim Wales for North Walsham in Norfolk, in which parish a weekly dole of 6d was the norm in 1636.[46] At this level, then, we should not rush to characterize the North West as 'parsimonious' just yet.[47]

There are signs that the 1630s saw some significant widening of the scope of rate-funded poor relief, although given the evident prehistory of development one should be wary of ascribing this too squarely to the increase in governmental tempo. Most striking were the intense drives to

---

44   TNA, SP16/330/64, Report of the Justices of Amounderness Hundred, 22 August 1636.
45   TNA, SP16/397/69, Report of the Justices of Lonsdale Hundred, 20 August 1638.
46   Wales, 'Poverty, Poor relief and the Life-cycle', pp. 355–6.
47   King, *Poverty and Welfare*, p. 197.

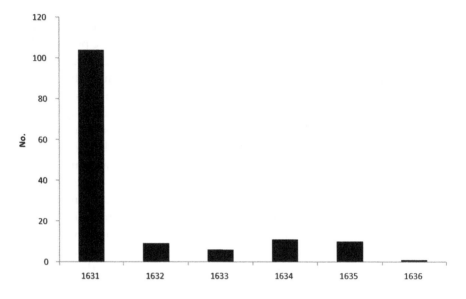

Figure 2: Pauper apprentices in Whalley parish, 1631–36

apprentice out poor children. Such projects were reported in Rochdale Division in 1626 and 1628 and in Blackburn Hundred in 1634.[48] Indeed, the degree to which this could mark a new beginning is highlighted by the returns made by an unnamed parish (probably Whalley) in 1637.[49] This contains a list of all those apprenticed in the parish since 1631 and the numeric importance of the initial drive strongly suggests that a significant backlog had built up before then (Figure 2). However, the best evidence for the entrenchment of poor relief during the Personal Rule comes from Lonsdale Hundred, this time the northern part.[50] As was noted above, a number of parishes in the Cartmel and Furness districts adopted a system whereby paupers were 'billeted' out to willing host families, a scheme that was, of course, rather different from the framework of relief stipulated by the law. In August 1636, billeting appears to have been widespread in North Lonsdale: eight out of nineteen parishes and townships surveyed

48   TNA, SP16/273/55, Report of the Justices of Blackburn Hundred, 18 August 1634; SP16/273/56, Report of the Justices of Rochdale Division, 18 August 1634; SP16/351/111, Report of the Justices of Rochdale Division, March 1637.
49   TNA, SP16/362/115, Report from an unknown parish, June 1637; Healey, 'Development', p. 563n.
50   TNA, SP16/330/99, Report of the Justices of North Lonsdale, 9 August 1636.

used this rather than poor rates as their preferred method of relief. Indeed, some townships put quite impressive numbers of their paupers out to hosts: Broughton-in-Cartmel relieved thirty-eight paupers this way, while there were thirty-nine in Allithwaite and another thirty-eight in Holker. Over time, however, billeting became squeezed out by moves to relieve the poor with pensions. When a similar report was made the following November, only one of the original eight, Kirkby Ireleth, still relied wholly on billeting.[51] Hawkshead, which in 1636 had put out eleven paupers to hosts, in 1637 certified 'that they doe provide for xiii poore people by way of bilittinge and all the rest of the poore is provided for by way of sessment and is not suffered to wander'. In August 1638, the parish was supporting five pensioners, each receiving either 4d or 6d per week.[52]

It is not clear whether the reports are showing a new urgency for enforcement in the 1630s, or merely the continuation of a longer period of incremental improvement which only came into view with the better source material available.[53] Meanwhile, the dearth in 1636–38 may also have been a factor in drives to ensure compliance.[54] There is, however, one tantalizing scrap of evidence which would suggest an important role for the Privy Council. This is the petition for relief, presented at Quarter Sessions in Epiphany 1633, of one Hugh Winstanley of Wigan.[55] The content of the petition itself is unremarkable: Winstanley claimed to be old and unable to work or beg alms in terms largely indistinguishable from other pre-Civil War appeals. What singles this document out for special interest is a note written at the foot of the page, in a different hand, dated to 28 September 1632 at Lever Hall and signed by one John Astney. It reads as follows: 'I desire Mr Lee in Ashurst and my brother to give order to the overseers that they give something weekely to this pooreman, the rather for that his Majestie hath lately called upon us to be carefull in the releif of the poore.' The specifics of the case are opaque, but it would seem to be indicative of some level of local understanding that central government was trying to implement poor relief policies more effectively, and that governors should act upon this.

51 TNA, SP16/382/10, Report of the Justices of Cartmel and Furness Liberties, 13 February 1638.
52 TNA, SP16/397/69, Report of the Justices of Lonsdale Hundred, 20 August 1638.
53 Cf. Langelüddecke, '"Patchy and Spasmodic"?', pp. 1247–8.
54 Ibid., p. 1239.
55 LA, QSB/1/114/56. There is a similar note, dated 22 May 1631, on a petition from Michaelmas that year: QSB/1/126/76.

To bring this evidence together, we might suggest the following synthesis. The 1598 and 1601 statutes brought an immediate response in some parts of the county, and there is clear evidence that *some* aspects of the formal poor relief system were in place in certain areas by 1620. To a certain extent this may have been imposed from above by Justices rather than developing out of the parishes themselves, but this is hard to tell, not least because most surviving documentation relates to the work of the magistracy. The 1620s probably saw rate-funded poor relief become even more entrenched, and by the later 1630s there were few parishes not implementing the key provisions of the Elizabethan Poor Laws. By 1655, at least one petition relating to poor relief had been heard from 83 per cent of Lancashire parishes, and most of the 'missing' ones were in North Lonsdale, where we know that rates had been imposed by 1638 at the latest.[56] In the space, then, of at most fifty years, rate-funded poor relief had become established across the county.

The Civil War and after

There is disagreement over what happened to poor relief during the Civil War years. Earlier historians' claims that the onset of Puritan rule brought with it a severe attitude to the needs of the poor have not proved durable.[57] However, there is virtually no evidence for any working system of poor relief in Lancashire during the war itself.[58] The court of Quarter Sessions ceased to sit between Easter 1643 and Epiphany 1646 inclusive.[59] Data from individual parishes is virtually non-existent. Fifteen paupers were relieved by the churchwardens of Prescot in the year ending Easter 1643, but the following year there is the record of just one pauper, Elizabeth

---

56   Healey, 'Development', p. 564.
57   R. H. Tawney, *Religion and the Rise of Capitalism: A Historical Study* (London, 1926), pp. 218–19; Webb and Webb, *English Poor Law History, Part One*, pp. 95–100; M. James, *Social Problems and Policy during the Puritan Revolution, 1640–1660* (London, 1930), pp. 249–51; H. N. Brailsford, *The Levellers and the English Revolution* (London, 1961), pp. 319–20; Jordan, *Philanthropy in England*, pp. 136–8; C. Hill, *The Century of Revolution, 1603–1714* (Edinburgh, 1961), p. 153; Beier, 'Poor Relief in Warwickshire', pp. 80–6.
58   Cf. D. Underdown, *Fire From Heaven: Life in an English Town in the Seventeenth Century* (London, 1992), p. 209; Gough, *History of Myddle*, p. 60.
59   LA, QSO/2/18–19.

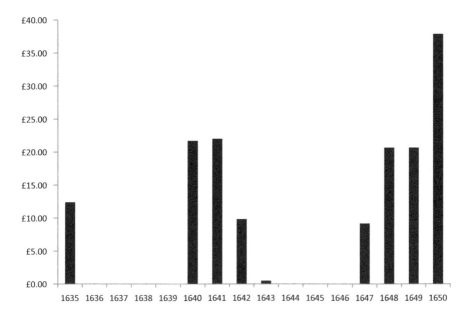

Figure 3: Poor relief expenditure by Prescot churchwardens, 1635–50

Case a 'poore old blynd woman', who received 10s.[60] The record of doles in the parish then restarts in the year beginning Easter 1647 (Figure 3).[61] The reappearance of Quarter Sessions records in 1646 brought with it a number of petitions, suggesting that the mechanisms of the Poor Law had not totally broken down, yet there are clear signs that in some communities relief payments were not being made and overseers not appointed.[62] In 1646, William Towers of Scotforth petitioned that he had been ordered relief in April 1641, but that 'the churchwardens & overseers hath neglected the payment thereof for three yeares now past'.[63] The following year it was reported that two blind Lancaster women had 'beene formerly relieved forth of the parishe of Lancaster yet since theise troubles some

60   *Prescot Churchwardens' Accounts, 1635–1663*, ed. T. Steele (RSLC, cxxxvii, Stroud, 2002).
61   The amounts spent in 1648 and 1649 are recorded together in the accounts; thus the figures in the graph represent half of the total for the two years.
62   It is worth noting, too, that Wrightson found evidence that the system of petty constables was breaking down in parts of Lancashire in the aftermath of the First Civil War: Wrightson, 'Puritan Reformation', pp. 200–1.
63   LA, QSB/1/270/20.

tymes not regarded nor no helpe hath had'.[64] And such problems were not confined to the north of the county either, for in 1646 James Kirkby of Downholland complained that he had not been relieved for the space of four years.[65] The following year a group of twenty-five 'inhabitants' of Croston complained that although the parish had many poor, 'wee have no overseers nor collectors nor collections for them, by reason whereof they all goe a begging daly among us and abroad in the country; and most of them are in a most miserable condicion and ready to perish for want of necessary mayntenance'.[66] Their tale was similar to that told by Mary Platt of Culcheth, who asked that same year for a relief order to be 'directed to the constables of the parish of Winwicke, in respecte of the troublesome tymes, there is but few churchwardens and overseers in the said parish but are dead'.[67] In 1648, Justices sent the complete text of the 1601 statute to the overseers of Bolton, urging them to make special provision for the impotent poor, and a similar order was made to the officers of Eccles the following year, suggesting that the court of Quarter Sessions was having to intervene to ensure full compliance with the law.[68] The catalyst in this regard was almost certainly the exceptionally severe dearth and trade depression which beset England between 1647 and 1650, and which seems to have hit Lancashire especially hard.[69] Indeed, Hindle has argued with great conviction that the dearth pushed local officers into enforcing the Poor Law where it had collapsed during the war, with the impetus often coming from parishes upwards to Quarter Sessions rather than necessarily the other way around.[70]

As it happens, it is in the immediate aftermath of the Civil War that we get our first sustained set of overseers' papers for Lancashire. Starting in Easter 1646, the accounts for the parish of Prestwich in the Manchester region run up to 1683, and those for five of the parish's eight townships are virtually continuous (Figures 4–6).[71] Records for all eight townships

64   LA, QSB/1/286/18.
65   LA, QSB/1/276/27.
66   LA, QSB/1/292/19.
67   LA, QSB/1/296/43.
68   Fessler, 'Official Attitude', p. 92; LA, QSP/12/2.
69   LA, QSP/4/6; see below, pp. 218–21.
70   Hindle, 'Dearth and the English Revolution', pp. 78–91.
71   MALS, L160/2/1, Prestwich Churchwardens' and Overseers' Accounts, 1646–83; The township of Duxbury also has accounts from 1653, which have recently become available, however the amounts dispersed were so low as to render quantitative analysis statistically suspect: LA, DDX/1834/1, Duxbury Overseers' Account Book, 1653–1820.

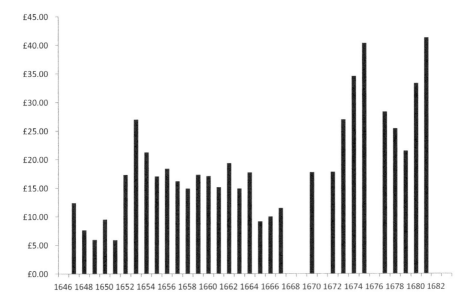

Figure 4: Poor relief expenditure in Prestwich, Heaton, Heaton Fallowfield, Alkrington and Tonge, 1646–83

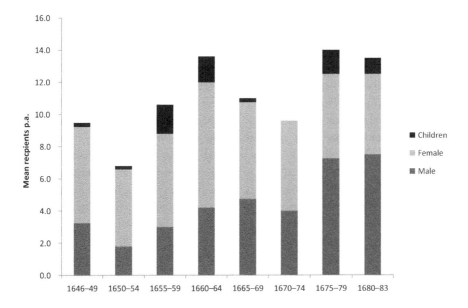

Figure 5: Mean number of named recipients of poor relief in Prestwich, 1646–83

Figure 6: Annual mean dole per named recipient in Prestwich, 1646–83

do survive in some years, and these show a gradual increase: an average of £44 was spent in 1652–60, but in 1675 expenditures had almost reached £100, though this was a year of dearth. Funding in the 1650s was already mostly from rates ('leys'), though the accounts also record contributions by funeral doles, one-off collections in the church, and money gathered at the sacrament. Relief was given by the individual townships rather than the parish, but the fact that the accounts can be found together in the papers of the latter suggests some supervisory role by the larger jurisdiction. They show a fairly typical array of doles, from weekly pensions through house rents to 7s 8d in 1675 to buy 'diet drinke and for 2 bottels of oyntement' for a lame boy. Interestingly, the mean number of recorded recipients of poor relief does not seem to have increased so noticeably over the period: a mean of 10.3 persons were recorded as in receipt of doles between 1646 and 1669, rising to 12.1 between 1670 and 1683. Overall, then, the increase in expenditure seems to have come about largely in the form of an increased dole per recorded recipient, with the annual mean roughly doubling from £0.38 between 1646 and 1669 to £0.80 after 1670.

Parish and township

By this time, Lancashire was grappling with what was – perhaps – a rather surprisingly bitter controversy, something which turned out to be one of the major teething problems for the county's first century of welfare. According to the Elizabethan statutes, the administration of poor relief in England and Wales was to take place at the level of the parish. It was this civil jurisdiction which was supposed to appoint overseers of the poor, and it was this unit which was to be the basic geographical basis of the property tax that was to fund them. In northern England, however, where the parochial framework had evolved to cater for a sparse medieval population and an impoverished early Church, many parishes were exceptionally large.[72] Manchester parish spread from the River Irwell in the north to the River Mersey in the south; Lancaster parish covered massive areas of lower Lonsdale and Wyresdale. Even these were dwarfed by the parish of Whalley, which covered some 160 square miles, contained forty-eight townships, and included Burnley, Clitheroe, and Colne. As a result of the practical problems caused by this topographical fact, the administration of poor relief gradually came to be invested in sub-parochial jurisdictions such as the township, hamlet or vill.[73] This alteration began to take place in the first half of the seventeenth century, was temporarily enshrined in statute law in 1662, and then confirmed permanently in 1685.[74] The process of change, while fairly confusing, tells us much about the local politics involved in the development of Poor Law administration.

The pace of the shift varied between jurisdictions. In Northumberland it was apparently only in the 1770s, when an energetic Clerk of the Peace took up the cause, that the township superseded the parish as the critical unit of local Poor Law administration.[75] By contrast, the West Riding seems to have implemented this arrangement almost immediately following the 1598 statute, while parts of Westmorland had clearly done

---

72 Higham, *Frontier Landscape*, pp. 215–20.
73 *Abstract of the Returns made by the Overseers of the Poor* (London, 1777), pp. 78–85.
74 See: Oxley, 'Old Poor Law', pp. 27–8; C. Watson, 'The Early Administration of the Old Poor Law in Leyland Hundred, Lancashire: the Importance of the Township', *Local Historian*, 40 (2010), 266–80.
75 N. McCord, *North East England: an Economic and Social History* (London, 1979), p. 87.

so by the 1630s at the latest.[76] In Prestbury, a 63,000-acre Cheshire parish, the constituent townships were administrating poor relief by the 1630s, when this 'constant practice past the memorie of man' was challenged, but the authorities ruled on the side of custom rather than the strict letter of statute law.[77]

In Lancashire, the evidence suggests that – in the immediate aftermath of the 1598 statute – poor relief was usually administered at the level of the parish. As was noted above, the earliest evidence we have of poor rates in the county is for the *parishes* of Bolton-le-Moors and Deane. Early orders for relief made by the court of Quarter Sessions show a similar evidence of parochial administration, with Melling, Garstang, Ormskirk, Lancaster, Eccleston, Prescot, Standish, Winwick, Kirkham-with-Goosnargh, Poulton and Wigan all mentioned in this context before 1605.[78] Even at this early stage, however, it seems that some townships were beginning to work independently. We first see this in Whalley parish, where the Shuttleworth accounts show a poor rate payment to Ightenhill township as early as 1600.[79] Similarly, the townships of Pendle, Burnley and Padiham were all collecting their own poor rates by the second decade of the seventeenth century.[80] Indeed, according to the lost parish book of Deane, consulted during a lawsuit on the issue in Charles II's reign, the individual townships were looking after their own poor by 1601, at which point Heaton had been 'ordered to releve their own poor and a tax made'.[81]

The process may have been hastened by the early involvement of some manor courts (which tended to be coterminous with townships rather than parishes) in the appointment of overseers. In Tottington in 1631, it was recorded that 'the pore people within the *manor* of Tottington have made great complaint to the churchwardens & overseers of the poore within the

76   *West Riding Sessions Rolls, 1597/8–1642*, ed. J. Lister, 2 vols (Yorkshire Archaeological Society Record Series, iii, liv, Leeds, 1888–1915), vol. 1, p. xxix; TNA, SP16/388/7, Report of the Justices of Kendal Ward, 18 April 1638; CRO (K), WPR/62/W1, Troutbeck Overseers' Accounts, 1640–43.

77   Hindle, *State and Social Change*, p. 154.

78   *Lancashire Quarter Sessions Records*, pp. 102, 138, 147, 149–50, 155, 167, 190, 200, 211, 219, 223.

79   *House and Farm Accounts*, vol. 1, pp. 128–9.

80   Ibid., vol. 1, pp. 224, 229–30, vol. 2, p. 236.

81   LA, DDKe/2/6/3, Breviate to defend a motion by Farnworth, Kearsley, and Westhoughton, 1682.

said towneshipp', suggesting some involvement of the former unit.[82] As late as 1667, all of the township officers of Anglezarke (Bolton-le-Moors) were appointed at the 'Courte Leete & Court Baron', as they had been 'for all the time whereof the memory of man is not to the contrary'.[83] Given that it allowed the appointment of four overseers, the law provided some flexibility to do this: where a parish had four townships or fewer, it was simple enough to attach one officer to each. Where the parish had more than four townships, it could be rationalized into 'quarters' for administrative purposes; alternatively the petty constables, technically officers of the leet, could take the lead in taxing and laying out money for the poor.[84] In fact, as the first half of the seventeenth century progressed, there were an increasing number of references to parishes subdividing into townships for the management of poor relief. The Quarter Sessions petitions of the 1630s primarily refer to townships rather than parishes, although on the other hand, the reports to the Privy Council of the same decade usually refer to parish-level administration. In Bury, a small urban community to the north of Manchester, even townships had proved too large, with Poor Law administration vested in the *hamlet* by an agreement of 1638 between 'the churchwardens overseers, & the most of the inhabitants' of the parish.[85]

But sub-parochial administration in itself could cause problems. While the parish was often an impracticably large unit, its size at least helped mitigate the problems caused by pockets of extreme deprivation. Thus, in those parishes in which small areas were suffering from heavy poverty and a weak rate-base, attempts might be made to maintain a certain degree of parochial administrative control, effectively constituting a rate-in-aid from the wealthier to the poorer parts of the parish. Unsurprisingly, this became a cause of inter-community conflict. The inhabitants of Shuttleworth (Bury parish), for example, were only willing in 1631 to pay a parochial rate if their contribution was guaranteed to go to their own poor, not those of impoverished Tottington.[86] The large parish of Melling, whose townships would fight an exceptionally long-drawn-out legal contest over rates well into the eighteenth century, had its first taste of such contention in 1643 when the 'poore distressed inhabitants' of Claughton petitioned that they had

---

82 LA, QSB/1/83/58. My italics.
83 LA, QSP/295/22.
84 Oxley, 'Old Poor Law', pp. 20–3.
85 LA, QSB/1/203/67.
86 LA, QSB/1/83/58; QSB/1/95/54.

107 needinge persons who have nothinge to relieve themselves withall but what the[y] get by day labour & 80 of them & more are children or impotent lame and aged people that cannot worke whereby the rest of the towne not beinge past five houses that are able to give or relieve.[87]

On this occasion the justices refused to reinstate parochial taxation, but on others such rates-in-aid were imposed, and by the end of the 1650s this local flexibility had allowed the development of a complex mesh of administrative arrangements.

In 1662 the legislative situation changed, for a statute of that year (better known for its provisions for pauper settlement) decreed that poor relief in the large parishes of the North should henceforth be administered 'within every township or village'.[88] There is a sense that this move, in Lancashire at least, created more problems than it solved. The older parochial system had been, in many cases, so obviously inadequate that it had practically given communities *carte blanche* to use whichever approach they felt most appropriate. The problem with the enforcement of township administration under the Restoration statute was, paradoxically, that it was *too* widely practical without necessarily being the *optimal* solution in every case. Thus wealthy townships who had found themselves subsidizing their impoverished neighbours were able to seize upon the legislation and dismantle any surviving remnants of parochial rates. The overseers of Great Bolton, the urban core of the much larger parish of Bolton-le-Moors, summed this up well in 1674 when they complained that

since the makeing of the Act of the fowerteenth of this King the poore in this and other Northerne countys beeing to bee taken care for within their perticular towneshipp (if the towneshipp bee able) your petitioners haveing beene thereby seperate from the rest of the parish have beene put to a charge greater than they are able to continue for manteyning their said poore.[89]

In fact, there was a marked increase in the number of disputes between townships over parochial taxation *after* 1662, some of which became exceptionally bitter. As mentioned, the townships within the rural parish

87   LA, QSB/1/269c/8–9.
88   14 Charles II, c. 12.
89   LA, QSP/413/14.

of Melling-in-Lonsdale were at loggerheads for most of the second half of the seventeenth century and into the eighteenth.[90] In Bolton-le-Moors, the townships took their dispute as far as King's Bench in the 1680s before a rate-in-aid from the rural to the urban parts of the parish became accepted.[91] There were even accusations of distraints being undertaken 'in a violent manner' when a parochial rate was attempted in Bury in 1686.[92]

Things came to a head in the eleven years between 1674 and 1685. The first key development in this period was the petition of the overseers of Great Bolton, writing at the height of a major trade depression, for a rate-in-aid from the parish to help fund the creation of a stock with which to employ the poor.[93] In response, the Justices at the Sheriff's Table decreed that parishes could choose to implement the systems of rating and relief stipulated in *either* the 1601 or the 1662 statutes, presumably depending on local circumstances and the judgement of nearby magistrates.[94] Any consensus achieved by this mercifully commonsense decision did not – however – last long, for in 1678 Parliament allowed the statute of 14 Charles II to lapse.[95] Technically, parochial administration was back in force, and this was quickly reflected in an order by the Quarter Sessions for West Derby and Leyland hundreds that overseers and churchwardens were to meet the next Sunday 'in their severall parish churches' to fix rates and relieve the poor.[96] Immediately a number of townships to whom the previous compromise had not been advantageous tried to re-instigate parochial rates. At Warton-in-Lonsdale, which was a small rural community rather than a growing town like Great Bolton, the officers of the central settlement gleefully pointed out that 'by the lawes and statutes of this realme now in force every parish are to keepe and mantaine their owne poore', and thus claimed support from the rest of the

90   LA, QSP/245/12; QSP/249/17; QSP/261/2; QSP/281/9; QSP/289/1; QSP/297/9; QSP/341/3; QSP/377/2; QSP/393/12; QSP/397/4; QSP/442/13; QSP/491/8; QSP/496/12; QSP/544/10; QSP/560/4; QSP/596/3; QSP/606/1; QSP/772/1–2; QSP/825/1; QSP/838/19; QSP/910/8; QSP/926/16; QSP/946/11.
91   LA, QSP/413/14; QSP/429/45; QSP/461/1; QSP/469/30; QSP/530/14–15; QSP/547/17; LA, DDHu/53/36, Order of Lancaster Assizes Concerning Payments for the Relief of the Poor in Bolton, 1687; BALS, PBO/2/1, Bolton-le-Moors Vestry Minutes, 1655–1744, p. 67.
92   LA, QSP/626/10.
93   LA, QSP/413/14.
94   *Proceedings of the Lancashire Justices*, pp. 132–3; cf. Botelho, *Old Age*, p. 40.
95   Oxley, 'Old Poor Law', pp. 27–8.
96   LA, QSP/509/23.

parish.[97] In Tarleton and Croston, previous orders to the contrary were
set aside and the parish ordered to collect and distribute poor rates.[98] The
township of Hawkshead, meanwhile, provoked an angry petition from
neighbouring Claife and Satterthwaite when they tried to tax the whole
parish for the relief of 'the wyfe of one Mr Henry Nicholson herefore
vicar of Hawkshead who is lately fled & left his wyfe & two children'.[99]
Up until now, and indeed 'by an antient custome used tyme out of mynd',
the constituent divisions had looked after their own poor.

In fact, these moves proved only temporary. In response to a dispute
about practices in the parish of Deane, beginning in 1682, four Justices
investigated and reported on the methods employed across the whole
county.[100] Their findings, reported to Petty Sessions by three of their
number (one was off sick with the gout), survive in the papers of the High
Constable, Roger Kenyon. They provide the first systematic investigation
into poor relief practices across the whole county since the 1630s, albeit
with a rather more restricted aim than the earlier surveys. The justices
received reports from the hundreds of Lonsdale, Amounderness, Leyland,
Blackburn and the parish of Eccles, each of which stated that the poor
were exclusively maintained by townships.[101] They also examined past
practices in Deane, concluding that since 1601 the constituent townships
had maintained their own poor. Collating the gathered information, a
brief in defence of township administration recorded that:

> There are in the County of Lancaster 64 parishes in sixty of which the
> poor are maintained each in his particuler town vill or hamlett, some
> of these parishes containe above 30 townshipps many of them are vastly
> spatious, to unhinge the settlements of the poor in soe many towns
> vills and hamletts might prove a more fatall consequence than is easy
> to foresee or perhaps would bee easily endured.[102]

The townships in question, meanwhile, were not suffering any greater
need than their neighbours, although 'it is not to bee disputed but if the

97   LA, QSP/511/7; Mourholme Local History Society, *How it Was: a North Lancashire
Parish in the Seventeenth Century* (Carnforth, 1998), pp. 119–25.
98   LA, QSP/513/10.
99   LA, QSP/515/1.
100 LA, DDKe/2/6/4, Quarter Sessions Orders, 1682.
101 LA, DDKe/2/6/6, Quarter Sessions Confirmation, 1683.
102 LA, DDKe/2/6/3, Breviate to defend a motion by Farnworth, Kearsley, and
Westhoughton, 1682.

towne and hamlets that move for this parish to be laid together were really poor or necessitous that they would have law and reason on their side'. It was an argument with which Quarter Sessions agreed, repeatedly.

Thus it appears that by 1683, notwithstanding the recent lapse of the 1662 statute, the township's position as the fundamental unit of poor relief administration in Lancashire was unassailable. Indeed, when the statute was renewed in 1685 it appears there was no corresponding peak in litigation. Rates-in-aid continued in several locations, but apart from this minor qualification the township was to remain supreme until 1834. In general, indeed, although it was the cause of ill will between townships, the working out of the contradictions of the statutes, local topography and the human landscape took place in a largely rational way, overseen by JPs, the Assizes and ultimately King's Bench, based on some conception of who could afford to pay what to whom: on 'law and reason'.

Obtaining relief: meeting needs to resources

It is unnecessary to go into much detail about the different types of relief offered by Lancashire's sixty-four parishes and their constituent townships, for the county was little different in this regard from the rest of the country.[103] Put briefly, relief came as either regular payments, notably pensions (or 'collections'), house rents and tabling fees, or as occasional doles such as for medical treatment, foodstuffs, trade tools, clothes and any number of other items deemed necessary. Payments to individual paupers generally followed an upward trend, with the recipient getting a greater amount of support as he or she declined in health or increased in age. On occasions, however, pensions could be reduced in the face of improved circumstances. In 1677, officers of Rainford petitioned to reduce the allowance of Edmund Lowe, 'now the rates of all sorts of provisions are become moderate and to bee had at reasonable values'.[104] Similarly, in 1699, the 'principall inhabitants' of Farnworth, Rumworth and Kearsley townships (Deane parish) reported to Quarter Sessions that

103   Several works exist detailing types of outdoor expenditure, for example: Leonard, *Early History*, pp. 206–36; Webb and Webb, *English Poor Law History, Part One*, pp. 149–313; Oxley, *Poor Relief*, pp. 61–78; Brundage, *English Poor Laws*, pp. 9–36; L. Patriquin, *Agrarian Capitalism and Poor Relief in England, 1500–1860: Rethinking the Origins of the Welfare State* (Basingstoke, 2007), pp. 100–3.
104   LA, QSP/472/10.

by reason of the scarcity or rather dearness of provisions for the time past the inhabitants of the said townes have beene extreamely burthened with the reliefe of theire poore but in regard provisions are become more reasonable and cheape tis hoped theire poore might subsist with lesser alloweances ...[105]

Overall, though, the general trend was for the costs of relief to increase.

From the 1690s onwards we start to see many more surviving poor accounts. Figure 7 comprises a composite average of total overseers' expenditures in seventeen townships for which decent accounts survive.[106] It suggests two points relating to costs from the 1690s to the 1740s. First, they clearly increased, with the average suggesting that costs in the county slightly more than doubled between the 1690s/1700s and the 1740s. We can take this process of estimation one step further using the Parliamentary Poor Rate Returns for the last years of the 1740s and projecting them backwards.[107] Thus, while the county is recorded as spending an average of £21,236 on poor relief per year between 1748–50, the best guess from back projection would suggest a total-county spend of around half this in the 1690s: just over £10,000 per annum. According to the best estimates, the number of people living in Lancashire rose from around 190,000 in 1690 to perhaps just below 300,000 in 1750.[108] This would give us an

105   LA, QSP/837/28.
106   LA, PR/2890/2/1, Accrington (New and Old) Parish Accounts, 1691–1800; LA, PR/872, Alston Churchwardens', Overseers' and Constables' Accounts, 1712–1817; WA, TR/Ath/C/2/1–8, Atherton Overseers' Accounts, 1692–1751; LA, PR/2592/2, Bispham Town's Book, 1722–1808; Bury Hamlet Overseers' Accounts, 1692–1760, microfilm copy in LA; LA, PR/499–500, Caton Township Accounts, 1714–95; MALS, M/10/7/2/1, Cheetham Overseers' Accounts, 1693–1791; MALS, M/10/9/2/1, Chorlton-on-Medlock Overseers' Accounts, 1718–94; LA, PR/256, Croston Township Accounts, 1717–1855; MALS, L82/2/1, Goodshaw Overseers' Accounts, 1691–1741; LA, PR/264–5, Halsall Township Accounts, 1694–1885; CRO (K), WPR/83/7/3, Hawkshead Overseers' Accounts, 1690–1750; CRO (K), WPR/83/7/6–8, Monk Coniston and Skelwith Overseers' Accounts, 1691–1808; LA, PR/2667, Nether Wyresdale Town Accounts Book, 1685–1837; WA, TR/Pe/C/1/1–37, Pennington Overseers Papers, 1699–1750; LA, PR/3168/7/9, Tarleton Overseers' Accounts, 1708–67. In each township a mean annual disbursement figure was calculated, covering all surviving years. This was taken as 100, with each year's disbursement total recalculated as a proportion of 100. A mean was then taken of all extant annual values to make up the composite mean for the sample as a whole in each year. Evidently this is a blunt instrument, and thus the results are indicative and in no way definitive.
107   Parliamentary Papers, 1818, vol. 5, Report from Poor Law Committee, p. 9.
108   Phillips and Smith, Lancashire and Cheshire, p. 67.

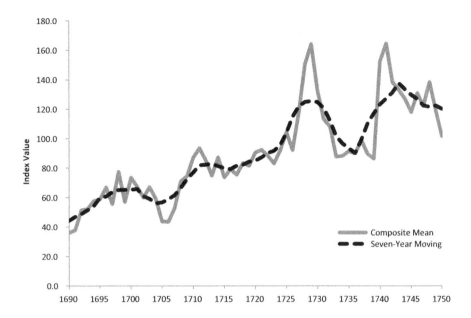

Figure 7: Composite of poor expenditure in Lancashire townships, 1690–1750

increase of 40 per cent from £0.05 per head in the 1690s to £0.07 by 1750. One would not want to put too much emphasis on these figures, although the overall increase in spending is fairly clear. If they are correct, though, Lancashire's spending per capita was lower than the national average, which lay at around £0.12 in 1748–50.[109]

The second point is that secular changes in the amount of money spent on running the Poor Law were clearly accompanied by some very marked periods of exceptionally high costs. Indeed, the degree to which poor expenditure fluctuated year by year, while often acknowledged by historians, is rarely displayed with such clarity as here. Two 'crises' stand out very prominently in our period: one in the late 1720s, one in the early 1740s, and if the graph was to extend forward another decade then a third crisis would be seen hitting the county in the late 1750s. There was, then, a pattern of slowly rising 'background' levels of poverty combined with short bursts of exceptionally high expenditure.

In England as a whole, there were frequent attempts to curb rising

109   Slack, *English Poor Law*, p. 22.

costs. On occasions, notably after a 1697 statute theoretically made it compulsory, relief was conditional on the pauper in question 'taking the patch', i.e. wearing a badge, usually comprising the letter 'P' (for 'pauper') and the initial of the township of settlement.[110] Another development was the growth in the number of workhouses. There is little evidence, apart from the abortive county scheme from the 1580s, of many workhouses existing in Lancashire before the 1723 'Knatchbull's Act', which allowed communities to make relief conditional on paupers moving into such establishments. The closest equivalent, save the two Houses of Correction at Manchester and Preston, was the house set up for the poor of Preston in 1674 in order to 'keepe them from wandering and begging', and the 'charity school' for 'work and labour' which was reported to exist in Liverpool in 1725.[111] Rising costs in the late 1720s seem to have led to calls for more workhouse schemes. One of earliest was that at Kirkham, agreed upon in 1726, while the vestry of Burnley agreed to found one in June 1730, and it was operational the following year.[112] In Lancaster, local shopkeeper William Stout told of a workhouse being created, with some success, as a way of clawing back costs that were spiralling at the time. 'The last year', he wrote of 1730,

> being a dearth of corn, encreased the poor, soe that our poor tax was advanced from one hundred to two hundred pounds a year. Upon which a house was hired to entertaine the poor in, to be maintained without goeing a begging, and to imploy such as were able to worke in some imploy; and a person to set them on to worke. Upon which, many that used to beg, finding themselves stopped from begging, fell to work, rather then to be confined to the poor house.[113]

By 1731, Lancaster, Warrington and Ashton-under-Lyne had houses for their poor, the latter towns reporting (so said a pro-workhouse publication) that they had

---

110   Webb and Webb, *English Poor Law History, Part One*, p. 161; Hindle, 'Dependency, Shame and Belonging'; Hindle, *On the Parish?*, pp. 433–45.

111   D. Hunt, *A History of Preston* (Preston, 1992), p. 82; *An Account of Several Work-houses for Employing and Maintaining the Poor*, 1st edn (London, 1725), p. 111.

112   P. Shakeshaft, *The History of Freckleton* (Lancaster, 2001), p. 58; W. Bennett, *The History of Burnley*, 4 vols (Burnley, 1946–51), vol. 3, pp. 60–1.

113   Stout, *Autobiography*, p. 207.

felt an advantage from it, even before it was finished; the dread of what is called confinement, having spurr'd on several of our poor to labour for a livelihood, which they would never have endeavoured, as long as they could have been relieved by the parish-rate, or by alms at our doors ...[114]

By the end of the following year there were new houses at Liverpool, Atherton and Windle (also serving Parr).[115] Furthermore, although Manchester's scheme broke down in the face of Whig-Tory and Dissenter-Anglican animosity, the comprehensiveness of the moves to getting a house in the town gives added support to the notion that these years were a turning point.[116] In Furness, meanwhile, the parishes of Cartmel and Dalton both had workhouses by the middle of the 1736.[117] Thus, the end of our period saw the beginnings of the great wave of Lancashire workhouse foundations that left the county with at least fifty-three establishments containing over 3,300 individual places by 1777.[118]

Conclusion

This chapter has sketched the broad outline of developments in poor relief practices in Lancashire from the late sixteenth century to the middle of the eighteenth. The process by which rate-funded poor relief became entrenched in the county was one of perpetual negotiation between vested interests including not just the central state but the wider patchwork of individual communities. Lancashire was also, however, probably a low-spending county, with both pension sizes and average relief costs per head often low by national standards. This, then, was the institutional landscape in which those in poverty – the main focus of this book – lived.

---

114   *An Account of Several Work-houses for Employing and Maintaining the Poor*, 2nd edn (London, 1732), pp. 143–4. Note that neither the Kirkham house nor that at Burnley is amongst those listed in this account. Also: Slack, *From Reformation to Improvement*, p. 134.
115   WA, TR/Ath/C/2/5, Atherton Overseers' Accounts, 1724–33; T. C. Barker and J. R. Harris, *A Merseyside Town in the Industrial Revolution: St. Helens, 1750–1900* (London, 1959), p. 133.
116   K. Kondo, 'Church and Politics in "Disaffected" Manchester, 1718–31', *Historical Research*, 80, no. 207 (2007), 100–23 (pp. 113–23).
117   Marshall, *Furness*, p. 137.
118   Even this Parliamentary survey was incomplete, missing at least one house (at Hawkshead). *Abstracts of the Returns*, p. 81.

3

Pauper Tales

And your peticioner at some former sessions applyed herselfe by her peticion to your good worships who was pleased to grant her first eight pence per weeke and after that was pleased to grant her four pence more addicionally per weeke for fyreing, shee being soe old and not able to provide her selfe fyer; and when your peticioner had soe obtained your said order and shewed it to the then overseer of the poore there, one John Braithwaite who paid your peticioner twelve pence per weeke accordingly for about tenn weekes, and then desired a sight of the said order whereupon your peticioner shewed it him, and he putt the same up in his pocket and would never redeliver the same againe to your peticioner. Since which your peticioner has been hindered of her said allowance, and kept from her subsistance soe allowed by your good worshipps.

Petition of Agnes Braithwaite of Field Head (Michaelmas 1702)[1]

The operation of the Poor Law left an impressive documentary trail. Overseers kept accounts and compiled censuses, the poor themselves launched petitions for relief, JPs undertook local investigations, settlement examinations were taken and certificates produced.[2] Removal orders and apprenticeship indentures were lodged in parish chests across the country, while occasional references to the system pepper many diaries, letters and autobiographies. It was a system in which written documentation was critical, hence Agnes Braithwaite's safe keeping of her relief order, and hence her difficulty in claiming her pension once it had been confiscated. As a result, the operation of official poor relief ensures that the very poor in early modern England are better documented than many further up the

---

1   LA, QSP/882/27.
2   W. E. Tate, *The Parish Chest*, 3rd edn (Cambridge, 1969), pp. 187–239; see also: J. Baker, I. Levitt and R. Pope (eds), *A Guide to the Lancashire Records: The Poor Law, 1750–1850* (Preston, 1996).

social scale. Before embarking on a survey of poverty and poor relief, we must look in rather more detail at the kinds of sources available and the uses to which they may be put.

Records of relief: the accounts of overseers of the poor

The most obvious set of documents are the accounts of overseers of the poor. According to the 1598 and 1601 statutes, these were to be presented at an annual parish meeting every Easter.[3] Additionally, from 1692, overseers were supposed to keep a 'book or bookes' of the poor, into which the names of all those receiving relief were to be written.[4] Some monthly accounts survive, especially for the later period, but the majority of records comprise the end-of-year accounts submitted at the Easter meeting, either incorporated into a book or as separate bundled sheets. Fairly often the surviving records for a parish or township comprise just a figure for total expenditure; when complete, however, they contain lists of names of recipients with a varying amount of detail as to the character of their need and relief.[5] In general, even when the documents are specific and complete, the emphasis is very strongly on details of relief: they record what was given, not why it was needed.

Since overseers' accounts are amenable to detailed quantification, they have proved popular with historians. But they are not unprob-lematic, and reliance on them has provided an incomplete view of the causes of need and the character of poverty in early modern England. Essentially the problems are of two kinds: practical and fundamental. On the practical side, although overseers' accounts were – nationally – quite impressively standardized for the time, they were still inconsistent and imprecise. Recording practices varied from place to place, and might even differ from officer to officer *within* communities. Worse, one cannot usually even tell *when* documents were consistent with others and when they were not. And they could lapse into quite serious imprecision. Some paupers were recorded by nicknames and vague descriptions: the officers of Halliwell, for example, spent money on 'a pye for the old man' in

3   39 Eliz. I, c. 3; 43 Eliz. I, c. 2.
4   3 William and Mary, c. 11.
5   The township book of Halliwell contains both years in which a single annual amount was recorded and those in which there is considerably more information: *The Township Booke of Halliwell*, ed. A. Sparke (CS, New Ser., lxix, Manchester, 1910).

1737.[6] In Atherton, we find picturesque names like 'Lame Jack', 'Barefoot Jane', and 'Liverpool Dick'.[7] Even when accounts are more precise, there are often multiple possible interpretations of single entries. In particular, it is usually impossible to determine the pauper's specific family circumstances. In cases of medical care, the individual named in the overseers' papers could be either the sick person themselves or the head of their household. Equally confusing are the numerous occasions when relief is recorded as being given to somebody's wife (as in 'to John Benson's wife'), which may or may not be evidence that the husband was absent. Moreover, since key welfare goods were often provided in kind, disbursements to individuals may have occasionally been retail purchases rather than doles, the two being indistinguishable in the accounting record. Thus we have the case of Hugh Cowperthwaite, recipient of £2 6s 5d from the township of Monk Coniston with Skelwith in 1737/38.[8] From internal evidence there is nothing to suggest this record is of anything other than a dole for Cowperthwaite's relief. It is only when we link this data to information from other sources that we find he was a prosperous innkeeper of a prominent local family.[9] In fact, Cowperthwaite had been *overseer* of the poor for Hawkshead the previous year – perhaps he had run up some kind of credit from the township of Monk Coniston with Skelwith which then needed repayment.

These practical issues notwithstanding, there is the more fundamental problem that these accounts are records of *relief* rather than of *poverty*. Thus there is an analytical chasm to cross before one can attempt to answer some of the most interesting questions about forms of need and reasons for poverty. In theory, this should be less of a problem than it is in practice, for under the terms of a 1692 statute, overseers were supposed to record, for each pauper, the 'occasion which brought them under that necessity'.[10] Had this happened with any regularity, then historians would have been presented with an exceptionally useful set of sources for conceptions of need and the character of deserving poverty in the early modern period. Unfortunately, however, the practice does not seem to have been widely adopted, so a certain degree of ingenuity is required if historians

6   Ibid., p. 115.
7   WA, TR/Ath/C/2/3, Atherton Overseers' Accounts, 1712–16.
8   CRO (K), WPR/83/7/6, Monk Coniston and Skelwith Overseers' Accounts, 1691–1808.
9   *Second Register Book*; CRO (K), WPR/83/7/3, Hawkshead Overseers' Accounts, 1690–1750.
10   3 William and Mary, c. 11.

are to make the leap from records of relief to an understanding of poverty itself.

One way to do this is to use the technique of nominal record linkage to get from overseers' accounts to the actual causes of poverty.[11] This involves cross-referencing names recorded in accounts with other source material referring to the same people. In particular, historians have been able to link poor accounts to vital events recorded in parish registers in order to produce 'family reconstitutions' – reconstructions of the life histories of paupers within family and kin groups. This research has helped provide data about the age, family circumstance, and availability of local kin for the relieved poor. Taken as a whole, the work has suggested that the poor were comparatively likely to be (in turn) old, in broken families, and with low levels of locally available kin. There are, however, serious problems with relying too heavily on nominal record linkage exercises and family reconstitutions; indeed, as Steven Ruggles has pointed out, 'family reconstitution methods usually exclude most of the parish population from analysis'.[12] First, geographically stable families are intrinsically easier to reconstitute than mobile ones, thus biasing the sample against the many who moved.[13] Secondly, linkage with parish registers limits historians to the reconstruction of social characteristics recoverable from such documents. Registers contain information about life-cycle progression and the formation and eventual breakdown of family units. They generally do not tell us about more short-term, non-demographic forms of hardship such as unemployment or sickness. Finally, in the North, there is another layer of difficulty. Vital registration in the region was undertaken at the level of the parish or (at the very best) the chapelry, yet poor relief and therefore overseers' accounts refer to *townships*, so registers and accounts rarely even cover the same territorial unit. Meanwhile, the North West in general, and the upland parts of the region in particular, suffered from a high degree of 'name clustering', with certain surnames being exceptionally prevalent in specific areas and parishes.

---

11   E.g. Wales, 'Poverty, Poor relief and the Life-cycle'; Newman-Brown, 'Receipt of Poor Relief'; D. Levine and K. Wrightson, *The Making of an Industrial Society: Whickham, 1560–1765* (Oxford, 1991), pp. 163–4; Smith, 'Ageing and Well-being'; King, 'Reconstructing Lives'; King, *Poverty and Welfare*, pp. 166–70, 211–15; Botelho, *Old Age*; Williams, *Poverty*.

12   S. Ruggles, 'The Limitations of English Family Reconstitution: *English Population History from Family Reconstitution, 1580–1837*', *Continuity and Change*, 14 (1999), 105–30 (p. 114).

13   Cf. Levine and Wrightson, *Making of an Industrial Society*, p. 176.

There are also serious problems of record survival. Before the 1690s, only a tiny proportion of Lancashire townships have surviving Poor Law accounts. Indeed, I am aware of just three sets of papers containing detailed and sustained overseers' accounts. One of these, the church-wardens' accounts of Prescot, has been published but covers only a handful of years in the 1630s and 1640s.[14] Another set, that for the township of Duxbury, survives for a long period (1653 onwards) but contain such a small number of doles per year that they are scarcely quantifiable.[15] Much the best set of accounts is that for the parish of Prestwich, lying immediately to the north of Manchester.[16] Covering all five of the constituent townships, these contain the names and total doles of individual paupers (with limited information about the character of the doles in question) from 1646 to 1683. From the 1690s onwards there is more survival, and most of the good accounts from the county after this date have been used. But the aim of this book is to unpick the character of 'deserving poverty' in more detail than a simple focus on overseers' accounts would allow. We will, therefore, have to look elsewhere for our main source material.

Censuses of the poor

Amongst the most interesting sources we have are the censuses of the poor compiled by the town of Bolton in 1674, 1686, and 1699.[17] Containing information (improving in scope over time) about paupers' age, household composition, infirmities, employment status, weekly income and the size of their doles, these censuses are exceptionally detailed, and were compiled by overseers, churchwardens and probably magistrates on the basis of regular 'views' or inspections of the poor.[18] They also represent

14   *Prescot Churchwardens' Accounts.*
15   LA, DDX/1834/1, Duxbury Overseers' Account Book, 1653–1820.
16   MALS, L160/2/1, Prestwich Churchwardens' and Overseers' Accounts, 1646–83.
17   LA, DDKe/2/6/2, Survey of the Poor in Bolton, 1674; BALS, PBO/1–2, Bolton Parish Records.
18   There are references to 'views' in the 1699 census. An order survives in the papers of the court of Quarter Sessions ordering justices living in and around the townships of Rivington, Lostock, Anglezarke, Turton, Longworth and Edgworth to 'take an accompt of the number of the poore of the said townshipps and theire necessities and to report the same to this courte at the next sessions' in October 1674. This I take to be one part of a general investigation into poverty in Bolton-le-Moors parish, which also led to the compilation of the first census: LA, QSP/429/45.

an apparently unique survival of a *series* of censuses in early modern England.[19]

The reason behind the initial compilation of the census is hinted at by an order from the parish vestry in 1681 that 'the poore of the said townshippe and parish of Bolton hence forward shall be sufficiently releeved and provided for from tyme to tyme by a tax equally to be rated and assessed upon all the inhabitants of the whole parish of Bolton'.[20] An article by Steve King, based upon the censuses, implies that this represented the parish's first ever poor tax, but the reality is more complex, for this was actually a rate-in-aid from the rural townships of the parish to support the poor of its urban centre. In fact, the census apparently represents a benchmark of need at a time when urban Bolton was trying to persuade (or compel) the rest of the large parish of Bolton-le-Moors to provide financial support, in circumvention of the clause in the 1662 statute that the relief of the poor in the seven northern counties be undertaken by townships rather than parishes. It thus relates to the controversies described in more detail in chapter 2. The three censuses are of a quality that means they can be subjected to detailed quantitative analysis, and we will return to them frequently.[21]

Voices of the poor? Pauper petitions

As much as these censuses are astonishingly rich sources, however, they remain in their essentials a kind of overseers' account, albeit in a more systematic form. Pauper petitions are an altogether different proposition. Literally thousands of individual appeals for aid survive in the papers of Lancashire's court of Quarter Sessions, especially for the period between the 1620s and the 1710s. The petitions were shared between each of the county's four sittings of Quarter Sessions, in Lancaster (covering Lonsdale Hundred), Preston (Amounderness and Blackburn), the alternating Sessions at Wigan and Ormskirk (Leyland and West Derby), and Manchester (Salford Hundred).[22] Usefully, these were broadly conterminous

---

19   Cf. Slack, *Poverty and Policy*, pp. 73–80.

20   BALS, PBO/2/1, Bolton-le-Moors Vestry Minutes, 1655–1744, p. 53.

21   They are analysed in more detail in: Healey, 'Poverty in an Industrializing Town'.

22   On the general form of Lancashire Quarter Sessions, see: P. Taylor, 'Quarter Sessions in Lancashire in the Middle of the Eighteenth Century: the Court in Session and its Records', *THSLC*, 139 (1989), 63–82.

with the county's economic subregions. Manchester Sessions served the textile region in the south-east, while the metalworking zone was represented by the alternating Wigan and Ormskirk Sessions. Finally, Lancaster and Preston together covered the county's northern, most purely agricultural region. The distribution of petitions roughly followed the county's population geography, though relatively few survive from North Lonsdale or Blackburn hundreds, reflecting – no doubt – their greater distance to the nearest Sessions. The largest proportions were from the south of the county: 32.6 per cent of the petitions in the sample were presented at Wigan or Ormskirk, 31.7 per cent at Manchester. Preston Sessions accounts for 22.1 per cent, while just 13.7 per cent were presented at Lancaster.[23] Towns were ever so slightly underrepresented. The vast majority of petitions have information about the parish or township of origin, and of these some 17.5 per cent were urban, whereas the 1664 Hearth Tax suggests an urban population of 20.8 per cent – a figure that will have grown as the century progressed.[24] Of the remainder, just 8 per cent came from locations above the 150m contour line, meaning that the county's lowlands accounted for 92 per cent of all non-urban petitions. A rough attempt at classifying communities by economic type found that 22 per cent of petitions came from the flat plains in the west of the county, 18 per cent from mineral-working areas in the south-west, 24 per cent from the fustian-manufacturing textile zone in the south-east (running up to Blackburn), and 6 per cent from the woollen-working region of the eastern uplands. The remaining 29 per cent came from the rolling agricultural lands that made up the rest of the county and dominated the north of it.

All told, the petitions constitute a unique and wonderfully vivid set of source material for reconstructing the experience of poverty, yet they currently lie largely untapped. This book incorporates a detailed analysis of all the roughly three thousand first-time petitions lodged at Lancashire Quarter Sessions between 1626 and 1710. Each petition contains a short statement of a pauper's case for support, including details of why they were poor and – less often – information about attempts to make shift or about their relations with their neighbours and officers. This archive is, quite simply, one of the most astonishing sets of material for the history

---

23   A very small number were heard at other locations when Sessions had been adjourned away from its main home. The only two additional locations were Prescot and Bolton (for the south-western and south-eastern sittings respectively).

24   Stobart, *First Industrial Region*, pp. 35–6.

of poverty in the pre-industrial world. This book is not the first one to make use of Poor Law petitions – indeed there is an important section of Hindle's *On the Parish?* which looks at a similar (though much smaller) set from Cumberland, as well as some of the Lancashire material.[25] But this is the first time that such a large set of these documents, and the unique perspective they give, has been allowed to take centre stage in a study of poverty.

Generally, most petitions originated in an appeal that had been denied at the township level. This was not, however, always the case. In the early and mid seventeenth century it is possible that some townships expected paupers to get an order from a JP before they were allowed relief. Each decision as to whether a pauper deserved or needed poor relief will have been especially hard to make in the early days, when there were fewer precedents to go by, and thus it is understandable that townships will have looked to Quarter Sessions for guidance. In a list of sixteen paupers in Prescot in 1641, fourteen were described as being relieved 'by Quarter Sessions order', with only two supported 'without an order', while the 1650s saw a notable cluster in the number of petitions to Quarter Sessions that were actually endorsed by local officers themselves, suggesting local uncertainty as to who should qualify for relief.[26]

It was, indeed, not uncommon in earlier petitions for paupers to state that overseers were unwilling to give relief without an order. The uncle of six-year-old Grace Davison of Melling, for example, told Lancaster JPs in 1638 that the parishioners were refusing to relieve her 'unless your worshipps give Order and Warrant soe to doe'.[27] In 1659, Alice Hornby of Oldfield Lane in Salford recounted that she had gone to the church-wardens and overseers, but that they had refused to relieve her without an order from Sessions.[28] Similarly, Alice Gaskell of Upholland was denied relief by the overseers in 1667 'with this only apologie that they will doe nothinge without order from this Honorable bench'.[29] This does not necessarily mean that the pauper was refused outright when they first appealed to their township, merely that the officers wanted the backing of a justice before they opened their purse, perhaps because the cases were – or were likely to be – controversial. This was probably what was at issue

25   Hindle, *On the Parish?*, pp. 407–28.
26   Oxley, 'Old Poor Law', pp. 11–12; Fessler, 'Official Attitude', p. 94.
27   LA, QSB/1/196/17.
28   LA, QSP/184/4.
29   LA, QSP/299/6.

with William Westhead of Lathom, for example, who had been a soldier in the Low Countries and petitioned in 1669 that he had applied to the overseers but, 'by reason of his long absense the officers refuse to afford him any reliefe without an order'.[30] Perhaps in the relatively early days, petitions were as much a way of insuring overseers against the sniping of their neighbours as they were about paupers forcing townships to give pensions.

As the seventeenth century wore on, however, those who appealed to Quarter Sessions will have increasingly been those who were refused point-blank in the first instance, or those who were unhappy with the size of their current pension. The normal way of getting poor relief by this stage was for them to apply to the township: this was probably the process recorded by the overseers of Hawkshead, for example, when they noted in 1752 that Elizabeth Knipe was relieved 'upon complaint of poverty'.[31] Indeed, that the parish or township should be the first port of call was actually enshrined in a statute of 1722, which stated that paupers *must* go to the overseers before approaching a justice (a 1692 statute had stipulated that no-one was to be added to the relief lists without ratification from a JP, except in times of emergency); though in Lancashire – where there were relatively large distances between active justices – such statutory enforcement was probably unnecessary by then.

Officers might also perform their own investigations into the conditions of the local poor. In 1632 the overseers and churchwardens of Rochdale reported that after taking a 'speciall view and notice ... of the goodes and estate of Gabriell Holte of Church Lane' they had concluded that he was in need of poor relief.[32] Similarly, the overseers of Chadderton reported in 1669 that they 'do not onely monethly but oftner when need requireth veiw and relive their poore accordinge as need requireth'.[33] Two viewings of the poor were made in 1682 in Prestwich, the first of which took three days, and it appears from the census of the poor for Bolton in 1699 that at least three similar investigations were performed that year.[34] In 1727,

30   LA, QSP/343/7.
31   E.g. LA, QSP/299/6; QSP/343/7; QSP/500/13; CRO (K), WPR/83/7/4, Hawkshead Overseers' Accounts, 1750–98.
32   LA, QSB/1/107/67.
33   LA, QSP/344/14.
34   MALS, L160/2/1, Prestwich Churchwardens' and Overseers' Accounts, 1646–83. Overseers' Accounts, 1646–83; BALS, PBO/1/1, Bolton Census of the Poor, 1686.

meanwhile, the overseers of Cheetham laid out five shillings for 'charges in going to review the poor'.[35]

But these processes evidently left some people disappointed. John Lomax of Bolton, for example, recounted in 1679 how 'the Overseers have refused to releeve his necessities although hee hath made his complaint for two yeares last past', while in 1683 Margaret Willasie of Woodplumpton went to JPs because the township 'have refused severall of your petitioners addresses'.[36] And there were those who were getting relief, but were unhappy with it, or who had seen it stopped. Sarah Byrom of Kenyon, for example, petitioned in 1675 that she had been given 12d per week, but 'about two moneths agoe shee desired to have an increase of allowance because of the scarcity and dearenesse of provision'. She was refused, so she went to Sessions.[37] Ellen Crookall of Kirkham, fifty years old and blind, complained in 1688 that she had been given a little house and seven loads of turf every year, 'but the present overseers have upon some particular disgust to your petitioner refused either to pay her house rent or find her any fire, which forced your petitioner to pawn her clothes'. They had, she said, 'no other pretence for it but your petitioners refusall to live with another old deaf woman in Kirkam who she could not live with, the one being deaf & your petitioner almost blynd'.[38]

Unhappy poor folk such as these had, in fact, three options. They could appeal to individual justices sitting out of sessions, who might be able to put pressure on townships in which they had influence to give out a dole. Or they could appeal to justices at Petty Sessions, a regular meeting – usually at the level of the hundred – which theoretically sat every six weeks to deal with minor local administrative and criminal matters. Petty Sessions (sometimes 'Privy' or 'Private' Sessions) was developing as a major organ of local government in the seventeenth century, and an increasing number of petitions contain oblique references to it as the period progressed. Unfortunately we have exceedingly little evidence of their proceedings for this period and thus, as Poor Law business increasingly leaked down the documentary plughole of Petty Sessions, we lose sight of it (although there is a rare survival of seven relief orders given at

---

35   MALS, M/10/7/2/1, Cheetham Overseers' Accounts, 1693–1791.
36   LA, QSP/500/13; QSP/569/1.
37   LA, QSP/428/38.
38   LA, QSP/656/9.

a Petty Sessions held at an inn in Rumsworth in December 1682).[39] The strength of the institution, and the growing importance of justices acting out of sessions, are probably the main reason for both the decline in the volume of surviving pauper petitions from the early eighteenth century onwards in Lancashire, *and* the general lack of similar material in most other counties.[40] It was a process that made appealing for relief over the heads of overseers considerably easier for the poor, but it has resulted in a void of information for the historian.

The third way of appealing was, then, to go to Quarter Sessions. This was the most senior court which regularly dealt with individual poor relief cases, and it is the court which has bequeathed us the records on which this book is largely based.[41] We do not know very much about what petitioning actually involved. It would appear from stray references in the documents that there was a general expectation that supplicants would attend with their petitions. Agnes Braithwaite of Hawkshead was clearly travelling down to Lancaster to present her numerous petitions around the start of the eighteenth century: Justices could see, griped one township officer, that 'she can travel to do mishcheef'.[42] In a fascinating appeal from 1693, Elizabeth Pilkington of Brindle told of her lameness and sickliness, and recounted how she 'hath severall times made application to the Overseers of the Poore of Brindle who knowing her not able to goe or ride to the sessions will allow her noe relief'. But now, she wrote, 'your petitioner procureing a friend to bring her in a cart to Ormeschurch', she 'presents yow with this petition'.[43] In another explicit statement, husbandman Robert Latham of Bispham insisted in 1699 that he and his family were 'really objects of charity as to your worships will appear when they are called to the barr'.[44] The following year, widower James Hoyle of Bacup even brought his children to Sessions and presented them before the justices, informing them that he was 'left with four small

39   LA, DDKe/2/6/5, Orders made at Private Sessions, 1682.
40   It is just possible that some cases were heard by JPs at Quarter Sessions but which were not recorded, and that these might have increased in numbers as the process became more regularized. There is, however, so far as I have been able to tell, no evidence for this in the post-1710 Order Books.
41   The odd Poor Law case did apparently end up in front of the Assizes. Richard Travers of Nateby, for example, told of being relieved by Assizes previous to his 1641 petition to Preston Sessions. He may well have been referring to the Sheriff's Table. LA, QSB/1/241/23.
42   LA, QSP/926/9.
43   LA, QSP/734/3.
44   LA, QSP/832/43.

children which your petitioner has brought hither to this sessions to shew them to your worshipps'.[45] Indeed, when she was unable to attend Sessions, Esther Tattershall of Rochdale made a point of apologizing that, 'haveing three children and at her tyme of the fourth', she was 'not able to neither come nor ride thus farr her selfe' and thus 'presumes to petition to your worships for an order'.[46]

Each petition survives as a single document, presumably archived by the court itself. The handwriting strongly suggests that the vast majority were written by someone *on behalf* of the petitioner, rather than the petitioner themselves. Occasionally, the handwriting in two petitions from different individuals is identifiably the same, proving that in at least one case the document was written on the appellant's behalf. In a particularly striking example, two petitions from the same parish (dated 1674 and 1678), but for different individuals, contain the same evocative phrase and are written in the same hand.[47] Presumably neighbours, professional scribes, and perhaps local clergymen were called upon to write them; and presumably their willingness to do so showed tacit support for the pauper's case (though possibly some scribes had more mercenary motivations). But it also means that petitions almost never constitute the purely independent words of the poor themselves: turns of phrase, literary tropes, outward displays of deference, might well have been added, or at least gently suggested, by the person who actually wrote the petition. They are, then, 'hybrid voices', between petitioner and scribe, influenced by the experiences of the petitioner, the cultural worlds of the scribe, and (as Hindle points out) a broad idea of what it was thought justices wanted to hear, too.[48]

On the other hand, there are a tiny handful of documents which do appear to be autograph. The spelling and script are so scrappy in, for example, the petition of Jean Eaton, a migrant to Liverpool in the 1690s, that it was almost certainly written by her. She told of coming to the kingdom 'aboute sume bisniss', where she was 'tacken very ill'. She claimed she would have liked to go home to her own country but 'ame not eabell for want for I was forst too sell what close I hade to relive me in my sicknes soo that my condition is very misirable'.[49] Nonetheless, such cases

45   LA, QSP/847/25.
46   LA, QSP/599/16.
47   LA, QSP/418/10; QSP/474/5.
48   Hindle, *On the Parish?*, p. 414.
49   LA, QSP/727/29.

are extremely rare – the overwhelming majority were almost certainly written by others.[50]

Each document set out why the petitioner thought they deserved poor relief. Specifically, they focused on the personal contingencies that had brought them to need support from their parish. They told tales of creeping old age, of cruel sickness, of widowhood and family breakdown, of personal misfortune and of hard times. Some petitioners, crucially, also told of how they were trying to make shift, and usually why this was not working out. So they described the help they got from kin, neighbours and 'friends', and their attempts to get by through selling their goods, pawning their livestock, or simply wandering about begging. They sometimes recounted details of their previous work, occasionally even their former good standing in the community or their past contributions to their poor neighbours' relief.

Once the appeal had been heard, justices gave order. Their decree was recorded in a rough book, which was then transcribed in fair copy on the Sessions Rolls. In many cases, the JPs' decision was also endorsed on the bottom of the petition itself, though these endorsements were often vague. It is very common for the endorsement to say simply 'Ch & Os', which could mean that the case was referred back to churchwardens and overseers, or it could be an order for relief. Indeed, in some cases justices clearly did simply refer the case back to more local officers or gentlemen. In a very revealing order from 1688, for example, William Winstanley of Preston Sessions – presented with a petitioner from the town itself – hoped that the town's government would 'spontaneously' offer relief 'when you consider how lothe I and the other above written his Majestys Justices of the Peace are to intermeddle in the Corporation over in this juncture'.[51] But in general it is very difficult to deduct what happened next, especially given the lack of surviving overseers' accounts. A quick sampling exercise shows this perfectly. Taking four sample years (1655, 1670, 1680 and 1697, chosen because they saw relatively typical levels of petitioning), a total of 154 first petitions survive, forty-five of which clearly resulted in orders for relief (including one that was given relief until the case could be fully heard and another that was given only partial relief in the form of a child's apprenticeship); there are also sixteen cases in which JPs referred back to the overseers with some stipulation that they should provide relief, albeit

50   Other possible cases are: LA, QSP/311/37; QSP/398/8; QSP/400/14; QSP/543/17; QSP/673/6.
51   LA, QSP/652/7.

framed in very vague terms, plus one case in which relief was *probably* being ordered but the sense is unclear. Then there are three cases that were 'recommended' back to local officers, which would *appear* to mean that the appeal was being upheld, though it is impossible to be completely certain. This makes a total sixty-five petitions or 42 per cent that were likely to have been initially successful. The remainder include five that are too faded to interpret or torn, twenty in which there is no pertinent information, and thirty in which the outcome is unclear, including those which state – simply – 'Ch & Os'. There were twenty-seven that were 'referred' to local officers, Privy Sessions, or other gentlemen, which could mean that JPs were ordering relief or it could mean that they were passing the decision back to local officers. Finally, six were refused point-blank, while in one case a petitioner's children were ordered to support them. Clearly there is too much uncertainty here to make much quantitative use of these recorded outcomes. Theoretically it would be possible to get further with this by cross-referencing the petitions with the surviving order rolls, but this would be another book's worth of work, and such a study might well tell us more about record-keeping practices than poverty.

The key point, though, is that in most cases, justices apparently found for the pauper. In our sample of 154 petitions, only seven can clearly be shown to have been refused. Nonetheless, it is important to remember that some appeals *were* unsuccessful, for reasons now lost to us. Usually in such cases, the pauper was sent on their way with the petition endorsed – 'nothing'. Others received a pension, but not the amount that they had requested. In at least a couple of cases, petitions drastically backfired. Richard Broadbank of Salford asked for relief from Manchester Sessions in 1697 on account of his wife's pregnancy and his own unemployment, but something clearly irked the magistrates, for the surviving petition was endorsed with the order that 'that Broadbank refuseing to worke be sent to the House of Correction and well whipt and kept to hard labour'; clear proof that JPs were using the ability to work as a crucial indicator of deservingness.[52] Twenty years earlier, Alice Knowles of Rainford had petitioned for relief for her three children, but was promptly dispatched to the House of Correction, 'all of these being bastard children'.[53]

The core of this book will involve the analysis of these petitions. Where possible, they have been quantified. It is, for example, useful to know

52   LA, QSP/796/1.
53   LA, QSP/464/5.

what proportion of the petitions evoked different kinds of hardship – how many petitioners claimed to be old; how many sick. Annual fluctuations in the numbers of surviving petitions provide useful clues as to which years were particularly tough for the poor. But the true interest of the petitions is really qualitative, even perhaps narrative. Although they were physically written by wealthier neighbours, and although they generally arose in cases where relief had initially been refused, they are the closest thing we have to voices of the poor themselves. And even if the language of the petitions will have been influenced by the scribe, the tales they told of hardship, resilience and destitution will have come from the petitioners themselves. They are also sources with time depth, since petitioners were quite free to describe their descent into destitution over a period. Together, this means that these petitions are a uniquely revealing source for the character of poverty in early modern England. Quite simply, with the arguable exception of settlement examinations, nothing like them survives until we start to get pauper letters, asking for 'out-relief', surviving from the late eighteenth century.[54]

But their individuality also means much of the most revealing evidence in petitions is not quantifiable for our purposes. Importantly, there is a basic distinction between information that was *expected* to be provided, which can be meaningfully quantified, and information which was *incidental* to the main appeal. With the latter, since there was no expectation that the petitioner would include such information, the numbers of cases largely reflect norms of petitioning and tell us little about poverty. Thus, while statements about the causes of poverty can be carefully quantified, figures relating to attempts to make shift, language used, details about downward social mobility, and so forth, must be treated in largely qualitative fashion.

---

54   Studies based on pauper letters include: J. S. Taylor, 'Voices in the Crowd: the Kirkby Lonsdale Township Letters', in Hitchcock, King and Sharpe (eds), *Chronicling Poverty*, pp. 109–26; Sokoll, 'Old Age in Poverty'; Boulton, 'It is extreme necessity'; *Essex Pauper Letters, 1731–1837*, ed. T. Sokoll (RSEH, New Series, xxx, Oxford, 2001); *Narratives of the Poor in Eighteenth-Century England, Vol. I: Voices of the Poor: Poor Law Depositions and Letters*, ed. S. King, T. Nutt and A. Tomkins (London, 2006); Williams, *Poverty*, pp. 86–91. For a useful discussion of petitioning (in this case, for pensions for ex-servicemen and war widows), see: G. L. Hudson, 'Ex-servicemen, War Widows and the English County Pension Scheme, 1593–1679' (Univ. of Oxford DPhil thesis, 1995), pp. 187–91; studies of pauper petitions in (respectively) Cumberland and Westminster can be found in: Hindle, *On the Parish?*, pp. 407–28; also, Boulton, 'Going on the parish', pp. 26–32. The classic study to use settlement examinations is: K. D. M. Snell, *Annals of the Labouring Poor: Social Change and Agrarian England, 1660–1900* (Cambridge, 1985).

The politics of petitioning

Such petitioning was, of course, an intensely political process. It was, as Hindle has pointed out, a 'weapon of the weak' by which those in a subordinate social position were able to nudge society's rulers towards treating them better. But it *was* a process of appeal, rather than – as a recent legal historian would have it – an assertion of the right to relief.[55] The implication of a right not to starve can be read into them, and some petitioners did, as we shall see, choose to invoke a language of legal rights. But these are petitions not writs. They were framed as supplications rather than the activation of a right. The documents aimed to persuade JPs that the petitioner was genuinely destitute and unable to relieve themselves through work.

They also throw up some intriguing cases of politics that were fraught and sometimes strikingly devious. Margaret Crooke, for example, was alleged by Euxton township in 1692 to have gained a pension by going to Ormskirk Sessions 'after a surreptitious manner, takeing an oportunity when shee well knew the Overseers weare absent & consequently the court could not possibly bee rightly informed in behalfe of the said towne, nor anything objected against her said complaint'.[56] On the other hand, some petitioners claimed for their part to have been tricked or abused by overseers. In 1683, Anthony English alleged that when he asked Ralph Holt of Breightmet, overseer, for relief he merely 'beateth & abuseth your poore petitioner', and 'threatneth him if hee make any complaint against him hee will nayle his ears to the crosse'.[57] According to Edward Hampson of Eccles, the overseer – around 1685 – 'did come unto your petitioners house when hee was from home, and desired your petitioners wife to shew him the order which this same overseer did receive from her & tooke it away with him and now denyes your petitioner of releefe'.[58] As we saw at the beginning of this chapter, Agnes Braithwaite of Hawkshead told a similar story in 1702. In 1667, fourteen-year-old Elizabeth Goodson of Pemberton and her two siblings told how the overseers did not 'take any care but rather threaten me with discourageble words'; 'especially', she petitioned, 'one of the overseers wife'.[59] Deborah Bowyer complained

55   Charlesworth, *Welfare's Forgotten Past*, p. 116.
56   LA, QSP/722/2.
57   LA, QSP/563/21.
58   LA, QSP/595/14.
59   LA, QSP/303/1.

in 1684 that when she applied for relief to the township of Upholland, whilst her husband was in gaol, all she got was a lecture. Her indigent condition was 'well knowne' to the inhabitants, 'yet notwithstanding they choose rather to fill the eares of your poore petitioner and children with reproachfull words, then their bellyes with food'.[60] In 1692, Preston JPs were told by Robert Ingham that the overseers of Rossendale had been 'obdurate and crosse' with him and his family.[61] When his wife went to an overseer of Dalton, said Henry Draper in 1701, the officer refused to help, for, 'sayes he', the 'custom in our country is when any one comes for relief to an Ovarsear they make noe more words but sends them to the house of Correction'.[62]

Another aspect of this 'politics' is, of course, the language of petitions. We must resist the temptation to use petitions as an easy guide to the cultural mindset of the poor themselves, for the specific language is more likely to have originated from the scribe rather than the pauper. Nonetheless, the language employed does tell us *something* about how poverty was understood at the time.[63] The terms used to describe poverty often involved calling it 'hard', 'sad', or (less frequently) 'cold'. It was characterized by 'nakedness' and 'misery', 'ruin' and 'beggary'. According to a petition from the ministers and classis of Warrington in 1647, former Parliamentary soldier William Cowper 'sitts weepeing over his sadd condition with a naked back and often an emptie belly'.[64] Misery, cold and filth were evoked by Ann Whitaker, a minister's widow from Downham. Tragically, her young daughter had cancer, she had a young son, and the 8d weekly pension they were receiving in 1661 would 'doe little more where your petitioner liveth then find fuell for a little fire to warme your poore petitioners miserable daughter & the little child, or heat a little water to wash her filthy rages withall'.[65] Perhaps this evoked some of the emotional difficulties that came with being poor: even Roger Lowe, who was hardly destitute, recorded coming home one Monday in 1663 and feeling 'very

60   LA, QSP/578/1.
61   LA, QSP/713/10.
62   LA, QSP/868/5.
63   Cf. P. D. Jones, '"I cannot keep my place without being deascent": Pauper Letters, Parish Clothing and Pragmatism in the South of England, 1750–1830', *Rural History*, 20 (2009), 31–49; J. Bailey, '"Think wot a Mother must feel": Parenting in English Pauper Letters, c.1760–1834', *Family and Community History*, 13 (2010), 5–19.
64   LA, QSB/1/292/50.
65   LA, QSP/202/1.

pensive and sad in consideration of my povertie', though he felt better once he had sung the 24th Psalm.[66] Thomas Heigham of Ince described 'misserable poverty & want' in 1686; Priscilla Butler of Rochdale was in a 'sad condicion' in 1657.[67] Richard Hodgson of Carleton was, in 1649, 'brought to miserable povertie and a labyrinth of necessitie and wante'.[68] The same year Margaret Salesbury of Chaigley, who had been plundered by Prince Rupert's men, was likely to be 'exposed to the miseryes of this wide and woefull world'.[69] In 1705, meanwhile (in what was undoubtedly an unusual case) Elizabeth Bovell evoked misery and rootlessness. She had married in New York, and when her husband died his will left her an estate in Lancashire. Leaving America, she was captured by the French, but found her way to England only to discover the will was 'a fake thing', and that neither her husband 'nor any of his predicesors before him never had a foot of land or teniment but what they paide for yearly rent'. She needed money to keep her before she went to Ireland, asking JPs to 'yeild relife to the comfortles and most miserable wido who wanders like a pilgrim in a wildernes'.[70]

Quite unsurprisingly, many petitions describe horrifying material deprivation. Mary Healey of Castleton told in 1693 of being left 'destitute of any thing save the cold earth'.[71] The children of labourer Henry Sharples of Hothersall were, in 1698, 'naked but for theire shifts'.[72] By 1669, widow Mary Rigby of Salford and her two children had just one bed between the three of them.[73] Thomas Hunt, meanwhile, lamented in 1674 that he was 'constrained for meare want to goe barefooted & bareleged this last winter in all the pinchinge frost and snow'.[74] Elizabeth Hoole of Livesey, abandoned, lame and with a child afflicted with the Evil said in 1683 that she 'hath nothing but strow & a few rags to lye in', and even these were 'sore spoyled with virmin'.[75] In 1690, husbandman John Worsley of Longworth had sold everything his family had 'so that he hath almost nothing to put on for clothing either for wife or children & hath no bed

---

66   Lowe, *Diary*, p. 3.
67   LA, QSP/625/32; QSP/152/1.
68   LA, QSP/10/16.
69   LA, QSP/22/12.
70   LA, QSP/927/7.
71   LA, QSP/731/6.
72   LA, QSP/806/26.
73   LA, QSP/332/25.
74   LA, QSP/416/15.
75   LA, QSP/569/6.

close but 2 blankets for them all'.[76] John Taylor of Walmersley and his
family of seven had, in 1697, 'neither dish spoone nor bed to lay them
downe upon'.[77] In 1698, Thomas Astley of Aughton had a wife and four
children but 'not a morsell of bread to put in their mouths'.[78] The same
year, 92-year-old James Friscoe of Broughton and his wife 'hath drunk
litell but water a long time'.[79] Widow Alice Roberts of Ince had, in 1708,
'noe habitation noe bed to lye on, but the cold frosty ground, nor a penny
of money to buy her a mouthfull of bread to put into her hungry belly'.[80]
In 1709, Sarah Hatton, with her husband away at war, told of how she
and her children had been 'many tymes forc't to sit downe with a piece of
bread & a little salt & water'.[81]

Petitioners asked not just for money but for charity, mercy, and benevolence. Their mother dead, their father run away, the Smalshaw children of
Ormskirk were being relieved by 'the charity of well affected neighbours'
in 1649.[82] Ralph Leach of Woodplumpton had, in 1663, 'noe estate but
the charity of good people'.[83] In 1664, Ellen Bozer of Speke had nothing
but the charity of 'well disposed Christians'.[84] In 1632, Jane Garths of
Lydiate evoked justices' 'accustomed clemencies & mercies heretofore
extended towardes widowes and fatherles chyldren'.[85] Edmund Chew of
Church Kirk had, up to 1661, been provided lodging 'through the mercye'
of Thomas Foster, a local farmer.[86] Ellen Woodhouse, the next year, was
likely to perish 'but by the mercifull goodnesse and love of her friends
and neighbours'.[87] At a more basic level still, they asked that magistrates
would act to ensure they survived. George Horner of Claughton and his
wife wanted relief in 1680 'to keep them alive'.[88] Elizabeth Rothwell of
Bickerstaffe, who suffered a sore leg, needed relief in 1683 'or else the losse

76   LA, QSP/683/2.
77   LA, QSP/792/8.
78   LA, QSP/815/5.
79   LA, QSP/820/4.
80   LA, QSP/980/2.
81   LA, QSP/988/9.
82   LA, QSP/11/25.
83   LA, QSP/234/14.
84   LA, QSP/259/17.
85   LA, QSB/1/106/90.
86   LA, QSP/202/46.
87   LA, QSP/223/29.
88   LA, QSP/520/1.

of her life or limb or both are likely to ensue'.[89] Many said they would
starve without relief.

Some petitioners implied that there were basic standards of living
that even society's poorest should expect, hinting at notions of social
justice. Elizabeth Heaton of Whittingham petitioned in 1688 that her
husband had run away, and that although she was 'very industrious', 'her
endeavors will not extend to halfe the sufficiency of mantainance that
Christians ought to have for pitys sake'.[90] Five years earlier, William Smith
complained that the overseers of Widnes not only 'did lett your petitioner
lye without a whole night for want of a howse att May last', but once
they did finally provide him somewhere to live it was a house 'fitter for
a swyne then a Christian whoe is of the age of 65 yeares and lame'.[91]
Widow Mary Roe of Crumpsall had a similar complaint in 1696: the
overseers, she said, had put her in a house that is 'unfinished soe that the
grass growes within the house, which endangers her life being soe antient
and not able to bear cold now as shee formerly hath done'.[92] In 1702, by
which time petitions for increased relief were becoming common, John
Shepard of Manchester, sixty-nine years old, informed JPs of the basic
goods he needed to buy each week. He was, he said, getting 6d a week,
'out of which your petitioner payd 3d a week for his bed & 1d a weeke for
washing his shirt, soe that your petitioner hath but 2d a weeke towards his
mantaynance with food'. This was not, he thought, enough.[93] In the early
weeks of 1703, Mary Collinge told Manchester JPs that she needed 4d a
week plus house rent for the winter season, for 'I think 4d a week towards
fire is not unreasonable'.[94] A sense of an entitlement to basic comfort
came through even stronger in a petition from Elizabeth Partington of
Tyldesley in 1702, in which she complained that the overseers had put her

> into the end of a kitchin without haveinge any thinge at all to use neither
> chimney to make a fire in nor one bitt of fire, nor soe much as a dish
> or spoone to eate her meat in when she hath any, neither bedstockes
> nor one bitt of beddinge to lay her downe in but lies upon the cold
> floore in a bitt of straw and can gett noe releife of the overseers soe that

89   LA, QSP/566/5.
90   LA, QSP/648/6.
91   LA, QSP/570/2.
92   LA, QSP/775/9.
93   LA, QSP/885/20.
94   LA, QSP/889/4.

your petitioner by reason of the coldnesse of the nightes and haveinge nothinge to cover herselfe with growes lamer and lamer.[95]

Neither was she the only one who complained about her accommodation. Alexander Lewthwaite of Shakerley had been put by the overseers 'into a house with a common strumpet', but so intolerable was this that he 'chose to goe to another place', where he lived in 'noe better lodgeing then a beast'. In fact, the overseers were proving unwilling to allow him a weekly allowance, 'nor cloths nor bedding fitt for a Christian to lye downe on'.[96]

Other petitions made more direct statements of distributional justice. Interestingly, many of these framed their appeals in terms of the *legal* obligation for the wealthy to support the poor, rather than the older moral right of subsistence in extreme necessity. Thus they were more statements about the Poor Law than they were echoes of the older theological notion that, in cases of extreme want, all material goods became common property.[97] Anne Rosse of Manchester, having been abandoned by her Scottish husband when the two realms went to war in 1648, petitioned for relief in 1651 'as may stand with justice and equitie and as is usuall in such cases'.[98] In 1656, Anthony Higginson, a 68-year-old waller from Priest Hutton, asked for poor relief 'as law requireth'.[99] Henry Owsey of Golborne was even more forceful in 1662, claiming relief 'by the overseers & churchwardens of the parish, whoe by the lawes of this land ought to releive & maintaine the poore & impotent people'.[100] Some paupers were quite confident, indeed, that they had law – and statutes – on their side. Elizabeth Heap of Downholland asked for maintenance in 1640 'according unto his majesties Statute in that behalfe'.[101] Widow Taylor of Thurnham, meanwhile, had been sick all through the winter of 1679/80, and would starve, she said, unless given relief 'according to the laws and statutes of this land'.[102] Such petitions give some support to Charlesworth's argument that the Poor Law had at its heart a common-law entitlement to relief, but

95   LA, QSP/880/1.
96   LA, QSP/980/1.
97   Swanson, 'Medieval Foundations'.
98   LA, QSP/52/14.
99   LA, QSP/129/5; cf. QSP/197/15.
100 LA, QSP/219/39.
101 LA, QSB/1/230/36.
102 LA, QSP/515/6.

it is worth remembering that such statements were rare. Even if such a right to relief existed in legal doctrine by this point, few paupers chose to invoke it in their petitions.

Some, indeed, chose to use the language of charitable rather than legal obligation. The 1674 petition of Jane Shaw of Warton-in-Lonsdale, for example, contained a striking exhortation that justices 'looke upon your poore petitioner with the eye of pitty (being soe often taught that the strong should helpe the weake, the rich should helpe the poore) and as an act of charitye give order that your poore petitioner may have something weekely'.[103] A petition of 1694, meanwhile, in support of Longton orphan Hugh Robinson, reminded JPs of the Beatitudes: 'blessed', it said, 'are the mercifull for they shall obtain mercy'.[104] The extent to which these statements reflected the sentiment of the petitioner rather than the scribe is uncertain. In the case of Jane Shaw noted above, it was certainly the penman's turn of phrase for there is an identical statement in a 1678 petition from Silverdale (also in Warton parish), which is in the same handwriting.[105]

It seems likely that each time a pauper was relieved by a parish, it became more difficult to refuse the next one, as such support became embedded in local custom. Ellin Wilson, a lame child of Halewood petitioned in 1652 for 'such allowance … as other impotent people & orphans in the said parish have'.[106] Similarly, James Noblett of Warton-in-Amounderness drew attention in 1656 to his disabled wife and six children, and asked for relief 'as is alowed to otheres in the parish of the like condition'.[107] Perhaps the strangest appeal was that of Lawrence Maddison of Fazakerley, a former soldier, who asked for relief from the town in 1668 by pointing out that it had just been 'freed from a greate charge by the death of an olde widdow'.[108] Other petitioners alluded to custom more generally. The 1659 petition in support of Martha Astley of Tyldesley-cum-Shakerley asked justices to exercise the 'accustomed goodnes and clemency unto the needy and parentles infants', while in 1667, Robert Sharples of Mawdesley petitioned JPs for assistance in his old age and infirmity 'according to your laudable customes'.[109]

103   LA, QSP/418/10.
104   LA, QSP/746/7.
105   LA, QSP/474/5.
106   LA, QSP/71/29.
107   LA, QSP/130/4.
108   LA, QSP/323/25.
109   LA, QSP/183/8; QSP/299/5.

Petitions also shed some light on the idea that poor relief worked as a form of social control. Appeals, of course, reflected discourses of deservingness, with petitioners highlighting those aspects of their character and situation which they felt were most likely to gain the sympathy of the magistracy. Thus, if poor relief was consistently predicated on conformation to outward behavioural mores, we would expect petitions regularly to contain protestations of morality and, to use Steve Hindle's phrase, 'fear of God'. Unfortunately, only two large cohorts of petitions have been analysed: those by Hindle for Cumberland (1686–1749) and those for Lancashire studied here (1626–1710), and it may be dangerous to argue too stridently from such a regionally specific sample. Nonetheless, it seems extremely telling that in these two samples, religious observance hardly seems to feature at all. More significant are the occasions in which petitioners claimed to have been 'good neighbours' and peaceable characters, but even these represented only a fairly small proportion of all appeals. In Hindle's Cumberland sample, only 4.5 per cent of petitions contained references to a supplicant's 'good reputation'.[110] In Lancashire we see the odd case: Elizabeth Astley of Blackburn claimed in 1650 to have been 'borne of good parentage and alwayes being of good behaviour of honest conversation and good report amongst hir neibors'.[111] Similarly, when the incumbents of Croston and Eccleston churches asked for relief to be given to Huskell Sumner in 1635, they interjected the word 'godly' between the first and second words in their description of him as 'a poore yong man'.[112] In 1656, Mary Speake of Twiston, backed by eleven of her neighbours, pleaded that she had lived for twelve years in the township, during which time she had 'demained herselfe modestly and civilly as become an honest woman without the least blemish of her reputation'.[113] Henry Cottom of Chipping told justices in 1657 that he had 'served the Comonwealth in England and Scotland and never revolted'.[114] Ralph Standish of Anderton, meanwhile, claimed to have been of 'good goverment & carrige' when petitioning for relief in 1691.[115] But overall the critical characteristics highlighted by petitioners, in both counties, were not moral or behavioural, but related to need.

110   Hindle, *On the Parish?*, p. 410.
111   LA, QSP/30/6.
112   LA, QSB/1/150/48.
113   LA, QSP/130/20.
114   LA, QSP/138/19.
115   LA, QSP/694/18.

Another telling set of documents are those petitions *against* poor relief, from parishes who believed a pauper was undeserving. As yet these have not been studied in any detail, but the Lancashire examples provide a useful starting point. Of these, I have only uncovered a handful apparently moralistic in tone, and even these are usually framed within the terms of wasteful expenditure (including a proclivity to drink) or unwillingness to work. In 1671, the officers of Blackrod asked for a reduction in the relief of some of their paupers, 'haveinge some of them cattell, others followinge games and others imployinge what the[y] gett by their labour in riotous and debaucht expences'.[116] Similarly, a 1679 petition from Lathom complained that James Browne, a pensioner, was 'very idle & debauched', while others' 'extraordinary allowances serve onely to support their riotous & extravagant expences'.[117] A 1668 petition aimed at reducing the relief given to Henry Hesketh of Lathom focused largely on his ability to work, though it also noted that his wife was 'a great gossoper'.[118] Thirty-year-old widow Anne Seeds of Arkholme, said a petition to Lancaster Sessions in 1695, had picked up a 'habit of laysiness', and was pretending lameness by 'wrappinge a parcell of old raggs about her leggs'.[119] Only one case has surfaced of townships using religion as grounds for refusing relief, and then only as part of a suite of enormities: this was in 1701 when the officers of Caton asked JPs to cancel Dorothy Wayman's pension because she was 'a popish recusant an idele woman and of abilitie to maintaine her selfe'.[120] Particularly rich is the series of petitions by the vestry and 'inhabitants' of Hawkshead against the relief of Agnes Braithwaite, an aged widow of Field Head.[121] These highlighted her 'drunkenness', and the fact she was 'very able to releve her selfe without any allowance', both implying wastefulness. But they also described Braithwaite as 'abusive', 'very contentious and ill', a 'troublesome and vexatious woman' and a 'troublesome person'. Forty years earlier, meanwhile, an overseer of Tyldesley-cum-Shakerley asked for a pension given to William Wilkinson and his family to be discontinued on several grounds. These included that he kept an alehouse; that his wife had 'spent out of her owne house xijd at

---

116   LA, QSP/364/10.
117   LA, QSP/509/5; also: QSP/640/5.
118   LA, QSP/327/26.
119   LA, QSP/756/4.
120   LA, QSP/858/6.
121   Healey, 'Poverty, Deservingness and Popular Politics', pp. 134–46.

a shott;[122] & alsoe gave to a musitioner six pence boastinge that they had noe neede of the[i]re weekely allowance'; that she was a 'most deboiset swearer slanderer & drunken person, whoe for her false slanders hath latelie received punishment & is not thereby reformed'; and finally, adding insult to the parishioners' injury, the couple had just built an extension to their house![123]

Here, it seems, we have relatively clear attempts to prevent paupers from getting relief partially on account of their bad neighbourliness. Yet even here we must exercise care, for such petitions were often designed to paint the pauper as dishonest and unreliable. The original relief had by definition usually been obtained by a petition to the bench, and the validity of the pauper's claims was always partly predicated on their personal reliability. Attempts to portray paupers as morally unwholesome thus might have had a clear political edge to them, and are therefore not incompatible with attempts to reduce their allowances largely on perceived need. Furthermore, in the only other attempt at analysis of petitions against relief, once again by Hindle on Cumberland, it was stated that of the twenty-nine extant appeals, the grounds given were that

> pensioners or their children always had been, or were now sufficiently recovered from illness to be, able to work; that they had reliable networks of kin support; that, if widowed, they had remarried; that they were idle, drunk, or dissolute; that assets had in fact been bequeathed to them by will or trust.[124]

These factors, essentially, can be put down to the need for residuality – the idea that poor relief was a last resort. Or, to put it another way, that no person who was able to work for a living should depend on the rates.

Understanding poverty and poor relief

Given the complex politics involved in producing the thousands of petitions now sitting in the Lancashire Archives, we need to be careful about how we use them. They are, quite simply, documents of advocacy: personal appeals with a very direct purpose – to convince justices that

122   An alehouse bill.
123   LA, QSP/296/1; cf. QSP/327/26.
124   Hindle, *On the Parish?*, p. 397.

the petitioner was a 'deserving pauper'. They will contain exaggeration, inattention to uncomfortable detail, and even downright distortion. It is hard not be sceptical when petitioners profess to be 127 years old, while it is similarly difficult to accept Roger Blakeley of Tyldesley's claim in 1663 that he was eighty-five while his daughter was 'but of seaven yeares of age'.[125]

Still, this is no reason to discard petitions as useful source material for the study of actual poverty. There are, indeed, several reasons we can be confident of the documents' usefulness. Even if we take an extreme view of the problems inherent in pauper petitions, and elect not to trust a single actual descriptive statement, then they are telling us about what kinds of need were believable and acceptable. Thus in an abstract sense, petitions tell us something about a cultural conception of deservingness which petitioners believed was held by magistrates. This in itself is a kind of historical truth, but it can also be taken to be indicative of actual events, for believability was likely – ultimately – to be tied to experience. Thus, when John Cawson of Quernmore petitioned in 1649 to have 'had greate losse by the Scots armie hee liveinge in the high rode at a place called Posteren Yate', this was believable to justices at Lancaster because the Scots *had* invaded the county the previous year, and they *had* passed through that area on their way to defeat at Preston.[126] I would, however, like to claim rather greater *specific* reliability for petitions than this necessarily allows, on three further grounds. First, many petitions were endorsed by neighbours, sometimes including local officers.[127] Even when no list of supporters is appended, the basic fact remains that the petitioner would almost always have had to get at least one individual, the scribe, to back their appeal. There may have been local conflicts, now lost to us, which could have led to the endorsement of some dubious claims, but this will have been the exception rather than the rule. Those who made false statements to the court presumably risked arraignment for contempt or – at the very least – severe community disapproval. In the light of this, the following chapters will refer to statements made in petitions counter-signed by neighbours as if they were true, while maintaining a note of

---

125   LA, QSP/34/7; QSP/244/2.
126   LA, QSP/21/7; S. Bull and M. Seed, *Bloody Preston: The Battle of Preston, 1648* (Lancaster, 1998), pp. 59–60. Postern Gate is at the intersection of the roads between Lancaster, Quernmore and Halton.
127   E.g. LA, QSP/79/25; QSP/122/19.

caution with those which are not countersigned.[128] But more generally, the process of petitioning itself – by which an illiterate pauper needed to convince at least one literate neighbour of the validity of their claims – lends some credence to the information contained in the petitions.

The second point is that, as discussed above, petitioners appear to have been expected to make their appeals in person, and magistrates in effect had the chance to interview those making petitions, something which ought to have prevented the most outrageous claims from even reaching the petition stage. And this process is closely related to the third point, namely that if paupers made demonstrably false assertions about their condition, the opportunity existed for the aggrieved overseers to fight them in the courts, either by attending Quarter Sessions at the initial reading of the petition, or by launching counterpetitions. The overseers' accounts of Atherton, for example, contain reference in 1714/15 to money 'Spent at Wiggen sessions to prevent the poor from getting orders'.[129] Around eighty years earlier, the parish of Prescot had fought an acrimonious battle with widow Jane Smith over her relief, while a similarly bitter dispute arose in Hawkshead between 1701 and 1706 over the relief of Agnes Braithwaite, one of whose petitions opened this chapter.[130]

So petitions provide an extremely useful and vivid source for reconstructing the social history of poverty in the 'first century of welfare'. The key approach here is to peer into the world of pauper petitions – with the occasional glance at the censuses of the poor – to see what they tell us about the nature of poverty in a pre-industrial society. In order to make the study manageable, I have focused on first petitions (this meant excluding petitions from someone whom we know had already petitioned Quarter or Petty Sessions, and thus prevented the sample being biased towards the most controversial cases), and I have excluded petitions for habitation orders[131] as well as those petitions which were for something *other* than a dole from the township, even where there was a stress on poverty. These

---

128   Thus in 1653, Ann Wallwork was a widow with five small children whose husband died in a mining accident, while John Edrington of Lancaster *claimed* to be sick and of 'great age': LA, QSP/76/13; QSP/77/1.

129   WA, TR/Ath/C/2/3, Atherton Overseers' Accounts, 1712–16.

130   Hindle, *On the Parish?*, pp. 421–3; Healey, 'Poverty, Deservingness and Popular Politics'.

131   These were cases in which JPs were being asked to provide a house – usually on the manorial waste – for a pauper, rather than a pension, on which see: J. Broad, 'Housing the Rural Poor in Southern England, 1650–1850', *AgHR*, 48 (2000), 151–70.

included appeals for military pensions, for relief from errant husbands or neighbours, for licences to beg for relief after some catastrophe, or for relief from taxation. On the other hand, the sample *includes* petitions for an increase in an existing dole, and those cases where a township had *stopped* a dole, so long as this was the first identifiable brush with Quarter Sessions. I have also had to exclude some petitions on grounds of illegibility, though fortunately the number is not large. Overall, this has left a sample of 3,169 appeals between 1626 and 1710.[132]

There would be any number of ways of sampling the source material, of which mine, focusing on first petitions for poor relief, is just one. Its logic is that it looks at a relatively standardized set of cases, such that individuals hopefully do not recur (though there may well be cases not picked up), which not only gives a rough idea of the numbers of petitioners claiming different types of poverty, but also more importantly showcases the wonderfully vivid personal stories recounted before the county's magistrates. The body of material can be subject to some rough-and-ready quantification, though I have tried to keep it basic to avoid giving any spurious appearance of precision; but their real glory – and why the Lancashire petitions constitute such an important set of historical sources – is the startlingly evocative *qualitative* picture they present of the lives of the poor. This picture is an altogether richer, more textured, and certainly more colourful one than the bare sketch we can get from overseers' accounts. I would venture that it was also – partly in the light of all this – a more realistic one.

132   Inclusive. Some appeals survive from after 1710, and these have been consulted but not included in the sample.

PART II:
MARGINALITY

.

4

Marginal People: Descending into Poverty?

Men tumble up and downe in the world.

The Diary of Ralph Josselin (1653)[1]

The first question we must ask ourselves is, *who were the poor*? In subsequent chapters, it will be suggested that the deserving poor were those suffering certain contingencies, certain 'crosses and losses'. But before we look at this, we must ask whether the poor were part of a distinctive group within English society, living lives of marginality across their life cycle, or whether they were ordinary people fallen on especially hard times. The answer, as it turns out, is that they could be either.

The position of the poor within English society has been an important historiographical subtheme. Keith Wrightson, for example, has suggested that England's Old Poor Law embodied a balance between 'communal identification' on the one hand, and 'social differentiation' on the other.[2] Parochial poor relief strategies represented both the acceptance of paupers into a community as legitimate objects of charity, but also their obvious social difference from those who were wealthy enough to give relief. It is a view that implies the existence of two distinct groups within rural society: the 'poor' and the comparatively wealthy, who were then subject to these paradoxical relationships towards each other. Indeed, Wrightson's work has argued forcefully that rural England *circa* 1580–1680 saw its 'middling sort', amongst whom most parochial officers were found, become increasingly – culturally and economically – differentiated from their poorer neighbours.[3] And he has also suggested that the Poor Law itself 'identified and isolated the poor as a group', serving to emphasize their otherness.

1   R. Josselin, *The Diary of Ralph Josselin, 1616–1683*, ed. A. Macfarlane (RSEH, New Ser., iii, London, 1976), p. 294.
2   K. Wrightson, *English Society, 1580–1680* (London, 1982), p. 181.
3   K. Wrightson, 'Aspects of Social Differentiation in Rural England, c.1580–1660', *Journal of Peasant Studies*, 5 (1977), 33–47; C. Lis and H. Soly, 'Policing the Early Modern

Thus even communal identification – the other side to Wrightson's coin – was based on an unequal vertical relationship between clearly distinguishable 'superior' and 'inferior' groups.

Such a picture is, to an extent, bolstered by studies of the scale of poverty in early modern communities. Poverty in early modern times, as today, was a concept with multiple meanings. Although the phrase 'labouring poor', a shorthand for those working for precarious wages, is apparently first found in a 1724 pamphlet by Daniel Defoe, many earlier commentators similarly referred to wage labourers as 'the poor', or 'the poorer sort'.[4] It has, moreover, become clear that those individuals actually receiving poor relief were a mere subset of those actually considered 'poor'. Tom Arkell has argued, using a variety of tax and poverty relief records from Warwickshire, that while some 30 per cent of the population were in households exempted from the hearth tax, only 5 per cent were in households receiving formal poor relief.[5] Thus, if this was a period of a widening gap between the middling and poorer sorts, and if the relieved poor were only a small subset even of the latter group, then we might expect very little overlap between those on relief and the more comfortable members of early modern society. Put simply, those who ended up supported by the parish are likely to have lived lives of marginality, amongst the mass of the 'poorer sort'.

It is, however, possible to make an alternative case, namely that a certain level of economic *affinity* could exist between the rural middling and poorer sorts. First, there might be regional nuances to the social differentiation suggested by Wrightson.[6] In the North West, for example, the standard picture is of a much more egalitarian rural society, with a larger proportion of households enjoying some access to land and few really wealthy capitalist farms.[7] Secondly, it is not necessarily the case that actual social differentiation would have eradicated *fears* of a descent into poverty by members of the rural middling sort. W. Newman-Brown has suggested

Proletariat, 1450–1850', in *Proletarianization and Family History*, ed. D. Levine (Orlando, 1984), pp. 163–228 (p. 176).

4 Muldrew, *Food, Energy and the Creation of Industriousness*, pp. 19–20; K. Wrightson. 'Estates, Degrees and Sorts: Changing Perceptions of Society in Tudor and Stuart England', in *Language, History and Class*, ed. P. J. Corfield (Oxford, 1991), pp. 30–52.

5 T. Arkell, 'The Incidence of Poverty in England in the Later Seventeenth Century', *Social History*, 12 (1987), 23–47.

6 Wrightson, 'Puritan Reformation', p. 180; Gritt, '"Survival" of Service', pp. 34–8.

7 Beckett, 'Decline of the Small Landowner', pp. 100–7; Healey, 'Agrarian Social Structure', pp. 73–7.

that 'some ... overseers would have been sensible of the fact that, given some misfortune, they too would be likely to have need of assistance from the parish.'[8] Samantha Williams has recently discovered considerable overlap between ratepayers and paupers in two Bedfordshire villages – albeit from the later eighteenth century, a period of spiralling poor relief costs, and a concomitant expansion of the ratepayer base to fund them.[9]

Certainly Defoe worried in 1729 that the spread of workhouses would lead to formerly respectable folk rubbing shoulders with the dangerous poor:

> We all, alas, are subject to misfortune. And if an honest gentleman or trader should leave a wife or children unprovided for, what a shocking thing it is to think they must be mixed with vagrants, beggars, thieves and night-walkers; to receive their insults, bear their blasphemous and obscene discourse, to be suffocated with their nastiness, and eat up with their vermin.[10]

Paul Fideler has recently noted repeated concerns about the plight of paupers *verecundi*, the formerly well-off poor, whom he considers may have been 'singled out for particular care' in the Middle Ages; indeed, Christopher Dyer has recently found evidence that the wealthier members of medieval rural society did not consider the poor *so* different from themselves.[11] More generally, Craig Muldrew has shown that the transitory nature of wealth and prosperity was – rightly it seems – a constant worry even for those possessed of relatively impressive financial resources, and Michael Mascuch has argued from middling-sort diaries and autobiographies that 'the openness of the abyss of poverty, into which providence might at any moment cast whole families, was more awesome than the openness of the elite into which individuals might climb'.[12] Indeed, Peter King's research on inventories of pauper goods in eighteenth-century

---

8   Newman-Brown, 'Receipt of Poor Relief', p. 419.

9   Williams, *Poverty*, pp. 126–9.

10 Quoted in: Webb and Webb, *English Poor Law History, Part One*, p. 248.

11 Fideler, *Social Welfare*, pp. 23, 45, 150; Dyer, 'Poverty and its Relief', pp. 65–6.

12 C. Muldrew, *The Economy of Obligation: The Culture of Credit and Social Relations in Early Modern England* (London, 1998), pp. 272–312; M. Mascuch, 'Social Mobility and Middling Self-Identity: the Ethos of British Autobiographers, 1600–1750', *Social History*, 20 (1995), 45–61 (p. 61); as is often the case, some of the best examples are in: Gough, *History of Myddle*, pp. 92, 97–8, 100, 109, 162, 191–2, 202, 203, 230–1; recently also: Boulton, 'It is extreme necessity', p. 60. On insecurity as a general feature of social life in

Essex suggests that amongst the relieved were a number of individuals of formerly comfortable standing.[13] And any dichotomous relationship between middling and poorer sorts would be complicated anyway by the existence of ties of kinship and friendship across social gulfs. According to Keith Snell, 'the old poor law allowed much scope for face to face relief between taxpayers and recipients who knew each other well and were sometimes of comparable status'.[14] Indeed, the diary of one mid-eighteenth-century overseer, Thomas Turner of East Hoathly in Sussex, actually records his friendship with a local pauper called Sam Jenner. It would be astonishing if this case was unique.[15]

As it happens, Lancashire's pauper petitions do contain instances of crossover between relative wealth, and severe poverty. In a number of cases, albeit a proportionally small one, petitioners actually described a previous existence of relative economic security. In others, petitioners recorded old occupations, which had previously allowed them to get by but which now – for whatever reason – had failed them. These narratives of social descent, then, can tell us much about the degree of downward social mobility amongst the ordinary men and women of early modern England.

Decayed households? Social mobility in pauper petitions, 1626–1710

When asking for relief, many petitioners felt it was relevant to include certain details about their life histories to date. While often this was banal and stereotyped, such as the frequent protestations of 'painful labour', this was not always the case. Petitioners might continue to describe themselves with reference to their previous occupation or might report details about the reasons for their poverty which shed light on a former existence of some security or even prosperity.

the period, see: K. Thomas, *Religion and the Decline of Magic: Studies in Popular Beliefs in Sixteenth and Seventeenth Century England* (London, 1971), pp. 5–24.

13   P. King, 'Pauper Inventories and the Material Lives of the Poor in the Eighteenth and Early Nineteenth Centuries', in *Chronicling Poverty: the Voices and Strategies of the English Poor, 1640–1840*, ed. T. Hitchcock, P. King and P. Sharpe (London, 1997), pp. 155–91.

14   Snell, *Annals*, p. 108.

15   N. Tadmor, *Family and Friends in Eighteenth-Century England: Household, Kinship and Patronage* (Cambridge, 2000), pp. 198, 209–10.

Table 2: Recorded occupations of first-time petitioners, 1626–1710

Occupation	Male occupations		Female occupations	
	No.	%	No.	%
Gentry and professional*	33	4.6	–	–
Yeomen	4	0.6	–	–
Husbandmen	129	18.1	–	–
Textiles	131	18.4	2	8.3
Coalmining	25	3.5	1	4.2
Metalworking	4	0.6	–	–
Trades	140	19.7	–	–
Midwifery	–	–	2	8.3
Carrying and peddling	13	1.8	–	–
Service	10	1.4	17	70.8
Soldiers	25	3.5	–	–
Labourers	197	27.7	2	8.3
Unknown	1	0.1	–	–
Total	712		24	

* Women whose husband or father have recorded occupations are recorded under 'male occupations'; this means that all of the 'gentry and professional' entries are counted as male.

Taking those petitioners who presented an obvious occupational title, including the titles of fathers and husbands, we can get some idea of the employment background of the county's poor. There were 735 such titles used by first-time petitioners between 1626 and 1710 (Table 2). The picture that emerges is one in which the petitioners were overwhelmingly drawn from the ranks of the small tradesmen and craftsmen, husbandmen, textile workers and day labourers, these groups in combination accounting for 84 per cent of all titles. There were also significant numbers of servants and a small number of coalminers and metalworkers. The most striking row in Table 2, however, is the top one. This shows, quite unexpectedly, that some 4.5 per cent of male occupational titles referred to gentlemen, professionals or the upper middling sort. These included four clerks, two curates, two ministers, a reverend, a vicar, a doctor, two freemen, six schoolmasters and teachers, an usher of a grammar school, plus thirteen others specifically referred to as gentry.[16] A word of caution is needed, as

16   Cf. R. Mitchison, 'Who Were the Poor in Scotland, 1690–1830?', in *Economy and*

it is probable that gentry petitioners were more likely to mention their former status than plebeian ones were to detail former occupations. Thus, while gentry and professional occupations constituted some 4.5 per cent of *recorded* occupations, a more useful statistic is perhaps that they accounted for thirty-two out of the total petition sample of 3,169, or 1.0 per cent. Even so, the fact that one out of every hundred petitioners claimed such high status is in itself an impressive finding.[17] We will return to these 'elite paupers' shortly.

Such bald statistics tell us part of the story, but it is the miniature 'life histories' offered by some petitions which are most interesting. Usually these contained very scanty detail about the previous economic lives of the petitioner, often confined to a statement to the effect that he or she had been self-sufficient, hard-working and of no trouble to his or her neighbours. But occasionally more detail was offered about these lives on the margins. As will be noted in the next chapter, several petitioners mentioned holding cottages with gardens or a tiny amount of land, or that they had one or two cows for milk. Such individuals were probably never far from dependence, and it cannot have taken much of a reduction in earning power to push them into serious hardship.

Other petitioners, however, told of rather more impressive falls from economic security, with several claiming to have been of good local standing, even if they were often rather vague in their description of it. Robert Cowper of Nether Burrow, for example, petitioned for relief in 1650 claiming to have 'formerly beene a man of very good estate'.[18] In 1686, Lawrence Charnley of Haighton reported to Preston Quarter Sessions that he was 'formerly a man of an estaite but through debts and severall of the inconveniences which haith light upon him through the providence of almighty God haith beene forced to sell & parte with all his

Society in Scotland and Ireland, 1500–1939, ed. R. Mitchison and P. Roebuck (Edinburgh, 1988), pp. 140–8 (p. 141).

17   In fact, there were more gentle households who came to need poor relief after disputes around property had failed to be resolved in their favour. These are found in Quarter Sessions papers petitioning for some kind of restitution of property, but whose appeals led magistrates to order relief by the overseers. The figure quoted here is of those who petitioned for township relief as their first resort. For other examples of crossover between gentility and poverty see: J. T. Cliffe, *The Yorkshire Gentry from the Reformation to the Civil War* (London, 1969), pp. 145, 156–7; P. Sharpe, 'Poor Children as Apprentices in Colyton, 1598–1830', *Continuity and Change*, 6 (1991), 253–70 (p. 263).

18   LA, QSP/25/11.

estaite soe that hee haith nothing lefte to relieve himselfe upon'.[19] Alice Keckwick of West Derby claimed in 1690 that she had previously enjoyed a 'considerable stocke of goods' until hard usage by her landlord and 'other casualties' had intervened.[20] John Hargreaves of Twiston was, he recounted in a petition of 1696, 'born of honest parents to a good estate not far from the place where I live'.[21] In 1649, Thomas Webster of Nether Wyresdale told of a social descent that came in several stages. Originally a yeoman, his estate 'decayed' and he came to 'releeve himselfe by educating & teachinge of children'.[22] By the year of Charles I's execution, however, he was old and had become blind, and so 'now beinge deprived of his sight is also disappointed of that helpe'. In 1661, Mary Chow reported that though she had been possessed of an estate of £20 per annum, her husband had now run away and she was destitute.[23] Even this was small compared with the estate lost by Ellen Valentine of Pilkington. Her husband, so she petitioned in 1690, had farmed a tenement worth £47 per annum, but he had become indebted and had run away, such that she had 'neither dish nor spoone left nor bed to lay her downe inn, soe that shee and her two poore children at present lyes upon a little straw'.[24]

Some petitioners simply pleaded that they had previously paid their own way without burdening their neighbours, continuing their lives in comfort and decency until misfortune intervened. William Dickenson of Adlington, for example, petitioned in 1688 that he had been 'a very civell, painefull, and laborius workman: and lived very handsomely amongst his neighbours, and not chargeable unto any'.[25] Nor was he the only one to claim 'civility' for a couple of years earlier Adam Aspull of Hindley had petitioned for relief, stating that he had 'civily demeaned himselfe amongst his neighbours'.[26] Not dissimilarly, Jane Barlow of Bury recounted in 1680 that she had maintained her family in a 'decent and comly manner not chargeable nor burdensom to anyone'.[27] In 1684, labourer John Berry and his wife Margaret reported to justices that they had 'heretofore lived very

19   LA, QSP/611/14.
20   LA, QSP/686/15.
21   LA, QSP/777/17.
22   LA, QSP/10/6.
23   LA, QSP/212/5.
24   LA, QSP/679/3.
25   LA, QSP/653/7.
26   LA, QSP/625/1.
27   LA, QSP/523/10.

commendably amongst their neighbours' and had 'brought up a great charge of children in decent manner'.[28] Perhaps decency was the best that most of the labouring poor could hope to claim, though 86-year-old Richard Hilton of Tonge described himself in 1686 as a yeoman who had 'of late lived fashionabley amo[ngst] his neighbours'.[29]

Others emphasized that they had made financial contributions to the local community. Blind eighty-year-old Humphrey Bury of Rainford claimed in 1651 to have previously contributed twenty shillings a year to provide for a preacher at the township's chapel.[30] Several told of supporting their poor neighbours. Isabel Garner of Eskrigg in Gressingham claimed in 1656 that she had formerly 'beene a woman of ablitie to helpe & relieve the poore & needie', though she was 'at this present through disasters[,] theis times & ould age' unable to subsist.[31] One poor Bolton felt-maker, James Younghusband, claimed in 1677 to have formerly been a 'releever of the poore' though he was now old, infirm and nearly blind.[32] In 1678, William Ayre of Greenhalgh-with-Thistleton reported having 'formerlie beene the owner of a verie competent estate whereby hee was enabled not onlie to releeve himselfe & familie but others in want', though now it had 'pleased god to alter your petitioners condition'.[33] John Tonge, a Manchester chapman, had – he claimed in 1680 – been an 'industrious workman and a free releever of the poore, whilst he was able to follow his labour', though now he and his wife were old, impotent and weak.[34] Given the importance of neighbourly charity to the Lancashire poor, described in the next chapter, it would be unwise to suppose that all of those who claimed to have previously been 'helpers' were actual ratepayers. However, there are also clear statements of former ratepaying by paupers. Samuel Midgley of Crompton told JPs in 1652 that he had 'formerly lived in good fashion & in repute & beene helpfull to others paying all taxes & contributions in the place of his abode'.[35] Margaret Bowker of Moston had, she said in 1659, paid all taxes in her township, but had spent all of her money

28   LA, QSP/591/46.
29   LA, QSP/622/6.
30   LA, QSP/43/4.
31   LA, QSP/125/6.
32   LA, QSP/461/16.
33   LA, QSP/483/21.
34   LA, QSP/523/15.
35   LA, QSP/64/15.

in sickness.[36] Twenty years later, John Lomax of Bradshaw petitioned that he had 'formerly lived in a plentifull condicion and hath paid taxes towards King and poore'.[37] Thomas Banks, finally, claimed in 1706 that he had lived in Poulton-le-Sands for thirty years, where he had 'paid his equall share and proportion of Assessments both to the Church and poor and severall other publick taxes'.[38]

One petitioner, Priscilla Butler of Rochdale, told not of ratepaying, but of how her family had left an unusually large endowment to the poor. Her uncle, so her petition states, left no less than £100 to the town's poor. This was before her 'wastfull and prodigall' husband left her 'troubled with the dropsie and … a running issue in her brest' and petitioning for poor relief in 1657.[39] She had her facts slightly wrong, for her generous uncle was the late Dr Samuel Radcliffe, erstwhile Principal of Brasenose College, Oxford, who left £50 to the poor of Rochdale (his place of birth) as well as £20 to be used for loans to tradesmen of the town. In reality, though, Radcliffe was an even greater friend to the poor than Butler appears to have known, leaving the sum of £400 for the founding of an almshouse in the Oxfordshire parish of Steeple Aston, of which he had been rector and where he had already founded a school.[40]

Neither was she the only example of a member of the elite being forced to petition for poor relief. Indeed, as mentioned above, the number of 'elite paupers' unearthed is both surprising and impressive. While only ever a tiny minority, of course, it is rather the fact that *any* members of Lancashire's social elites came to depend on the Poor Law which is important, showing as it does the potential for cataclysmic social descent. Robert Singleton, for instance, a schoolmaster and gentleman of Broughton-in-Amounderness, was found amongst supplicants for aid at Preston Sessions in Easter 1650, claiming age and lameness.[41] Another example is that of Mr James Molyneux of Wigan, who had been usher of that town's Free Grammar School for twenty-seven years before he became sick, was turned out of his job, and required poor relief.[42] Nicholas Bray,

---

36 LA, QSP/176/18.
37 LA, QSP/500/13.
38 LA, QSP/934/22.
39 LA, QSP/152/1.
40 Jordan, *Social Institutions*, p. 26; C. C. Brookes, *History of Steeple Aston and Middle Aston* (Shipston-on-Stour, 1929), pp. 101, 120–2, 303, 306–9, 324–7.
41 LA, QSP/30/9.
42 LA, QSP/135/1.

meanwhile, had been vicar of the parish church of St Michael's on Wyre, but after his death his daughter Elizabeth found herself on a downward spiral into poverty.[43] Then fourteen years old, she lived with her mother in Catterall for three years, but when the latter became unable to look after her, she was sent to work as a domestic servant with her brother William in Bolton. Seven years later, when falling sickness left her incapacitated, William sent her back to their mother, and she is found petitioning for poor relief in 1662. That year also saw a petition by the wife and children of William Hulton, Esq., of Chorley, who were left begging relief from their neighbours when he absconded.[44] In 1682, John Comsell's petition described him as a gentleman, but told of how he had 'beene a souldier in the Low Countries and att severall engagements in England' and was now eighty-seven years old and 'reduced to povertie', living in Manchester.[45] Another gentleman, Alexander Shireburn of Chipping, found the costs of a lawsuit too much to bear, and ended up petitioning for poor relief in 1691. Two of his neighbours petitioned that he had been

> a greate sufferrer in a suite commenced against him by one William Parker and others in forma pauperis, and had a continuance both at lawe and equitie above five yeares; which maye plainly appeare, by such relations of the whole proceedings in the said suite, as the bearer is able to give: which, with such other misfortunes as he hath met with in the world, have brought him into povertie and want.[46]

Shireburn was a prominent local Catholic, whose family had been sequestered Royalists during the Civil Wars, and who descended from the Stonyhurst Shireburns. He had held a significant estate at Wolfhouse in Chipping, but had either mortgaged or sold it in 1678, and by six years later it had been sold to two men, William Patten and Thomas Naylor, who were probably trustees for a third man, Thomas Patten of Preston.[47] He was awarded 2s 6d per week until further order, an unusually high sum, which might be taken to suggest that JPs thought he deserved a higher standard of living than the mass of the poor.

A further case, about which we can say rather more, comes from

43   LA, QSP/230/9, 13, 15.
44   LA, QSP/219/4.
45   LA, QSP/551/26.
46   LA, QSP/697/9.
47   *VCH Lancs*, vol. 7, pp. 26–32.

Hawkshead in the reign of Charles II. Mr Henry Nicholson had been minister of nearby Colton from 1673 (at the latest) to around 1677.[48] By the latter year he had been installed as vicar of Hawkshead parish, and in 1679 his wife gave birth to a daughter, Judith, at which point the couple lived in the small settlement at Walker Ground.[49] By 1680, however, he had apparently deserted his wife and two children, thus triggering a dispute between Hawkshead bailiwick and the neighbouring townships of Claife and Satterthwaite over responsibility for the family's poor relief.[50] The next we know of Nicholson was his replacement as vicar by Thomas Bell, MA, in 1682. Intriguingly, however, he seems to have been back in the parish in 1683, when he signed the affidavit certifying that Elizabeth Nicholson, the daughter of William of Keen Ground, had been buried in woollen.[51]

As it happens, even some of the most prominent members of the county's aristocracy can be found amongst those asking for relief in our period. According to the antiquarian research of Reginald Sharpe France, scions of at least six of the 'leading families of the county' petitioned magistrates for relief in the seventeenth century: the Whittinghams, the Shireburns (whom we have discussed), the Hindleys, the Byroms, the Brettarghs, and (most astonishingly) the Bickerstaffe branch of the Stanley family.[52] In the latter case, France found two cases of Bickerstaffe Stanleys (created baronets in 1628) having brushes with the Poor Law in the early 1680s. The first, resulting from a dispute between the three surviving daughters of the Third Baronet, Sir Edward Stanley (1643–71) and their mother and grandmother, had seen the girls approach the township's overseers of the poor, only to be rebuffed – not unjustly – on account of their grandmother's considerable estate.[53] The second instance, involved Isabel, the daughter of Henry Stanley, gent. of Rainford, a close relative of

---

48   LA, QSJ/8/1/201–3, Sacrament Certificates, 20 July 1673; *VCH Lancs*, vol. 8, p. 386 and n. Nicholson is not mentioned in the list of incumbents of Colton, but a new minister was installed in 1678, a date which roughly agrees with his first mention as vicar of Hawkshead in 1677.

49   This was the location of the vicarage: H. S. Cowper, *Hawkshead (the Northernmost Parish of Lancashire)* (London, 1899), pp. 412, 548; *Oldest Register Book*, p. 315.

50   LA, QSP/515/1.

51   *Oldest Register Book*, p. 328.

52   R. S. France, 'On Some Stanley Cadets in the Reign of Charles II', *THSLC*, 96 (1944), 78–81; R. S. France, 'The Poor Brettarghs of Penketh', *THSLC*, 99 (1947), 89–93 (p. 93).

53   France, 'Some Stanley Cadets', pp. 78–9; P. E. Stanley, *The House of Stanley: The History of an English Family from the 12th Century* (Edinburgh, 1998), p. 267.

the Bickerstaffe family.[54] Henry had, sometime before 1683, been drowned in the Irish Sea, after which Isabel had petitioned Quarter Sessions for poor relief, a request they duly granted. The township of Rainford then agreed to pay her 6d per week, but around Christmas time in 1682 apparently reduced their offer to 4d or nothing. Thus Isabel was, she claimed, forced to petition to Ormskirk Sessions at Easter 1683, an appeal which again resulted in an order for 6d, although it took yet another petition to Midsummer Sessions for the township eventually to comply. And these were not the only occasions that Stanley cadets asked for poor relief either, for in 1703 Ursula Stanley of Broughton, whose husband had been an esquire, was petitioning at Manchester Sessions for relief. By this point her husband's lands had been alienated to the Chethams of Turton and Smedley, but she claimed she had the use of a tenement in Broughton for her own life and that of her daughter Arabella. She complained, though, that her son Henry had taken the land (and four milk cows), and was given a pension of 12d a week.[55]

The point is that poor relief in the seventeenth century was not just confined to those of immediately 'marginal' backgrounds, but was sometimes claimed by those from middling or even professional and gentry households.[56] It is even possible to find examples of cadet branches of major noble families needing relief from their townships and parishes. Presumably some of this fluidity can be related to the considerable poverty of the Lancashire gentry in comparison with other regions, and many of the county's gentry families suffered decline in the late seventeenth century.[57] Additionally, the social structure of farming at the time, with large numbers of smallholders and few full-time agricultural labourers, must have meant that aged and sick husbandmen accounted for a higher proportion of those on relief than in those communities where a larger rural proletariat had already developed.[58] The political turmoil of the mid seventeenth century may also have been a powerful force for downward social mobility in some cases, although Blackwood's research suggests

54 France, 'Some Stanley Cadets', p. 81.
55 LA, QSP/901/25.
56 Cf. Muldrew, *Economy of Obligation*, pp. 272–98.
57 Walton, *Lancashire*, pp. 27–8; Blackwood, *Lancashire Gentry*, pp. 160–2.
58 Gritt, '"Survival" of Service', pp. 34–8; cf. B. Stapleton, 'Inherited Poverty and Life-cycle Poverty: Odiham, Hampshire, 1650–1850', *Social History*, 18 (1993), 339–55 (pp. 347–50).

this was not the norm.[59] It was, however, the experience of the Hollands of Clifton.[60] Having, like most of the Lancashire gentry, backed the wrong side in the 1640s, they found their lands sequestered by the Republic, and failed to recover after 1660. Thus while Thomas Holland had been titled an esquire before the Civil Wars, his daughter Frances was, by 1663, receiving 12d per week from the township in which her family had been lords of the manor since the fourteenth century.

Conclusion

In 1656, the wife of Lawrence Wilding presented a petition, countersigned by some fourteen of her neighbours, for poor relief at Ormskirk Sessions. Wilding's husband had been forced to take up military service overseas to pay off his father's debts, leaving her poor. What was more, she was struggling to support their children through school, petitioning that she

> hath done to her poore power what shee could to obtaine them learneinge; Insoemuch that the one boy is attain'd to well reedinge, & att present is learneinge to write, Notwithstandinge they beeinge and groweinge both to high statures that shee is through want & great impoverishment forced to take them from learneinge & seeke there livelyhoods in the country.

The Wilding children, then, were unable to complete their education for reasons of sheer poverty. Such poor children were unlikely to grow up possessing the social capital that was essential to make headway in a society in which such a large proportion of transactions were undertaken on credit and in which personal reputation was critical to both economic and social advancement.[61] Indeed, the fact that her father-in-law's debts were still causing Wilding difficulty shows the potential for intergenerational poverty to bite hard.

This chapter has been all too brief, but it has shown that poverty did not always cross generations as it clearly did in this case. In fact, a number of petitioners for poor relief in seventeenth-century Lancashire

---

59   Blackwood, *Lancashire Gentry*, pp. 111–48, esp. pp. 147–8.
60   *VCH Lancs*, vol. 4, p. 405; Blackwood, *Lancashire Gentry*, p. 114; LA, QSP/240/11; QSP/264/16–17; QSP/268/16.
61   Muldrew, *Economy of Obligation*, pp. 149–56.

had enjoyed previous lives of some comfort. Some had lived amongst the more prosperous peasantry, the yeomen and wealthier husbandmen who formed the backbone of English rural society. Some petitions show many of the poor regarded themselves not simply as 'paupers', but as also being contributors to their community when times were better. They noted their occupations, even when they were old and past labour; they told of helping their neighbours, of paying poor rates, and of giving to charity. The image that comes out of the petitions is not of an isolated group, but one in which paupers saw themselves as ordinary people who had fallen on hard times. Some paupers were even decayed gentry.

And yet, the mass of petitioners made no such claims. Some highlighted collapses of fortune that seem trifling to posterity but which must have been devastating to those who already had little, such as the loss of a cow, or the spiralling debts of a labouring husband. The majority did not mention any such descent. Presumably in most cases they had lived out lives of back-breaking marginality, with little hope of scratching together enough to avoid poverty in their elder years, and none of ever ascending the social scale. Nonetheless, the small number of cases in which the social gulf between local elites and the poor was bridged may have been of disproportionate importance. These cases, such as those in which township officers or ratepayers came to be poor, or when farmers of sizeable tenements petitioned for relief, or when gentlewomen were forced onto the charity of their town by the currents of misfortune, might have had a powerful impact on the attitudes of their comfortable neighbours. For the ranks of the marginal contained many not born to them.

5

Resourceful People: Survival Strategies
of the Lancashire Poor

Sheweth, That your petitioner being about three score & ten yeares of age, formerly lived in good & credible condition, but aboute foure yeares since it pleased God to visit him with an ague & other sore sicknes, which continued on him aboute three yeares, in which time all his estate & meanes was spent, & consumed, & likewise being stricken with a palsie, soe that all his right side is uselesse, he now lyeth in a miserable condition not able to helpe himselfe in any thinge, his very bed being all rotten under him by reason of a laske[1] that hath houlden him above three yeares, & his impotencie not being able to move himselfe: in this lamentable condition he is like to perish, unless some releefe be granted for him, for being destitute of both meanes & able frends to releeve him, he for a longe time this winter hath had noethinge but what pittifull neighbours have sent him, and likewise none are willing to be trobled to looke to him, & helpe him in this his loathsome condition, onely a kinswoman of his hath out of naturall affection thus far beene with him, but she beinge of small estate unable to releeve him & greeveinge to see his dayly miserie is discoraged & almost wearied out.

Petition of Thomas Nailor of Standish (13 April 1662)[2]

When Thomas Nailor fell seriously ill in around 1658, he did not immediately seek relief from the overseers. Instead, his first response was to draw upon the charity of his neighbours and his kin. It was their support that – initially at least – insulated him from the economic shock caused by his sickness. In other words, he 'made shift', and his descent into poverty was cushioned by the existence of people willing and able to help him.

In seventeenth-century England, there was an ingrained culture of

---

1   I.e. diarrhoea.
2   LA, QSP/223/19.

'making shift'. Not only the poor, but middling households drew income from multiple sources, perhaps working for wages here or grazing a cow on the common there, and families had a number of avenues to explore should they experience a temporary hardship. Credit from neighbours, the selling of household goods, and a busy interchange of gifts, favours and patronage ensured that short-term difficulties were cushioned by peoples' social environments. But although such networks existed across the social spectrum, they were particularly essential to the poor. The purpose of this chapter, then, is to explore how paupers 'made shift': in other words, how they drew upon their social environment in order to hold off dependency on formal poor relief. It builds upon a developing tradition of scholarship on the 'economy of makeshifts' that has done so much to highlight the importance of multiple incomes to impoverished households. In focusing on pauper petitions, however, the chapter offers an unusual perspective. There are no systematic sources which detail 'total' individual or household strategies of making shift, and so historians have been forced to draw together conclusions from research on such diffuse topics as enclosure, crime, charity, and of labour and wages.[3] This leaves room for a more 'pauper-centred' approach, something that petitions – which allowed paupers themselves to detail their own survival strategies – provide.[4]

Petitions need, to a certain extent, to be read against the grain, since they do not necessarily recount attempts to make shift. Rather, *some* petitioners saw fit to mention that they had previously enjoyed some form of income source which had cushioned them from destitution, but that now it had failed. There was clearly no *expectation* that such information would be offered, and thus any quantification of the data might be highly misleading. Petitions only allow us to catch stray 'whiffs of theme' against a background white noise, but there are enough of these to get a sense of the overall structure of the pauper 'economy of makeshifts'. It is also the case that certain more 'deviant' income strands, particularly illegal ones, are unlikely to have been divulged. Even so, the descriptions of survival strategies and why they had failed provide a vivid qualitative picture of the ways in which ordinary households tried to get by.

---

3   Recently: Hindle, *On the Parish?*, pp. 15–95.
4   For a similar approach, see: Boulton, 'It is extreme necessity'. In addition, Alannah Tomkins has called for a greater exploitation of petitions and letters in this way: A. Tomkins, *The Experience of Urban Poverty, 1723–82: Parish, Charity and Credit* (Manchester, 2006), pp. 14–15.

Self-sufficiency: land, property and labour

In 1661, six inhabitants of Bickerstaffe launched a petition to Wigan Quarter Sessions complaining about the support given to one Henry Topping, a local pensioner.[5] The complaint was that Topping had little need of the allowance he was getting for 'hee hath a tenement of sixe acares during the terme of three lives now in beeing & likewise that hee hath two kine and one heffer stirke[6] and one swine and also getteth his fier within his one [i.e. own] ground which is more then any of us his neighbors hath'. In other words, the petition claimed, he had enough access to productive property to be at least partially self-sufficient.

(1) Access to land and natural resources
Topping's holding of land was probably his most effective safety net against poverty. Land was not only a productive resource in itself, but it could – if owned outright or held by secure customary tenures – be sold or leased to provide ready cash, or offered as security on loans in times of difficulty.[7] Over 2 per cent of petitioners mentioned the possession of cottages or small plots of land, either to say that this was all they had, or that they used to have land but had somehow lost it. George Noblet, a labourer of Broughton-in-Amounderness, reported in 1659 that he 'hath a little cottage wherein he now inhabiteth and a rood[8] of land which is all that this petitioner hath towards the maintenance of himselfe, his said wife and children besides your petitioners wages which he receives for day workes'.[9] Thomas Thornton of Borwick had, by 1691, sold off his 'poor cottage and a smale backside' to maintain himself in the face of old age and lameness, and gone to live with his brother.[10] Margaret Callon of Ashton-in-Makerfield told in 1687 of how her husband was sick, and the eldest of her seven children had been stricken with a cancer for two years; apparently, in order to get by, the family had leased out their house to their neighbour John Crank.[11] It seems as if land did not even have to

5   LA, QSP/215/19.
6   I.e. a heifer.
7   Cf. P. R. Schofield, 'The Social Economy of the Medieval Village in the Early Fourteenth Century', *EcHR*, 2nd Ser., 61, Supplement 1 (2008), 38–63.
8   A linear measure of between six and eight yards.
9   LA, QSP/174/29.
10   LA, QSP/700/19.
11   LA, QSP/633/14.

have been of especially good quality to have constituted a useful resource (though we must be wary of exaggeration). Thus, with a tangible sense of indignation, Anne Aynsworth of Pleasington petitioned for relief in 1669, claiming that she and her late husband had drawn income from five acres of 'blacke barren moore ground (beinge all her tenement) which had never had any tillage or husbandry on it', but that at her spouse's death their landlord had been 'glad to take [it] into his owne hands'.[12]

It is likely that in many parts, changes to the structure of landholding were reducing access to land. In upland areas there is evidence of a gradual reorganization of landholding into fewer hands in the seventeenth and eighteenth centuries, while some communities had a growing population of subtenants up to the early seventeenth century and (to an extent) beyond.[13] In industrializing areas, subdivision of holdings and an expansion of the population of cottagers living on the edge of manorial wastes led to an increase in the number of households having very limited access to land.[14] Furthermore, the general growth in the county's population, much of it concentrated in towns, will similarly have increased the number of households divorced from the land, though not necessarily from house ownership.[15] For many, however, it was probably not broad alterations in the agrarian economy which led to loss of landed resources, but the simple pressures of the life cycle. John Walker, for example, a husbandman from Claughton-in-Amounderness, stated in 1674 that he had possessed a cottage and half a roodland but was not now able to work it on account of his sickness and old age.[16] On the other hand, land held by a secure tenure could be alienated, often to a family member, in return for a fixed pension – usually in old age. Medieval historians have uncovered evidence of these arrangements well before the age of the Poor Law.[17] Evidently, however, they sometimes went wrong, and it is when they

12   LA, QSP/334/7; cf. QSP/435/20.
13   E.g. Hoyle and French, 'Land Market'; Healey, 'Agrarian Social Structure'; Healey, 'Land, Population and Famine'.
14   Tupling, *Economic History*, pp. 42–97, 161–8.
15   Urban common fields did exist, however: see, for example: H. R. French, 'Urban Common Rights, Enclosure and the Market: Clitheroe Town Moors, 1764–1802', *AgHR*, 51 (2003), 40–68.
16   LA, QSP/415/7.
17   E. Clark, 'Some Aspects of Social Security in Medieval England', *Journal of Family History*, 7 (1982), 307–20; R. M. Smith, 'The Manorial Court and the Elderly Tenant in Late Medieval England', in Pelling and Smith (eds), *Life, Death and the Elderly*, pp. 36–61; P. Horden, 'Household Care and Informal Networks: Comparisons and Continuities from

had broken down that we often catch a glimpse of such agreements.[18] In 1669, for example, John Rylough of Heysham lamented that

> when his eldest sonne came to be a man your petitioner thought to[o] good of his said sonne[,] conveyed his whole estate to him and in consideration thereof was content to cast him selfe upon the care and providence of his said sonne who in a short time wasted and mortgaged all or the most parte of the estate aforesaid [and] left his cuntrie and his ould father your petitioner both sorrowfull and poore.[19]

His grievance would have struck a chord with Elizabeth Cudworth of Moston, who eight years earlier complained that she 'haveinge formerly bestowed most of her substance uppon her sonne & his wife is nowe by them and their unnatural dealinge toward her enforced to leave her former habitacion and gett her relieffe out of the charity of her neighbors'.[20] Such petitions are not in themselves suggestive of a successful system of support for the aged, but we can reasonably assume that they were unrepresentative, and that in general such schemes must have worked, otherwise people would presumably have avoided them.

Common resources offered another potential source of income. It is well established that the poor were able to supplement their meagre incomes through gleaning, the gathering of wood, the collection of peat and the grazing of livestock on common land, amongst other traditional practices.[21] Moreover, when common lands were enclosed in this period, their privatization often incorporated the allocation of some of the new fields for the specific use of the poor, surely suggesting that the loss of access was of some immediate detriment.[22] And yet, surviving petitions

---

Antiquity to the Present', in *The Locus of Care: Families, Communities, Institutions and the Provision of Welfare since Antiquity*, ed. P. Horden and R. Smith (London, 1998), pp. 21–67 (p. 43).

18   Cf. A. Shepard, *Meanings of Manhood in Early Modern England* (Oxford, 2003), pp. 241–3.

19   LA, QSP/337/1; cf. LA, QSP/220/17.

20   LA, QSP/204/17.

21   E.g. P. King, 'Customary Rights and Women's Earnings: the Importance of Gleaning to the Rural Labouring Poor, 1750–1850', *EcHR*, 2nd Ser., 44 (1991), 461–76; Hindle, *On the Parish?*, pp. 27–48.

22   E.g. Hoyle and Spencer, 'Slaidburn Poor Pasture'; J. Broad, 'The Smallholder and Cottager after Disafforestation: a Legacy of Poverty?', in *Bernwood: the Life and Afterlife of a Forest*, ed. J. Broad and R. W. Hoyle (Preston, 1997), pp. 90–107 (pp. 92–101).

yield virtually no evidence of the use of common land by Lancashire's poor. Occasional exceptions do exist, but they are either ambivalent or oblique. During the dearth of the late 1640s, the son of blind 88-year-old Nicholas Bradell recounted how the poor in his home of Ribchester had traditionally collected wood in fields around the town.[23] However, while doing so recently, he had been threatened with indictment for theft before he could even 'get halfe a burden'. In the same parish, half a century later, John Dodds told in 1697 that he had a 'small peece of ground tacken of the common', however the enclosure would not pay for his wife and children because his house, lands and goods had been taken up by James Ettiforth for debt.[24] Agnes Braithwaite of Hawkshead, meanwhile, claimed in 1704 that she needed extra relief to pay 'to hire men to get turfe or fewell', undoubtedly referring to the peat she had previously collected from that township's extensive common fell.[25] But it is striking how infrequent are such references, and also how ambiguous; and this in a county which, at the time, had vast areas of common. Presumably this reflects the technical illegality of many cottagers using the commons. One needed to possess a commonable tenancy to do so, and Angus Winchester has shown that a number of upland manors were setting by-laws explicitly restricting the common rights of the poor (though this in itself shows such usage cannot have been unheard of).[26] Nonetheless, when local officers used the cottage-building clauses of the 1601 Poor Law to provide housing for the impotent, the land they used was – of course – the manorial wastes.[27] Thus, the surprising view from the petitions should not lead us to write common resources out of Lancashire's 'economy of makeshifts', though it clearly cautions us against placing too much emphasis on the common rights of the early modern poor.

Closely associated with access to land was the possession of livestock. It seems likely that some of the poor kept pigs and chickens: pigs, if allowed some space to roam, were incredibly – even notoriously – easy to feed and could thus be killed for a welcome bit of pork; chickens could be kept without hassle on a small plot, and provided a fairly consistent stream

23   LA, QSP/2/10.
24   LA, QSP/794/3.
25   LA, QSP/914/3.
26   Winchester, *Harvest of the Hills*, pp. 48, 79–81, 104, 115, 129, 132–3, 136; cf. L. Shaw-Taylor, 'Labourers, Cows, Common Rights and Parliamentary Enclosure: the Evidence of Contemporary Comment, c.1760–1810', *PP*, 171 (2001), 95–126 (p. 126).
27   Broad, 'Housing the Rural Poor'.

of eggs. Yet almost the only livestock mentioned in petitions were cattle. The reason for this was undoubtedly that cows were the most lucrative of animals. Jane Humphries, looking at the late eighteenth century, has calculated that possessing a cow could contribute as much as 40 per cent of a household budget in dairy produce.[28] So long as space could be found to graze them, then, cattle could be a major source of income for the poor. One petitioner in 1687, Jane Kellet of Brockholes, even wrote evocatively (perhaps proverbially) of how her one cow provided her the 'releeffe that cometh of beastes'.[29] In 1661, Alice Pemberton and her neighbours of Mawdsley reported that her family had possessed a cottage, a rood of ground, and a cow, but that now she was poor because her husband and her cow were dead.[30] James Whittaker, a cobbler of Tottington, claimed in 1663 to have 'sustayned greate losse by the death of three melch kyne which were the most part of your said petitioners substance and liveliehood'.[31] From another angle, this was one assumption behind the petition promoted against certain pensioners by the authorities of Blackrod in 1671, 'haveinge some of them cattell, others followinge games and others imployinge what the[y] gett by their labour in riotous and debaucht expences'.[32]

(2) Wages
It seems likely, however, that waged labour was a more important source of income than access to land. In fact, the gradual economic and specifically industrial growth in our period will undoubtedly have increased the availability of waged work, though the growth of employment will have been running in a constant race with population growth (which will have helped keep wage rates down).[33] There is a certain conceptual difficulty here, for a fully employed weaver was not really marginal, just as a household possessing an economically viable farm was not. Nonetheless, wage work will be treated here as a strategy of 'making shift' for three reasons. First, there is a large body of evidence showing a

28   J. Humphries, 'Enclosures, Common Rights, and Women: the Proletarianisation of Families in the Late Eighteenth and Early Nineteenth Centuries', *Journal of Economic History*, 50 (1990), 17–42 (pp. 21–32).
29   LA, QSP/636/4.
30   LA, QSP/211/16.
31   LA, QSP/236/53.
32   LA, QSP/364/10.
33   Muldrew, 'Th'ancient Distaff'.

close relationship between industrial work and the poor; not for nothing did industrialists often describe their workers as 'the poor'. Secondly, pockets of industry were able to maintain a large number of households whose economies were significantly more fragile and marginal than those of small farmers.[34] And thirdly, as will become clear from what follows, industrial work was available to many of those who were too weak for most farmwork.

Textile manufacture was especially suitable for the poor because many of its strands, spinning in particular, were relatively low skilled and suitable for weak hands.[35] As the anonymous *Ease for Overseers of the Poore* put it in 1601, the spinning of flax into thread for linen, the carding and spinning of wool into yarn for woollen, and the bunching of hemp, were especially recommended for the poor, 'as they are workes soone compassed by any that are capable of wit', as well as being 'things very vendible to put away when they are done'.[36] Quite apart from this, they did not require much physical strength, making them especially important to those whose bodies were aged and weak, or to children. Indeed, a number of eighteenth-century commentators (most obviously Daniel Defoe) highlighted the opportunities for child employment in manufacturing.[37] And there are plenty of specific references to the role played by the textile industries in employing Lancashire's poor.[38] Several petitioners mentioned spinning, occasionally with the very strong implication that it was a trade for the physically weak. Alice Simpson, a Skerton petitioner, told Lancaster JPs in 1658 of how she had worked as a servant but 'when she did grow an age and lesse able to serve, she gott her relieffe by spninge and other her hand labour', though even this had become too hard in her stricken years.[39] Despite being 'very weake, and sometimes lame by the Evill', and being 'constrained to keepe her bed 2 or 3 dayes together

34 D. C. Coleman, 'Proto-industrialisation: a Concept Too Many?', *EcHR*, 2nd Ser., 36 (1983), 435–48; L. A. Clarkson, *Proto-Industrialization: The First Phase of Industrialization?* (Basingstoke, 1984), pp. 39–41; Walton, 'Proto-industrialisation'.

35 Muldrew has recently suggested that we should not underestimate the skill involved in spinning: Muldrew, 'Th'ancient Distaff', p. 500. This said, as the following hopefully illustrates, it was nonetheless often viewed as relatively unskilled, and it remained far less lucrative than many other forms of employment.

36 *An Ease for Overseers*, p. 21.

37 H. Cunningham, 'The Employment and Unemployment of Children in England, c.1680–1851', *PP*, 126 (1990), 115–50 (pp. 128–9).

38 E.g. Hill, *Century of Revolution*, p. 19.

39 LA, QSP/153/7.

sometimes longer', and 'not able to come to the fyre without helpe, nor forth of the doore for any use', Elizabeth Berry of Dalton still apparently earned money by spinning in 1687.[40] Similarly, in 1699, Sarah Crompton of Kearsley petitioned that she was weak and unhealthy, her husband lame, and that neither of them were able to work at anything 'save only spinynge of fustian when they can get anye'.[41]

There is other evidence, too. In the 1630s, justices of Bury Division reported that they had not needed to put poor children out as apprentices thanks to the employment provided by the town's woollen industries.[42] According to a letter by John Assheton, the poor around Clitheroe in the 1690s spent the winter spinning flaxen yarn to raise extra cash.[43] Similarly, William Stout noted the impact that fluctuations in the textile industries could have on the livelihoods of the poor, recounting in 1723, for example, that 'our linnen manufactors and spining at good prices, the poor subsisted well this year'.[44] More generally, he reported that year that the 'late act for prohibiting the wearing of calicos and other East India goods has very much advanced our linnen and woollen manufactores, and advanced spining 3d in a shilling', which was 'a great encuragement to the poor'.[45]

Some of the best evidence comes from the cotton-manufacturing region. In 1637, the justices of Bolton-le-Moors and Deane parishes reported that they had not needed to put forth many poor children as apprentices 'by reason of the greate tradeing of fustians and woollen cloth ... whereof the inhabitants have contynuall imployment for their children in spinning and other necessary labor about the same'.[46] Nearly four decades later, a similar claim was made by the town of Bolton, whose overseers petitioned to Manchester Sessions that 'when the fustian trade went well most of them [i.e. the poor] were employed as spinners or weavers of fustian and lived very well thereby without beeing burdensome'.[47] Finally, during the dispute over the plan for a workhouse in Manchester in 1730–31,

40 LA, QSP/629/20.
41 LA, QSP/833/31.
42 TNA, SP16/383/55, Report of the Justices of Bury Division, 17 August 1637.
43 HMC, *Kenyon*, John Assheton to Roger Kenyon, 10 January 1695, pp. 372–3.
44 Stout, *Autobiography*, p. 189.
45 Ibid., p. 188, cf. p. 231.
46 TNA, SP16/364/122, Report of the Justices of Bolton Division, July 1637; cf. *Seventeenth-Century Economic Documents*, p. 258.
47 LA, QSP/413/14.

opponents of the scheme claimed that 'the variety of manufactures carried on in the town, affords a constant supply of work to the poor of both sexes, of what age soever'.[48]

The listings of the poor compiled for the small town of Bolton in the late seventeenth century allow us to quantify some of the support provided by textile industries, in this case to those explicitly in receipt of poor relief.[49] The censuses record the occupations of the majority of household heads, and while the specific area of textile manufacture they were engaged in was rarely mentioned, we can be fairly certain that most were making fustian. Some 64 per cent of male heads receiving regular relief in 1686 and 1699 were working in textiles (predominantly weaving), while the comparative figure for female heads was as high as 83 per cent. All but one of these women were spinners.

In fact, the figures show that not only were many of the 'poor' engaged in textile work, but also that it was relatively successful in providing them with an income. The censuses give figures for the total 'weekly get' of each pauper household, and the amount that they were paid by the parish. It is possible, therefore, to work out what proportion of their recorded income was provided by their work, and what came through poor relief, and these calculations are presented in Tables 3–4. Of course, there are various complicating factors which prevent the simplistic reading of these data. For example, while the seventeen male spinning households were apparently less self-sufficient than the eight headed by labourers, this was no doubt affected by the much higher average age amongst the former. Moreover, the very fact that individuals were included in such lists shows that their efforts to subsist through work had been unsuccessful. This all said, the data do suggest that waged textile work could make a significant contribution to the livelihoods of the poor. If Craig Muldrew is correct in his estimation that up to 650,000 married women could have been spinning wool by the middle of the eighteenth century, then this will have acted as a major cushion against poverty for many of England's most marginal people.[50]

There is, as we might expect, further evidence relating to wage labour in the pauper petitions and censuses. In the Bolton censuses in 1686 and 1699, there were ten households headed by individuals undertaking

48   Walton, *Lancashire*, p. 91.
49   BALS, PBO/1/1, Bolton Censuses of the Poor, 1686 and 1699.
50   Muldrew, 'Th'ancient Distaff', p. 518.

Table 3: Household poverty by occupation (male-headed households) in Bolton, 1686 and 1699

Occupation of household head	No.	Mean age	% of income provided by parish
Husbandman	13	45	19
Labourer	8	44	27
Weaver	46	48	20
Other textile	6	55	21
No recorded occupation	25	56	38
Others	17	53	23
Spinner	17	61	47
Past labour	6	79	100
Overall	138	53	26

Table 4: Household poverty by occupation (female-headed households) in Bolton, 1686 and 1699

Occupation of household head	No.	Mean age	% of income provided by parish
No recorded occupation	18	69	82
Spinners (and one carder)	89	55	37
Overall	107	56	42

various irregular work.[51] Some petitioners, meanwhile, told of engaging in odd jobs and irregular forms of employment. Mancunian Anne Harmson, whose husband had been pressed to the forces, could only earn money (she petitioned in 1651) on 'such daies as some neighbores hath neede to sett her to worke', suggesting that she did odd jobs in the neighbourhood.[52] In his petition of 1654, Thomas Rothmell, alias Cooke of Blackley, described his work as incorporating cooking, gardening and husbandry.[53] Anthony Higginson of Priest Hutton recalled in 1656 that, when able of body, he

51 Cf. LA, QSP/413/8.
52 LA, QSP/56/10.
53 LA, QSP/100/22.

had undertaken 'soe hard a labour or another lawfull calling as killing of foxes, badgers and other devouring creatures which he much used when he was not otherwise imployed'.[54] John Dawson of Hornby reported in 1663 that while his eyesight was good he had lived by 'digin grubinge and getinge and setinge of quickwoode and such like labours'.[55] John Simpson of Haigh lived even more precariously. His 1681 petition to justices at Manchester was backed by a personal appeal from Sir Roger Bradshaw, who witticized that Simpson 'hath a (lowd) calling, though not a lowdable one, being only a pittifull pyper'. However, said Bradshaw, '(except at my house in a Christmas) I beleeve hee gets very little by it'.[56] Ale-selling was another form of petty employment undertaken by the poor. According to Wrightson, the licence to sell ale was 'a pension which cost the parish nothing and allowed the poor the dignity of maintaining themselves in a manner useful to the community'.[57] But it was always subject to regulation and restriction. This peaked during the Interregnum when a sustained campaign by Lancashire justices appears to have reduced the number of functioning alehouses, but there were also later complaints of the detrimental impact of government regulation.[58] Margaret Thornton of Pilling, for example, claimed poverty in 1674 because the exciseman had seized her goods when she tried to sell ale.[59] The same year, Richard Nicholson of Silverdale stated that his wife had sold ale but had 'desisted from that profession and practice ever since Midsummer last or longer by reason of the excessive demaundes and charge of excise', though he admitted that another factor lay in the 'verie small sale of her comoditie, dwelling in a place not apt and commodious to bee frequented or resorted unto'.[60]

Service, like ale-selling, was a common form of employment amongst poor women. Alice Fawcett of Over Kellet petitioned for relief in 1652, recounting that she 'hath beene a sarvant above forttie yeares' but was now grown old, 'into great decay and misserie'.[61] Contracts for servants were often short, so they might find it difficult to gain a settlement; such was the lament of Agnes Burrow of Priest Hutton, who told justices in

54   LA, QSP/129/5.
55   LA, QSP/245/17.
56   LA, QSP/530/9–10.
57   Wrightson, 'Puritan Reformation', p. 85.
58   Ibid., pp. 142, 188.
59   LA, QSP/415/5.
60   LA, QSP/414/18.
61   LA, QSP/61/5.

1673 that she had 'for severall years by past beene willing to officiate as a servant where shee could gett imployment; but not beeing able to officiate as a servant either for a yeare or halfe a yeare (for the space of seaven years last past) shee hath beene tossed up & downe from place to place without any settled residence'.[62] In the parish registers of Whittington, meanwhile, the clerk took it upon himself to note the life of household service of Jane Canfield, when she was buried in June 1676. She died at the age of eighty-four, being 'most of her time a true servant in divers good houses, some few years in her old age had her reliefe out of the parish poore stock[,] never married'.[63]

(3) Migration

Many marginal people migrated in search of work. The extent to which the Poor Laws, and especially those relating to settlement, either hindered or facilitated labour movement has exercised pens from contemporary times to the present.[64] Famously, Adam Smith argued that the law of settlement restricted the poor's freedom to move, but there have been opposing voices too. James Stephen Taylor, for example, drawing to a significant extent on evidence from the North West, argued that townships in the early nineteenth century were prepared to support labour migration through

---

62 LA, QSP/393/11.

63 *The Registers of the Parish Church of Whittington in the County of Lancaster, 1538–1764*, ed. F. Wrigley and T. H. Winder (LPRS, iii, Rochdale, 1899), p. 111.

64 E.g. A. Smith, *The Wealth of Nations*, New edn (New York, 2003), pp. 191–4; N. Landau, 'The Laws of Settlement and the Surveillance of Immigration in Eighteenth-century Kent', *Continuity and Change*, 3 (1988), 391–420; N. Landau, 'The Regulation of Immigration, Economic Structures and Definitions of the Poor in Eighteenth-century England', *Historical Journal*, 33 (1990), 541–72; N. Landau, 'Who Was Subjected to the Laws of Settlement? Procedure under the Settlement Laws in Eighteenth-Century England', *AgHR*, 43 (1995), 139–59; cf. J. S. Taylor, 'The Impact of Pauper Settlement, 1691–1834', *PP*, 73 (1976), 42–74; Snell, *Annals*; K. D. M. Snell, 'Pauper Settlement and the Right to Poor Relief in England and Wales', *Continuity and Change*, 6 (1991), 375–415; K. D. M. Snell, *Parish and Belonging: Community, Identity and Welfare in England and Wales, 1700–1950* (Cambridge, 2006); D. Feldman, 'Migrants, Immigrants and Welfare from the Old Poor Law to the Welfare State', *TRHS*, 6th Ser., 13 (2003), 79–104. On migration: P. Clark and D. Souden (eds), *Migration and Society in Early Modern England* (London, 1987); I. D. Whyte, *Migration and Society in Britain, 1500–1830* (Basingstoke, 2000). Specifically on pauper migration: P. Slack, 'Vagrants and Vagrancy in England, 1598–1664', *EcHR*, 2nd Ser., 27 (1974), 360–79; Beier, *Masterless Men*; J. R. Kent, 'Population Mobility and Alms: Poor Migrants in the Midlands during the Early Seventeenth Century', *LPS*, 27 (1981), 35–51.

the mechanisms of 'out-relief'.[65] This constituted a practical solution to the problem of local variations in demand, and involved an individual or family's parish of origin agreeing to support them should they become poor by endorsing a 'settlement certificate'. This they did in the knowledge that their migration to locations with more vibrant economies meant that the chances of this situation arising were significantly reduced.[66]

There is much less information for the earlier period: overseers' accounts are few and far between, and where extant they tend to be less detailed than nineteenth-century papers. Indeed, it has been suggested that the lack of circulating cash before the later eighteenth century imposed major practical difficulties on parishes wishing to deploy such out-relief.[67] This said, the accounts for Atherton do contain some references to paupers clearly living outside the township, including James Aldred of Wakefield (West Riding) in 1714/15 and regular payments to widow Mary Harrison in Ireland between 1711 and 1725.[68] Petitions, on the other hand, frequently show evidence of migration amongst the poor, notably when supplicants claimed to have lived in their current township for a period of years lower than their age. Movement can also be inferred from cases such as the 1640 petition of Elizabeth Heap of Ormskirk, who stated that two of her children had been born in Prescot, one in Ormskirk and one in Halsall.[69] On the other hand, it was unusual for petitioners to recount their movements in much detail, presumably to avoid awkward questions about settlement. There is, however, one explicit case of out-relief, from 1706. A petition by Thomas Banks, a Bolton fustian-weaver, was sent to Wigan Sessions with the support of the parish officers, asking that the township of Golborne relieve him. He had two small children, a pregnant wife, and was in bad health and weak of body; moreover, at the time – the petition stated – 'the fustian trade goes very badly'. It seems that Banks hailed originally from Golborne, but had been apprenticed as a fustian-weaver in Tottington within Bury parish. He had married five years ago in Bolton, where he evidently now lived, but

65   J. S. Taylor, 'A Different Kind of Speenhamland: Nonresident Relief in the Industrial Revolution', *Journal of British Studies*, 30 (1991), 183–208.

66   Ibid., pp. 192–207; Taylor, 'Voices in the Crowd', pp. 109–26; King, *Poverty and Welfare*, p. 186; S. King, '"It is impossible for our Vestry to judge his case into perfection from here": Managing the Distance Dimensions of Poor Relief, 1800–40', *Rural History*, 16 (2005), 161–89.

67   Muldrew and King, 'Cash, Wages and the Economy of Makeshifts', p. 160.

68   WA, TR/Ath/C/2/2–5, Atherton Overseers' Accounts, 1704–33.

69   LA, QSB/1/230/36.

trade was bad, and he was too weak to work in husbandry. Were Golborne not to pay a pension, the petition stated, the officers of Bolton were likely to remove him there. However, he pointed out, 'if your poore petitioner bee removed into Golborne where there is no tradeinge in fustians', and 'your petitioner being unable to worke at anythinge else', then he 'is either like to starve or bee exceedingly burdensome to them there'. If, on the other hand, 'hee remaine in Bolton', then 'both hee and his wife can both of them doe somthing towards a livelihood'.[70]

In reality, of course, poverty, migration, and the law existed in a complex symbiosis. Poverty might force people to migrate, but their migration itself might leave them in a position of vulnerability, far away from their kin. The law, meanwhile, might either restrict their ability to move, or force them on to the road to return to a place of 'settlement' many miles from their actual home.[71] Economic fluctuations might impact upon the politics of labour mobility too. Alice Howorth's petition for a house in Livesey, submitted to Preston Sessions in 1662 just after the laws of settlement had been codified, gives some sense of this.[72] It claimed that Howorth and her husband John had lived there for two years after their marriage but, 'by reason of the decay of tradinge and beinge in want were forced since the first of May last to seeke relief where wee could[,] but the lawe beinge more strictly put in execucion by cause of theis hard tymes your poore petitioner was forced againe to her native countrie'.

The extent to which the poor engaged in *seasonal* migration is very hard to gauge: such movement rarely left a documentary trail. Olwen Hufton found it to be one of the chief ways in which the French poor 'made shift' in the late eighteenth century, but evidence for seventeenth- and eighteenth-century Lancashire is very sparse.[73] Humphrey Leathwaite of Ainsdale stated in 1661 that he had made his living 'following the sea, and keepeing the marketts all about the country in or neere this country', which suggests a migratory life.[74] Anne Bradley's husband, from Bailey, went as a harvest worker to Lincolnshire and Cambridgeshire, where he

70 Taylor, 'Different Kind of Speenhamland'.
71 M. E. Fissell, 'The "Sick and Drooping Poor" in Eighteenth-century Bristol and its Region', *Social History of Medicine*, 2 (1989)', 35–58 (pp. 38–9, 49–50); King, 'Reconstructing Lives', pp. 330–8; S. Barrett, 'Kinship, Poor Relief and the Welfare Process in Early Modern England', in King and Tomkins (eds), *Poor in England*, pp. 199–227.
72 LA, QSP/226/3.
73 Hufton, *Poor of Eighteenth-Century France*, pp. 69–106.
74 LA, QSP/207/37.

fell sick and died – but it is uncertain from her petition (in 1692) whether he would ever have returned.[75] One of the Bolton paupers in 1699, meanwhile, was recorded as 'gone a haymaking', leaving his lame wife at home.[76] But such clear examples are rare.

(4) Sales, credit and cost-cutting

A life of labour generally allowed poor households to build up a stock, however meagre, of personal and household goods which could then be sold for emergency cash.[77] In fact, the sale of acquired goods emerges from our petitions as a significant survival strategy. Nearly 6 per cent of first-time petitioners claimed to have sold all or most of their goods before asking for relief from their township. When, for example, the wife of John Woorall of Skelmersdale was left lame by complications at childbirth some time before 1652, he 'spent and sould all his goodes hee had for and towards the recovery of hir health upon phisicke and surdgery as long as hee could make shift'.[78] Jane Scolfield of Bury, widowed for twenty years by 1663, told justices that she had now 'sould upp her goods beddinge and apparrell for to bye foode'.[79] Henry Hilton of Samlesbury petitioned for relief in 1679, being old 'and almost dark sighted', stating not only that he had 'sustained greate loss by death of cattell', but that to stave off indigence he had sold all of his and his wife's goods.[80] In 1693, Jane Eaton found herself stranded in Liverpool when, 'coming in too this Kingdom aboute sume bisniss', she was taken ill. She was sick for four months, and although she had since recovered and 'wolde faine goo home too my one cuntry if posible I colde', she was unable because 'for want for I was forst too sell what close I hade to relive me in my sicknes soo that my condition is very misirable'.[81] At Easter in 1699, justices at Manchester heard of Robert Drinkwater, a labouring man of the town, who had been forced to sell all his 'best goods' to maintain himself and his wife, so he had 'nothing left now for to sell but the bed that we lye on'.[82] By the turn of

---

75   LA, QSP/708/9.
76   BALS, PBO/1/1, Bolton Census of the Poor, 1699.
77   Cf. King, *Poverty and Welfare*, p. 78.
78   LA, QSP/63/24; for a similar case, see J. Bailey, *Unquiet Lives: Marriage and Marriage Breakdown in England, 1660–1800* (Cambridge, 2003), p. 189.
79   LA, QSP/240/7.
80   LA, QSP/508/13.
81   LA, QSP/727/29.
82   LA, QSP/828/7.

the century, some of the poor may even have sold their hair to wigmakers for cash.[83] Material possessions were thus not just held for immediate functions, they were – in a world before savings banks – perhaps the best way for those of limited means to store their meagre wealth. Certainly this was the explicit sentiment of Christopher Cundliffe of Salford, when he claimed in a 1669 petition that he had for four years 'lived on those goods which in fortymes by providence and great labor hee had reserved for such a tyme as old age when labor is past'.[84] He was echoing the words of the agriculturalist Thomas Tusser, who rhymed that 'youth bids us labour, to get what wee can, for age is a burthen to labouring man'.[85]

Credit was another way to raise cash. Studies of probate records have highlighted the constant stream of borrowing between neighbours: cash swirled around villages and communities as the desire to buy and sell outstripped the supply of coin.[86] Thus the marginal often had surprisingly open access to credit and petitions abound with references to borrowing and indebtedness. John Oldham of Moston, for example, reported in 1664 that he was 'indebte unto severall persons for sustenance and other necessaries'.[87] George Sedden, a butcher from Kearsley, petitioned in 1668 that he had 'run into dett to severall neighbours towards his manetey-nance' after he had become bedridden.[88] Labourer William Haslome of Breightmet, asking for relief for himself, his lame wife and seven children in 1682, reported how 'by reason of his great charge and bread corne beinge soe deare' he was 'now become much indebted'.[89] A number of petitioners mentioned that they had put goods in pawn in order to raise cash.[90] John Woorall had, in 1652, pawned ten shillings worth of bedding

83   E. Cockayne, *Hubbub: Filth, Noise and Stench in England, 1600–1770* (London, 2007), p. 67.
84   LA, QSP/336/15; cf. QSP/350/10; Gough, *History of Myddle*, p. 191.
85   T. Tusser, *Five Hundred Points of Good Husbandry*, 1614 edn (London, 1614), p. 16.
86   Muldrew, *Economy of Obligation*, pp. 98–103.
87   LA, QSP/252/6.
88   LA, QSP/324/13.
89   LA, QSP/555/18.
90   B. Lemire, *The Business of Everyday Life: Gender, Practice and Social Politics in England, c.1600–1900* (Manchester, 2005), pp. 95–105; There is surprisingly little mention of pawning in literature on the early modern period, but see: K. Wrightson, 'Alehouses, Order and Reformation in Rural England, 1590–1660', in *Popular Culture and Class Conflict, 1590–1914: Explorations in the History of Labour and Leisure*, ed. E. Yeo and S. Yeo (Brighton, 1981), pp. 1–27 (p. 17); P. Clark, *The English Alehouse: A Social History, 1200–1830* (London, 1983), pp. 137–8, 229; Muldrew, *Economy of Obligation*,

to help pay for the treatment of his sick wife.[91] Before petitioning in 1658, John Percivall – a blind blacksmith from Manchester – ran himself 'much in debt and ingaged his worke tooles to severall persons who have lent your petitioner severall great sumes of money'.[92] Elizabeth Brookes of Reddish stated in 1672 that she had pawned her only cow to one John Ardene 'for more than shee is worth'.[93]

Notwithstanding the above, the availability of credit undoubtedly had limits. Margaret Halworth, a widow of Catterall, complained in 1687 that her husband, 'ungratious & cruall' as he was, had left her in debt and unable to get credit.[94] The same year John Heaton, a 58-year-old Whittingham labourer petitioned that he was poor, and that although he had a cow, he needed to rent ground to keep her on, but was no longer able to do so, 'his creadit beinge gone by reason of his povertie'.[95] Agnes Braithwaite found that when her allowance was stopped by Hawkshead's overseers, she was left thirty shillings in debt, petitioning in 1705 that she could 'no longer subsist by reason shee cannot any further upon credit buy things necessary for her maintenance unless that shee have ready money to pay withal'.[96] Quite obviously, the poor were less likely to repay their debts than the more economically secure. Indeed, so risky were those loans to poor relatives, friends and neighbours, that – if Muldrew's calculation is correct – more money was redistributed to the poor through the forgiving of bad debts than through the formal Poor Law.[97]

Finally, a rather different strategy was for poor households to trim back their income in line with falling incomes. The willingness of people to 'trade down' from expensive grains such as wheat to cheaper ones such as barley is well known to historians of dearth.[98] In the North West,

---

pp. 303–4; Hindle, *On the Parish?*, p. 80. For the later eighteenth century see: A. Tomkins, 'Pawnbroking and the Survival Strategies of the Urban Poor in 1770s York', in King and Tomkins (eds), *Poor in England*, pp. 166–98; Tomkins, *Experience of Urban Poverty*, pp. 204–34.

91   LA, QSP/63/26.
92   LA, QSP/156/7.
93   LA, QSP/384/14.
94   LA, QSP/636/12.
95   LA, QSP/636/5.
96   LA, QSP/930/1.
97   Muldrew, *Economy of Obligation*, pp. 304–5.
98   Appleby, *Famine*, p. 113; A. B. Appleby, 'Diet in Sixteenth-century England: Sources, Problems, Possibilities', in *Health, Medicine and Mortality in the Sixteenth Century*, ed. C. Webster (Cambridge, 1979), pp. 97–116 (pp. 112–13); A. B. Appleby, 'Grain Prices and

however, these cheaper grains were already the staple foodstuffs; so while living costs in general were lower, the ability to trade down during a crisis was in all likelihood seriously curtailed. Moreover, the research of Carole Shammas suggests that up to the middle of the seventeenth century the northern labourer had exceptionally little 'spare' income with which to absorb fluctuations in the cost of food.[99] The appearance of the potato by the 1670s is almost certainly of great significance, for it provided another source of cheap sustenance.[100] It is uncertain whether potatoes were common enough at this point to provide much extra security for the poor against the failure of the main winter-sown crops, but the appearance of a specialized market at Wigan by the 1680s suggests their widespread use in that district at least.[101] In 1701, Henry Draper of Dalton, a township within Wigan parish, mentioned in his petition for relief that he had 'set a few potatos and soed a little corne towards the relieveing of him and his poor familly this wintar', though he had subsequently been forced to sell them.[102] By the 1720s, potatoes were well established and in 1727 William Stout recorded that despite rising prices generally they proved 'plenty and cheap ... which was releife to the poor'.[103]

Savings could also be made on other essential goods. It was in no way desirable, but when poor households found the cost of housing too high they could sometimes board in single rooms or even outbuildings.[104] In 1642, one young man from Billinge near Wigan even claimed that he had 'noe habitation but lives in a hole under the ground'.[105] Perhaps he was exaggerating his predicament, but his case convinced justices at Ormskirk, who ordered him relieved forthwith. Much more acceptable to modern sensibilities, and presumably also to paupers of the time, was the

Subsistence Crises in England and France, 1590–1740', *Journal of Economic History*, 39 (1979), 865–87 (pp. 871–87).

99   C. Shammas, 'Food Expenditures and Economic Well-being in Early Modern England', *Journal of Economic History*, 43 (1983), 89–100 (p. 97).

100   There are numerous references to potatoes in: Fell, *Household Account Book*, *passim*.

101   Salaman, *History and Social Influence*, pp. 451–2.

102   LA, QSP/868/5.

103   LA, DDCl/400, Steward's Accounts, 1707–29; Stout, *Autobiography*, pp. 201, 204, 206, 213, 231. On the other hand, it was not until the 1730s that potatoes were being sold regularly at Kendal market: Bingham, *Kendal*, p. 145.

104   Mitchison, 'Who Were the Poor', p. 140; Ben-Amos, 'Gifts and Favors', pp. 317–19; Boulton, 'It is extreme necessity', p. 56.

105   LA, QSB/1/266/73.

purchase of second-hand clothing.[106] There is little direct evidence of this in petitions, but the fact that many paupers claimed to have sold items of clothing ('both bed clothes and back clothes', as some put it) bears testimony to an active market for such material.

Dependence on others: kin, neighbours and charity

So far we have discussed ways in which the marginal poor tried to maintain self-sufficiency. But sometimes this was not possible, and individuals and households were forced to look to others to support them. Apart from the Poor Law, there were also other avenues of redistributive support which could be exploited. As one historian has put it, 'organized and institutionalized relief in all its forms was probably only the tip of the iceberg in a range of support that was provided through webs of much less formal relations'.[107] In particular, help might be forthcoming from kin, from neighbours, or begged from complete strangers. At the same time, more formal or institutionalized forms of charity such as funeral doles, gifts in wills, and local endowments might also contribute.

(1) The support of kin
Kin support was an obvious way of making ends meet for the seriously poor, as much as for anyone else, and over 3 per cent of petitioners mentioned being helped by their kin or 'friends'.[108] According to a petition in 1654, endorsed by his neighbours, ninety-year-old Bryan Byrom of Windle would have starved without the support of his son.[109] When the Pennington children of Billinge were orphaned, it was reported in 1652, they were maintained in the first place by their aunt.[110] Fifteen-year-old orphan Jane Parke of Out Rawcliffe told justices in 1675 that she was being looked after by her uncle out of 'love & respecte'.[111] One petitioner from Hornby even stated with refreshing honesty in 1659 that he and his wife

---

106   B. Lemire, *Fashion's Favourite: the Cotton Trade and the Consumer in Britain, 1660–1800* (Oxford, 1991), pp. 61–76, 176–9.

107   Ben-Amos, 'Gifts and Favors', pp. 295–6. Also, Ben-Amos, *Culture of Giving*.

108   Cf. Gough, *History of Myddle*, p. 101; Hindle, *On the Parish?*, pp. 48–58; Boulton, 'It is extreme necessity', pp. 57–64; Hudson, 'Ex-servicemen', pp. 47–8, 296–7.

109   LA, QSP/103/7.

110   LA, QSP/63/39.

111   LA, QSP/431/5.

had 'twoe sonnes whome ... [they] tenderly brought up and nourished and dearly loved in hope they should have had comfort in them and help from them in this their decreped ould age'.[112] But the two had gone into Scotland during the wars and had not returned.[113] Such familial help might not always be directly monetary in character. According to his 1652 petition, Edmund Sudell, a blind weaver of Fishwick, was forced to 'entreate his brother which is a poore workeman to lead him from dore to dore to gett a livelyhood'.[114] In 1661, Lettice Gleast claimed that in her old age and blindness she was forced to rely upon a grandchild who 'doth daily beg for her releefe'.[115]

Some of these supportive relationships were specifically enforceable under the terms of the 1601 statute. According to the Act, vertical kin (except grandchildren) were directly responsible for the upkeep of their poor relatives:

> the father and grandfather, and the mother and grandmother, and the children, of everie poore olde blinde lame and impotent person, or other poore person not able to worke, beinge of a sufficient abilitie, shall at their owne chardges releeve and mantaine everie such poore person ...

Indeed, JPs did enforce this provision, though apparently relatively rarely.[116] They intervened in the case of Esther Freeman of Salford, for example, whose yeoman husband had enlisted in the army, but before doing so had left her unable to work through his 'beateing & bruseing' of her. She had gone to live with her father, but his wife (her stepmother), had turned her out of the house and taken all her goods. On Esther's petition in 1692, magistrates ordered the stepmother to maintain her.[117] In practice, though, the net of support could also be cast much wider than that ordered by the 1601 statute.[118] The best summary, albeit in the negative,

---

112   LA, QSP/177/1.

113   Cf. A. Macfarlane, *The Family Life of Ralph Josselin, a Seventeenth-century Clergyman: An Essay in Historical Anthropology* (Cambridge, 1970), pp. 149–51, 167–92; A. Macfarlane, *Marriage and Love in England: Modes of Reproduction, 1300–1840* (Oxford, 1986), pp. 145–7.

114   LA, QSP/70/6.

115   LA, QSP/215/23.

116   Ottaway, 'Providing for the Elderly', pp. 397–8.

117   LA, QSP/711/9.

118   Cf. Slack, *Poverty and Policy*, pp. 84–5; Smith, 'Ageing and Well-being', pp. 64–5; Boulton, 'It is extreme necessity', p. 63.

comes from a petition in support of Edward Scorer, a sick journeyman-tailor from Leigh, which stated that he 'hath neither parentes, uncles, auntes, brother, sister, or any of his kinne now living to relye upon'.[119] I have found a total of ninety-three descriptions of kinship support in surviving petitions, almost always stating that such support *had* existed but was now exhausted or impossible. Of these, seven were unspecific references to support by and for relatives, seventeen involved parents supporting grown-up children, thirteen saw support by brothers and three support by sisters (including one sister-in-law). Three cases saw grand-mothers supporting grandchildren, while there is one example of a grand-father who did so. There are two cases of support by uncles, one by an aunt, one by a cousin, one by a nephew and another by a niece's husband. The most common supportive relationship, however, saw children giving support to their parents, of which there were forty-three cases. It is striking that seventy-six out of the ninety-three cases (82 per cent) saw support flowing between siblings or between parents and children. We should be a little circumspect about this – the fact that support between parents, grandparents, and children could be enforced by statute will have encouraged some petitioners to point out that such support was no longer tenable. Nonetheless, it does seem to suggest – perhaps paradoxically – that support existed beyond the immediate nuclear household, even if it tended to flow between kin who were *formerly* members of the same nuclear family.

Of course, long-term support of relatives could place intolerable burdens on those called upon to help. According to her 1654 petition, sick Margaret Bannister of Ashton (near Lancaster) 'wasted both her sisters substance and her owne in seekinge for remedie'.[120] In 1655, Ellin Law of Wheelton claimed that 'for three yeares and a halfe last past ... [she] hath beene mainteyned by her daughter who hadd gotten some smale meanes in service': however, the costs of supporting a blind, lame, 77-year-old widow had meant that she had 'now quit[e] consumed the same'.[121] Labourer James Livesey of Pleasington, who had 'no substance but what he gets by the sweat of his brow', had by 1698 been ruined by having his lame daughter-in-law and her two children placed with him by the overseers; 'by endeavouring to keep 'em he has reduced himself

119   LA, QSB/1/134/60.
120   LA, QSP/101/4.
121   LA, QSP/107/3.

to such strait poverty that, haveing but one cow, he hath been forced to sell her'.[122] Occasionally, petitioners stated explicitly that their offspring were having difficulty supporting their relatives in old age because they now had children of their own. Richard Smith has suggested that such a confluence was common in the demographic world of pre-industrial England, and there are a number of such cases in the petitions.[123] Thus, in 1631, William Ticole complained to Wigan Sessions that he had nothing but 'what meanes his childrene could afford them, and they now haveinge charge of children are not able to releive them as heretofore they have donne'.[124] In 1671, William Houghton of Eccleston successfully petitioned that he had hitherto been

> releeved & manteyned by the industry & handy labour of John Houghton his sonne but your petitioners said sonne hath a wife and two little children haveinge noe estate but what by his owne labour & dayly worke hee getteth is much depaupered & very poore & not able further to manteyne or releefe his aforesaid father.[125]

A similar problem was felt by Margary Martan, a lame spinster of Hutton, who claimed in 1664 that since her father's death she had been kept by her brother Robert, but 'hir said brother marrying, hath a charg of children & soe hath turnd your poor petitioner out of doores'.[126]

It was quite common, in fact, for petitioners to complain in general terms of a lack of nearby relatives, thus helping to explain their dependence on the Poor Law. Indeed, Mary Fissell has suggested, in her study of eighteenth-century Bristol, that a deficiency of local kin and 'friends' was a key factor in determining who needed poor relief.[127] Steve King's family reconstitution studies of Calverley in the West Riding, meanwhile, found that those with no co-resident kin were significantly more likely to need poor relief at some stage than those who *did* have relatives in the township.[128] This would have resonated with some petitioners. Thomasine Wood of

---

122   LA, QSP/818/1.
123   R. M. Smith, 'The Structured Dependency of the Elderly as a Recent Development: Some Sceptical Historical Thoughts', *Ageing and Society*, 4 (1984), 409–28 (pp. 417–19); Smith, 'Ageing and Well-being', p. 68.
124   LA, QSB/1/82/48.
125   LA, QSP/363/15.
126   LA, QSP/259/1.
127   Fissell, 'Sick and Drooping Poor'.
128   King, 'Reconstructing Lives', p. 331.

Withington, for example, claimed relief in 1657 when her husband ran away and while her 'good frends' were 'far of[f]'.[129] A petition representing the children of Rachel Mollineaux, meanwhile, pointed out that they had come over from Ireland, and therefore had no friends.[130] Indeed, a lack of 'friends' was perhaps something suffered with more frequency by the aged, who found that their kin gradually died around them. Hence the petition of 75-year-old Andrew Bury of Middleton, who told in 1698 of how he and his wife needed relief because 'their friends are dead which did releive them'.[131]

Whether there was a long-term decline in the capacity of kin networks to support the needy, and whether this was a factor in the increased reliance on the Poor Law is highly debatable. Such developments have, it has been pointed out, been detected in many periods, and there is conflicting evidence of the weakness of kin support before the seventeenth and eighteenth centuries, and of its strength in later times.[132] Indeed, a recent study by Ilana Krausman Ben-Amos, has argued for the continuing vitality of both kin and neighbourly support from the late sixteenth to the mid eighteenth centuries.[133] Increased geographical mobility may have put a strain on the flow of money between relatives, but there is also evidence that support could be maintained across impressively long distances.[134] Furthermore, King has suggested that proto-industrial development of the kind being experienced in much of Lancashire enhanced the density of local kin networks, improving the prospects for making shift.[135] It is an area in which there is still much work to be done.

A related but rather different resort was to reformulate economically dysfunctional household groups, aiming to ensure financial security. Recent work on the pre-industrial household has emphasized the flexibility of residential familial arrangements. Indeed, such was this flexibility that it is reckoned that only 1 per cent of people lived alone in pre-industrial

---

129   LA, QSP/144/20; also, Boulton, 'It is extreme necessity', p. 63; in this context 'friends' obviously meant relatives: cf. Tadmor, *Family and Friends*, pp. 145–7, 149–51, 167–92.

130   LA, QSP/211/12.

131   LA, QSP/820/3.

132   Horden, 'Household Care'.

133   Ben-Amos, *Culture of Giving*.

134   Boulton, 'It is extreme necessity', pp. 60–2; cf. the attempt to downplay the role of kin in: K. Wrightson and D. Levine, *Poverty and Piety in an English Village: Terling, 1525–1700*, 2nd edn (Oxford, 1995), pp. 82–94.

135   King, 'Reconstructing Lives', pp. 336–8.

England.[136] The evidence we have for pauper household size in the region suggests it was usually small. In Bolton, the mean pauper household size was 2.9 in 1674, 2.4 in 1686, and 2.6 in 1699; in Colne, the equivalent figure was 3.8 in 1663 and 3.7 in 1689; in Farnworth in 1682 it was 2.9. Similarly, listings of poor beneficiaries of an endowed charity from the rural parishes of Grasmere and Windermere, just over the border in Westmorland, show a mean household size of 3.0 in 1685 and 2.8 in 1687.[137] But few lived alone, and petitions show households evolving over time. Remarriage, living with siblings, even moving into the households of neighbours, were all strategies available to the poor. In 1696, for example, Joanna and Ann Davenport of Ardwick told JPs that they were both single and 'very antient', and were 'sisters & live both in a house together'.[138] According to her petition of 1653, Susan Fish of Castleton entered service when her husband died while fighting in Scotland, thus allowing her to provide for one child.[139] In a further complication, however, her 'friends' looked after two more of her children, and the churchwardens and overseers of Castleton provided for another. Fish's entry into service reflected what has been seen as a crucial survival strategy for vulnerable women in the period, while the spreading of her children between providers reminds us of the extent to which some nuclear families were forced into dissolution.[140]

A more drastic strategy involved simple abandonment of vulnerable members, although the surviving evidence for this practice in Lancashire is sparse.[141] One depressing case was reported to Manchester Sessions in 1660, and involved first the flight of one Francis Bridge of Dedwenclough from his pregnant wife,

---

136   P. Laslett, *Family Life and Illicit Love in Earlier Generations: Essays in Historical Sociology* (Cambridge, 1977), p. 199n.

137   Healey, 'Poverty in an Industrializing Town', p. 134; LA, QSP/238/11–12; QSP/668/10; DDKe/2/6/4, Notes and Orders Relating to the Poor of Deane, 1682; CRO (K), WD/Ry/Box 35/1, Lists of Poor Householders, 1685 and 1687.

138   LA, QSP/775/11.

139   LA, QSP/88/24.

140   A. Kussmaul, *Servants in Husbandry in Early Modern England* (Cambridge, 1981), pp. 75–7; T. Meldrum, *Domestic Service and Gender, 1660–1750: Life and Work in the London Household* (London, 2000), p. 18.

141   E.g. V. Fildes, 'Maternal Feelings Reassessed: Child Abandonment and Neglect in London and Westminster, 1550–1800', in *Women as Mothers in Pre-industrial England: Essays in Memory of Dorothy McLaren*, ed. V. Fildes (London, 1990), pp. 139–78; Boulton, 'It is extreme necessity', p. 55; A. Levene, 'The Origins of the Children of the London Foundling Hospital, 1741–1760', *Continuity and Change*, 18 (2003), 201–36.

insomuch that when she was in child bed, she had utterly sterved for want of convenient necessaries (as we have heard, and doe verely belive) had it not been for her kinred, and some of her charitable neighbores, who did looke upon her in that condition as an object of their pittie and charitie ...

But then, once she had recovered her strength, the mother herself ran off, abandoning the newborn child and its elder sibling.[142] In another, Edward Lucas of Pleasington told JPs in 1708 that he was lame and that his parents, 'very poor people', had nothing support themselves, 'and they being very unkind to your petitioner he is forced to beg abroad & lodge where he can and sometimes near starving'. He now, he said, 'begs his learning at a school in Preston'.[143] But the most common kind of household reformulation must have been through pauper apprenticeship, and some petitioners even asked directly that children be taken off their hands.[144] Margaret Croser of Silverdale, for example, told JPs in 1681 that she had

sixe smale children whereof one is gone to service the other fyve is all with her and shee being now very poore in keepinge them since her husband dyed that she is not able to maintaine her selfe & them therefore humbly beggs that three of them may bee taken of her hand and be put forth to bee apprentices where your good worshipps shall thinke most fitt'.[145]

The following year, meanwhile, Elizabeth Worrall of Salford called upon justices to apprentice one of her two children 'for the benefite of the child and her owne easement'.[146]

(2) The help of neighbours

Petitioners often wrote of getting help from their 'friends'. The word was – at the time – used rather amorphously and included both kin and 'friends' in the modern sense, as well as what we might term 'social allies'.[147] Indeed, the concept of the 'friend' seems to have held quite

---

142 LA, QSP/198/9.
143 LA, QSP/983/12.
144 Cf. Sharpe, 'Poor Children', p. 257.
145 LA, QSP/540/1.
146 LA, QSP/555/10.
147 Tadmor, *Family and Friends*, pp. 145–7, 149–51, 167–92. K. D. M. Snell, 'Belonging

some significance to the marginal poor, and was deployed with similar frequency to the term 'neighbours' and more often than the words 'kin' or 'relatives'. Robert Smethurst's brothers, left orphaned in Bury in 1627, were 'provided for in some smale sort by meanes of theyr mothers frendes & other well disposed neighbores'.[148] In 1656, Isabel Hey of Westhoughton told that she had been 'sustained by her one [i.e. own] worke and with the good helpe of her frends which now are not soe willing neither soe able'.[149] And Jane Tarleton, petitioning from Hesketh in 1662, reported that her 'poore friends' had 'already extended their hands of charity towards her farr beyond their abilityes'.[150] What this perhaps suggests is that some of the poor tended to have a social network comprised of relatives and neighbours to whom they were close, on which they could call in times of need. It was those instances when such networks did not exist that paupers found themselves in particular trouble.

But it was also common for paupers to get support from individuals to whom they apparently had little connection, or from the neighbourhood more generally. Indeed, informal neighbourhood support continued to be important long after official poor relief had become established.[151] The petition of Grace Rydings of Heywood in 1656 told a story which, if true, shows something of the willingness of neighbours to succour the destitute.[152] Rydings claimed to be eighty years old, and declared that she

> hath beene sicke about two monthes and haveinge but 3d a weeke alowance was enforced to goe abroad for reliefe and comeinge to one James Hardmans howse being in the parish of Middleton for an alms [*sic*] was soe sicke and weak that shee could not goe againe into the parishe of Bury neither hath any place of aboad but for the space of 12 dayes hath beene at the said James Hardmans house and put him to cost and trouble.

When her husband died 'in great debt' in 1680, lame Alice Moone of Newsham was left with two children to look to, but she had nothing but

and Community: Understandings of "Home" and "Friends" among the English Poor, 1750–1850', *EcHR*, 2nd Ser., 65 (2012), 1–25 (pp. 12–20).
148 LA, QSB/1/19/113.
149 LA, QSP/136/8.
150 LA, QSP/223/1.
151 Hindle, *On the Parish?*, pp. 48–58; Hudson, 'Ex-servicemen', pp. 48–9, 296–7.
152 LA, QSP/124/18.

what little she could earn, and 'the charitable benevolence of well disposed neigbours out of their tender pitty towards her said children'.[153] Again, help need not have been monetary. Alice Lea of Newton, for example, had broken her back in an accident, but in 1674 she was being 'carried from bed to fier with help of her nightbors'.[154] In fact, 8 per cent of our petition sample mentioned being relieved by their neighbours. Given that this information was not *expected* to be forthcoming, this is an impressively high figure. The precise forms of this relief are usually obscure, and statements will almost certainly conceal cases of formal poor relief, but they will have included gifts, favours, *pro bono* services, gratuities, and purchases above and sales below market rates.[155]

Most help almost certainly came from ordinary households – fellow husbandmen, weavers, small tradesmen and labourers – but there are also documented examples of substantial support being provided by local elite households and individuals. Alice Bordman claimed to have been helped by both a Worsley and a Chetham in 1630s Manchester, both members of important and rich merchant dynasties.[156] In 1671, Elizabeth Pemberton of Hindley stated that 'were it not for the charety of Abraham Longton Esq your petitioner mighte starve for want of foode'.[157] It is possible that the eagerness of some petitioners to name elite donors in their petitions reflects a desire to gain respectability by association, particularly when we bear in mind that the petitions were designed to be presented to members of the gentry sitting as JPs. But some of these instances probably also grew out of entrenched notions of elite hospitality, and potentially also from previous social and economic relations between donors and paupers.[158] John Kindsley of Haigh petitioned in 1704 on behalf of Ellen Baxendale, who was eighty years old and to whom he 'hath given for thirty yeares last past house rome ... without any maner rent and hath likewise found her fire because she lived a servant with your petitioner formerly'.[159] An uncommonly good example comes from the accounts of Sir Daniel Fleming of Rydal (Westmorland) and relates to one John Holme, a waller

153   LA, QSP/525/6.
154   LA, QSP/424/9.
155   Ben-Amos, 'Gifts and Favors'.
156   LA, QSB/1/143/66.
157   LA, QSP/363/10.
158   Heal, *Hospitality*.
159   LA, QSP/916/1.

from Monk Coniston at the very northern end of Lancashire[160] Holme had been employed by the Flemings when they built both Low Park barn (1659) and Rydal Hall Barn (1670). In 1660 he had married Elizabeth Jackson at his parish church of Hawkshead, and the wedding had prompted a gift from Sir Daniel of two shillings. By 1689, however, Holme had fallen on hard times, and according to Fleming he 'came a begging' on 12 December that year. On this occasion he left with a shilling, but he was back for more the following December when he received 6d, in September 1691 (6d), April and November 1693 (6d and 12d respectively), and finally in 1694 when he was given another 6d.[161] It seems certain that Holme's former employment by Sir Daniel helped oil the wheels of compassion.

Another form of benevolence could come in the lodging of paupers on the property of the wealthier, often in the seasonally underused outbuildings which scattered the countryside.[162] No doubt, in a society with such a close relationship with the land and with agriculture, the paupers who sheltered in barns were doing so with the acquiescence if not quite the indulgence of the farmers. When husbandman John Taylor and his family were thrown out of their house for debt sometime before 1697, he and his wife and children 'were forced to make a fier in the Kings high road in Walmisley', until 'out of pitty & meer compassion a neightbour there tooke them in & allowed them to ly in some out housinge'.[163] The following year, Richard Clough of Manchester, who had worked as a collier and a servant to a 'mineral man', told that he was old and lame and 'at this time is forced to lie in a barne in certain old rags that neibours out of pity threw upon him'.[164] Back in 1632, Anne Wolfenden of Chadderton claimed to have lived for a whole year in a barn – and

160   Holme's story has been reconstructed by Blake Tyson: D. Fleming, *Estate and Household Accounts of Sir Daniel Fleming of Rydal Hall, Westmorland, 1688–1701*, ed. B. Tyson (Cumberland and Westmorland Antiquarian and Archaeological Society Record Series, xiii, Kendal, 2001), p. 314.

161   Fleming, *Estate and Household Accounts*, pp. 100, 118, 136, 167, 180, 196. It is almost certain that this is the same John Holme who received poor relief from the township of Monk Coniston with Skelwith in 1691/92 and 1697/98: CRO (K), WPR/83/7/6, Monk Coniston and Skelwith Overseers' Accounts, 1691–1808.

162   Ben-Amos, 'Gifts and Favors', pp. 317–18; cf. Beier, *Masterless Men*, p. 223; Heal, *Hospitality*, pp. 384–5. Note that the rather different housing market of the capital may have curtailed this practice there: Boulton, 'It is extreme necessity', p. 64.

163   LA, QSP/792/8.

164   LA, QSP/820/1.

this with four children.[165] In 1633, it was reported to Lancaster Sessions that Agnes Denny of Halton 'for sixe of the last yeares ... hath dwelt in a little chamber in the end of a fyrehouse of Lawrence Huttons'.[166] But paupers could find themselves cold-shouldered if their presence became too much of a burden or otherwise inconvenient. In 1660, Hugh Morres of Tarleton complained with grim irony that he, his pregnant wife, and six children were 'destitute of succour' and 'lykely to be all starved' since they could no longer lodge in an 'ould barne' that was now filled up with grain.[167] Others managed to gain shelter in donors' houses. The parish register of Garstang, for example, records the burial on 13 May 1695 of 'a poor wandring man who died att Edward Adamson house'; in this case, the householder apparently providing a roof for an indigent stranger until the latter's death.[168] Similarly, in Hawkshead on 25 March 1720, parishioners buried 'A beggar who lodged at the Hill & died there'.[169] Widow Frances Bridge told Manchester JPs in 1661 that she had been 'half yeare in the house of Ellis Fletcher and hath paid noe rent nor is able to pay eny att all'.[170] In 1673, Elizabeth Leech of Ashton-under-Lyne was sick, widowed and old, but was being helped by Robert Leech 'a poore man' (and perhaps a relative), who had given her house room.[171] The same year, Anne Longworth of Sharples reported that 'Mr Henry Norres of Bolton of his free consent suffered her to inhabit in a howse of his for this winter tyme' though now he 'can no longer spare the same'.[172]

These innumerable petty acts of charity, often on the part of ordinary people, apparently formed a critical element of the 'economy of makeshifts'; indeed, Felicity Heal has argued that the support of one's neighbours was expected not just of the better yeomanry, but of husbandmen too.[173] Information from petitions indicates that this was a crucial way in which the 'collectivity' helped provide for those in need. Moreover, there are tantalizing scraps of evidence which suggest that support for the needy was entrenched enough in local society to have

---

165   LA, QSB/1/111/57.
166   LA, QSB/1/120/21.
167   LA, QSP/199/32.
168   *The Parish Registers of Garstang Church, 1660–1734*, ed. H. Brierley and A. Sparke (LPRS, lxviii, Preston, 1932), p. 208.
169   *Second Register Book*, p. 26.
170   LA, QSP/216/16.
171   LA, QSP/396/2.
172   LA, QSP/404/12.
173   Heal, *Hospitality*, pp. 377–81.

been considered 'customary', a term which could – at the time – carry quite significant force. In 1661, for example, Humphrey Leathwaite recorded that 'had not the tender affection of their good neighbours in Formby and Aynsdale releived them while they were able to come abroad amongst them (according to the custome of the said townshipps) they had utterly perished for want of food and mayntenance'.[174] In Furness in the eighteenth century it was apparently the tradition that, when someone fell sick, neighbours – particularly those who might have had disagreements with the affected household – would bring gifts to show that they were willing to help them in their difficulty.[175] It is, indeed, possible that contributing to the upkeep of one's poor neighbours was a way of 'investing' in the social capital of a community, and ensuring similar support should the donor become needy in later life, hence petitioners' claims to have been 'helpers' to the poor in the past.[176] As Richard Gough put it (in Latin), 'He who helps others in prosperity has allies in adversity: our charity to the poor is not a gift but capital.'[177]

Communal festivities could also help to support the poor and marginal. According to Wrightson, popular recreations such as ales, dances and wakes provided not only an expression of solidarity that brought together recusants and conformists, but also an occasion for the redistribution of the surplus wealth of a community.[178] Certainly such events seemed to have persisted in the North while they declined elsewhere.[179] Funeral doles, for example, can be found well into our period in the North West. In 1638, for instance, wealthy George Clark of Manchester provided for a funeral dole of £40 in his will.[180] When Adam Martindale's father was buried at Prescot in 1658, 'All men who came to the house to fetch

---

174   LA, QSP/207/37.
175   T. W. Thompson, *Wordsworth's Hawkshead*, ed. R. Woof (Oxford, 1970), p. 281. Thompson does not record his source for this observation, but it may have been the autobiography of John Ireland, a local inhabitant born in 1734, which was written between 1803 and 1805 and upon which much of *Wordsworth's Hawkshead* is based: ibid., pp. 153–4.
176   E.g. LA, QSP/176/8; QSP/224/25; QSP/396/19; cf. Bailey, *Unquiet Lives*, p. 190; Leeuwen, 'Logic of Charity', pp. 603–4; On the other hand, such statements could betoken contribution to official poor rates.
177   Gough, *History of Myddle*, p. 236.
178   Wrightson, 'Puritan Reformation', pp. 27–8; J. M. Bennett, 'Conviviality and Charity in Medieval and Early Modern England', *PP*, 134 (1992), 19–41.
179   Heal, *Hospitality*, pp. 364–76.
180   Jordan, *Social Institutions*, p. 19.

his corpse thence (beggars not excepted) were entertained with good meat, piping hote, and strong ale in great plentie', while the poor got leftovers from dinner in a local tavern.[181] At the funeral of his son Daniel in December 1698, the elder Sir Daniel Fleming of Rydal (Westmorland) distributed a 'Threepenny Dole' totalling £9 13s 6d. This was a substantial amount in the context of the region at that time, being around twice the sum spent on Poor Law relief at the nearby township of Hawkshead in 1696/97.[182] It would also, assuming one dole per pauper, suggest that 774 needy folk thronged around the small country church at Grasmere to pay their respects and receive alms.[183] In some cases funerals occasioned general benevolence from living attendees, too: Sarah Fell gave £2 7s 3d at the funeral of Rachel Yeamans in 1676, easily her largest single bequest for the period her accounts survive.[184] Many of the best later examples come from Westmorland and Furness, and it is not impossible that such practices continued for longer in this more culturally 'backward' region than they did further south in Lancashire.[185] Certainly we can be sure that there was at least one attempt to stamp out indiscriminate funeral doles quite early on further south. According to a set of orders laid down by several townships in Whalley parish in 1629:

> the doles usually given and distributed at funeralls and burialls in theis parts, do not only little or no good to the neighbouring poore (to whom the same doles are ment), but also drawe infinite numbers of other poore together from places farre remote, amongst which many wanderers, incorrigible rogues, and vacabands, do flocke in and unworthilie share in the devotions of the dead, never intended for them, as also do pester

181   A. Martindale, *Life of Adam Martindale*, ed. R. Parkinson (CS, Old Ser., iv, Manchester, 1845), pp. 119–20; Heal, *Hospitality*, p. 371.

182   CRO (K), WPR/83/7/3, Hawkshead Overseers' Accounts, 1690–1750.

183   Fleming, *Estate and Household Accounts*, p. 269. The 1674 Hearth Tax Assessment for the township of Grasmere lists sixty-two households, or a total population of 279 using a 4.5 multiplier. The funeral of Daniel Fleming the younger must have represented a major event for this remote upland community. *Westmorland Hearth Tax: Michaelmas 1670 & Surveys 1674–5*, ed. C. Phillips, C. Ferguson and A. Wareham (Cumberland and Westmorland Antiquarian and Archaeological Society, Extra Series, xix, London, 2008), p. 291.

184   Fell, *Household Account Book*, p. 285; Fleming, *Estate and Household Accounts*, p. 297.

185   E.g. S. H. Scott, *A Westmorland Village: the Story of the Old Homesteads and 'Statesman' Families of Troutbeck* (Westminster, 1904), p. 138.

and trouble those parts (where such funeralls happen to bee) for a longe tyme after, and manie tymes robberies and other outrages are committed ere the countrie bee quit of that disordered crew. And often tymes also wee see that great numbers of persons who are no needers in that kynd (nor take themselves to bee) do by pretext of a custome (but indeed an abuse) come themselves or send theire children, or both, to the said doles and partake thereof, soe as the true indigent poore, indeed, (for whom it was ment) do receave the least part.[186]

In response to this problem it was ordered than any future such doles would be paid into the hands of the churchwardens of the parish and then administered more carefully.

On the other hand, neighbourly support was unlikely ever to provide for the all needs of the poor. Families which agreed to host paupers could find an unacceptable strain placed on their own domestic economies. Henry Atkinson Junior of Pennington, for example, had nothing in 1665 'but what good people out of pittie doe releeve him with, soe that nowe they takeinge him to bee a great burthen to them their charitye reapeth every day lesse and lesse'.[187] And strains went beyond mere financial costs: the same year, Ellen Sedden of Rumworth, who said she was eighty-four years old, petitioned that although she was living at the house of one John Marsh, 'hee and his family are overburdened with her not onely in providing for her[,] but wakeinge everie night with her which is a greate hindrance to their vocacion and livelyhood'.[188] Moreover, difficulties like these seem to have motivated some of those petitions for relief to which neighbours added their signatures: the appeal thus looks like an attempt to enforce the sharing of the burden of support across a township. That of Isabel Debdell of Eccleston, endorsed by a number of her neighbours and presented in 1633, told very candidly of how her twelve years of lameness had meant she 'hath lyen very sore on her nexte neighbors; whoe begin to bee weary of the burthen'.[189] It would require more research to be certain, but there is also a possibility that these 'group petitions' contained the names of many who were not ratepayers, and were hoping to absolve themselves of the costs of looking after their poor neighbours.

Indeed, lest we develop too rosy a picture of communities full of

186   HMC, *Kenyon*, 'Alms for the Poor of Whalley', pp. 38–9.
187   LA, QSP/279/3.
188   LA, QSP/280/10.
189   LA, QSB/1/118/48.

helpful neighbours, there are also recorded instances of apparently harsh and parsimonious behaviour towards the poor.[190] In 1629, for example, Elizabeth Flitcroft of Prestwich reported that she and her husband had been 'putt and driven' away from Oldham when they tried to settle there.[191] Thirty years later, Margaret Bowker of Moston complained that the inhabitants of the township had 'unmercifully' tried to bar her out of her own cottage.[192] Relatives, even, could show considerable cruelty. According to his 1691 petition, Evan Shaw of Walton-le-Dale, who was both deaf and mute, had gone for support to his sister-in-law, Ellen Shaw, and she had kept him for several years. But all that time he 'was kept at hard worke and labour', with Ellen 'useing great severity against your petitioner', leaving him weak, stricken in years, and a 'miserable poore creature'.[193]

There is also a hint that the spread of compulsory rates for the poor may have dampened the charitable imperative amongst some potential donors. The Poor Law manual, *An Ease for Overseers of the Poore*, implied in 1601 that there was a negative relationship between charity and formal poor relief, pointing out that '[i]f the rule of charitie toward the poore were observed, the establishing of statutes for releeving the poore might be omitted.'[194] And conflict between taxes and charity is indeed evident from the petition of old John Rydeing of Walton-le-Dale in 1657, which claimed he was

> exposed to the charity of his neighbours & other good people, amongst whom, the good old Lady Hoghton hath bene a principall reliever of him who hath of her Ladyshipps free bounty & charity kept your supplicant from begging for neare three yeres last past; but soe it is that her Ladyshipp (being charged in her estate with unusuall leyes by the constables & overseers of the poore) doth now leave off her former keeping of your supplicant.[195]

And over forty years later in 1699, James Shelmerdine of Ardwick made a similar point when he told Manchester JPs that, were he to beg, 'peoples

190   Cf. Hindle, *On the Parish?*, pp. 300–60; Boulton, 'It is extreme necessity', p. 65.
191   LA, QSB/1/59/91.
192   LA, QSP/176/18.
193   LA, QSP/701/19.
194   *An Ease for Overseers*, p. 22.
195   LA, QSP/150/1; cf. Horden, 'Household Care', p. 30.

harts are soe nought that the[y] will bestowe nothinge of mee the[y] say the[y] pay great leyes and every thinge is soe dear that the[y] cannot keepe theire owne familyes and then the[y] thinke the[y] shall not give it to others'.[196]

(3) 'Wandering up and down'

Itinerant begging constituted another way in which the poor could tap the resources of charitable sentiment, and it is not always clear – especially in the vague terms used by petitioners – of where neighbourly support began and begging ended. Technically, of course, the system of poor relief introduced in 1601 was supposed to end the itinerant seeking of alms; indeed, acts against 'Rogues Vagabondes and Sturdie Beggers' reached the statute book in 1598 and 1604.[197] Nonetheless, the evidence that unlicensed begging continued well into the seventeenth century is abundant, indeed Thomas Ady, writing over half a century after 43 Elizabeth, observed that 'no man of ability is long free from poor coming to his door'.[198] In 1671, for example, Thomas Fitton of Heaton-in-Prestwich recounted getting 'releife at the howses of the inhabitantes in Heaton soe longe as hee could goe for it'.[199] Destitute of friends, seventy-year-old Woodplumpton spinster Jane Almond was – she claimed in 1683 – 'forced to gaine her releife by beginge onely', while in 1686, Anne Dods of Samlesbury recounted having 'nothing to live upon but what she gets of her charitable neighbours by begging'.[200] She was ninety years old and 'not able to worke'. Such statements are repeated many times over. Sir Daniel Fleming, Sarah Fell, and William Blundell all record numerous one-off gifts to the nameless and begging poor in the second half of the seventeenth century.[201] Moreover, Blundell records two cases in which begging became a form of empowerment, with paupers manipulating the consciences of those better off. One individual was recorded by Blundell

---

196   LA, QSP/828/25.
197   39 Eliz. I, c. 4; 1 James I, c. 7.
198   Cf. Gough, *History of Myddle*, p. 146; Heal, *Hospitality*, p. 378; T. Ady, *A Perfect Discovery of Witches* (London, 1661), p. 129.
199   LA, QSP/376/24.
200   LA, QSP/573/2; QSP/611/16.
201   Fell, *Household Account Book*, *passim*; F. Tyrer, 'The Poor Law in the Seventeenth and Early Eighteenth Centuries, with Case-histories in Crosby and District in the County of Lancashire', unpublished volume, Lancashire Archives (1956), pp. 15–21; W. Blundell, *A Cavalier's Notebook*, ed. T. E. Gibson (London, 1880), pp. 86, 137, 160, 214–15, 241–2, 283–4.

Figure 8:
*The Cunning
Northerne Begger,*
by permission of
University of
Glasgow Library,
Special Collections

as begging 'in a rhetorical bold way at the races on Crosby marsh', where he 'would flatter the noble gentlemen, and tell aloud what gallant houses they kept'.[202] 'His importunity there', Blundell recorded, 'was insufferable. For I did once see a gentleman cast a shilling unto him, saying, "A pox o' God take thee!"'. Even more colourful was the tale Blundell had heard of 'an old wandering beggar, by name Hesketh', who

> understood one time that a company of young gallants (most or all of them Catholics) were passing through Downholland, towards Scarisbrick. It was in the times of usurpation, and in the summer season. The man, being very old, had his grandson to attend him, whom he commanded to go aside; then he threw himself into a puddle, and wallowed therein. The gallants, coming to the place, asked him what he was. He replied, 'I will never deny myself to be a Catholic, and because I am so, your comrades the troopers that went before you have beaten and used me thus; and now I do expect you will kill me outright.' Hereupon the soft-hearted gallants made a contribution of twelve or fourteen shillings. Which when he had got, and the gentlemen passed away, he called to his boy and said, 'Here is a trick to help you when you grow to be old.'[203]

But unlicensed begging was tolerated rather than legal, and it could cause considerable annoyance. The inhabitants of Scotforth, for example, complained in 1670 that Jennet Kew had 'denied the good will of the inhabitants and become a great trouble to them whereby they cannot rewle her[,] and wanders up and downe the township [and] neere abouts like a vagrant person to the great anoyance of his Majesties loyal subjects'.[204] Some petitioners expressed a profound reluctance to beg, though perhaps such protests were rhetorical. Richard Browne of Tunstall, for example, claimed in 1638 that since his wife died he had been 'enforced to begg from doore to doore with & for his sayd children, which manner of life is as irkesome to him, as it is contrary to law'.[205] The same year, Mary Kennison of Gorton worried that she might bring shame on her kin if she took to the road, 'beinge greatly abashed & dismayed to begg, for the

202 Blundell, *Cavalier's Notebook*, pp. 214–15.
203 Ibid., pp. 283–4.
204 LA, QSP/353/5.
205 LA, QSB/1/200/45.

disgrace of her friendes'.[206] In 1663, meanwhile, Jane Seed of Ribchester stated that she went begging for relief, but was 'ashamed' to have to do so.[207]

Even where begging was tolerated it was an inefficient way of redistributing money to the neediest. There were occasions on which petitioners reported that their localized begging was an excessive burden on their nearest neighbours, a problem that became especially serious if a pauper became incapacitated and thus unable to travel far. Edward Holme, a labourer of Scarisbrick, reported in 1631 that as a result of his lameness, 'many of his neere neighbours [were] much troubled through his mayntenance in regard hee is not nor hath bine able for 6 yeares last to begge in remote places'.[208] Similarly, Jane Fieldhouse-alias-Punder of Cockerham lamented in 1662 that she could not 'goe any abrode' due to sickness, 'except to some neighbours that dwell near to her; to which said neighbours she is become a burden'.[209] And there was the potential for rejection, though complaints of this are rare. One unnamed woman from Ribchester claimed that in 1634 'in these tymes strangers are butt hard of hartt', a statement that may reflect recent clampdowns in response to directives of the Privy Council during Charles I's Personal Rule.[210] In 1695, meanwhile, widow Ellen Radcliffe had been told by overseers in Culcheth (where she had her settlement) that she should go around begging for her keep, but – she pointed out – this was banned in Warrington where she now lived.[211]

It may be that in years of economic difficulty, when the poor needed most support, their neighbours actually hardened their attitudes towards begging. Winchester found cases of manorial courts tightening their indulgence of beggars during the famine of 1623.[212] In the tough year of 1650, John Dawson of Blackley complained that he had 'little favour from the neighbours', something he implicitly linked to the fact that 'trades are bad and wages little as manie can wytnes'.[213] His sentiment was mirrored

206   LA, QSB/1/203/77.

207   LA, QSP/234/16; cf. Hindle, *On the Parish?*, pp. 75–6.

208   LA, QSB/1/86/60.

209   LA, QSP/229/6.

210   LA, QSB/1/137/36; Fletcher, *Reform*, p. 209; K. M. Sharpe, *The Personal Rule of Charles I* (London, 1992), pp. 478–82.

211   LA, QSP/770/10.

212   A. J. L. Winchester, 'Responses to the 1623 Famine in Two Lancashire Manors', *LPS*, 36 (1986), 47–8.

213   LA, QSP/32/4; cf. QSP/32/29.

by Samuel Dickinson of Heaton, who in 1674 noted 'the present hardness of the time' and complained that he had 'sought reliefe by other charitable means, but being disappoynted therein'.[214] And James Shelmerdine, quoted above, had his neighbours tell him that 'every thinge is soe dear that the[y] cannot keepe theire owne familyes and then the[y] thinke the[y] shall not give it to others'.[215] Such evidence, though, goes against the advice given in a pro-Christmas tract from 1647, which stressed the charitable aspects of the festival, 'and this year requireth more charity then ordinary, because of the dearness of provision of corn and victuals'.[216] Presumably attitudes depended to a large extent on the mindset of the giver. Sarah Fell, for example, apparently gave more doles to individual paupers in 1674 and 1675 than she did in the better years of 1676 and 1677.[217] By contrast, Sir Daniel Fleming's expenditure on charitable doles was no higher in lean years (1693, 1699) than it was in fatter ones.[218]

Intriguingly, positive references to begging (i.e. those in which a pauper admits to begging, or describes themselves as unfit to beg, implying they would do so under normal circumstances) and to the informal charity of neighbours, were more common in the earlier petitions than later ones. Around a third of petitions made such references before the Civil War, but only about 15 per cent did so after 1650. They were also less common in petitions to Manchester Sessions than to the other three sittings: between the 1620s and 1670s, around 12 per cent of petitions in Manchester referred positively to begging or neighbourly support; in Lancaster, Preston, Ormskirk and Wigan, this number was around a fifth. These patterns might well simply reflect local fashions and trends in petitions – certainly petitions tended to get more laconic as the period wore on. But it might also hint that begging was becoming less common as a makeshift strategy, and that it was always more tightly controlled in the south-east of the county.

(4) Formal charity: endowments and gifts

There were also more formal types of charity available, although Lancashire was perhaps less well endowed in this regard than many others. W. K. Jordan estimated that by 1660 there was enough capital stock invested in

214   LA, QSP/417/10; cf. Fessler, 'Official Attitude', p. 110; Hindle, *On the Parish?*, p. 407.
215   LA, QSP/828/25.
216   'T.H.', *A Ha! Christmas* (London, 1647), p. 4.
217   Fell, *Household Account Book*, *passim*.
218   Fleming, *Estate and Household Accounts*, *passim*.

the county's charities for the poor to produce an annual return of nearly £900.[219] This would represent around 6d per household per annum if the population of the county is taken as around 160,000 (assuming household size of 4.5) at this date, or – if we assume that only around 5 per cent of households were deemed poor enough to benefit – something like 9s 6d per poor household per annum.[220] In fact, it appears that overt concern for the poor was low amongst the priorities of Lancastrian testators, certainly in comparison with other charitable causes, notably education. Thus, Jordan found the county's bequests to the poor 'inadequate', and felt that 'the care of the poor ... did not weigh heavily on the consciences of Lancastrians'.[221] The fact that Jordan's coverage ends in 1660 means that we must guess how this figure might have altered over the ensuing century. It seems possible, given the generally rising prosperity in the county, that it rose significantly. However, even allowing for an exceptionally high estimate of the total annual distribution to the poor out of these endowments (say, between £4,000 and £5,000 per annum by 1750), the contribution of such benevolence to meeting the needs of the poor was not especially large, compared with the £21,236 a year reported as spent through rate-funded poor relief.[222] Moreover, figures produced by Nigel Goose for Colchester suggest a waning of the 'charitable impulse' in the second half of the seventeenth century, with a fall in the available rate of interest combined with a drop in the total annual value of one-off cash bequests resulting in a decrease in the amount of money available.[223]

This is, of course, just part of the story of charitable assistance in seventeenth- and eighteenth-century Lancashire. Official licences to collect charity in the form of church briefs, or the passes given by Quarter Sessions to beg in specific hundreds, also provided the opportunity for relief, as did the established Church.[224] There were poor boxes in parish churches of the region, while one-off collections could be held in order to aid specified individuals. In 1627, Isabel Halsall of Standish stated that she had not been burdensome to her neighbours for five years, 'saveinge

219   Jordan, *Social Institutions*, p. 21.
220   See above, p. 39.
221   Jordan, *Social Institutions*, pp. 12–26, quotation on p. 26.
222   *Parliamentary Papers, 1818*, vol. 5, Report from Poor Law Committee, p. 9.
223   N. Goose, 'The Rise and Decline of Philanthropy in Early Modern Colchester: the Unacceptable Face of Mercantilism?', *Social History*, 31 (2006), 469–87 (pp. 480–1).
224   On briefs: M. Harris, '"Inky Blots and Rotten Parchment Bonds": London, Charity Briefs and the Guildhall Library', *Historical Research*, 66 (1993), 98–110.

onely some well effected people in the church in Wigan & Wynwicke parishe procured theme some gatheringes in the churches for & towardes theire payinge of there rent & provision for fyre'.[225] When the house and barn of Cuthbert Brearely of Booth Hollins in Butterworth burnt down a few years later, his neighbours organized collections in the churches of Rochdale, Whitworth and 'twoe other places'. Unfortunately these only raised a fraction of the sum required and so he applied for licence to beg across Salford Hundred.[226] The seventeenth-century accounts of the churchwardens and overseers of the poor of Prestwich parish show regular collections in the church for individual paupers in addition to rate-funded relief and collections at the sacrament.[227] Dissenters and Recusants might also have strategies for relieving those of their own faith. Sarah Fell and her Quaker associates from Furness ran a very early form of women's friendly society in the 1670s, while in 1699, Ann Houghton of Bardsea set up in her will a trust for – amongst other purposes – 'binding poore boys and girls who are or will become catholicks to be instructed in trades and handicrafts'.[228]

(5) Crime

We must finally say something about crimes of necessity. Such illicit behaviour was obviously unlikely to be brought up in petitions, though this was at least representative of theft's position within individual makeshift strategies relative to petitioning: promoting an appeal at Quarter Sessions, as onerous as it may have been, was probably a course of action more palatable than criminality. Unfortunately, there is relatively little secondary literature on crime in the North West.[229] Wrightson has tabulated instances of prosecution for theft (amongst other criminal activity) in south Lancashire in the first half of the seventeenth century, though it is naturally impossible to say what proportion of thefts arose out of desperate need.[230] There was an increase in the number of prosecutions

---

225   LA, QSB/1/30/43.
226   LA, QSB/1/95/55; cf. QSP/256/2.
227   MALS, L160/2/1, Prestwich Churchwardens' and Overseers' Accounts, 1646–83.
228   Fell, *Household Account Book*, *passim*; LA, RCLn/10/7, Spiritual Will and Testament of Ann Houghton, 1699.
229   Though see: W. J. King, 'Prosecution of Illegal Behavior in Seventeenth-century England, with Emphasis on Lancashire (Univ. of Michigan PhD thesis, 1977); G. Walker, *Crime, Gender, and the Social Order in Early Modern England* (Cambridge, 2003).
230   Wrightson, 'Puritan Reformation', appendix 1.

in Salford Hundred in the hard years of 1631 and 1638, but this was not replicated in West Derby and Leyland, so the overall picture is obscure.[231] To a certain extent we can co-opt studies of other regions. In particular, a number of historians have argued that economic crises could result in rising levels of property crime, although the waters are muddied by the possibility of heightened prosecution at times of social dislocation.[232] There is also a sense in which theft could shade into custom, notably in the case of gleaning and industrial embezzlement.[233] The first of these was facing restriction in England as a whole, while the second may have increased in scale concomitantly with the rise of putting-out, especially in industrializing regions like Lancashire.[234]

Conclusion

There was, then, a diverse array of income sources to which marginal households might turn so as to prevent (or at least delay) dependence on official poor relief. This chapter has described some of those sources, notably those which we see recounted in petitions for relief. There are, of course, issues which have been covered only in passing. But the general picture is clear: there existed a complex network of support available to marginal people. This was often piecemeal, irregular, and temporary, and it might come at a social cost, but it was there, and in many cases it was seen as preferable to drawing upon the enforced – tax-funded – support of the parish. It did, however, often fail to provide adequate support, leaving households – so they said – forced to apply for formal relief. And it is to the reasons for such failure that we must now turn.

---

231   There was a peak in prosecutions during the 1594–97 harvests crisis: J. Walter and K. Wrightson, 'Dearth and the Social Order in Early Modern England', *PP*, 71 (1976), 22–42 (p. 24).

232   D. Hay, 'War, Dearth and Theft in the Eighteenth Century: the Record of the English Courts', *PP*, 95 (1982), 117–60; P. Lawson, 'Property Crime and Hard Times in England, 1559–1624', *Law and History Review*, 4 (1986), 95–127; Gough, *History of Myddle*, p. 100.

233   King, 'Customary Rights'; Hindle, *On the Parish?*, pp. 35–42, 85–7.

234   J. Styles, 'Embezzlement, Industry and the Law in England, 1500–1800', in *Manufacture in Town and Country before the Factory*, ed. M. Berg, P. Hudson and M. Sonenscher (Cambridge, 1983), pp. 173–205.

PART III:
MISFORTUNE

6

Dependent People: Endemic Poverty

Humbly sheweth, That your petitioner hath formerly lived in a plentifull condicion and hath paid taxes towards King and poore, But had some yeares ago his house broken and fourtie pounds of readie money stollen from him and hath sustained other greate losses by his trade & (being formerly a drovier) through which and other misfortunes your petitioner is so distressed that hee is forced to wander abroade and begg, having nothing of his owne left to manteyne him with nor howse to dwell in, and the overseers have refused to releeve his necessities although hee hath made his complaint for two yeares last past your petitioner is fourescore and two yeares of age and is no longer able to begg ...

Petition of John Lomax of Bradshaw (May 1679)[1]

Although John Lomax had failed to convince the overseers of Bradshaw of his need, he found relief in the adjourned court of Quarter Sessions for Salford Hundred, held at Bolton in May 1679. Endorsing his petition, the Bolton justices ordered that he be provided for 'according to his wants'. The next stage, then, is to explore the kinds of 'wants' experienced by paupers like Bradshaw, which were either relieved or expected to be relieved by the Poor Law. The chapter will discuss the different forms of poverty in turn using both qualitative and quantitative data from petitions (with the occasional glance at some overseers' accounts), and the censuses of the poor for the town of Bolton, which I have analysed in more detail elsewhere.[2] These documents, particularly given their sheer volume, provide a new perspective on some of the underlying causes of poverty in the period – indeed, they are the only sources which come close

---

1   LA, QSP/500/13.
2   Note that the petition data is based on appeals for parochial and township relief, and excludes those war widows and ex-servicemen who asked for pensions from the county fund. On the censuses: Healey, 'Poverty in an Industrializing Town'.

to allowing paupers something like their own voice, and they are the only ones which give *narratives* of poverty.

What emerges is that petitioners asked for support in moments of personal economic hardship caused by the inherent risks entailed in life in a pre-industrial society. Indeed, many of these difficulties are endemic in *all* societies. Quantitatively, the main forms of hardship they asked for support through were old age, sickness, and the breakdown of the nuclear household (or the failure to form it), though hardships relating to the wider economy such as high prices or unemployment, and the more general hazards of the social and natural environment constituted important subsidiary risks. Thus, formal poor relief can be characterized not just as a form of support towards life-cycle hardships, nor merely as a transfer of wealth to a mass of chronic poor (though there is much truth in both of these), but as a more comprehensive system of social insurance against risk. It functioned to prevent total destitution at times of personal emergency when people simply could not scrape together enough cash to support themselves. It was not the only source of such 'social insurance' at the time. There were church briefs, for example, which provided support for those who had lost through misfortune, and some of the elderly could hope to find support in an almshouse: perhaps around 1.21 to 1.53 per cent of the population aged over sixty were housed in such institutions at the start of the seventeenth century.[3] Moreover, the first port of call for most was to 'make shift', as detailed in the last chapter and in numerous other studies. Meanwhile, formal relief was *redistributive* rather than contributory insurance in the modern sense (excepting the fact that petitioners who could point to a history of ratepaying seem to have used this in support of their claims for assistance). It was *needs based* rather than contingency based: paupers were not given fixed doles when they experienced certain set categories of hardship, such as reaching old age or having a child to support. And formal poor relief was *residual*: unlike most British welfare payments today, it was aggressively means-tested and a recourse of the last resort. But, with all these caveats, relief under the Poor Law nonetheless acted as a flexible system of social insurance for the marginal. Even given the occasional documented attempt to use it for cultural control, the fundamental determining factor in its distribution was need, and thus its operation came to reflect the actual contours of early modern 'deserving hardship'.

---

3   N. Goose, 'The English Almshouse and the Mixed Economy of Welfare: Medieval to Modern', *Local Historian*, 40 (2010), 3–19.

Multiple hardships

The following chapter discusses the main forms of such 'deserving hardship' in turn: old age, ill health, nuclear family breakdown, economic and environmental risk. But one of the implications of the system's basis on need (rather than specific contingencies), was that many paupers were actually suffering from several different forms of hardship when they asked for relief. The importance of 'multiple hardship' emerges if we take the three obviously identifiable forms of difficulty (sickness, old age and household failure) from the Bolton censuses of 1686 and 1699.[4] Here, just 5 per cent of poor households suffered only from sickness, 6 per cent only from old age and 24 per cent from family failure or breakdown alone. Overall, 35 per cent of poor households were suffering one of these identifiable contingencies, as compared with 38 per cent suffering two and 16 per cent all three. We need to refine these figures slightly to account for those with no obvious hardship (assumed to be single-hardship households); and also to incorporate those who were overburdened with children.[5] This recalculation gives 42 per cent of households suffering single hardship, as compared with 58 per cent suffering two or more. It is an obvious point, but personal misfortunes were more devastating when they stacked up.

Meanwhile, nearly 30 per cent of pauper petitioners claimed to be suffering from two or more of the same hardships. Such evidence, however, has to be read critically, for when applying for relief on account of – say – old age, a pauper had nothing to lose by mentioning the fact that she was also widowed and lame, even if she was coping adequately with both of these. To a certain extent then, the inclusion of multiple hardships tells us more about the kinds of contingency which were *seen* as deserving of relief rather than the actual causes of poverty in individual cases. Nonetheless, there are certain occasions where – by following personal histories in overseers' accounts – we can prove that a pauper was suffering from more than one kind of difficulty, each of which had an independent impact. The sparseness of the county's accounts renders any large study problematic, so some individual case studies must suffice. One example is Alice Haslam, a single woman of Prestwich, who received relief from the township between 1661 and 1680. Her dole was raised in 1675/76 and

4   BALS, PBO/1/1, Bolton Censuses of the Poor, 1686 and 1699.
5   Defined here as households with four or more resident children under the age of fourteen.

1676/77 when she was sick, and then again under similar circumstances in 1679/80.[6] In 1702/03, Widow Bury of Cheetham got extra money when her daughter's leg required treatment.[7] Christopher Fisher of Hawkshead received poor relief in the early eighteenth century, in part presumably on account of his old age (he was in his seventies), but he received extra help in 1712/13 'when his wife [was] out of health'.[8] Finally, Anne Tilling of Atherton was in regular receipt of a small pension (usually 6d a week) in the 1710s, but received a number of additional doles, including 7s in 1717/18 to pay for mending her chimney.[9]

Old age

An exceptionally large proportion of those who received or petitioned for poor relief claimed to be old, and this reinforces the findings of many other scholars of pre-industrial poverty.[10] According to Richard Smith, by 1700 there was a 'detectable sentiment that the elderly were entitled to communal support'.[11] Indeed, of Hindle's sample of 453 adult petitions from Cumberland between 1686 and 1749, around 40 per cent made some reference to old age.[12] The mean age of pensioners in the parish of St Martin's in the West End of London stood at sixty-eight in 1707 and sixty-six in 1716, while both Susan Ottaway and Lynn Botelho have focused on the close relationship between agedness and pre-industrial poor relief.[13] Urban censuses from the sixteenth and seventeenth century consistently show old age as a major identifier amongst the poor. In Bolton in 1686 and 1699, 46.7 per cent of poor households were headed by people aged over fifty, and 34.2 per cent by those over sixty. Having a household head over sixty years old, according to regression analysis, raised the proportion of recorded household income taken from the Poor Law by 11 per cent.

In our sample of petitions, nearly 43 per cent made some reference to

6   MALS, L160/2/1, Prestwich Churchwardens' and Overseers' Accounts, 1646–83.
7   MALS, M10/7/2/1, Cheetham Overseers' Accounts, 1693–1791.
8   CRO (K), WPR/83/7/3, Hawkshead Overseers' Accounts, 1690–1750.
9   WA, TR/Ath/C/2/1–8, Atherton Overseers' Accounts, 1692–1751.
10   E.g. Wales, 'Poverty, Poor Relief and the Life-cycle'; Smith, 'Ageing and Well-being'; Botelho, Old Age.
11   Smith, 'Ageing and Well-being', p. 82.
12   Hindle, On the Parish?, p. 409.
13   Boulton, 'It is extreme necessity', p. 50; Ottaway, Decline of Life, pp. 173–276; Botelho, Old Age.

being old. The specific ages they gave are highly unreliable, as they were usually rounded to the nearest decade, and indeed contain some very questionable claims. In the 1670s, for example, John Nichols of Eccles claimed to be 104, Anne Rigby of Ormskirk 105, while James Robinson of the same town similarly declared his age to be an impressive 105.[14] No doubt some individuals did enjoy a lengthy existence: Deborah Penny, a pauper of Hawkshead whose life can be followed through the parish registers, definitely lived to the age of ninety-seven (she died in 1759) but others were clearly stretching the bounds of credibility. The Lancashire record for unrealistic longevity, for what it is worth, is held by 'Ould' Simon Aloftus, a poor petitioner of Goosnargh, who claimed in 1650 that he had reached the thoroughly venerable age of 127.[15]

Whatever the truth of these particular cases, the problems of old age were undoubtedly real. Ageing brought serious and worsening infirmity and bodily afflictions, amongst which creeping lameness and poor eyesight were mentioned with most frequency. In 1655, Oliver Wilson of Walton-le-Dale complained that he was 'blind through the infirmity of ould age', while the agedness of Robert Cowper of Nether Burrow had left him – he claimed in 1650 – 'very decrepit, weake and infirme'.[16] Less specific was Gawen Simpkin of Lonsdale Hundred, who in 1650 petitioned that he was 'very feeble & ould'.[17] William Oldham of Heaton Norris summed the problem up when he claimed poverty in 1691 through the 'weaknes in body and other infirmities always attendinge upon ould age'.[18] He was eighty-two. The key problem was simply that it was very hard for the aged to earn their living. John Burrow of Skerton was explicit about this in 1649 when he complained that 'of late infirme and decrepitt ould age hath taken his worke from him that he cannott neither will people have him to worke as formerlie'.[19] Alice Simpson, also of Skerton, petitioned in 1658 that she was 'nowe farr stricken into yeares, and of late growne blynd, soe that she is not any longer able to labour for her liveinge or to helpe herselfe in any sorte'.[20] Such examples could be multiplied many times over.

In fact, the aged often struggled to 'make shift' of any sort. In Hawkshead,

14   LA, QSP/384/4; QSP/448/8; QSP/367/19.
15   LA, QSP/34/7.
16   LA, QSP/114/8; QSP/25/11.
17   LA, QSP/33/11; also QSP/8/20.
18   LA, QSP/699/3.
19   LA, QSP/9/2.
20   LA, QSP/153/7.

paupers were apparently able to dig peat and turf on the common fell for use as fuel, but this was of little use to those who were too weak.[21] Thus, when Agnes Braithwaite petitioned two Lancaster justices in 1704 that she was 'not able to hire men to get turfe or fewell whereby to relieve her selfe in the winter season', she did so to show that her age was forcing her to pay able-bodied men to gather fuel for her.[22] Presumably, the same factors explain why Hawkshead's overseers laid out regular sums of money for providing fuels for many of their paupers between the 1690s and the end of our period.[23] Even the ability to travel around the neighbourhood in search of neighbourly charity could be seriously impaired. In 1633, Ellin Gerrard of Ormskirk claimed she had 'growne soe weake & fible in regard of her ould age & lameness' that she was 'not nowe able to goe abrode in to the towne and countarie … to gett her anie relife or sustenance or the charitable rewardes of well disposed people'.[24] In 1650, 89-year-old Thomas Aughton of Penwortham found himself 'not able to labour or travaile [i.e. travel] for releefe amongst his neighbours without danger of beinge drowned in pitts & ditches beinge lately in hazzard of his life if passengers & neighbours had not releeved him'.[25] Similarly, Robert Burne, a 95-year-old man of Woodplumpton, claimed in 1657 to be 'not able to begge from doore to doore without a guide'.[26] And those with such limited mobility could end up a particular burden on those who lived close by. In 1666, for instance, John Fletcher alias Jovill of Bury petitioned that he was old and by

> the comon calamityes thereupon attending is not at all able to earn his liveing, neither by hand labour, nor by going from house to house (as of late he hath donne) to receive the charity of good people, but is become a double charge to his next adjacent neighbours, by reason of his said imbecility …

Despite this, had they not relieved him out of 'mear charity', then he would – he said – have been 'quite lost'.[27]

---

21   On this aspect of the upland economy see: Winchester, *Harvest of the Hills*, pp. 123–38.

22   LA, QSP/914/3; Healey, 'Poverty, Deservingness and Popular Politics', pp. 144, 151–2.

23   CRO (K), WPR/83/7/3, Hawkshead Overseers' Accounts, 1690–1750, *passim*.

24   LA, QSB/1/118/55.

25   LA, QSP/31/27.

26   LA, QSP/138/6.

27   LA, QSP/284/21.

Falling incomes, from workplace earnings or the wider 'economy of makeshifts', were not the only problem. Senility and weakness of body also meant that individuals needed help to complete previously simple domestic tasks. Sometimes this help could be offered as charity by well-meaning neighbours, but if this was not available, domestic assistance had to be paid for. Old age could thus also lead to the partial marketization of the household. Such a large number of petitioners co-opted the language of helplessness as to suggest it was something of a cliché amongst appeals, so we need to be careful. But there is a sense of authenticity about petitions such as that of Jane Bridge of Fazakerley, who pleaded in 1662 that she was 'now some what aged & growne soe infirme & weake of body, that your petitioner is not able to worke for her liveinge, & many times your petitioners said weaknes is soe extreame that had she meat your petitioner were not able to feed hir selfe'.[28] Thirteen years earlier, Anne Howsman of Lancaster had evoked a relatively commonplace image when she claimed to have been ninety years old and as a result 'soe infirme that shee is not able to put on her cloathes much lesse to seeke for reliefe'.[29] And in 1694, William Makater of Upholland provided a graphic image of old age, with him 'nowe scarce able to performe a dayes worke, and his wife soe extreame impotent that she is scarce able to crawle or goe about'.[30] We should perhaps be wary of taking such statements too literally, but they do at least show that there was a conception that old age increased dependence on others, and that this could necessitate the purchase of care.

The Lancashire evidence thus clearly shows that agedness was a major characteristic of the poor. On the other hand, as we shall see, the importance of old age within our sample, comparative to nuclear family breakdown and sickness, was perhaps rather less than we would have expected given the emphasis placed upon it by many previous historians. For example, David Underdown has stated that in Dorchester the 'elderly' constituted the 'main recipients' of poor relief in the first half of the seventeenth century.[31] Similarly, Tim Wales found that in Hedenham (Norfolk), in the second half of the seventeenth century, 'ageing was the most significant identifier' amongst the poor.[32] Nonetheless, the proportion of petitioners claiming old age was higher here than is suggested by Ottaway

28 LA, QSP/223/20.
29 LA, QSP/21/12.
30 LA, QSP/742/2.
31 Underdown, *Fire From Heaven*, p. 123.
32 Wales, 'Poverty, Poor Relief and the Life-cycle', p. 365.

and Botelho's recent work. This has the proportion of regular recipients of relief defined as 'elderly' ranging between 4 and 33 per cent in eighteenth-century Terling (Essex) and Puddletown (Dorset), 7 per cent in late-seventeenth-century Poslingford and 20 per cent in Cratfield (both Suffolk).[33] It is possible that the discrepancy comes from the rather liberal definition of old age employed by paupers when highlighting their own need. On the other hand, our evidence fits rather better with Steve King's finding that in nine parishes in the third quarter of the eighteenth century, people over sixty years old accounted for more than half of the total relief bill.[34]

Another question is whether it was old age *as such* which qualified paupers for support. This, for example, is the case with present-day old age pensions, which are payable once the individual in question has reached a certain age. In fact, for all the scholarship showing the high proportion of poor relief given to the elderly, there is powerful evidence to the effect that old age *in and of itself* was not a necessary and sufficient condition for poor relief. Richard Smith's estimate of 40–50 per cent of those over sixty receiving poor relief in eighteenth-century Whitchurch (Oxfordshire) is, for example, impressive, but it still leaves most of the elderly supporting themselves in other ways.[35] In my recent study of the small town of Bolton in the late seventeenth century, meanwhile, I tentatively estimated that around 35 per cent of those over sixty were in receipt of poor relief.[36] To be sure, these are sizeable proportions, and show a wide-ranging, perhaps even 'generous' system of support for the poor; but they do not show agedness *necessarily* conferring any right to relief.

One of the reasons that so many of the elderly did not receive poor relief was the system's residuality. It was support of the last resort, only aimed at those who had no other means of being self-sufficient; and the previous chapter showed these other means were exhaustively deployed. But there was probably another reason, which was that it was not old age as such which was seen as a cause of poverty, but the impact that

---

33 Ottaway, *Decline of Life*, p. 243; Botelho, *Old Age*, p. 108.

34 The nine parishes were Farthinghoe and Aynho (Northamptonshire), Ashwell (Hertfordshire), Paxton (Cambridgeshire), Calverley and Farsley (West Riding), Cowpe (Lancashire), Middleton (North Riding) and Sutton Bonnington (Nottinghamshire). King, *Poverty and Welfare*, pp. 168, 213.

35 R. M. Smith, 'Some Issues Concerning Families and their Property in Rural England, 1250–1800', in Smith (ed.), *Land, Kinship and Life-cycle*, pp. 1–86 (p. 74).

36 Healey, 'Poverty in an Industrializing Town', p. 138.

old age had on the body. Ageing was likely to cause physical infirmity: indeed, eventually, it *inevitably* did. It was this infirmity which reduced the capacity to work, and to look after oneself, so it was infirmity that underpinned the deservingness of the elderly. This is reflected in the debate amongst contemporaries as to when 'old age' started, with ages from thirty-five to sixty suggested. One 1612 tract even stated that old age was 'nothing els but a kinde of sicknes'.[37] More subtly, indeed, the issue is partly one of how societies define 'old age'. Today we tend to do so quantitatively – after a certain number of years we become 'old'. But in the early modern period, old age was – as Alex Shepard puts it – 'as much a product of incapacity as accumulated years, and it was more often judged in functional rather than chronological terms'.[38] Thus, there is a powerful argument to be made that studies of the Poor Law which highlight the way it tended to support the old are missing the obvious point, that poor relief was generally targeted at the bodily infirm. A large, perhaps overwhelming, proportion of these tended to be elderly, but this was because old age usually resulted in infirmity. The *infirmity* was the proximate cause of the poverty.

Ill health

Old age, then, should in part be seen as a subset of a wider category of bodily infirmity: 'impotence' being the word most used by contemporaries to describe such a condition. In any case, other forms of ill health also constituted a root cause of much of the poverty recorded in the period. Almost exactly 50 per cent of Lancashire's petitioners claimed to be suffering some sort of physical or mental incapacity, aside from simply noting their old age (and excluding those aged paupers who used vague terms like 'infirm', 'almost blind', or 'decrepit'). It is not always easy, however, to tell whether a sick petitioner was merely describing the effects of old age, or whether they suffered an independent health problem.[39] Indeed, the connection between old age and incapacity was itself emphasized by some petitioners. Edward Wilson of Hambleton, for example, claimed to be suffering from the 'sicknes and infirmitys

37 Shepard, *Meanings of Manhood*, p. 44.
38 Ibid., p. 217.
39 Cf. Fessler, 'Official Attitude'.

inseparably accompanying old age' in 1659.[40] Francis Bridge of Chorley was eighty years old in 1660 and 'by reason thereof, decrepitt full of sores ulsers and imperfections', while William Foster of Pennington suffered seven years later from 'many infirmities incident to old age'.[41] It is worth, therefore, trying to factor out this problem, and so a dataset was created of those petitioners *not* claiming old age and here some 55 per cent of appeals contained some reference to sickness in the household. In Bolton, meanwhile, 40.1 per cent of all households were reported as sick, although regression analysis only has sickness responsible for a 6 per cent increase in the proportion of income taken from poor relief – a figure that is not statistically significant. This probably partly reflects the nature of the census, as a report on *regular* poor relief: presumably a large proportion of expenditure on the sick came in the form of occasional doles, often for treatment.

To some extent the quantitative importance of ill health in determining who was poor has been overlooked by historians. In contrast to old age, there is relatively little extant work on the relationship between sickness and poor relief in the pre-industrial period, though its importance is not doubted. But medical costs were clearly an important component of total relief expenditures in the period, although this is obviously an imperfect gauge of the actual level of ill health. Between 5 and 20 per cent of total irregular payments in the communities studied by King from 1730 to 1770 were related to medical treatment of some kind.[42] On the other hand, work on pauper listings has generally suggested that only limited numbers of the poor were affected by illness. Pelling, for example, has shown that just 7.1 per cent of all recorded paupers in the Norwich census of 1570 were categorized as sick.[43] Similarly, according to Slack, sickness was only the 'most obvious cause of impoverishment' in 9 per cent of poor Norwich families, although the census of the poor compiled for Salisbury in 1635 gives a larger figure of 27 per cent.[44] More broadly, it seems that – in various European communities from around 1450 to 1800 – between 10 and 25 per cent of those in receipt of outdoor relief were sick.[45] Yet,

40   LA, QSP/174/5.
41   LA, QSP/199/13; QSP/299/21.
42   King, *Poverty and Welfare*, pp. 157, 199–200.
43   M. Pelling, *The Common Lot: Sickness, Medical Occupations and the Urban Poor in Early Modern England* (London, 1998), p. 74.
44   Slack, *Poverty and Policy*, p. 79.
45   Jütte, *Poverty and Deviance*, p. 24.

Pelling and Jütte's estimates are likely to understate the actual economic importance of sickness to pauper households, for the real impact of ill health would have been felt not just by the individual in question, but by their whole household. Their data also, like the Bolton census, refers to regular pensions and excludes occasional payments. Thus, it is worth being sensitive to the proportion of households *affected* by sickness. In view of this, the level of reported household sickness in the Lancashire petitions is not greatly at odds with those found elsewhere.

Given the vagueness of the petitions, and the unsophisticated medical knowledge of the time, we cannot read too much into the different diseases reported. Lameness and blindness were very common complaints, but others told of palsies, agues, the King's Evil (scrofula), falling sickness, and mental incapacity. Elizabeth Dandy of Tarleton told JPs in 1701 that she was troubled with 'a maisines in her head that shee is ready to fall if shee doth not suport herself by takeing hould of some table or stoole to help her'.[46] Isabel Hardman of Manchester had – in 1699 – 'a mellen-cholly man to her husband', and as a result 'none of your petitioners familly hath had or eaten any bread for the space of 3 dayes last past'.[47] One couple suffered a 'surfett of cold', while another man told of being 'very sore broken in his privat partes'.[48] Anne Orrell of Pemberton was given poor relief in 1700 after being poisoned by her lover, the toxin being administered in a cup of sugary water he had given her to toast their marriage.[49] Pregnancy, whilst not – of course – a sickness, was often written about in similar terms: in its final stages it acted as a form of bodily infirmity, reducing one's ability to work. William Hindley of Aspull reported in 1682 that his wife was 'at this tyme great with child & unable to doe anything towards a mantaynance'.[50] In 1688, Elizabeth Renshaw of Stretford petitioned that she had been widowed, and 'is not able to work any longer by reason of her bigness with child'.[51] Just under 2 per cent of petitioners referred to current or recent pregnancy.

Mental incapacity could be as devastating as any physical infirmity, and petitions recounted cases of people who had suffered from birth, as

---

46 LA, QSP/860/51.
47 LA, QSP/833/18.
48 LA, QSP/828/37; QSP/630/17.
49 LA, QSP/848/17.
50 LA, QSP/551/20.
51 LA, QSP/646/4.

well as those enduring acute bouts of mental illness.[52] In 1662, 85-year-old
Edmund Knowles of Gorton complained that his middle-aged son was
'deprived of most of his understandinge, whereby hee is unprofitable to
himselfe and his aged parents'.[53] Even more seriously, the 1670 petition
of Jane Bostock of Rainhill stated that her husband was suffering from
severe lunacy and that the family had 'beene att chardges for one to watch
& looke to him'.[54] However, without his earnings from shoemaking they
were unable to afford this, so they asked for relief so that he 'may bee
looked unto for destroyeinge himselfe or doeinge harme to any other'. In
Bolton in 1674, it was recorded that Elizabeth Alleains was 'soe simple as
not fitt to worke or begg', while in 1681, John Sandholme of Inskip-with-
Sowerby petitioned that

> his wyffe is exterordinary troubled with melancollie distemper in soe
> much that shee is in danger to distroy herselfe if shee should be left in
> the house allone but for the space of halfe an houre and he hath a child
> that is but about a month above halfe a yeare old which he nurseth and
> hee is a very pore mann and hath nothinge to maintayne himselfe nor
> his wyffe and child but his owne hand laboure & he can not leave his
> wyffe to worke unlesse he hier an able person to stay & looke to his
> wyffe for feare shee distroy herselfe ...[55]

In 1706, Mary Hill of Manchester told of how her husband 'has been
melancolly for thirty years last past and now is wholy distracted and
raveing mad', leaving her fully 'imploy'd in attending and looking after
him'.[56]

Many petitioners told of accidents. William Gille, an aged weaver from
Scarisbrick, complained in 1633 that two years earlier he had 'receyved
such a cruell fall that his body was soe bruysed therby, that sythence
hee was never able to sit at his woorke but hath since spent up former
gotten goodes & bine troublesome to his neighbours for his releeffe'.[57]

---

52   A. Fessler, 'The Management of Lunacy in Seventeenth Century England. An
Investigation of Quarter Sessions Records', *Proceedings of the Royal Society of Medicine*,
49 (1956), 901–7; P. Rushton, 'Lunatics and Idiots: Mental Disorder, the Community and
the Poor Law in North East England, 1600–1800', *Medical History*, 32 (1988), 34–50.
53   LA, QSP/240/37.
54   LA, QSP/359/21.
55   LA, DDKe/2/6/2, Survey of the Poor in Bolton, 1674; QSP/537/6.
56   LA, QSP/945/5.
57   LA, QSB/1/118/51.

In 1658, John Singleton – a servant from Broughton-in-Amounderness – needed poor relief after he was lamed by falling off a ladder.[58] In 1654, John Ashton, a blind man of eighty years residing in Ashton-in-Makerfield, petitioned for relief, noting that he had 'received severall hurts & crushes of bodie in marle pitts, by the fall of marle, and other accidents through his hard toyle and labor'.[59] John Renshall of Stretford claimed in 1655 that he was doubly unlucky.[60] Having been blind in one eye for ten years, 'being at worke making hedge for Sir Cecill Trafford Knight hastily stoopeing downe chanced to hitt his [other] eye upon an hasle sticke & thereby lost the sight thereof'. There were also cases of injuries in coal mines, carting accidents and at least one individual was hurt building a bridge.[61] Eleven weeks before Easter Sessions in 1682, William Hindley was out driving a plough, when 'one of the horses in the said plow struck your petitioner upon his left leg & with the said stroake broke his leg'. Thanks to this, Hindley 'never rose out of his bed for the space of one month & hee is still unable to worke or anywayes get his livelyhood'. His wife was pregnant and unable to assist, and he needed forty shillings to pay for the services of Thomas Baron the bone-setter.[62] All told, just over 1 per cent of all petitions referred to some kind of accident or wounding, though this figure – perhaps unsurprisingly – was higher at nearly 3 per cent in the mineral-working part of the county. In each case, it seems that this was seen either by petitioners, by justices or by both as being a legitimate reason for needing poor relief.

It is clear that sickness of whatever form could devastate the household economy. Like old age, it could lead to incapacity, reducing one's ability to work, to 'make shift', or even to feed oneself or one's family. But there was a further cost, too, for illness could force sufferers to spend large sums of money on treatment, and – like old age – it might necessitate the employment of carers to maintain something like an acceptable standard of living. This twin assault on the household economy was a recurrent theme in petitions. Thomas Greene, for example, a collier of Chorley, petitioned in 1653 that he had a

---

58 LA, QSP/162/1.
59 LA, QSP/103/1.
60 LA, QSP/120/8.
61 E.g. LA, QSP/224/6.
62 LA, QSP/551/20.

visitation of sickness, and hot favour [i.e. fever] which hath and as yett infecteth many famallys and inhabitants in these partes to the great weaknes of many ... wherby he hath not only spent and wasted all his estate, but alsoe hath debarred and doth still with hould him from all workes, and imployments.[63]

Similarly, in 1670, Abraham Hall of Heap complained that sickness and lameness left him 'not able to worke to mainteyne himselfe' as well as needing 'some competency to pay the surgion'.[64]

Many supplicants concentrated on their inability to make shift, to work, or provide for their families. In one of the more vivid descriptions of the impact of illness, Elizabeth Huddleston of Huyton petitioned in 1675 that she

> hath had the falling sicknesse during seaven & fortye yeares last past, falling at every full moone, & change, & somtymes oftner, & hath been many tymes in great perill of her life, both by fire, & water, in those her said trances, but especially about one month since a fall which shee then had, hath so disabled her, that shee cannot goe to seeke releife amongst good people.[65]

William Pendleton of Crumpsall, meanwhile, had worked as a linen-weaver, but by 1682 he had 'suffered a tedious visitation of painfull impotency for many years now last past, wherby he hath been rendered uncapeable of imployment, and helpless to himself, notwithstanding the best means he was able to procure in order to his recovery'.[66] Christopher Nuttall, an eighty-year-old labourer from Rochdale, told justices in 1687 that he was 'very sore broken in his privat partes that hee cannot goe abroad for to begg for a living'.[67] Edward France's wife, he petitioned in 1698 from Blackrod, had lost the use of one side through a 'palsie so that whereas before tyme shee could have gotten eighteene pence a weeke with spinning shee can not now get a penny'.[68] Robert Cowper of Broughton's wife was, he claimed in a 1690 petition, 'so lame that shee cannot rise nor

63   LA, QSP/75/17.
64   LA, QSP/356/4.
65   LA, QSP/436/22.
66   LA, QSP/547/12.
67   LA, QSP/630/17.
68   LA, QSP/812/1.

go to bedd of herselfe nor eate her meate without the helpe of one to feed her'.[69] According to Oliver Seedall of Worsley, his wife had been lame for three years by 1682, and 'thorrow her lamenes and infirmities her suck went from her', leaving her unable to nurse the couple's young baby. In fact, she was 'soe lame that she is not able to lay it on a bed nor to take it out of bed soe that the poore infant is in such a vere poore and feeble condicion that it would pittie any mans hart to bee hold it'.[70] Possibly more heartbreaking even than this was the case of Richard Harrison, a Skerton weaver. In 1691, Harrison appealed to the Lancashire bench in a petition that reminds us of just how little most of the poor must have understood the afflictions they bore, and how helpless they were in the face of them; he states that he 'for the space of six months last past hath been greevously afflicted with a swelling & pain in his neck which as your petitioner is informed is called a cancer by reason of which your petitioner being deprived of his strength and in such misery that he is not able to doe anything at all for his family'.[71]

The costs of caring for those who were so sick they could not look to themselves could be a major worry for the poor, and some were forced to stop working to look after their ailing spouses. Adam Pendlebury of Collyhurst saw his wife visited with sickness at Christmas 1680, 'so that shee could neither goe to bed nor rise without help neither can shee goe as yet but of a payer of crutches and is in danger to bee lame as long as shee liveth'. The sickness was, he said, 'a great hindrance to your poore petitioner in his worke by reason hee was not able to hire anie person to tent hir but was forsed to help hir as often as need required his selfe and your poore petitioner is cast into a deale of debt with being taken of his worke night and day'.[72] Ten years later, Thomas Dobson, a labourer from Whittingham, reported that his wife was so lame she could not move, meaning that 'all he can do is to looke and take care of his wife so that if your petitioner could work there must be one to take care of his wife'.[73] In 1699, meanwhile, Alice Leigh of Urmston reported that her husband was 'sore afflicted with mellencholly & very boystrouss and unruly', leaving her 'forced to wait on him & looke to him'.[74] Others tried

69   LA, QSP/678/18.
70   LA, QSP/555/5.
71   LA, QSP/696/6.
72   LA, QSP/535/11.
73   LA, QSP/693/27.
74   LA, QSP/833/23.

to buy in care, but were unable to afford it, such as blind Edward Sudell of Fishwick, who appealed for money in 1659 'towards the payment of the rent of his restinge place and the wages to her who washeth for him and attends upon him'.[75] Similarly, of the 9d she received a week in poor relief in 1667, Mary Hamer spent 6d 'every weeke for one to helpe her and her child to bed & from bed and upon all other necessary occasions'.[76] James Mawdesley of Middle Hulton, meanwhile, petitioned in 1690 that his wife was lame and so he was forced to hire a servant to look after her while he worked in husbandry; he only earned about 4d a week, though, and that was not enough.[77] For husbands who could not afford such a servant, the only option might be to give up work. Thus, in 1685, Robert Farnworth of Kearsley told of how he had a family with five children, and his wife was 'continually visited with very bad health soe that your petitioner is often forced to leave his worke and stay at home amongst them (not being able to hire a servant)'.[78]

Others focused on the way the costs of treatment had destroyed their wealth. Jane Tarleton of Hesketh 'wasted all her small stocke in physicke, and other things which shee procured for the recovery of her health' when she was hit by a disease of the back from around 1659 to 1662.[79] Samuel Dickenson, a linen-weaver of Heaton, claimed in 1674 to have suffered a long sickness and to have 'spent much in seeking remedy'.[80] The following year, despite the surgeon's willingness to waive his fee in regard of his patient's poverty, Ann Mercer of Great Woolton claimed to owe £6 10s 3d to an apothecary after her daughter had had a limb amputated.[81]

Few petitioners ventured much specific detail about their treatment. Alice Holt of Tottington petitioned in 1687 for ten shillings to relieve her granddaughter, afflicted with the King's Evil, for she had consulted Drs Grundy and Loe about the distemper and 'they think that a dyat drink and some other physick might be very beneficiall for her and tend much to her health', but her specificity was relatively unusual.[82] Probably most

---

75   LA, QSP/182/21.
76   LA, QSP/308/31.
77   LA, QSP/679/10.
78   LA, QSP/604/21.
79   LA, QSP/223/1.
80   LA, QSP/417/10.
81   LA, QSP/432/1; Richard Gough recalled that the amputation of a neighbour's leg cost the parish some £20: Gough, *History of Myddle*, p. 221.
82   LA, QSP/638/21.

were treated locally, though there is a 1636 case in which a woman from as far north as Over Kellet reported getting treatment in St Bartholomew's Hospital in London.[83] A small number mentioned having to pay for trips to London in order to be touched for the King's Evil. According to his successful petition of 1669, for example, Thomas Morecroft of Scarisbrick was forced to borrow twenty shillings in order to pay for the trip, he 'haveing no friends nor any estate or other mantanieance'.[84] However, of seventy-four petitioners who mentioned the Evil, only six stated explicitly that they had travelled to the capital, or asked for money to make the trip, all dating from the reign of Charles II. One of them, Thomas Charles of Worsley, reported – perhaps not surprisingly – that 'though the last springe your petitioner & to his greate costs procured a touch from his Majestie yet his distemper still growes faster & faster upon him insoemuch that hee is totally disinabled to worke'.[85] Nor was he the only one who noticed the apparent ineffectiveness of the King's divine touch: Hannah Williamson complained to the Manchester bench in 1683 that her child suffered the Evil, but 'tho his majesty has been pleased to touch the sayd child yet shee still breakes forth againe'.[86]

Indeed, much of the money on cures can, with hindsight, be said to have been wasted – at least in purely medical terms. Petitioners often mentioned the failure of attempts to treat them, and while in some cases this was probably due to the incurable nature of their disease, one does wonder about the expectations that were placed on the medical care provided. It might legitimately be asked, for example, why the employer of Edward Scorer of Leigh sent him in the early 1630s – on charity – to 'a strange Doctor in Phisick or chirugion who about that time sojourned in Manchester' in order to treat an unnamed sickness.[87] The stranger's attempt at cure proved ineffectual. In 1688, meanwhile, after a Christmas in which his daughter Ellen suffered some kind of mental breakdown, James Woodcock of Wheelton reported how she 'continues so mad that wee are constrained to loke her to a post', a 'treatment' only likely to have made matters worse.[88] It is, indeed, especially hard not to feel sorry for Nicholas Knott, who sometime before 1638 was

83 LA, QSB/1/164/27.
84 LA, QSP/331/5.
85 LA, QSP/441/6.
86 LA, QSP/563/16.
87 LA, QSB/1/134/60.
88 LA, QSP/653/12.

under the hands of George Cloughe and John Cloughe phisitians for to have my sores cured, and therupon they searched and in my theegh they found a sore seaven ynches deepe and in the cuttinge of it withe a penknife George Clough turned his hand round aboute in it which was verie great payne unto mee and great coste & charges, for they came unto mee constantelie a whole quarter of a yeare.[89]

Perhaps the two Cloughs had Knott's best interests at heart, indeed they even countersigned his petition to Quarter Sessions, but their cure hardly seems to have done much help.

In fact, sickness could even leave paupers vulnerable to the avarice of their neighbours, whether counterfeit healers or simply opportunist scammers. When blacksmith John Percivall of Manchester fell blind in the 1650s, 'his apprentice takinge the advantage of your petitioners afflictions [did] run away from your petitioner and left him void of any assistance'.[90] Most reprehensible was the behaviour of the neighbours of Thomas Grayson of Rainford, whose wife complained in 1665 that he

hath for severall yeares last past beene lunatick and deprived of his understanding within which tyme severall neighbours and inhabitants of the townshipp of Rainford well knowing his defect of reason and understanding and through an unjust and greedy desire to advantage and enrich themselves have by theire practices and endeavors obteyned from your petitioners husband for very inconsiderable sommes of money severall graunts of the lands and tenements of your petitioners husband soe that not any parte thereof is left for or towards the releefe or mateynance of your petitioners husband her selfe and theire children[91]

A list of eight neighbours who had taken advantage of Grayson in this manner was appended to his wife's petition, and the justices at Wigan were sufficiently convinced of the case to order these eight to be specially taxed by the overseers to ensure his maintenance. There is a hint of exploitation in other petitions, too. Ellen Graystock of Preston claimed in 1688 that she was a 'poor lunatick womane not of her self able half so much to mantain herself she being so much an idiot that she

89 LA, QSB/1/195/78.
90 LA, QSP/156/7.
91 LA, QSP/267/6.

will worke a full weeke for one penny whereas she pays two pence for her bed & fier'.[92]

It is possible that the poor were more prone to sickness than wealthier members of society. We can assume that they tended to live in more crowded accommodation and performed more dangerous jobs than those higher up the social scale, and they may have had worse diets, too. But this is exceptionally hard to prove, for any attempt to compare levels of sickness amongst 'the poor' against the 'non poor' is inevitably circular. Nonetheless, there are two statements by petitioners which appear very significant. First, Isabel Taylor of Haslingden reported to Preston Quarter Sessions in Midsummer 1675 that her eldest child had '*through poverty* become maimed & not able to worke or walke abroad to seeke releife'.[93] Then, in 1684, an appeal from fourteen-year-old Robert Willasy of Ashton told of how he had 'by cold and inevitable poverty contracted soares and those distempers that at present make him languish in a condition so deplorable that he can neither goe nor ride and is now neer starved'.[94] These are two statements out of a large sample, but it would appear in these cases petitioners were suggesting a link between being poor and getting ill, rather than the more obvious reverse.

The nuclear household: formation and breakdown

Bodily infirmity, then, either as a result of old age or some other form of ill health, lay at the root of most petitions, but a third major characteristic of those petitioning for poor relief was rather different. This was their tendency to be single.

The nuclear household was the dominant form of social organization in pre-industrial England.[95] This basic fact, which is often supposed to have distinguished Western Europe from other pre-industrial societies such as those in Asia and Africa, has given rise to the suggestion that the greater emphasis on collective and state poor relief in the West was a product of the looser familial ties and smaller potential for risk-pooling

---

92   LA, QSP/648/8.
93   LA, QSP/435/11. My italics.
94   LA, QSP/585/3.
95   J. Hajnal, 'European Marriage Patterns in Perspective', in *Population in History: Essays in Historical Demography*, ed. D. V. Glass and D. E. C. Eversley (London, 1965), pp. 101–43; Laslett, *World We Have Lost*, pp. 90–9.

amongst kin-groups here.[96] On the other hand, we must realize that however inadequate the nuclear household was as a locus of mutual support, it did provide some kind of economic safety net for vulnerable individuals. It was, quite simply, better in economic terms to be in a two-adult partnership than it was to be alone.[97] And nuclear households also served to mitigate, for each family, the gender imbalances of the labour market, while concurrently helping to pool supposedly 'male' and 'female' productive activities, notably paid employment and unpaid domestic work.

Given this, it is perhaps not surprising that the breakdown of nuclear households, or the failure of people to form them, was one of the most salient social characteristics of the county's poor, being mentioned in just over 40 per cent of all first petitions. In Bolton, 70.1 per cent of poor households in 1686 and 1699 had fewer than two adults, making this the most common identifier; and, whilst the average two-adult household received 21.1 per cent of its recorded income from the township, single women took 42.4 per cent, single men 52.7 per cent, and those households with no adults 74.9 per cent. Regression analysis suggests that having only one adult in the family increased the proportion of income taken from the township by 24 per cent.

Essentially, there were three problems related specifically to the nuclear household. First, there were always some people who failed to form them, with statistics from demographic studies suggesting, for example, that around a quarter of women born in 1606 never married.[98] Secondly, every nuclear family eventually broke down, either through some kind of separation (notably abandonment by one spouse) or more usually through death. Thus widows, widowers and deserted wives (and just occasionally deserted husbands) were prone to fall into poverty, and their prevalence in the Lancashire petitions reinforces the findings of other studies. For example, the proportion of relieved households judged by Slack to have been poor on account of the death or desertion of the main breadwinner lay at 17 per cent in Norwich (1570), and 14 per cent in Salisbury (1635).[99] In fourteen case studies from seventeenth-century Norfolk as recounted by Wales, the mean proportion of pensioners who were widows stood at

96   Laslett, 'Family, Kinship and the Collectivity', pp. 153–8.
97   Cf. Ottaway, 'Providing for the Elderly', p. 395.
98   Wrightson, *Earthly Necessities*, p. 223.
99   Slack, *Poverty and Policy*, p. 79; cf. Bailey, *Unquiet Lives*, pp. 168–92.

50.1 per cent.[100] Similarly, in 1660s Biddenden (Kent) and St Peter's Bywell (Northumberland) in the 1720s, widows were markedly over-represented amongst the poor.[101] Thirdly, child-rearing, by temporarily introducing new dependants to the household, could tip the balance from self-support into indigence as a household became 'overcharged with children'.[102]

In all this, it is crucial to emphasize the disproportionate vulnerability of single women to poverty. By contrast, single men are extremely hard to detect. They are usually invisible in petitions as wives are frequently not mentioned even when clearly present.[103] Spinsters, on the other hand, occur relatively often, accounting for nearly 6 per cent of all adult female petitions.[104] Similarly, there are more widowed and deserted females than males.[105] A total of 54 per cent of female petitions claimed widowhood, compared with the 6 per cent of males who explicitly mentioned being widow*ers*. Deserted wives, or wives forced apart from their husbands, accounted for 13 per cent of female petitions, of which 5 per cent had husbands in prison, 32 per cent had husbands in the armed forces, while 63 per cent had simply been abandoned.[106] The number of deserted husbands in the petitions could be counted on the fingers of one hand. Although the economics of family breakdown has still not been fully explored by historians, support for these figures is not hard to find.[107] Pelling found just one widower in the 1570 census of the poor for Norwich, and in 1590s Ipswich, a mere 4.9 per cent of households were headed by single men, with the equivalent figure of 13.1 per cent for 1630s Salisbury only slightly higher.[108] Indeed, calculating from figures presented by Newman-Brown for Aldenham (Hertfordshire), it

100   Wales, 'Poverty, Poor Relief and the Life-cycle', p. 361. My calculation.

101   Poole, 'Welfare Provision in Seventeenth-Century Kent', pp. 260–1; Rushton, 'Poor Law, the Parish and the Community', p. 150.

102   Wales, 'Poverty, Poor Relief and the Life-cycle', pp. 374–6.

103   Cf. Hindle, *On the Parish?*, p. 409. Hindle found 36 per cent of Cumberland petitions were from single men, compared with 45 per cent from single women.

104   This could also be an occupational title, as in the case of Margaret Hunt of Nateby (1669) who was both a 'spinster' and a 'widow'. Nonetheless, internal evidence of family circumstances within petitions leaves no doubt that in the vast majority of cases the term was being used in the sense of a single woman.

105   Cf. Boulton, 'It is extreme necessity', p. 53.

106   Cf. Snell, *Annals*, p. 361; D. A. Kent, '"Gone for a soldier": Family Breakdown and the Demography of Desertion in a London Parish, 1750–91', *LPS*, 45 (1990), 27–42 (p. 29).

107   Although, see: Snell, *Annals*, pp. 359–64; L. Stone, *The Family, Sex and Marriage in England, 1500–1800* (London, 1977), p. 38; Kent, 'Gone for a soldier'.

108   M. Pelling, 'Finding Widowers: Men without Women in English Towns before 1700', in *Widowhood in Medieval and Early Modern Europe*, ed. S. Cavallo and L. Warner

appears that while an average of 32.8 per cent of resident widows at any point between 1641 and 1681 might be receiving poor relief, the equivalent figure for widowers was much lower at 13.2 per cent.[109] In Colyton (Devon) in 1682, just 22.5 per cent of pauper males over fifty years old were widowed, as compared with 67.5 per cent of equivalent females.[110]

The vulnerability to poverty of female-headed households is also attested by their regular prevalence in lists of those receiving or asking for relief, where women were very much *over*represented compared with other lists of household heads such as tax returns or censuses. Whilst around 10 per cent of households were normally headed by women, just over half of all adult petitions were by females. And of the twenty-one 'very poore distressed' households in Tottington in 1629, ten were headed by women.[111] Similarly, in Lonsdale Hundred in 1638, just under half of pensioners were women, although here there is a tantalizing and inexplicable difference between the northern (69 per cent female) and southern (82 per cent *male*) divisions.[112] The female-dominated pattern is repeated in other accounts: in Prestwich township, the ratio of named male to female paupers (taking each year separately) was 0.7 between 1646 and 1681; in Atherton from 1710–23 it was 0.8, while in Hawkshead (1690–1730) and Cheetham (1695–1730) the equivalent figures were 0.5 and 0.9 respectively.[113] It also fits in with the bulk of previous work on poor relief, such as King's work on nine parishes for the later eighteenth century.[114] Amongst petitioners the ratio was just under 1.0, but – intriguingly – the male to female ratio was particularly high in the south-east of the county: at Lancaster Sessions it was 0.7, at Preston 0.9, and at Wigan/Ormskirk 0.8, but at Manchester it was as high as 1.3.[115] This may well represent the unusual ability of the textile-based economy

---

(Harlow, 1999), pp. 37–54 (p. 42); *Poor Relief in Elizabethan Ipswich*, pp. 122–40; *Poverty in Early-Stuart Salisbury*, pp. 75–80.

109   Calculated from: Newman-Brown, 'Receipt of Poor Relief', p. 412.

110   P. Sharpe, *Population and Society in an East Devon Parish: Reproducing Colyton, 1540–1840* (Exeter, 2002), p. 225; also, cf. Fissell, 'Sick and Drooping Poor', p. 47.

111   LA, QSB/1/59/86.

112   TNA, SP16/397/69, Report of the Justices of Lonsdale Hundred, 20 August 1638.

113   MALS, L160/2/1, Prestwich Churchwardens' and Overseers' Accounts, 1646–83; CRO (K), WPR/83/7/3–4, Hawkshead Overseers' Accounts, 1690–1798; MALS, M10/7/2/1, Cheetham Overseers' Accounts, 1693–1791; WA, TR/Ath/C/2/1–5, Atherton Overseers' Accounts, 1692–1733.

114   King, *Poverty and Welfare*, pp. 167, 212; Jütte, *Poverty and Deviance*, p. 41.

115   If 10 per cent of household heads were female, then this would be represented by a male to female ratio of 9.0.

of the south-east to provide employment for women. Indeed, using a rough economic categorization for each petition's township of origin, the relationship comes out even more strongly. Here, the male to female relationship was 0.7 in the plains and 0.9 in both the mineral-working region and the rolling agricultural parts of the county. But it was 1.3 in the areas of fustian manufacture, and as high as 1.8 in the woollens region.

As interesting as these local variations are, however, the bigger story is that – across the county – single women were over-represented amongst the poor, and the most fundamental reason for this was that in early modern England, as with most human societies, past and present, women earned less than men did.[116] Women's wages were generally markedly lower than men's, partly because their efforts were often restricted to the less well-paid jobs such as carding and spinning, but also because they tended to be paid less for doing similar jobs.[117] There is a sense from the surviving petitions that the lower earning power of women was taken for granted. It was often stated that a household had been self-sufficient while the father was alive, with little questioning of why it should be that male earnings were so critical. A typical example is the petition of Mary Buckley of Leigh, read at Ormskirk in 1628.[118] Buckley's husband, George, had fathered three children by her in the 1620s:

> the which her sayd husband (during his lyffe) did by his paynes taking in the trade of a fustian weaver in a decent maner mayntayne. But her sayd husband (In Lent last) to the inspeakeable greeffe of your pore petitioner departed this lyffe, leaving your petitioner with those 3 children without meanes to keepe them on …

Similarly, many male petitioners wrote of 'relieving' their wives, as if to suggest a net redistribution of income from husband to wife within couples. The vulnerability of single women to poverty was a function of the patriarchal assumptions underpinning the labour market.

---

116 J. M. Bennett, 'Medieval Women, Modern Women: Across the Great Divide', in *Culture and History, 1350–1600: Essays on English Communities, Identities and Writings*, ed. D. Aers (Hemel Hempstead, 1992), pp. 147–76 (pp. 161–2); also: A. Fletcher, *Gender, Sex and Subordination in England, 1500–1800* (London, 1995), pp. 223–55.

117 Bennett, 'Medieval Women, Modern Women', pp. 155–64; C. Shammas, 'The World Women Knew: Women Workers in the North of England during the Late Seventeenth Century', in *The World of William Penn*, ed. R. S. Dunn and M. Maples-Dunn (Philadelphia, 1986), pp. 99–116 (pp. 104–10).

118 LA, QSB/1/42/63.

But there were other reasons too. Women, even then, tended to live slightly longer. Widowers were also, thanks to their economic position, sometimes more likely to find new – younger – partners than widows.[119] In addition, legal factors related to the holding and transmission of property can only have served to increase the hardship of single women.[120] When a man's wife died there was no immediate impact on his material possessions; by contrast, the death of a husband was likely to entail the loss of access by his wife to a considerable share of the household's property. This was especially true after Parliament in 1670 reduced the proportion passed on to widows from childless intestate men from the whole of his movable goods down to just one half (where there was a next of kin).[121] Furthermore, the so-called 'widow's portion', the third part of a man's goods that he was unable to alienate by will and which was to revert to his spouse, was abolished for the northern province in 1692. This legislation left a man theoretically free to disinherit his wife completely. Given the importance of property as a security against hardship, discussed in the last chapter, women's disproportionate lack of access to it was a critical economic disability. On the other hand, a share in customary lands, often of a third, sometimes devolved upon the widow on the death of the husband, but the impact of this on the very poorest is doubtful, and even those with at least some wealth seem to have found it hard to hang on to their property.[122] Paupers were probably most likely to live in small leasehold cottages paying market rents, and these would often revert to the landlord if the husband died. Thus, the simple fact remains that the death of a husband had a much more serious impact on the financial position of his widow than vice versa.

Similar factors probably explain why, in the vast majority of cases of abandonments in petitions, it was husbands who had left their wives and not the other way around. In terms of the economics of poverty, the impact of an abandonment was similar to that of bereavement, although there was some small hope of tracking down the offending party and forcing him

---

119   Pelling, 'Old Age', pp. 87–90.

120   S. Cavallo and L. Warner, 'Introduction', in Cavallo and Warner (eds), *Widowhood in Medieval and Early Modern Europe*, pp. 3–23 (pp. 12–15); A. L. Erickson, 'Property and Widowhood in England, 1660–1840', in ibid., pp. 145–63.

121   Erickson, 'Property and Widowhood', pp. 152–3.

122   W. Butler, *The Customs and Tenant-right of the Northern Counties* (Millom, 1925), pp. 11–24; B. H. Toft, 'Widowhood in a Market Town: Abingdon, 1540–1720' (Univ. of Oxford DPhil thesis, 1983), p. 293.

to offer financial support.[123] On the other hand, abandonment might not necessarily entail the same loss of wealth as death, for there was no will or devolution of property involved. Nonetheless, some errant husbands found a way around this by simply selling off household property before fleeing. According to her petition of 1654, Katherine Chamney's husband had sold their 'little house in Lancaster' before running away.[124] Elizabeth Swift of Burscough complained in 1675 that sixteen years previously her husband had fled into Ireland, but not before mortgaging their tenement, worth £12 per annum.[125] Similarly, the petition of Anna Browne of Nateby stated that her husband left her for the army in 1678 with 'three small children and nothing wherewithall to maintaine them, for before hee went hee made over all his goods to severall neightbours, to whom hee ought some money'.[126] Few, though, could claim to have been as unlucky in marriage as Elizabeth Gaskell of Orrell. Her first husband, she recounted, had been executed for treason, forfeiting all of his goods and leaving her – she claimed – with nothing. By 1684 she had remarried to one Edward Gaskell, but he 'hath since left your petitioner and betaken himselfe to another woman and hath been with the said woman since Mayday'. She was left with four children.[127]

It was common for abandoned wives to state that it was to escape creditors that their husbands had fled.[128] Isabel Taylor of Haslingden reported to Preston Sessions in 1675 that her husband had, as a result of debt, been 'forced to leave this county'.[129] Four years earlier the wife of Robert Booth of Denton reported that her husband was forced 'by reson of his depts and the rigor of his creditors to leave his owne home, being in the place aforesaid, and he being now in or about London'.[130] Less understanding was the wife of John Ryding of Little Crosby, who in 1669 noted her spouse's 'bad husbandrie' in getting himself 'into such debtes that hee was forsed to flee into Ireland'.[131] A similar tale had been told at Manchester Sessions two years previously in which Martha Pilkington recounted that

---

123 E.g. LA, QSP/198/9.
124 LA, QSP/89/6.
125 LA, QSP/436/36.
126 LA, QSP/479/4.
127 LA, QSP/586/24.
128 Cf. Gough, *History of Myddle*, pp. 226, 228; B. S. Capp, *When Gossips Meet: Women, Family and Neighbourhood in Early Modern England* (Oxford, 2003), pp. 40–1.
129 LA, QSP/435/11.
130 LA, QSP/368/4.
131 LA, QSP/335/8–9.

about seaven years since she married one James Pilkington of Salford whoe had in marriage with her at least threescore pounds[.] But soe it is that the said James Pilkington haveinge wasted & spent the said moneys & runn into debt about twoe yeares & an halfe since left your petitioner with twoe small children & went to London where hee now is. Since which tyme of his departure your petitioner hath paid almost £20 of her husbands debts which shee raised by the sale of her goodes and what was remaineinge thereof she hath hitherto releeved herselfe & children[,] her said husband allowinge her nothing ...[132]

Even without debt being a factor, the emotional difficulties resulting from a hard life in poverty might have encouraged some people to abandon their families and seek better lives elsewhere. Thus Bridget Hesketh of Aighton petitioned in 1649 that her husband had run away after losing his goods in the Civil Wars, he being 'not willinge to partake with his wife & children in want & miserye'.[133]

Abandonment during pregnancy or lying-in must have been especially traumatic. Elizabeth Ogden's husband, a Manchester packer, had left her infirm and with a young child (not eight weeks old) he having – she claimed in 1683 – 'over gone her to live in some remote place unknowne to your petitioner'.[134] In 1687, Margaret Albin of Whittingham had been abandoned with six children, 'whereof fower of them are in a manner infant', left 'in a forlorne and destitute condition by an ungratious & cruall husband'.[135] The following year Elizabeth Walker of Kirkland told Preston JPs that her husband John, shortly after their wedding, 'rann his country & left your petitioner miserably poor & great with child allmost at down lyinge'.[136] Margaret Owen's husband, a Walton-le-Dale woollen-webster, left her just a fortnight before her pregnancy was due to come to term, so said her 1689 petition, as did Rebecca Penketh's husband (a labourer from Great Sankey) the following year.[137]

It is possible to wonder, especially in cases where debt was a prominent cause, whether marital breakdown might have been a greater problem amongst poor households than it was in the population as a whole.

132   LA, QSP/304/14.
133   LA, QSP/22/18.
134   LA, QSP/575/12.
135   LA, QSP/636/12.
136   LA, QSP/644/1.
137   LA, QSP/668/45, QSP/686/11

Martin Ingram has drawn attention to the comparative volatility of marriages amongst the poor, while Joanne Bailey highlights the 'instability of the marriages of those vulnerable to poverty'.[138] On the other hand, there may be an element of circularity here, for – as Muldrew has suggested – existing disorder in a household even before a desertion could lead to a loss of credit and therefore eventually poverty.[139] Indeed, abandonments could clearly occur as a result of a simple breakdown in the personal relationship between the couple, regardless of their economic position. In 1651, for example, the wife of Edward Brand of Lancaster petitioned magistrates in the town, alleging that he had not only denied her relief from his estate of £20 per annum, but had also 'caused proclamation to be made in severall market townes that noe person or persons should credit or truste [her] … for anie moneyes goods chattels or corne'. Worse still, Edward had 'threatned to bynd your petitioner to a post and for to burne the howse over her heade or else to put her downe at the Bridge'.[140] Moreover, Diane O'Hara's suggestion that marriages amongst the relatively poor were entered into with extreme care should warn us against seeing them as necessarily transient for simple economic reasons.[141]

One quite striking facet of the petition sample is the increasing number of women who claimed to have been left by husbands who had joined the armed forces, especially from 1689 onwards.[142] This is hardly surprising, given the large-scale recruitment of men to fight the wars of King William and Queen Anne against Louis XIV. Indeed, it is a timely reminder that the seventeenth century saw two great periods of military mobilization – the Civil Wars and the War of the League of Augsburg (1689–97), followed almost immediately by the War of the Spanish Succession (1702–13). These were not just distant battles in faraway lands: they had real consequences at home, not only in terms of extra taxation and trade disruption, but also because a large number of England's families lost men to the fighting. Indeed, enlistment may well have been – as Keith Snell suggests – 'the institutionally acceptable form of familial desertion', though of sixty-seven petitioners in the sample whose husbands were away in the forces, twenty-nine of them stated that he

138 M. J. Ingram, *Church Courts, Sex and Marriage in England, 1570–1640* (Cambridge, 1987), pp. 148–9; Bailey, *Unquiet Lives*, pp. 6, 171–2.
139 Muldrew, *Economy of Obligation*, pp. 124–5.
140 The petition asked for relief out of his estate rather than poor relief. LA, QSP/41/4.
141 D. O'Hara, *Courtship and Constraint: Rethinking the Making of Marriage in Tudor England* (Manchester, 2000), pp. 219–20.
142 Cf. Capp, *When Gossips Meet*, p. 42.

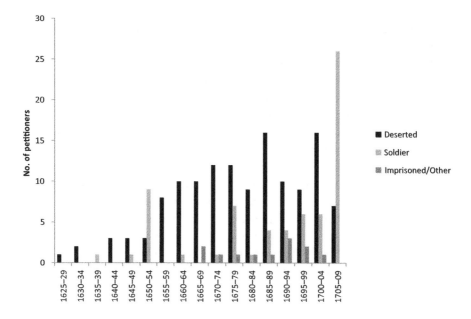

Figure 9: Desertions, imprisonments and enlistments by half-decade, from Lancashire pauper petitions, 1625–1709

had been impressed, and only fourteen explicitly stated that the enlistment had been voluntary.[143] Certainly the War of the Spanish Succession seems to have brought a particularly heavy toll (Figure 9).

Exceedingly few petitions relate tales of runaway wives. This was no doubt a product of two factors: such an occurrence was less frequent as women had more to lose economically from family breakdown, and when it did happen it was less likely to lead to immediate hardship. Indeed, this presumably explains why, when reform of the Poor Law was suggested in the Parliament of 1626, one new clause would have been to make the abandonment of wives and children by husbands or the abandonment of children by men or women a punishable offence, yet nothing was said of the abandonment of husbands by wives.[144] There were exceptions, however.[145] In Atherton in 1714/15, the overseers' accounts contain a payment of 2s 9d

143   E.g. LA, QSP/483/4; QSP/485/22; QSP/489/5; Snell, *Annals*, p. 362; cf. Kent, 'Gone for a soldier'.
144   *Proceedings in Parliament, 1626*, vol. 4, p. 123.
145   Cf. Bailey, *Unquiet Lives*, pp. 191–2.

for 'Tabling a child of John Youngs when his wife had laft him'.[146] Over half a century earlier in 1665, the wife of John Pennington of Ince ensured his poverty by running away and taking with her 'not onely your petitioners household goods but alsoe the very cloathes which your petitioners children did then weare[,] leaveing some of the same children naked all of them being very little and one of them a sucking childe'.[147] More simply, in a petition endorsed by a number of his neighbours, Thomas Moreton of Barton stated in 1671 that he was 'a verie poore man (his wife beinge over runne him)'.[148] There is not the evidence here to support Bernard Capp's assertion that runaway wives (on account of their cruel husbands) were 'commonplace', but there are *some* cases of abandoned husbands. Whether they had been cruel is lost to us forever.

Men recounted the *death* of their spouse much more frequently than abandonment, although still not as often as women did. More than one out of every twenty male petitioners made a point of mentioning it, bearing testimony to the very real economic importance of female labour within the domestic world of the poor.[149] Women made significant monetary contributions to the household economy; indeed, a study of their activities in the far north of the county shows women involved in a wide range of economic activities outside the household.[150] But they also undertook exceptionally important and laborious unpaid domestic work, as well as playing a critical role in the upbringing of children.[151] This fact is not always obvious from reading the work of economic historians (usually male), but it would have been to Hugh Walsh of Heskin, who in 1648 described himself as 'very weake thorow his lamenes and not able to work as formerly', and petitioned for poor relief when 'it pleasing good [i.e. God] aboute Christmas last to take to himselffe your petitioner['s] said wyffe'.[152] John Simpson, the 'pittifull pyper' of Haigh, told justices in 1681 how his wife had died 'and hath left him three or four children to manteyne & he hath nothing to manteyne them with' (though quite how he was unable to say *exactly* how many children he

---

146   WA, TR/Ath/C/2/3, Atherton Overseers' Accounts, 1712–16.

147   LA, QSP/279/10.

148   LA, QSP/376/11.

149   Williams notes a number of cases in which widowers started receiving poor relief immediately following the death of their wives: Williams, *Poverty*, p. 113.

150   Shammas, 'World Women Knew'.

151   For a summary see: C. Peters, *Women in Early Modern Britain, 1450–1640* (Basingstoke, 2004), pp. 45–67.

152   LA, QSP/3/35.

had is hard to know).[153] In 1687, Broughton shoemaker Richard Wilkinson described suffering an ague for two years making it difficult for him to work, '& to increase his troble your petitioners wife dyed about 12 monthes agoe & left your petitioner a young child, not yet two yeares old which he has fostered up till now'.[154] The removal from the domestic economy of the wife, as the principal provider of unpaid 'household' work, might leave the husband with the choice of whether to pay someone else to undertake that work, or to do it himself, with the associated opportunity costs then impacting on his ability to earn.[155] One case of the former strategy is the 1657 petition of James Hart, a husbandman widower of Westhoughton, who claimed that he did not earn enough money to hire somebody to look after his three children while he worked.[156] In a similar manner, John Kellett of Walton-le-Dale told in 1683 that he was lately widowed and, 'not being able to pay for nurseing his youngest child nor haveing any subsistance for the other two', his children were 'likely to be starved'.[157] John Howard of Chadderton, meanwhile, petitioned in 1670 that

> his vocacion is what hee can gett with following and dryving of two little horses loaden with coales or other loading what hee can procure from one place to another so as your petitioner by his calling is much forced to bee from his children and cannot bee without some one amongst his children to dresse and order them.[158]

Not for nothing did the Manchester wigmaker and diarest Edmund Harrold describe his wife, when she died, as his 'dear assistant'.[159]

It may well be that, given the very forceful cultural expectations about gender roles in the period, men were often reluctant to perform household tasks deemed more suitable for women, such as housework and child-rearing. According to a popular work by the Marquis of Halifax, published in 1688, the 'Oeconomy of the House' was indecent to the husband, whose 'Province is without doors'.[160] Capp, indeed, found a

153   LA, QSP/530/9–10.
154   LA, QSP/636/18.
155   Cf. Horden, 'Household Care', p. 37.
156   LA, QSP/144/7.
157   LA, QSP/565/11.
158   LA, QSP/360/13.
159   E. Harrold, *The Diary of Edmund Harrold, Wigmaker of Manchester, 1712–15*, ed. C. Horner (Aldershot, 2008), p. 52.
160   Quoted in Bailey, *Unquiet Lives*, p. 78.

seventeenth-century Cambridgeshire villager who was roundly mocked for staying home and minding the child and cleaning the floor, while his wife went about having an affair with their servant.[161] And Bailey, surveying matrimonial lawsuits, found that 'a domestic double-standard prevailed with husbands' involvement restricted to emergency situations like illness, their wives' lying-in, or periods of male unemployment'.[162] This being said, the fact that some men who lost their wives' household labour were forced to supplicate for poor relief does nicely illustrate Bailey's point that the indispensability of female work helped take some of the edge off patriarchy – enforcing a 'marital relationship of co-dependency'.[163]

There was also a simpler economic function played by partnerships, too, for couples were inherently more insulated against shocks to the earning power or living costs of one spouse. Thus, as unromantic as it sounds, marriage served as a form of risk-pooling between two individuals. According to a 1638 petition, supported by her neighbours, lamed Anne Vaux of Ormskirk was maintained by her husband until he became too old.[164] William Nicholson of Ulverston recounted in 1659 that, as he aged and his eyesight failed, his wife had been 'his helper and the best cumforeth he hade under God'.[165] Similarly, when John Leigh of Crompton fell ill with an ague in 1674 – so he petitioned that year – his wife Anne was able to maintain him and their children for eighteen weeks by her 'diligent and hard labour'.[166] Finally, expressing the same sentiment from a rather different angle was Thomas Singleton of Wharles, who in 1660 lamented that he and his wife had become so destitute that 'neither of them [were] able to looke to one another when in any sicknes or misery'.[167] Indeed, the importance of having two incomes could only get greater as paupers got older. Age brought increasing infirmity, and thus more times when one needed a partner to rely upon, both for income and care. As Francis Bacon put it, with characteristic pith, 'Wives are young men's mistresses; companions for middle age; and old men's nurses'.[168]

---

161   Capp, *When Gossips Meet*, p. 246.
162   Bailey, *Unquiet Lives*, p. 78.
163   Ibid., pp. 78–84.
164   LA, QSB/1/198/32.
165   LA, QSP/173/7.
166   LA, QSP/425/15.
167   LA, QSP/198/36.
168   F. Bacon, *The Essayes or Counsels, Civill and Morall, of Francis Lord Verulam, Viscount St Alban* (London, 1626), p. 39.

In the light of all this, the practice whereby parishes *prevented* marriages amongst the poor seems short-sighted. This phenomenon has been focused on by Hindle and is taken to represent one of the more extreme forms of exclusion under the Poor Laws.[169] It has to be said that relatively few cases of the prevention of marriage have been unearthed, although this hardly renders the subject unimportant. The Lancashire evidence is sketchy, but there are two comparatively well-known cases from Ashton-under-Lyne in the 1630s.[170] In fact, it would be unwise to focus too heavily on attempts to prevent marriage in the face of clear evidence that parishes actually tried to make failing unions work. In at least one case, from Atherton in 1720, officers actually seem to have subsidized the marriage of a pauper, while in Padiham in 1726 they paid for a single mother to marry the father of her child.[171] In addition, errant husbands were often pursued and either forced to return to their wives or at least to pay for their upkeep.[172] The key point is probably that officers were not necessarily against pauper marriage *per se*, but were wary of those marriages which might confer a right of settlement on future children. Prevention of marriage was really the prevention of *settlement*.

Children, indeed, could bring considerable hardship, even to two-adult families. Particularly difficult were periods in which households included children considered too young to work, which by definition came at times when the mother had temporarily (though perhaps partially) withdrawn from the labour market.[173] Cases of large families requiring assistance appear in virtually any set of poor accounts.[174] Adam Chorlton and his wife of Little Bolton, for example, were given an allowance of 9s a week for themselves and their seven children in 1674.[175] Three years later it was reported by the

169   Hindle, 'Problem of Pauper Marriage'; Hindle, *On the Parish?*, pp. 337–52; Ingram, *Church Courts*, pp. 130–1.

170   TNA, SP16/404/96, Report of the Justices of Ashton-under-Lyne and Oldham, 18 December 1638; Hindle, *On the Parish?*, p. 342.

171   WA, TR/Ath/C/2/4, Atherton Overseers' Accounts, 1717–24; LA, PR/2863/3/7, Padiham Overseers' Accounts and Papers, 1696–1829. Williams finds that Bedfordshire parishes encouraged, and even forced, single paupers to marry, though it seems that in all cases the bride was either pregnant or had already given birth to an illegitimate child: Williams, *Poverty*, p. 108.

172   Bailey, *Unquiet Lives*, pp. 35–7.

173   H. Medick, 'The Proto-industrial Family Economy', *Social History*, 3 (1976), 291–315 (pp. 304–6).

174   E.g. Wales, 'Poverty, Poor Relief and the Life-cycle', p. 373; J. Boulton, *Neighbourhood and Society: A London Suburb in the Seventeenth Century* (Cambridge, 1987), p. 125.

175   LA, DDKe/2/6/2, Survey of the Poor in Bolton, 1674.

overseers of Tonge that Thomas Hilton and his wife were overburdened with nine children, while James Browne of Lathom petitioned for relief in 1678 on account of his having ten.[176] In the Bolton censuses of the poor from 1686 and 1699, thirty-four out of 245 households with an adult head (14 per cent) had four or more children.[177] Petitions frequently complained of households having a 'great charge' of children, and these were often singled out as a major cause of hardship. In our sample of petitions, 43 per cent mentioned having one child or more to support their case, though – as petitioners had a habit of including children they had already raised and who had already flown the nest – this figure is not a reliable indicator of how many of the poor had dependant offspring still living with them (but perhaps it does illustrate the belief that raising children cost you money you would never get back).[178] In addition, some of the most severe cases of poverty were those of the orphans recorded amongst petitions. As the protection of children was one of the basic functions of the family, orphaned children represented an extreme form of family breakdown, and this was clearly widely accepted as a form of deserving poverty. Some 2 per cent of petitions were on behalf of parentless children, and these appear to have been treated with great sympathy by the county bench. Indeed, these figures probably do not reflect the total level of poverty caused by such parental loss, as orphans were probably less likely to have been rejected by overseers in the first place.

Much of the problem was, of course, that children cost money to raise. As Jane Erleham of Pilkington put it in 1629, her children were 'verie yonge and not able to helpe them selves nor to gett their liveinge'.[179] On the other hand, children were apparently expected to make some contribution from an age which the modern world would consider very young. In late-seventeenth-century Bolton, for example, children as young as five were employed as spinners – perhaps in part reflecting the particular vibrancy of that town's textile industries and a resulting shortage of labour. Here, indeed, children apparently made unusually useful contributions to the household economy.[180] The information in petitions, alas, is considerably less reliable, as most children were simply described as 'small' rather than being of specific ages. That said, the petition of Rossendale weaver Oliver

176   LA, QSP/469/30; QSP/488/3.
177   TNA, SP16/388/7, Report of the Justices of Kendal Ward, 18 April 1638; BALS, PBO/1/1, Bolton Censuses of the Poor, 1686 and 1699.
178   Cf. Hindle, *On the Parish?*, p. 409.
179   LA, QSB/1/63/58.
180   Healey, 'Poverty in an Industrializing Town', pp. 139–40.

Haworth, in which he described the youngest five of his nine children as unable to earn anything, may well be typical of childhood working practice. The eldest of the five children deemed unable to earn was eight years old.

But young children also required looking after, and this brought opportunity costs to their mothers. In 1692, labourer William Hoole of Preston told of how he had suffered sickness for half a year, and that he had two small children, of whom 'one whereof sucks at the brests of its mother and thereby disables her to labore'.[181] Similarly, widow Margaret Bretherton of Golborne petitioned that she had three small children, she 'not being in a capacity of doeing much att present towards their maintainance by reason of her youngest child sucking off her brest'.[182] These costs were especially damaging to single women. Widowed Isabel Hey of Dalton, for example, complained in 1684 of how she had two small children to look after, she 'haveing not time to worke being wholly employed in the attending of her said children'.[183] Similarly, in 1707, Jane Watson of Warton – widowed with three children – told of how her day work was 'very uncertaine', and 'besides shee haveing a young child it cannot be expected that she can performe a day worke so well as those that have none'.[184]

Economic risk

As well as the personal contingencies detailed above, households could also fall victim to shifts in the broader economy. Essentially, these worked in two ways: some economic changes served to reduce the volume of employment available while others caused the cost of living to rise. A collapse of industrial production might lead to widespread unemployment, while a poor harvest might cause prices to increase. Just over 4 per cent of petitions contained reference to such economic problems.

It has to be said that there is relatively little evidence of structural unemployment in the petitions, but this may partly be a trick of the documentary light. It was not in petitioners' interests to stress any lengthy jobless periods as that might leave them open to accusations of idleness. But some petitioners did allude to local cases of economic difficulty, such as raised rents or unfavourable labour markets. John Cawson, for example,

181   LA, QSP/713/7.
182   LA, QSP/836/11.
183   LA, QSP/586/30.
184   LA, QSP/954/12.

complained in 1637 that he was eighty-four years old, his wife blind, and was 'sore chardged with the yearely payment of a racke rente to Lawrence Copelande' for his little house and ground.[185] Considerably later, in 1690, Alice Keckwick of West Derby petitioned that her husband had run away: he had possessed a 'considerable' stock of goods, but 'what with hard usage from his landlord and other casualties hee was unable to pay his rent and maintaine his familie'. Presumably that 'hard usage' entailed an increase in his rent.[186] Labourer Roger Seddon of Bolton, meanwhile, asked for relief in 1681 because he could 'gett no work being neither husbandman nor artificer'.[187] In 1652, William Laborer of Barnacre reported to JPs that he (ironically) had 'noe trade'.[188] In a rather unusual example of detrimental economic change, Margery Gill of Winmarleigh blamed a shift in the local educational landscape for her destitution in 1686. When eight years old, her son Robert (apparently illegitimate) lost the use of his left hand and all of his left side 'by blasting or otherwise as it pleased god'. Fearing a life of penury, his mother 'took all the paines possible by her dayly and hard labour to mantayne him & gett him learning to teach English schollers on purpose to keep him from beging'. This he then did for nine years, helped by his mother's work and a dole from the township, but now she was sixty years old, and meanwhile his customers were 'falling in number from what they formerly were by reason of severall schooles being nere adjacent, and parents takeing their children from this school this somer season'.[189] One also wonders just what the story is behind the poverty of James Shackley, a miller from Euxton, who complained in 1692 that he was 'now out of imployment and not capable to follow other imployment not beeinge brought up in husbandry'.[190] Or the rather audacious attempt by Jane Lomas of Edgworth to get a pension in 1703. Her husband had enlisted, leaving her 'in a strange country and unaquainted with their work there', so she was 'not able to maintaine herselfe and child without releife'. She failed to impress the Manchester bench.[191]

It might be possible to gauge patterns of seasonal unemployment by assessing the timing of petitions to Quarter Sessions, in a similar manner

185   LA, QSB/1/176/32.
186   LA, QSP/686/15.
187   LA, QSP/530/25.
188   LA, QSP/66/2.
189   LA, QSP/620/5.
190   LA, QSP/718/9.
191   LA, QSP/893/6.

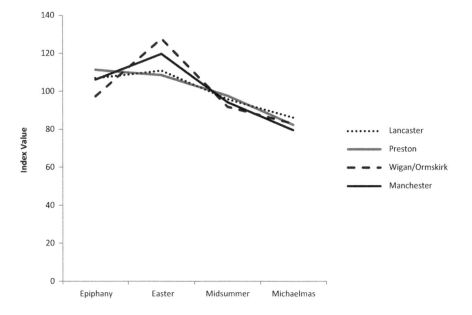

Figure 10: Seasonal distribution of first petitions for poor relief, 1626–1709 (indexed)

to Snell's use of settlement certificates (Figure 10).[192] This is a blunt instrument, since the extent of delay between the initial shock and the subsequent appeal to Quarter Sessions is uncertain, and appeals could only be heard at one of four dates annually, but three points do emerge. First, there is a marked trough at Michaelmas across all four Quarter Sessions divisions. This presumably coincided with the harvest, which would have provided temporary employment for many. Secondly, it is noticeable that the major peaks in the year are found at the Epiphany and Easter Sessions, i.e. in winter and spring. Given the fact that paupers – who were often physically weak – generally appear to have travelled with their petitions, we might expect appeals to cluster in the summer months. In reality, paupers tended to make the journey to Quarter Sessions at the very time when roads would have been most treacherous. It is thus more likely that the winter and early spring represented lean periods in the employment calendar. Thirdly, there is a strong Easter peak in the south which is not replicated in the north of the county. This may well arise from

192   Cf. Snell, *Annals*, pp. 15–66.

two factors. First, industrial employment in the south might have provided income during lean periods in the agrarian calendar, thereby ironing out the winter peak found elsewhere. On the other hand, in the northern and still predominantly agricultural region, it is likely that the spring lambing and calving season provided some temporary employment, dampening the peak at Easter Sessions.[193]

One final facet of our sample must also be highlighted, and this is the markedly higher number of 'economic' petitions found in Salford Hundred compared with the remainder of the county. Of the petitions heard at Lancaster, Preston, Ormskirk and Wigan Sessions, only 3 per cent were of this type, while the equivalent figure for Manchester was 6 per cent. This may well hint at the population of the south-east of the county being more vulnerable to periodic problems of unemployment and high food prices, something which almost certainly reflects its specialization in the textile industry. Indeed, whilst only 1 per cent of petitions from the county's plains referred to such economic problems, 6 per cent in the fustian- and wool-working areas did so.

Environmental risk

There were also environmental hazards (both natural and social), which could cause damage to or loss of property and thus leave previously self-sufficient households impoverished. In many cases these were relieved by other forms of assistance to the Poor Law, such as church briefs or (in the early days) licences to beg. Nonetheless, parishes and townships also had a role to play in mitigating such hardship, especially as this was a period in which commercial insurance was in its infancy and was apparently wholly unavailable to ordinary families.[194] In total, nearly 3 per cent of our petitions mentioned these kinds of difficulties, with around a third of these referring to broadly 'natural' factors and the remaining two thirds complaining of 'social' ones.

Of the natural environmental risks, the most commonly complained about were fire, the death of livestock and general wear and tear to property. Thus Thomas Taylor, a husbandman of Penketh, asked JPs in

193   By contrast, Botelho found no seasonal variation in occasional poor relief in dairy-farming Cratfield (Suffolk) in the late seventeenth century: Botelho, *Old Age*, p. 94.
194   B. E. Supple, 'Insurance in British History', in *The Historian and the Business of Insurance*, ed. O. M. Westall (Manchester, 1984), pp. 1–8.

1650 for 'some releef so as youe in your wisdomes shall thinke most meete & conveniant' after a fire had gutted his barn and caused £30 worth of damage.[195] In 1667, the inhabitants of Newchurch-in-Rossendale reported that Widow Fish was 'come to extreame povertie by reason that her house is fallen'.[196] Her case would have struck a chord with Martha Miles of Chadderton, who told in 1688 of how 'the house shee lives in is soe bad that it raines downe upon the bed, soe that shee & the poor children is forct to sitt up many nights by the fire side by reason the house being soe far out of repaire'. She asked for the overseers to provide repairs 'soe that shee may sitt dry from raine'.[197] Rather earlier in 1642, Thomas Holland of Prescot complained that he 'hath lately by mishapp or misfortune lost some sheep which were all his stocke of goodes'.[198] Similarly, John Worrall, a salt carrier of Skelmersdale, 'haveinge lately suffered great losse by death of his horses with which he was supported and maintained' petitioned for relief in 1675.[199] Edward Byrom of Windle had maintained himself and his family by carrying tobacco pipes, for which he employed three horses. But sometime before 1695 'it pleased God that all his horses dyed', and although his hard work and 'the benevolence of his friends and neighbours' had allowed him to get on his feet again with two horses plying the same trade, he had also taken on debt and the two horses ended up seized by his creditors, the latter 'being very severe and cruell'.[200]

Just occasionally wider changes and fluctuations in the natural environment were blamed as causes of poverty. In 1674, after a notoriously hard season, John Thorpe of Chadderton claimed his estate to have been 'exhausted by meanes of this late sore winter and sickenesse of my wife'.[201] John Leigh of Walton-le-Dale stated in 1678 that he and his wife were

> now reduced into poverty by reason of the two late great floods which happened in Walton aforesaid about the 11th of September a yeares agoe at which time your petitioner lost tenn acres & a halfe of wheat barley & oates besides the washinge downe of your petitioners hedges and your petitioner further sheweth that your petitioner the yeare after

195   LA, QSP/27/29.
196   LA, QSP/310/4.
197   LA, QSP/654/28.
198   LA, QSB/1/266/70.
199   LA, QSP/436/34.
200   LA, QSP/762/13.
201   LA, QSP/417/4.

for bread corne seed & other necessaryes became indebted in the some of fifty pounds by reason whereof your poore petitioner is cleerely ruined & undone ...[202]

Some unidentifiable (but perhaps connected) environmental change seems to have been to blame when Nicholas Ashton of Silverdale petitioned the same year that he was not able 'to follow any labour for to relieve himselfe withall except it be by fishinge or the like it being the whole sume and substance of his maintenance what as he can get of the sand which has beene so bad of these late yeares as has not been the like time out of mind'.[203] Finally, in 1698, Thomas Parkinson of Chatburn complained that he was eighty years of age and had nothing to relieve him 'in this sharp weather'.[204]

Social-environmental factors, on the other hand, could include loss by theft, war, or even simply the destructive behaviour of others. John Lomax, the drover from Bradshaw whose petition opened this chapter, appealed for and received relief in 1679, complaining that – as well as being old – he had lost £40 when his house was broken into.[205] Humphrey Atherton, a Pemberton nail-maker, similarly needed relief in 1686 after his house was burgled.[206] In 1636, Dorothy, the widow successively of Peter Heald of Tottington and Mr Charles Nuttall of Nuttall, was relieved by Manchester Sessions after being forced to fight a lawsuit over a plot of land.[207] In a tantalizing 1641 petition, Jennet Thompson of Kirkham claimed to have been 'driven into greatt poverty' not just by reason of her age but also the 'trobles shee haith beene putt unto by the said towne by the losse of her goods and good name by the cunstables there'.[208] Thomas Sagar of Alston-with-Hothersall told JPs in 1656 that when his wife had been imprisoned on some charge, his 'neighbors hadd like to have comme violentlie upon mee and bound mee againe in chaines, whose uncivill byndinge at the first was the greatest cause of my weakened sences and losse of witt'.[209]

202   LA, QSP/483/7.
203   LA, QSP/474/5.
204   LA, QSP/806/13.
205   LA, QSP/500/13; cf. Hudson, 'Ex-servicemen', p. 48.
206   LA, QSP/625/3.
207   LA, QSB/1/171/80.
208   LA, QSB/1/241/22.
209   LA, QSP/126/14.

The mid-century political and military upheaval clearly also took its toll, and was the root of over a quarter of these 'social-environmental' petitions. Plunder and pillage were obvious risks, with Prince Rupert, the Scots (especially after 1648), or simply 'the enemie' being blamed for destruction of property at various times.[210] Holders of Irish estates would have been especially vulnerable. Robert Bray's eighty-one years of age combined with the loss of his Irish lands and the death of two of his sons during the 1640s to leave him petitioning for relief from the parish of Poulton-le-Fylde in 1651.[211] Similarly, although it is unclear exactly how much this related to her immediate situation, Elizabeth Bashforth of Poulton-le-Sands (present-day Morecambe) recounted in 1657 that she emigrated to Ireland in 1616, marrying a man of good estate, but was subsequently ruined by the rebellion and fled to Lancashire in the early 1640s.[212] Even if one escaped damage to property by marauding forces, there was the threat of soldiers being quartered without paying their way. Frances Houghton of Manchester complained in 1656 that she had been forced to put soldiers up on free quarter and as a result had eventually been turned out of her house.[213] Others petitioned for relief on account of having to make substantial payments to avoid being pressed. William Euxton of Leyland lamented in 1662 of having to find 'a great deale of monie' in order to hire a replacement when he had been conscripted to fight.[214] In fact, this kind of problem apparently predated the mid-century commotions by some time, for in 1637 John Bateson of Melling petitioned that, as well as being sick, old, and having been repeatedly burgled, he had been 'pressed out for the warres against Ireland, so that he was glad to hire one thither in his stead, at a great rate'.[215] That he could still draw on this experience over thirty years after it took place bears testimony to (if nothing else) the emotive force of this kind of misfortune.

When hardship was obviously caused through the actions of others, poor relief might not be needed if those responsible could be forced to cease their harmful behaviour. Such petitions are not included in the sample here, but they can nevertheless give a vivid sidelight on the causes of hardship. Thus it was for the better conduct of one of his neighbours

210   E.g. LA, QSP/21/7; QSP/22/12; QSP/24/10; QSP/27/36; QSP/113/5.
211   LA, QSP/54/1.
212   LA, QSP/137/3.
213   LA, QSP/124/19; cf. QSP/156/16.
214   LA, QSP/223/14.
215   LA, QSB/1/180/20.

rather than parish relief which 'verie poore' Hugh Thropp of Ormskirk, petitioned in 1627.[216] Visited with 'extreame sickness' in 1626, Thropp had attempted to pursue his normal trade of a felt-maker and hat dealer as his health began to improve. However, his efforts to ply his trade at Ormskirk market were – he alleged – hampered when one James Morecroft, a butcher of the town, 'bassly & slanderouslye' abused Thropp and his wife, 'calinge him a coocolde & his wife a whore'. In addition, the petitioner complained, Morecroft 'doeth most desperatly & dangerously stricke your said petitioner with staves & other wepons'. Thropp had thus fallen into severe hardship because he was unable to pursue his trade, not daring to 'come into the streets for feere of his lyffe'. The immediate solution to this instance of poverty was not to reach for the parish purse, but to prosecute Morecroft. Perhaps this was also the solution to the poverty of widow Martha Thomson of Little Crosby, a petitioner in 1692 who complained of being turned out of her small tenement by the 'bad usage' of her neighbours.[217] But sometimes this kind of restorative action was impossible, as Alice Pendlebury and her brother found out in 1655. They had been given twenty shillings in poor relief by the town of Salford, but it was subsequently 'taken out of her chest by a neighboringe boy whoe was for soe doeinge sent to the howse of correction where hee yet is, but hee haveinge made away the said moneys your petitioner could not regaine any part thereof'.[218] The pair thus needed to petition for further relief.

Conclusion

The main causes of 'deserving poverty', then, were old age, ill health, and family breakdown or failure. Protection against these three emerges from the petitions as the key day-to-day function of the Poor Law. Other forms of misfortune – notably economic problems such as unemployment and high prices, and environmental contingencies (both social and natural) were important, but they were secondary. On some occasions, however, economic forces acted to drag whole communities into hardship. The mitigation of these crises was another of the Poor Law's critical functions, and it is to this issue that we will now turn.

216   LA, QSB/1/26/67.
217   LA, QSP/718/10.
218   LA, QSP/112/38.

7

Crisis Poverty

The condition of the nation and church is very sad. The pitiful uncertain
foot that things stand upon. Religion on tiptoes. Division out against
us, so as it hath rarely been, in such concurrence of so many things. 1. A
destruction of corn and hay, in the time of it. 2. Great loss of cattle. 3.
Great dearth. 4. Great want of money. 5. Inveterate deadness of trade.
6. The late sad storm, with the dreadful effects of it. 7. A threat in the
present great rain to prevent the fruiting of the earth. 8. A miserable
security and senselessness, among the people notwithstanding all this.
Autobiography of Henry Newcome (1 May 1674)[1]

The level of hardship in any economy will fluctuate, with certain years
seeing particular prosperity, others extreme difficulty and social dislocation, and this basic truism has informed some work on poor relief.
James Sharpe and Steve Hindle, for example, have highlighted the link
between the social experience of the dearth and famine of 1594–97 and
the Parliamentary codifications of the Poor Laws in 1598, amongst a
raft of other social legislation.[2] Yet little work has been produced on the
relationship between economic crises and the day-to-day operation of the
Poor Law.[3] Moreover, although there are studies of economic fluctuations
in both the early seventeenth and the eighteenth centuries, there is no
comparable literature on the later Stuart period.[4]

This final chapter will go some way towards tackling these problems,

---

1   H. Newcome, *The Autobiography of Henry Newcome, M.A.*, ed. Richard Parkinson,
2 vols (CS, Old Ser., xxvi, xvii, Manchester, 1852), vol. 2, p. 207.
2   J. A. Sharpe, 'Social Strain and Social Dislocation', in *The Reign of Elizabeth I: Court
and Culture in the Last Decade*, ed. J. Guy (Cambridge, 1995), pp. 192–211; Hindle,
'Dearth, Fasting and Alms', pp. 48, 81–4.
3   Walter and Wrightson, 'Dearth and the Social Order'; Appleby, *Famine*; J. Walter, 'The
Social Economy of Dearth in Early Modern England', in *Famine, Disease and the Social
Order*, ed. J. Walter and R. S. Schofield (Cambridge, 1989), pp. 75–128.
4   B. E. Supple, *Commercial Crisis and Change in England, 1600–1642* (Cambridge,

taking two approaches. First, it will use fluctuations in the volume of surviving first petitions, and the statements contained in those petitions, plus some overseers' accounts, to identify the main economic crises that hit Lancashire from the 1630s to the early eighteenth century. Secondly, it will look in more detail at the response of poor relief to two contrasting crises, those of the mid-1670s and of 1727–30. Both of these saw severe hardship in the region, and the latter saw one of the last great pre-modern mortality crises, killing a significant proportion of the county's population.

Poverty crises in Lancashire, 1630–1715: a chronology

Pauper petitions provide a fascinating dataset for reconstructing the timing of economic crises, as they can be counted – bad years saw more petitions – and because we can mine them for contemporary comment. Paupers, as will be seen, would complain in their petitions that provisions were dear, or that trading had stopped and work was difficult to get, or simply that the 'times' were 'hard'.

Figure 11 shows the fluctuating number of surviving first petitions from 1626 to 1710. There are some very marked peaks, most obviously in 1638, 1650, 1657–62, 1674–75, 1699, and 1706. There is also much textual evidence of hardship in 1709–10. Almost all of these years coincided with periods of high food prices, a connection made stronger when petitions are compared to the national series of grain prices compiled for the *AHEW* (Figure 12).[5] In addition, Figure 11 data have been disaggregated for specific date ranges, and for each of four subregions based on the location of Quarter Sessions: the south-eastern textile zone (Manchester), the south-western mineral-working zone (Wigan/Ormskirk), and two northern 'agricultural' regions (Preston and Lancaster). These first petition disaggregated data are presented in Figures 13, 15, 16, 19 and 21 as part of the discussion which follows.

These graphs provide some of the clearest evidence yet produced of the existence of 'crisis poverty'. On the other hand, the picture they provide of the ability of the Poor Law to respond to such conjunctures is rather more ambiguous, for had relief at both parish and township level been truly effective at meeting local need, then such appeals to Quarter Sessions

1959); T. S. Ashton, *Economic Fluctuations in England, 1700–1800* (Oxford, 1959); J. Hoppit, *Risk and Failure in English Business, 1700–1800* (Cambridge, 1987).

5   P. J. Bowden, 'Statistical Appendix', in *AHEW*, vol. 4, pp. 814–70 and vol. 5, pp. 827–902.

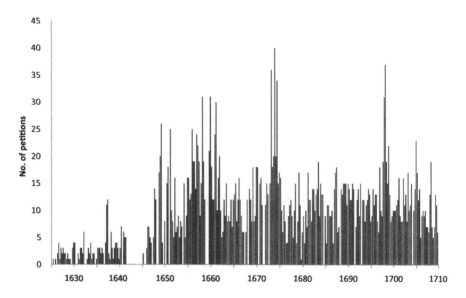

Figure 11: First petitions for poor relief in records of Lancashire Quarter Sessions, 1626–1710

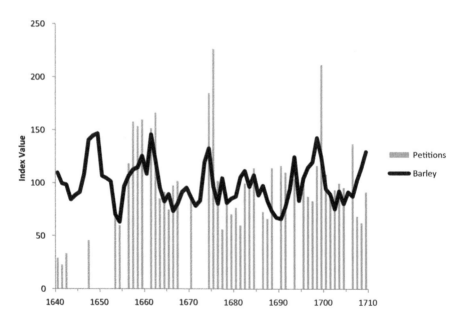

Figure 12: First petitions (complete years only) and barley prices, 1640–1710 (100 = mean of 1640–1710)

would have been unnecessary. It could therefore be argued that the peaks in petitioning actually show a *failure* of the Poor Law to mitigate economic crises. In reality, however, the situation was yet more complex, since it appears far that more of surviving petitions resulted in relief orders than outright rejections. Thus, just as Hindle has seen collective popular action as instrumental in reactivating parochial poor relief after the Civil War, petitioning during economic crises is perhaps best seen as a similar (albeit more individualist) form of bargaining, forcing recalcitrant overseers and vestrymen into performing their duties to the poor.[6] Here, as perhaps elsewhere, the *system* of poor relief, from paupers through overseers up to JPs, provided more comprehensive coverage than the sum of its parts might suggest. Certainly the jumps in petitions suggest that neither the 'economy of makeshifts', nor the more specific 'social economy of dearth', which scholars have seen as an important cushion against severe short-term hardship, were doing enough to maintain the poor.[7] Formal poor relief was being called upon to fill the gap.

Crises, 1630–70

The first crisis for which we have petition evidence was in 1637–38 and coincided with a severe regional dearth. There is a suggestion of shortages in 1636 in a report to the Privy Council from an unnamed Lancashire division, probably dating from early 1637, which recounted that

> At a meetinge the xith of October in Anno aforesaide [i.e. 1636] our harvest beeinge past, and there beeinge a greate dearth of corne and graine feared to be in our partes wee did give strickt charge and comand to the constables and appointed severall other persones in divers partes of our saide division, to see that none did regrate, ingrosse or forstall any corne or graine contrary to the statute in that case provided and had an eye ourselves to our marketts …[8]

Clearly the threat of shortages was palpable enough for justices acting in Petty Sessions to instigate the usual regulatory measures without central

6   Hindle, 'Dearth and the English Revolution', pp. 78–91.
7   Walter, 'Social Economy of Dearth'; for a more pessimistic view, see: Schofield, 'The Social Economy of the Medieval Village'.
8   TNA, SP16/351/108, Report of JPs of Unknown Division, undated (early 1637).

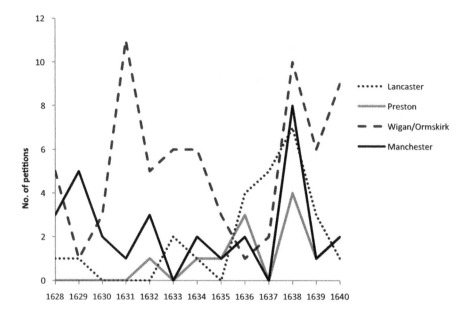

Figure 13: First petitions for poor relief, 1628–40

direction. Indeed, by October 1636, justices in Leyland Hundred were complaining of an 'inordinate concourse of wandering rogues strangers and beggers into theis partes of our countrey'.[9] Things got much worse the following year, with wheat prices hitting their highest point between 1630 and 1647. Oats and barley, the staple foods of the northern poor, were especially expensive.[10] A peak in petitioning ensued (Figure 13).

Surprisingly, the high prices of 1637/38 led to a much greater increase in the number of petitions than the better-known and supposedly much more serious dearth of 1629–31. In part this may have been a reflection of the small numbers of surviving petitions at this point. Interestingly, there is a peak at Wigan and Ormskirk Sessions, which between them have the highest level of survival for the 1630s as a whole. Similarly, it may reflect a lack of understanding or confidence in the ability of parochial poor relief

9   R. B. Outhwaite, 'Dearth and Government Intervention in English Grain Markets, 1590–1700', *EcHR*, 2nd Ser., 34 (1981), 389–406 (pp. 398–9); TNA, SP16/334/16, Report of the Justices of Leyland Hundred, 19 October 1636.
10   W. G. Hoskins, 'Harvest Fluctuations and English Economic History, 1620–1759', *AgHR*, 16 (1968), 15–31; Bowden, 'Statistical Appendix', vol. 4, pp. 814–70 (p. 821).

to mitigate hardship at this stage, especially in the south-east and north of the county. In particular, if we accept the early to mid-1630s as a turning point in the adoption of official poor relief by Lancashire townships and parishes, then it is possible to see the later crisis rather than that of 1629–31 as the first occasion on which high prices had the opportunity to affect the operation of a largely functional rate-funded relief system. On the other hand, these latter years may simply have seen a much more serious regional crisis than is yet appreciated.[11] Indeed, Wrightson felt that despite the widespread dislocation in the south-east, 1631 was 'not a particularly bad year in the north-west'.[12]

The years from 1640 to 1642, unexpectedly perhaps, saw no strong evidence of increased hardship. The political uncertainties that presaged the outbreak of Civil War are known to have severely disrupted trade.[13] Merchants, both English and alien, took money out of circulation, and woollen manufactures stalled across the country.[14] The degree to which these problems reached Lancashire is uncertain, but there was at least one complaint to Quarter Sessions of a 'scarcitie of worke', in this case from a poor Manchester labourer early in 1642.[15] That said, the crisis did not apparently cause heightened levels of petitioning. Meanwhile, the apparent breakdown of the system of poor relief, and the abeyance of Quarter Sessions, means that our sample has nothing to say on the immediate economic impact of the Civil War. As the fighting brought with it plunder, disease, food shortages and severe disruption of trade, we would expect its effect on the poor to have been baleful. In this sense, the petition of William Manchester of Radcliffe, who recalled in 1653 that 'our trade in time of wars being altogether downe I tooke up armes for the Parliament of England', is highly suggestive.[16] Paradoxically, however, the armies' ability to recruit marginal men may have not only provided work for the young and the underemployed, but also have reduced

11   Wrightson's description of this as a 'slightly deficient' harvest is not strong enough: Wrightson, 'Puritan Reformation', p. 180; cf. Outhwaite, 'Dearth and Government Intervention', p. 398.

12   Wrightson, 'Puritan Reformation', p. 189.

13   Supple, *Commercial Crisis*, pp. 125–31; *Seventeenth-Century Economic Documents*, pp. 39–48.

14   Supple, *Commercial Crisis*, pp. 129–31.

15   LA, QSB/1/259/62.

16   LA, QSP/80/7; cf. C. Duffy, *The Military Experience in the Age of Reason* (London, 1987), pp. 90–1.

the competition for work amongst those who did not join up.[17] On the other hand, the resultant break-up of families may have had a parallel and opposite impact, leaving more single women of child-bearing age vulnerable to destitution, but again this may have been qualified by an increase in female earning power associated with the withdrawal of many male hands from the labour market.[18]

Whatever the case during the actual fighting, the economic situation immediately after the Civil War appears to have become markedly worse.[19] The best data have food prices reaching their highest levels between 1640 and 1749 in the year following the 1647 harvest, and then remaining high for the following two years. There were reports of people having 'died in the highways for want of bread' in Cumberland and Westmorland.[20] In addition, it appears that these years saw one of the most appalling episodes of dearth in Scotland for the whole period between 1630 and 1780.[21] In fact, although it now seems unlikely that actual starvation was ever very widespread, there is little doubt that this was an exceptionally difficult period for the poor.[22] In Lancashire, this was reflected in a series of appeals to the county's Quarter Sessions, beginning around January 1647.[23] Early that year it was reported that 'famine' was 'much feared', while by 1648 the 'poor distressed people' of West Derby Hundred were reporting an 'exceeding dearth of corne'.[24] A petition the same year from the 'poore inhabitants within the towne of Salford' complained that the 'dearthe and scarcity of corne thereabouts at present hath much added to theire poverty & more especially to the augmentation or increase of

17   C. Holmes, *Why Was Charles I Executed?* (London, 2006), p. 11.

18   For a similar set of problems in the context of the wars of 1689–97 and 1702–13 see: Boulton, 'It is extreme necessity', p. 49.

19   Hindle, 'Dearth and the English Revolution', pp. 64–72.

20   *Seventeenth-Century Economic Documents*, pp. 48–52.

21   M. Flinn, *Scottish Population History from the 17th Century to the 1930s* (Cambridge, 1977), p. 150.

22   Wrigley and Schofield, *Population History*, pp. 660–1; Hindle, 'Dearth and the English Revolution', pp. 71–2. Appleby implies that there was starvation in the North West in 1649, largely on the basis of the reports from the North East printed in the Leveller newsbook *The Moderate*. However, given the lack of evidence amongst burial registers for widespread mortality, the suspicion must remain that these were politically motivated exaggerations. Appleby, 'Grain Prices', p. 867. The original report is published in *Seventeenth-Century Economic Documents*, pp. 51–2.

23   Wrightson, 'Puritan Reformation', pp. 181–9; Walter and Wrightson, 'Dearth and the Social Order', pp. 38–40.

24   Quoted in Wrightson, 'Puritan Reformation', p. 181.

34

May 24, 1649.

A true Repreſentation of the preſent ſad and lamentable condition of the County of *Lancaſter*, and particularly of the Towns of *Wigan, Aſhton*, and the parts adjacent.

THE hand of God is evidently ſeen ſtretched out upon the County, chaſtening it with a three-corded ſcourge of Sword, Peſtilence, and Famin, all at once afflicting it: They have borne the heat and burden of a firſt and ſecond War, in an eſpeciall manner above other parts of the Nation : through them the two great bodies of the late *Scottiſh* and *Engliſh* Armies paſſed, and in their very bowels was that great fighting, bloud-ſhed and breaking. In this County hath the plague of Peſtilence been ranging theſe three years and upward, occaſioned manifeſtly by the Wars. There is a very great ſcarſity and dearth of all proviſions, eſpecially of all ſorts of grain; particularly that kind by which that Countrey is moſt ſuſtained, which is full ſix-fold the price that of late it hath been. All trade (by which they have been much ſupported) is utterly decayed : it would melt any good heart to ſee the numerous ſwarms of begging poore, and the many families that pine away at home, not having faces to beg : Very many now craving almes at other mens dores, who were uſed to give others almes at their dores : To ſee palleneſſe, nay death appear in the cheeks of the poor; and often to hear of ſome found dead in their houſes or high-wayes for want of bread. But particularly the Townes of *Wigan* and *Aſhton*, with the neighbouring parts, lying at preſent under the fore ſtroak of God in the Peſtilence : In one whereof are full two thouſand poor, who for three moneths and upward have been reſtrained, no relief to be had for them in the ordinary courſe of Law, there being none at preſent to act as Juſtices of the peace : The Collections in our Congregations (there only ſupply hitherto) being generally very ſlack and ſlender, thoſe wanting ability to help who have hearts to pity them : Moſt mens Eſtates, being much drained by the Wars, and now almoſt quite exhauſt by the preſent ſcarſity, and many other burdens incumbent upon them : There is no bonds to keep in the infected hunger-ſtarved poore, whoſe breaking out jeapoardeth all the Neighbour-hood. Some of them already, being at the point to periſh through famine, have fetcht in and eaten Carion and other unwholſome food to the deſtroying of themſelves, & increaſing of the infection: And the more to provoke pity and mercy it may be conſidered, that this fatall Contagion had its riſe evidently from the wounded ſouldiers of our Army left there for cure.

All which is certified to ſome of the Reverend Miniſters of the City of *London*, by the Major, Miniſter, and other perſons of credit inhabitants in, or wel-wiſhers to, and well acquainted with the Town of *Wigan*, together with four godly and faithfull Miniſters of *Lanchaſhire*, by providence in this city at this preſent.

Now if God ſhall ſtir up the hearts of any or more Congregations in and about the City of *London* (the premiſes conſidered) to yeeld their charitable contribution to the neceſſities of theſe afflicted & diſtreſſed parts and places, it wil be carefully ſought after, and thankfully received by Mr. *Iames Wainewright*, Mr. *Thomas Markelande*, Mr. *James Winſtanley*, and Mr. *Iohn Leaver* or ſome of them, and faithfully diſpoſed according to Chriſtian diſcretion by Major General *Aſhton*, William *Aſhurſt*, Peter *Brookes*, Eſquires, Mr. *Iolly* Major of *Wigan*, together with Mr. *Richard Heyricke*, Mr. *Charles Herle*, Mr. *Alexander Horrockes*, and Mr. *Iames Hyet* Miniſters of the Goſpel, or ſome of them.

Ambroſe *Iolly* Major	*Iames Hyet*	
Iames Bradſhaw Miniſter	*Richard Hollingworth*	Miniſters of
Iohn Standiſh Bailiffs	of the Town of *Wigan*.	*Iſaac Ambroſe* *Lancaſhire*
Ralph Markland	*Iohn Tilſley*	

Figure 14: *A True Representation of the Present Sad and Lamentable Condition of the County of Lancaster …*, an anonymous broadside first printed in London on 24 May 1649, reporting famine in Lancashire. © British Library Board: London, British Library, Thomason Tract collection, 669.f.14 (34).

the poverty of those who have noe trade nor callinge whereby to obtayne money for theire relieffe'.[25] Most harrowing was the published report, *A True Representation of the Present Sad and Lamentable Condition of the County of Lancaster*, first printed in London on 24 May 1649 (Figure 14).[26] The county, and 'particularly ... the Towns of *Wigan, Ashton*, and the parts adjacent', had been chastened 'with a three-corded scourge of Sword, Pestilence, and Famin'. Disease, it lamented, had been prevalent for three years and had been 'occasioned manifestly by the Wars', while there was a 'very great scarsity and dearth of all provisions, especially of all sorts of grain; particularly that kind by which that Countrey is most sustained, which is full six-fold the price that of late it hath been'. Trade, meanwhile, was 'utterly decayed', and – the report stated – 'it would melt any good heart to see the numerous swarms of begging poore, and the many families that pine away at home, not having faces to beg'. Of course, the report was exaggerated, with the charitable contributions of London the ultimate aim, but it is still evocative of an exceptionally serious economic crisis. Indeed, the appeal for national support appears to have been successful, for a collection for Lancashire, 'much afflicted with famine and pestilence', was noted by the Essex clergyman Ralph Josselin.[27]

Some attempts were made by the authorities to reduce the severity of the dearth. In 1648, licences to deal corn were cancelled in Leyland and West Derby hundreds. The same year, the malting of barley was forbidden at Wigan, since malt was 'sould ... to alehouses and tippling houses where it is spent much to the dishonor of god and the hurt both of the souls, bodies and estates of the people'.[28] And, recognizing the impact of military demand for supplies in the county, the Council of State ordered that troops were not to take free quarter there because it 'tends to the famishing of many poor people'.[29] Nonetheless, Hindle has argued that the national response to the dearth was slow, and that it had to be forced by popular action through mass petitioning.[30] In Lancashire, though, the glut in the number of *individual* petitions was

25   LA, QSP/4/6.
26   *A True Representation of the Present Sad and Lamentable Condition of the County of Lancaster* ... (London, 1649): British Library, Thomason Tract collection, 669.f.14 (34).
27   Josselin, *Diary*, p. 172.
28   Wrightson, 'Puritan Reformation', p. 188.
29   Ibid., pp. 181–2.
30   Hindle, 'Dearth and the English Revolution', pp. 78–91.

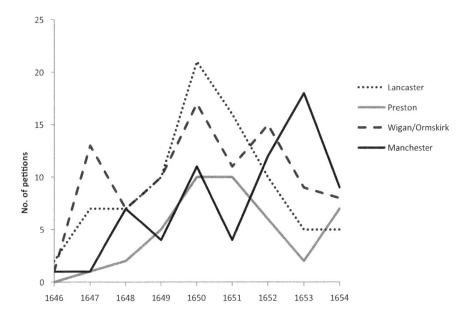

Figure 15: First petitions for poor relief, 1646–54

just as impressive (Figure 15). William Ward of Alkrington, for example, petitioned in 1648 that he and his wife were 'especiallie now of late by reason of the scarcitie of bread & hardnes of the tymes both of them … brought into extreame want & miserie'.[31] In 1649, Margaret Salisbury of Chaigeley reported herself to be in poverty 'by reason of this great dearth and scarsitye of corne'.[32] And to make matters worse, trade was evidently also hard hit, as John Dawson of Blackley complained in 1650: 'trades are bad and wages little as manie can wytnes'.[33] The peak in petitions was especially marked in the north of the county, with Lancaster Sessions seeing its second highest peak for the whole period under study. Presumably this reflected the northern parts' poverty, similar to that of the adjacent Lake Counties (which appear to have fared extremely badly).[34]

Harvests improved from 1651 onwards, although the import of corn and a 'plentifull and seasonal' crop in 1649 had allowed an earlier, if

31 LA, QSP/8/7.
32 LA, QSP/9/9; QSP/22/12.
33 *Seventeenth-Century Economic Documents*, pp. 52–64; LA, QSP/32/4.
34 *Seventeenth-Century Economic Documents*, pp. 51–2.

temporary, abeyance.[35] Fortunately, the period 1652–55 appears to have
been a bountiful one.[36] Nonetheless, there is still evidence for a continuing
industrial depression in the south-east of the county, and there was a
cluster of petitions complaining of low wages and poor trading from
Salford Hundred between 1652 and 1654.[37] In 1653, for example, Margaret
Bowker of Manchester complained of a 'decay of trade and comerce',
while a year later Robert Scoles of Ashton-under-Lyne worried about a
similar decay and the 'smale wages' it brought.[38] The location of these
references suggests that the problem related to the cotton-using textile
industries upon which so much of the area's economy depended. Indeed,
James Roylands of Westhoughton stated this specifically in 1653, noting
that he, 'being a fustian webster', found there was 'now litle to be begotten
with it'.[39] It was also in 1654 that Thomas Waring and others petitioned
to the Council of State 'in behalf of the poor of Lancashire' to complain
that 'the dearth of [cotton] wools this present year is worser undergone
by the poor in Lancashire than the famine of bread was (though that was
great) three years past'.[40] The petition blamed the depression on the high
prices of imported cotton, with low levels of production in the West Indies
leaving the country dependent on supplies from the Levant, which were in
turn dominated by the 'Turkey merchants'. But an additional problem was
the First Dutch War (1652–54), which caused significant disruption to a
Mediterranean trade already stuttering in the face of French hostility.[41] It
would not be the last time that the fragility of the intercontinental cotton
trade would hit the Lancastrian poor hard.

The trade depression of *circa* 1652 to 1654 does not register on the total
sample of petitions, with overall survivals remaining low between 1650
and 1655, however the disaggregated figures show a peak at Manchester
in 1653. Intriguingly, indeed, if we use the peak in petitions to Manchester
Sessions as our gauge, the stoppage in the fustian industry was indeed
'worser undergone' by the poor than the dearth of 1648–50. Nonetheless,

---

35   *Materials for an Account of the Provincial Synod of the County of Lancaster,*
1646–1660, ed. W. A. Shaw (Manchester, 1890), pp. 49–51; Walter and Wrightson, 'Dearth
and the Social Order', pp. 39–40.

36   Hoskins, 'Harvest Fluctuations', p. 16.

37   There is also a suggestion of economic problems in the capital in 1654: Muldrew,
Economy of Obligation, p. 297.

38   LA, QSP/80/26; QSP/92/3.

39   LA, QSP/80/14.

40   *Seventeenth-Century Economic Documents,* pp. 258–9.

41   A. C. Wood, *A History of the Levant Company* (Oxford, 1935), pp. 54–6.

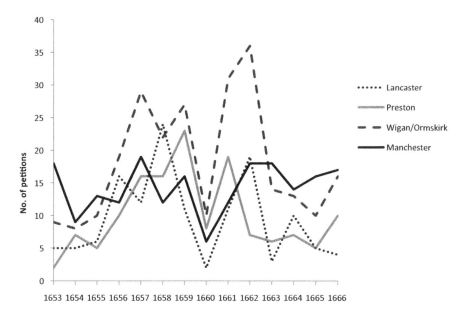

Figure 16: First petitions for poor relief, 1653–66

the next countywide crisis would wait until 1657–62 (Figure 16).[42] Again we get a cluster of references in petitions to adverse economic conditions: between 1657 and 1663, some thirteen first petitions mentioned scarcity of either corn or employment, both, or simply 'hard times'. The basic cause of the crisis was undoubtedly the run of poor harvests and the associated poor trading from 1656 to 1661 which, although apparently not as severe as the 1647–50 dearth, saw food prices reach exceptional levels after the harvest of 1661.[43] Restrictions were placed on markets and the victual trade, although there were apparently no repeats of the attempts to stamp out alehouses and the common peoples' sin.[44]

The ensuing years saw no evidence of any major poverty crises, although there were a relatively high number of petitions presented at Preston (and, to a much lesser extent, Lancaster) in 1669, something perhaps related to the mortality crises in these areas between 1667 and

---

42   Cf. Botelho, *Old Age*, p. 41. Note that the dip in 1660 reflects the fact that only Michaelmas Sessions sat that year.

43   *Seventeenth-Century Economic Documents*, pp. 65–8.

44   Wrightson, 'Puritan Reformation', p. 189.

1672.[45] In particular, the Second Dutch War (1667–68) does not seem to have led to a trade depression in the cotton region as had occurred during the First. This said, there are stray hints that all was not entirely well in these years. A petition for a habitation order by John Hill of Manchester complained in 1665 of 'all tradeinge being soe deade as for the present it is', perhaps alluding to the impact of restrictions imposed in response to the plague in London.[46] In addition, another habitation appeal of 1667 by Edmund Butterworth of Castleton referred to a 'decay of tradeing' and the 'hardnes of tymes', suggesting at least some local difficulties in the cotton region during the Second Dutch War.[47] But it was only during the Third Dutch War (1672–74) that things got markedly worse again.

Dearth and depression: the crisis of 1674–75

In the early weeks of 1674, the overseers of the poor for the town of Bolton launched a desperate petition to the Epiphany Quarter Sessions at Manchester.[48] Their town, they pleaded, 'hath for many yeares abounded with multitudes of poore inhabitants'. '[W]hen the fustian trade went well', they continued, 'most of them were employed as spinners or weavers of fustian and lived very well thereby without beeing burdensome'. Their town was able to circumvent the provision of the Poor Law of 43 Elizabeth that ordered parishes to provide a stock of goods to put the poor to work, and it did not need to bind out poor children as apprentices, for 'the tradesmen in the said towne have beene accustomed to take poore children apprentices gratis'. Indeed, 'the stock that was raysed was onely soemuch money as to releeve the lame impotent old blind and such other poore not able to worke'.

By the winter of 1673/74, however, things had gone horribly wrong. The fustian trade 'now fayles', continued the petition, while the 1662 Poor Law statute had placed responsibility for the maintenance of the Northern poor at the doors of each township, rather than the older system of parochial administration. In other words, urban Bolton had lost the tax revenues of the vast parish of Bolton-le-Moors: 'your petitioners haveing beene thereby seperate from the rest of the parish have beene put to a charge

45   Gritt, 'Mortality Crisis'.
46   LA, QSP/280/18; *Proceedings of the Lancashire Justices of the Peace*, p. 117.
47   LA, QSP/312/2.
48   LA, QSP/413/14.

greater than they are able to continue for manteyning their said poore vidzt neere 500li per annum'. Worse, the poor themselves were getting restless: 'the said poore are growne very unruly' and 'runn through the parish of Bolton and other neighboureing parishes dayly in great numbers a begging and will not notwithstanding their great allowance bee kept in'. Some were refusing to work, while others were making spurious claims for assistance to Quarter and Petty Sessions, which the overseers were then forced to honour. This was a deep crisis for the growing textile town.

It is not commonly acknowledged that the middle of the 1670s saw parts of England, including much of Lancashire, beset by major economic problems. Ralph Davis, for one, acknowledges a serious malaise in exporting textile industries especially between 1674 and 1677, which he attributes to problems in reaching war-torn foreign markets.[49] Peter Bowden, meanwhile, describes the 1670s and 1680s as a period in which the wool trade was 'chronically depressed' and this is certainly the impression gained from the series of prices presented by J. E. T. Rogers.[50] Yet the mid-1670s are conspicuously absent from histories of dearth, and this lack of attention has led Peter Laslett to state unequivocally that 1674 was 'not a crisis year nationally, not one of a fall in real wages, or of local emergencies', indeed, it was 'a time of relative plenty'.[51] However, in Lancashire at least, the middle of the 1670s saw exceptionally severe economic problems. These in turn led to a dramatic increase in the level of poverty, pulling many ordinarily secure households into dependence on the Poor Law. William Blundell, in his summary of his accounts for the year 1675, described the situation well: 'The poor have been in great want thes 2 dear years, & I either have or should have releeved the poor of our parish at a greater expence than formerly'.[52]

The decisive cause of the crisis seems to have been an especially poor harvest in 1674, which caused a massive increase in the cost of grain in the region. Statistics from *AHEW* suggest that the harvest year 1674–75 saw the highest grain prices in the period from 1661 to 1698. Nonetheless, the scale of the price increases found in the national series is not especially

49   R. Davis, 'English Foreign Trade, 1660–1700', *EcHR*, 2nd Ser., 7 (1954), 150–66 (p. 161n).
50   P. J. Bowden, *The Wool Trade in Tudor and Stuart England* (London, 1962), p. 7; J. E. T. Rogers, *A History of Agriculture and Prices in England*, 7 vols (Oxford, 1866–1902), vol. 5, pp. 590–1.
51   Laslett, *World We Have Lost*, p. 146.
52   Tyrer, 'Poor Law', p. 20.

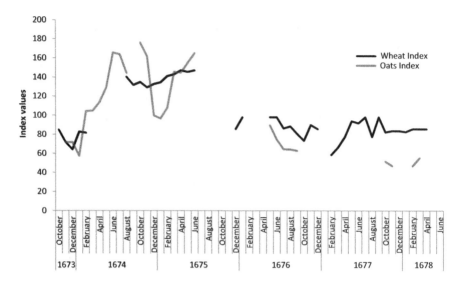

Figure 17: Grain prices at Swarthmoor, 1673–78

impressive, with the composite costs of grain significantly lower than
either 1661 or 1698, or the late 1640s for that matter. On the other hand,
Scottish data suggest much more significant rises in the prices of wheat and
especially oats, so perhaps the 'national' figures underestimate the degree
of regional shortage.[53] In fact, we are fortunate enough to be in possession
of a good series of local grain prices for the duration of the crisis. These
can be reconstructed from the papers of Sarah Fell of Swarthmoor Hall
(near Ulverston) who was involved in the marketing of foodstuffs as both a
producer and a consumer, and whose account book for the period between
1673 and 1678 has been published.[54] The grains she dealt in most frequently
were wheat and oats, and her transactions in these two crops have been
indexed and presented in Figure 17. The picture here is clear: prices roughly
doubled during the crisis, suggesting an increase far in excess of that
recorded in the *AHEW* series. In particular, the main increase came between
January 1674 and August/October that same year, hinting that it was the

53   A. J. S. Gibson and T. C. Smout, *Prices, Food, and Wages in Scotland, 1550–1780*
(Cambridge, 1995), pp. 16–17; K. J. Cullen, C. A. Whatley and M. Young, 'King William's
Ill Years: New Evidence on the Impact of Scarcity and Harvest Failure during the Crisis of
the 1690s on Tayside', *Scottish Historical Review*, 85 (2006), 250–76 (p. 258).
54   Fell, *Household Account Book*, *passim*.

depredations of the terrible winter, and especially a blizzard that harried the north in March, which devastated the year's crop. This then led to price rises in anticipation of a poor harvest that autumn. Finally, it is particularly important to note the degree of symmetry between wheat and oat prices, with both the expensive and the cheap grains badly affected by the crisis. This contradicts Appleby's assertion that the price of oats 'usually did not follow wheat prices, and after 1647 … remained remarkably stable, with the possible exceptions of prices for 1699 and 1728'.[55]

Even this is not the whole story. Although the evidence we have for Swarthmoor suggests that prices were not regionally very high before the late winter of 1674, it appears that the harvest of 1673 had been bad elsewhere. A north-eastern correspondent of Lady Lowther wrote to her on 22 October that year expressing concern at the 'sad sumer', for 'if their come a dearth god knows what will bee com of such poore people as I for I can't get that small rents that I have'.[56] Moreover, *AHEW* shows composite grain prices for 1673–74 at 23 per cent above trend, with especially marked increases in the cost of wheat and rye. In addition, there is strong evidence of problems in cotton-using industries from 1673 that predate both the price rises of 1674–75 and the more general industrial malaise detected by Davis between 1674 and 1677. The petition of the Bolton overseers, already cited, complained of failure in the fustian trade in early 1674 – several months before the great price rises found at Swarthmoor. James Hudson, a fustian-weaver from Oldham, reported to Epiphany Sessions that work was 'not onely ill to do but also little for the doinge of it', i.e. both scarce and poorly paid.[57] Meanwhile James Kirkall, of Bolton, petitioned to Easter Sessions that he was 'out of worke being a fustian dyer att which hee can get no imployment, by reason of bad tradeinge'.[58] By this time, petitioners had begun to complain specifically of dearth, though not with as much frequency as they would do after the summer, but it seems fairly clear that industrial depression in the cotton-using industries had already begun in earnest.[59] The cause of all this was almost certainly the Third Dutch War (1672–74), which once again disrupted imports from the Mediterranean.[60] In addition, the 'Stop of the

55   Appleby, 'Grain Prices', p. 880.
56   CRO (C), D Lons/L1/1/24/26, Mary Preston to Lady Lowther, 22 October 1673.
57   LA, QSP/413/21.
58   LA, QSP/417/39.
59   LA, QSP/415/9.
60   Wood, *History of the Levant Company*, pp. 102–3.

Exchequer' of early 1672 led to chaos in the London financial community and ruined a number of goldsmith-bankers.[61] It is hard to be sure whether this had much of an impact in Lancashire, but it would follow that cotton-using industries would have suffered more than most, as they remained heavily dependent on international merchants based in the capital.[62]

There is, therefore, clear evidence of both dearth and trade depression hitting the North West between 1673 and 1675. In turn, this poses the question as to whether there is evidence that the dearth ever developed into a famine. In theory, we have all the classic ingredients for a crisis of subsistence, and indeed the parallels with 1623, especially in the south-east of the county, are ominous. As in the earlier catastrophe, industrial depression was compounded by a serious shortage of grain, encompassing high prices in wheat and in cheaper cereals.[63] Moreover, there is little reason to suppose that the social-structural conditions in 1670s south-east Lancashire were any more favourable than those highlighted by Appleby for Cumberland and Westmorland in the 1620s. In particular, the Hearth Tax returns for 1664 suggest the existence of a sizeable population of marginal households in the region.[64]

And yet, taking a sample of fifty parish registers from across the county, the simple fact is that there is no evidence of any mortality peak coinciding with the 1674–75 crisis (Figure 18).[65] Indeed, although there was a peak in burials in the early spring of 1672 this looks very much like a part of the series of epidemics in the county that had begun around 1667 rather than anything connected to the economic crisis.[66] We must conclude that in this instance dearth did not, thankfully, become famine. And this has implications in turn for the question of why, after a last catastrophe in 1623, famine ceased in seventeenth-century England.[67] In particular, the clear symmetry of food prices between cheap and more expensive grains

---

61   A. Browning, 'Historical Revisions, 52: The Stop of the Exchequer, 1672', *History*, New Ser., 14 (1929), 333–7.

62   Wadsworth and Mann, *Cotton Trade*, pp. 30–3.

63   Appleby, *Famine*, pp. 50–66; Hoyle, 'Famine as Agricultural Catastrophe'.

64   TNA, E179/250/11/Part Six.

65   For the sources for this graph, see: J. Healey, '"The Tymes Being Soe Hard With Poore People": Poverty and the Economic Crisis of 1672–76 in Lancashire', *THSLC*, 162 (2013), 49–69.

66   Gritt, 'Mortality Crisis'.

67   On which, see: J. Walter and R. S. Schofield, 'Famine, Disease and Crisis Mortality in Early Modern Society', in Walter and Schofield (eds), *Famine, Disease and the Social Order*, pp. 1–73 (pp. 28–61).

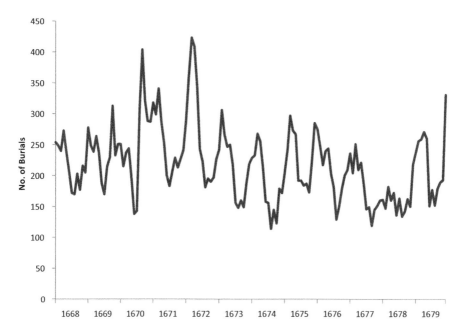

Figure 18: Monthly burial totals in fifty Lancashire parishes, 1668–79

is difficult to reconcile with Appleby's well-known suggestion that it was diversity between winter and spring-sown crops that guaranteed access to at least some affordable food.[68] It is also difficult to accept that regional specialization and the laws of comparative advantage were the critical factors in this case, given the evident social problems caused by the collapse of the area's industries and the resulting vulnerability of the 'specialized' population.

A large part of the explanation must lie with increased spending on society's most vulnerable through formal poor relief. As has been shown, the period 1674–75 saw a massive peak in the numbers of surviving first petitions for poor relief, especially at Manchester Sessions where the peak began in 1673 (Figure 19). This indicates both a great increase in perceived need, but also that the poor were looking to formal relief systems to ensure survival. That such relief was forthcoming is shown by existing sets of overseers' accounts. Those for Prestwich clearly show a response (Figure 20), with total dole expenditure peaking in 1673–75 before receding.

68   Appleby, 'Grain Prices'.

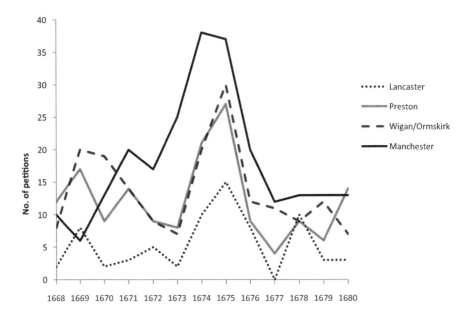

Figure 19: First petitions for poor relief, 1668–80

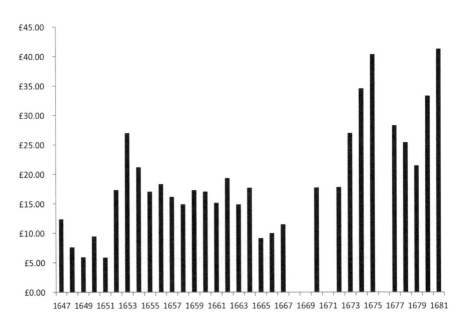

Figure 20: Poor expenditure in Prestwich, Heaton, Redditch Heaton,
Alkrington and Tonge, 1647–81

Table 5: Poor relief in Bolton, 1674–99

Year	No. of paupers	Total annual dole	Dole per capita per annum	Mean annual living costs per capita
1674	740	£1927.47	£2.60	£2.60
1686	333	£230.85	£0.69	£1.47
1699	430	£284.16	£0.66	£2.10

The most impressive set of sources, however, are the Bolton censuses of the poor. In particular, it is possible to compare the census compiled towards the end of 1674 with those from 1686 and 1699 in order to gauge the impact of the 1670s crisis on the town's poor. The year 1686 was not one of crisis; 1699, by contrast, was more complex. It was apparently a year of very high food prices (even famine in Scotland) after the seriously deficient harvest of 1698.[69] Yet, although there is some evidence of greater distress than 1686, the scale of need seems to have been hardly comparable to that a quarter of a century earlier. Why this should be is unclear, but it may relate to the apparent boom in cotton manufactures which followed the temporary cessation of hostilities with France in 1697. Taxation statistics suggest that 1699 was a strong year for retained imports of raw cotton, and as most of this would have been worked in the Bolton, Manchester and Blackburn regions, it is possible that this sustained many of the poor in reasonable security.[70] In particular, this would help explain why the 1699 census records a high cost of living (roughly £2 2s per capita per annum) amongst the poor, but a relatively modest mean dole at just over 13s (Table 5).

It appears, then, that we can use data from 1686 and 1699 as a comparison with that of the clear crisis year of 1674. At the most basic level, it is clear that the cost of poor relief in Bolton in 1674 was exceptionally high. In their petition to Epiphany Sessions that year, the overseers of the township of Bolton claimed to need some £500 to support the poor, a figure which – if true – represents a substantial increase on the figures for the 1650s, which rarely seem to have exceeded £100 for the whole parish.[71] It was also substantially higher than the annual level of expenditure in

---

69 Cullen, Whatley and Young, 'King William's Ill Years', pp. 260, 270–4.
70 Wadsworth and Mann, *Cotton Trade*, pp. 520–1.
71 BALS, PBO/2/1, Bolton-le-Moors Churchwardens' and Poor Relief Accounts, 1654–1711.

Table 6: Percentage of households by circumstance in Bolton, 1674–99

Household circumstance		1674 (a)	1674 (b)	1686	1699
	Two adults	34.3	57.0	26.4	32.3
	Single men	13.9	7.9	18.6	12.2
	Single women	42.6	27.2	40.0	32.3
	No adults	9.3	7.9	15.0	23.2
Adult-headed with:	1 child	9.3	20.2	6.4	3.0
	2 children	7.4	16.7	15.0	9.8
	3 children	13.0	14.9	12.9	12.8
	4 children	10.2	7.0	3.6	7.9
	5+ children	7.4	–	3.6	6.7
Age of head	Unknown/14–49	42.6	59.6	31.4	36.0
	50–59	7.4	11.4	16.4	9.1
	60–69	13.9	16.7	15.0	17.7
	70+	26.9	4.4	22.1	14.0
With infirmities	Total	37.0	5.3	47.9	34.1
Others	Two-adult, non-infirm	23.1	55.3	8.6	25.0
	Two-adult, non-infirm in 14–59 age group	17.6	45.6	6.4	20.1

both 1686 (£231) and 1699 (£284); yet apparently this turned out to be a drastic underestimate, for when the census came to be compiled in the late autumn or winter that year (i.e. after the great price rises of the spring) the weekly cash requirement for the support of the town's poor was recorded as reaching £37 1s 4d. This would, if continued for a year, have cost the town the astonishing sum of over £1900, or somewhere around 17–18s per head of the total urban population. Furthermore, the numbers needing relief were exceptionally high, with some 740 paupers recorded in 1674, probably representing around a third of the population.

The most interesting data, however, come from a more detailed study of the social characteristics of Bolton's poor households in 1674. The census of this year was unique in that it made the distinction between the regular poor, described as the 'aged decayed, blynde lunaticke and diseased beinge past labour, as also the fatherless, motherless and infant not able to labour and poor familys overcharged with children', and

Table 7: Characteristics of pauper households in Bolton, 1674

Household circumstance		Group A			Group B		
		No.	%	Dole per capita per week (pence)	No.	%	Dole per capita per week (pence)
	Two adults	37	34.3	12.6	65	57.0	7.9
	Single men	15	13.9	15.4	9	7.9	12.6
	Single women	46	42.6	18.6	31	27.2	9.0
	No adults	10	9.3	18.5	9	7.9	9.3
Adult-headed with:	1 child	10	9.3	16.0	23	20.2	8.5
	2 children	8	7.4	13.9	19	16.7	8.5
	3 children	14	13.0	14.0	17	14.9	7.5
	4 children	11	10.2	11.4	8	7.0	6.8
	5 children	8	7.4	11.2	0	–	–
Age of head	Unknown	46	42.6	12.4	68	59.6	8.0
	50–59	8	7.4	15.2	13	11.4	7.3
	60–69	15	13.9	19.3	19	16.7	9.6
	70+	29	26.9	21.0	5	4.4	14.3
With infirmities*	Total	40	37.0	16.7	6	5.3	13.7
Others	Two-adult, non-infirm	25	23.1	12.0	63	55.3	7.9
	Two-adult, non-infirm, not over 50	19	17.6	11.0	52	45.6	7.6
Overall		108		14.6	114		8.3

* Not including those recorded as 'weak', 'infirm' or 'impotent' unless there is positive evidence that they are under fifty years old. These terms were often being used to describe the weakness associated with old age. The word 'infirmity' seems to be used in the context of the 1686 and 1699 censuses to refer to the most visible cause of poverty and includes such misfortunes as being overcharged with children or abandoned by one's spouse.

another group comprising 'those not in the book but assisted with money and in kind at our doors and such also who are in great necessitie, being overcharged'. Thus, we can not only compare 1674 with the 'non-crisis' data, but it is also possible to look *within* 1674 to compare the two sets of poor households as delineated by the census-takers. Table 6 compares the percentages of paupers living under certain household conditions across all three censuses, and with that of 1674 divided into its two headings. Of these, the group comprising the regular poor is little different in its composition from the paupers of 1686 and 1699. It is the second group which is more interesting, and here the difference with the other censuses is very marked: two-adult households accounted for 57.0 per cent of the total, while it seems that only 32.5 per cent of pauper households were headed by those over fifty years old. Sickness was negligible, just six households (5.3 per cent of paupers) recording any kind of infirmity. Importantly, while in 1686 and 1699 just 13.8 per cent of all paupers households were neither broken, aged nor infirm, in the second group of the 1674 census this figure stood at over 45 per cent. The basic fact is that in 1674 a large number of families, although not suffering from some life-cycle, family-breakdown or health-related hardship, were nonetheless suffering from poverty, and thus it is evident that the year saw the incorporation of a significant number of apparently functioning families into the relief lists. This was a product of the greater demand for relief resulting from a very severe economic crisis. Additionally, although the 1674 census omits data on earning – the 'weekly get' – it does tell us the dole given to each household (Table 7). Doles were substantially higher here than those recorded in 1686 and 1699, and hence it seems that the omission of earnings from the 1674 census, though frustrating for the historian, may also be telling: at a time when the household economy of the poor had so completely broken down, there was little point in collecting data on pauper incomes. There was simply not enough money being earned.

Crises, 1680–1715

Although levels of both poor relief and petitioning tailed off after 1675, the economic crisis of 1673–75 apparently had a lasting impact. As late as 1677, two petitioners claimed to be still suffering as a result of their losses during the dearth. Richard Tomlinson, a husbandman of Broughton-in-Amounderness complained that through the scarsity of the late yeares your poore petitioner beinge forced to runne himselfe into debte for the relife of himselfe and his family whereby that hee is engaged unto severall persons which doth threaten to sease upon what goods hee hath and likewise to throw his body into the gaole ...[72]

Meanwhile, widow Isabel Waterhouse of Balderstone reported that 'in the time of the last dearth or scarcity was willing (& did) sell most part of those small goods they had to maintaine their selves & poore small children, lest they should too much oppresse or be troublesome to the said towne'.[73] Thus when they suffered fire in 1677 the family had nothing to fall back on. Presumably this kind of problem was relatively widespread, for there is evidence that the level of poverty remained elevated *after* the crisis. The registers of Colne, for example, saw an increase in the number and proportion of 'poor' burials recorded from eight per annum in 1670–73 (11 per cent of the total number of burials) to twenty-three per annum in 1674–75 (29 per cent). After this, however, the apparent level of poverty remained remarkably high, with twenty-four 'pauper' burials in 1676 (24 per cent) and seventeen per annum between 1677 and 1679, or 27 per cent. Similarly, levels of expenditure in Prestwich remained high in 1676/77, only dropping significantly the following year.[74]

In general, though, after the hardships of the mid-1670s there was a period of relative calm. A few petitioners mention difficulties – the 'deadnes of trading', the 'tyme of scarcity', and the 'hardnesse of the times' – between 1679 and 1682, perhaps reflective of uncertainties resulting from the Exclusion Crisis, in addition to a poor harvest in 1679 and a series of epidemics between then and about 1683.[75] The 1690s, meanwhile, were an infamously difficult decade, with recurrent high food prices, warfare in Ireland and the continent, as well as a devastating famine in Scotland. To top it off, there was a damaging loss of confidence in the country's money, especially in the North, which in turn forced King William's government to embark on the so-called 'Great Recoinage'

---

72   LA, QSP/459/6.
73   LA, QSP/471/13.
74   MALS, L160/2/1, Prestwich Churchwardens' and Overseers' Accounts, 1646–83.
75   Wrigley and Schofield, *Population History*, pp. 666–7, 679–81; LA, QSP/506/21, QSP/541/8, QSP/547/7.

with its predictable disruption to the economy.[76] One or two petitions did, indeed, complain of unemployment and economic difficulties in the early 1690s. Labourer Robert Booth of Manchester, for example, claimed poverty in 1691 with 'work being soe scarce & hee soe ancient'.[77] Two years later, widow Jane Ashworth of Hindley told of how she had nothing to maintain her child but her own industry, 'and since the times are now become soe scares of money that their is noe worke to be gotten'.[78] Adam Roscow of Blackrod was complaining of hard times in 1693, while labourer John Robinson of Whittingham told in 1695 of how there was no available work in his parish. In 1697, webster John Thorp of Bury noted the 'hardness of the times' when petitioning for relief for himself and his large family, while early in 1698, Mary Low of Coppull lamented her aged husband's decrepitude, but also how work was now 'very scarce and wages small'.[79] Later that year, Manchester silk-weaver Robert Robinson reported how his trade was 'att such a stand that he has had little or noe worke for theise twelve months last past'.[80]

But it was only in 1699 that there was another major peak in the *number* of petitions, coinciding again with a period of especially high food prices (Figure 21). In fact, the number of first petitions roughly doubled on the annual mean, even that for the 1690s. It is a startling fact that, in a decade of war, trade disruption, and the 'Great Recoinage', it was only as food prices rocketed (and during a brief interlude of peace) that the level of petitioning jumped in this way. Poor relief costs apparently rose too, although there are still – even by this point – few surviving accounts upon which to base this assertion. Most important are those for Bury, which show a significant peak in spending from 1697 to 1699 (Figure 22). Petitioners, meanwhile, started noting the high food prices from as early as Michaelmas 1698, the time of the harvest. John Sandiforth, a Manchester labourer, complained to JPs then of the 'scarcity of provisions'.[81] Early in the New Year, a slew of petitioners brought up the standard laments: 'the hardnes of the tymes', the 'scharenesse of provisions', 'provisions very dear', and that 'there is little or no worke to be had in this time'.[82] Again,

76 M. H. Li, *The Great Recoinage of 1696 to 1699* (London, 1963).
77 LA, QSP/707/4.
78 LA, QSP/738/7.
79 LA, QSP/792/4, QSP/807/29.
80 LA, QSP/820/5.
81 LA, QSP/820/6.
82 LA, QSP/823/15; QSP/822/30; QSP/823/16; QSP/822/32.

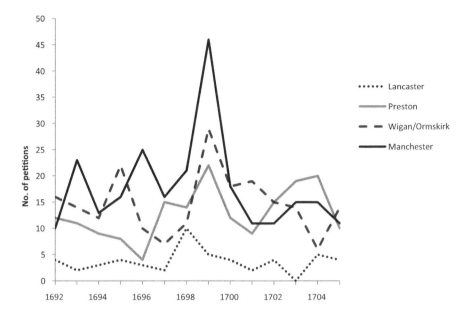

Figure 21: First petitions for poor relief, 1692–1705

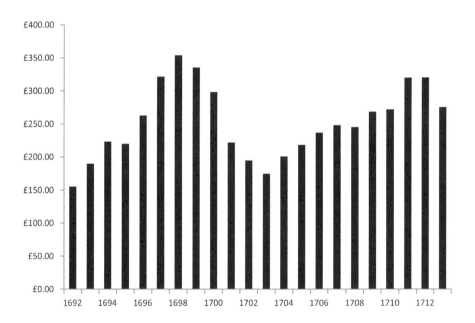

Figure 22: Poor law expenditure in Bury township, 1692–1713

as this last petitioner implied, high prices seem to have had their usual knock-on effect on the market for labour. Everything was dear, recounted James Shelmerdine of Ardwick at Easter, and he had been 'destitute of worke and imployment ever since the last Christmas'.[83] 'I have but very litle worke', Rebecca Hopwood told Manchester justices, 'and every thing is very dear'.[84] These were, William Rothwell of Winstanley petitioned in Easter that year, 'sad times of scarcity with poor people'.[85]

But after the 1700 harvest the price of food dropped, and the references to scarcity largely disappear. There were still a couple of complaints of the decay of trade into 1700, however, so it seems that some economic problems remained.[86] In early 1701, James Roscoe, a labouring man of Leyland told JPs of how his wife had been sick for eight years, and that 'the hardnes of the tymes hath constrened him to sell his cowe sheep & what hee hath for the relife which brought him in to a lowe condition'. Again, economic crises could cast long shadows for those who suffered through them. Warfare returned in 1702, and despite the British state's success on the battlefield this was another tough decade for those at home. There was a small peak in the number of petitions in 1706, possibly resulting from difficulties in the textile industries (the price of grain was not especially high). Early that year, Thomas Banks of Bolton told of how he had trained as a fustian-weaver but that 'the fustian trade goes very badly'.[87] Woollen-webster Richard Sharples of Pleasington had, by that year, married a widow with three children who was also pregnant, 'and the times groweinge hard and worke scarse to be had' he had come to need relief.[88]

This crisis passed, but a more serious one hit in 1709–10, when poor harvests again brought hardship. By this point, the volume of surviving petitions is small, and there was no peak at Quarter Sessions, but the textual evidence is clear enough. In Easter 1709, for example, Elizabeth Atkinson of Haighton was complaining of the 'scarcitye of provisions'.[89] Corn, wrote tailor Nicholas Rymer of Upholland, was 'very dear' and

83 LA, QSP/828/25.
84 LA, QSP/828/31.
85 LA, QSP/827/62.
86 LA, QSP/841/19; QSP/844/18.
87 LA, QSP/936/7.
88 LA, QSP/939/11.
89 LA, QSP/987/6.

work was 'scarce'.[90] Widow Ruth Harrison of Overton was getting 40s a year for herself and her three children, but 'now all provisions being dearer', this 'will not purchase so much bread as to nourish the said three children'.[91] Still in early 1710, corn was 'so very deare', petitioned John Tompson of Tarleton, while Robert Butler of Garstang wrote that Easter of how 'tymes' were 'very hard and every thing scarce'.[92] An allowance of 6s 6d a month was, complained Richard Tattersall of Newchurch-in-Rossendale, hardly enough for his lame wife and four young children, 'trade being dead & necessaryes at a great rate'.[93] Even in this last crisis, it is striking how the complaints of poor petitioners remained virtually the same. Provisions were dear, prices were high, times were hard and trade had stopped. It was the same litany of complaints that paupers had used in the crises of the 1640s and 1660s, and in the 1670s and 1690s. And it came, like the earlier crises, after a poor harvest. Lancashire no longer suffered famines in this period, but there were recurrent shortages of food, which themselves brought economic disruption. The words of the petitioners form a timely reminder that the Poor Law developed partly as a way of dealing with the shocks caused by poor harvests to a pre-industrial, agrarian economy.

Unfortunately from then on the number of surviving petitions drops off quickly, and there are very few extant from after 1710. By this point, however, enough poor accounts survive for the most severe and widespread crises to be detectable. If we return to the composite series of poor expenditure in the county, as discussed in chapter 2, then it is apparent that the most pronounced crises came at the end of the 1720s and the beginning years of the 1740s. Both of these were periods of high food prices, the latter seeing a famine in Ireland, perhaps more severe than the 'Great' one of 1845–51, as well as a spate of food rioting in England. The earlier crisis appears more complex, with high food prices compounded by a deadly spate of epidemics which resulted in England's most serious mortality crisis since the 1550s, and the second highest peak in burials between 1537 and 1871. It is this unique 'poverty crisis' that will occupy the final part of this book.

---

90   LA, QSP/988/22.
91   LA, QSP/990/6.
92   LA, QSP/1000/5; QSP/1003/4.
93   LA, QSP/999/8.

'Never so sickley a time known': the crisis of 1727–30

According to Wrigley and Schofield, the latter years of the 1720s saw
the second most serious mortality crisis in England between 1541 and
1871.[94] They noted a band of high mortality through the Midlands 'with
extensions into Lancashire, east Yorkshire, and East Anglia', although
many parts escaped. The crisis combined a series of peaks in burials,
general complaints of sickness, and a two-year run of high food prices.[95]
In fact, the strong coincidence of timing between exorbitant prices and
elevated mortality has led one commentator to describe the episode as
the '1727–9 *harvests* crises', suggesting that disease ravaged a population
already weak through malnutrition.[96]

Certainly Lancashire was very badly affected, and a number of contemporary comments attest to its local severity.[97] According to the diarist
Nicholas Blundell, in his entry for December 1727, there was:

Much damage don in many parts of England this year by thunder &
lightoning. Corne generally speaking proved small. Never so sickley
a time known in Lancashire as from May till the end of this year,
abundance died but generally those above 50 years old, the distemper

---

94 Wrigley and Schofield, *Population History*, pp. 652–3, 667, 681–4. The most serious
mortality crisis was that of the late 1550s.
95 C. Creighton, *A History of Epidemics in Britain*, 2 vols (Cambridge, 1891–94), vol.
2, pp. 66–74, 341–6; J. D. Chambers, *The Vale of Trent, 1670–1800: A Regional Study
of Economic Change* (London, 1957), pp. 29–30; Ashton, *Economic Fluctuations*,
pp. 144–5; D. E. C. Eversley, 'A Survey of Population in an Area of Worcestershire from
1660 to 1850 on the Basis of Parish Registers', in Glass and Eversley (eds), *Population
in History*, pp. 394–421 (pp. 408–10); J. A. Johnston, 'The Impact of the Epidemics of
1727–30 in South-west Worcestershire', *Medical History*, 15 (1971), 278–92; A. Gooder,
'The Population Crisis of 1727–30 in Warwickshire', *Midland History*, 1 (1972), 1–22;
A. B. Appleby, 'Epidemics and Famine in the Little Ice Age', *Journal of Interdisciplinary
History*, 10 (1980), 643–63 (p. 643); Hoppit, *Risk and Failure*, p. 107. On prices, see:
Bowden, 'Statistical Appendix', vol. 5, pp. 830–1.
96 Gooder, 'Population Crisis', p. 21. My italics.
97 J. Healey, 'Socially Selective Mortality during the Population Crisis of 1727–1730:
Evidence from Lancashire', *LPS*, 81 (2008), 58–74; E. M. Edwards, 'Crisis in Lancashire:
A Survey of the 1720s Demographic Crisis' (Univ. of Central Lancashire MA thesis, 2009).
Also: G. P. Jones, 'The Population of Broughton-in-Furness in the Eighteenth Century',
CW2, 53 (1953), 136–48 (pp. 142–3); G. P. Jones, 'Some Population Problems relating to
Cumberland and Westmorland in the 18th Century', *CW2*, 58 (1959), 123–39 (pp. 133–4);
Speake, 'Historical Demography', pp. 53, 59–60.

was an uncommon sort of a fever which eather took them off or ended in a violent ague which often lasted severall months & was scarce possible to be cuer'd and most who had these fits had them after different mannors so that they scarce knew when to expect them, being somtimes quartan, tersion &c: and som had an easy fitt and as soon as that was gon off had a most violent fitt; in som parts of England they fair'd not much better and beyond the seas it was a very sickley time. When the distemper began to abait the horses in severall places were ill, being seas'd with a runing at the nose & a cough of which som few died.[98]

Blundell's diary ends in 1728, but Lancashire's great early-eighteenth-century autobiographer, William Stout, recorded the whole period.[99] He described 1728 as seeing a 'very sickley summer, and great mortalety in the plaine country' though he noted that this was 'much more then in the towns'. 'The buryalls', he stated, 'were double this year to what they were last year'.[100] At the same time the parish authorities of Deane (near Bolton) felt compelled to explain, through a series of notations, why their registers contained such an extraordinary number of burials.[101] Thus, according to an interjection for September 1727, those buried that month 'dyed of a fever. But in some respects the disorder resembled the plague, and continued amongst us above two years.' The symptom most commonly recorded by contemporaries was a 'fever', and it has been suggested that typhus and relapsing fever were the main culprits, although there is clear evidence of widespread influenza, particularly in the winter of 1729/30.[102]

It is also clear that food prices were unusually high. Stout considered

---

98 Blundell, *Great Diurnal*, vol. 3, p. 230.

99 Stout, *Autobiography*, pp. 199–207.

100 Ibid., p. 201.

101 *The Registers of the Parish Church of Deane: Burials, 1604–1750*, ed. A. Sparke (LPRS, liv, Bolton, 1917), pp. 532–44.

102 Cf. *Trentham Parish Register*, ed. S. W. Hutchinson (Stoke-on-Trent, 1906): here fevers also feature prominently as stated causes of death. W. Hillary, *A Practical Essay on the Small-pox. To which is added, An Account of the Principal Variations of the Weather at Ripon, and the Concomitant Epidemical Diseases, From the Year 1726, to the End of the Year 1734*, 2nd edn (London, 1740); C. Wintringham, *Commentarius Nosologicus: a Treatise on the Study of Diseases: Embracing the Epidemic Diseases and Variations in Weather in the City of York and Neighbouring Places through Twenty Consecutive Years*, trans. E. Johnson (Pocklington, 1979).

the economic situation of the later 1720s in some detail, referring to shortages in the south of the county after the 1727 harvest, followed by widespread dearth after that of 1728, when grain was shipped in from as far away as Hamburg and America.[103] Some early relief was provided by a relative abundance of potatoes, but this did not last into 1729.[104] In the south of the county, Blundell acknowledged the unusual economic circumstances of the late 1720s in his 'Anecdote Book':

> Anno Domini 1728 and 1729 corn was very scarce in Lancashire, as well as in other parts of England. For which reason great quantitys of corne was brought into Leverpoole and I am informed from very good hands that from June the 24 1728 to May the 6th 1729 there was import into Liverpool 234562 bushels of corne, chiefly wheat and barly.[105]

We can also compare these statements to a set of farm stewards' accounts from Lytham,[106] which contain quantifiable grain prices, set out in Figures 23–4. Thus, the prices of potatoes, oats, and barley show no sign of increase until the months following the harvest of 1728 (though wheat prices seem to have risen slightly between early 1725 and mid-1727). From the 1728 harvest, however, there were significant increases in wheat, oat, and potato prices, and a rather smaller increase in the cost of barley. It is worth noting that the prices paid by the Cliftons' stewards did not rise as much as those recorded by Stout: perhaps their social power helped get them a discount.

The most dramatic evidence comes from burial registers. A broadly representative sample of forty-two parish registers shows an exceptionally marked swelling in the number of burials between August 1727 and the spring of 1730 (Figure 25).[107] Taking the thirty-six-month period from August 1727 to July 1730, the number of burials was roughly 90 per cent higher than we would expect from the mean annual total for the non-crisis periods between 1720 and 1735. Assuming a population of

103   Stout, *Autobiography*, pp. 201–4.
104   L. A. Clarkson and E. M. Crawford, *Feast and Famine: A History of Food and Nutrition in Ireland, 1500–1920* (Oxford, 2001), p. 125.
105   Blundell, *Great Diurnal*, vol. 3, p. 230n.
106   LA, DDCl/400, Steward's Accounts, 1709–29.
107   Healey, 'Socially Selective Mortality', p. 62.

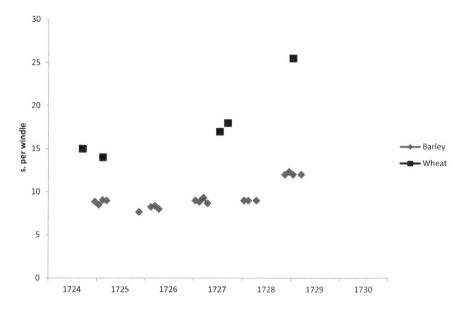

Figure 23: Prices of barley and wheat at Lytham, 1724–30 (shillings per windle)

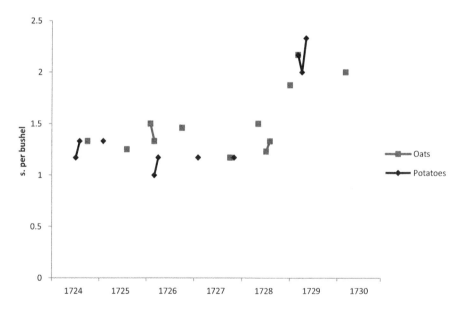

Figure 24: Prices of potatoes and oats at Lytham, 1724–30 (shillings per bushel)

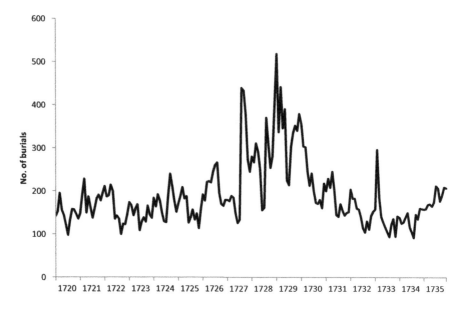

Figure 25: Monthly burial totals in forty-two Lancashire registers,
1720–35

Figure 26: Composite mean of poor account expenditures, 1710–39
(100 = mean of 1690–1750)

around 225,000[108]and a normal death rate of twenty-five per thousand,[109] this would mean an extra 15,000 or more deaths *in Lancashire alone* are attributable to the epidemics. All told, this would represent the loss of an extra 6–7 per cent of the county's population, making the crisis marginally more severe than the famine of 1623, which is reckoned to have killed 5 per cent.[110] And there is evidence for some social selectivity in mortality. Commentators in Yorkshire noted the particular sufferings of the 'labouring and poor people' and the 'common people', and a quantitative survey of burials, published elsewhere, seems to show that the gentle, mercantile and professional category experienced no increased mortality, suggesting at least some social differentiation in the incidence of death.[111] Nonetheless, outside this group, high mortality was general across almost all occupations.

In the face of this dearth and disease, poor relief costs rocketed (Figure 26). In fourteen townships studied, all showed increases in relief expenditure in the late 1720s, though in Hawkshead in the far north of the county this ran from 1724 to 1731, so that it would be difficult to ascribe this to the 1727–30 crisis alone. A number of townships show a very impressive increase in expenditure at the end of the decade: in Kearsley (near Bolton), for example, the overseers spent an average of £17.09 per annum between 1717 and 1726, but their costs rose to £47.72 in 1728 and £58.54 in 1729. Similarly, in New Accrington, mean annual expenditure lay at £23.88 between 1710 and 1726, but it hit £48.39 in 1727, rising to £55.13 in 1728 and then further to £64.85 and £63.58 in 1729 and 1730 respectively. Most impressive, given the large amounts being spent, were the accounts for the township of Bury. Here the annual cost of running the poor relief system came to a mean of £86.93 per annum between 1710 and 1726, but hit £194.00 in 1728, £219.98 in 1729 and peaked at £222.57 in 1730. Even many of those who did not fall sick as a direct result of the crisis, or who could ride out the high cost of food, would have been

108   According to figures in Phillips and Smith's history, the population of the county lay at just over 190,000 in the 1690s, while by 1750 it was nearly at 300,000; the figure of 225,000 for 1730 would make some allowance for geometric growth over the period: Phillips and Smith, *Lancashire and Cheshire*, pp. 66–70.
109   Wrigley and Schofield, *Population History*, p. 67.
110   Taking natural replenishment of the population under consideration. Cf. Rogers, *Lancashire Population Crisis*, p. 10.
111   Hillary, *Practical Essay*, pp. 11, 14; Wintringham, *Commentarius Nosologicus*, pp. 34, 38; Healey, 'Socially Selective Mortality'.

affected by the spiralling taxation that funded a significant redistribution of wealth.

The question is whether this expenditure was the product of the epidemic, or simply a result of high food prices. To a certain extent this is too simplistic: high food prices inevitably put stress on family budgets, making the costs of medical care much harder to bear. Thus a rise in medical costs *could* arise as a simple by-product of high food prices. It is worth noting in this context, however, that the evidence suggests a drop in the cost of provisions after the harvest of 1729, yet the mortality crisis continued after this. And while high mortality continued, so did the high poor expenditure. Of the eleven townships for which we have expenditures for the four years from 1727 to 1730 inclusive, and which suffered a crisis of expenditure, four saw costs peak in the accounting year of 1728/29 (i.e. Easter 1728 to Easter 1729), five in 1729/30 and two in 1730/31. In Kearsley, where the overseers rendered quarterly accounts, January to March 1730 saw costs higher than for any other single quarter between 1717 and 1734.[112] Meanwhile a number of townships were still experiencing high expenditure in 1730/31. In Bury, as we have seen, costs peaked in that year, as they did in Halsall and Halliwell.

Unfortunately, only three sets of accounts exist in enough detail to show us the specific costs of medical care: Hawkshead, Cheetham and Atherton. Of these, the Hawkshead accounts have been set aside as the high expenditure ran, as was noted, from 1724 to 1731, which was atypical. In Cheetham, meanwhile, where expenditure between 1727 and 1729 lay 43 per cent above trend, costs were generally so low that any serious quantification is fraught with difficulty. For what it is worth, the medical expenditure recorded in Cheetham in 1728/29 (£6.08) was the highest for any year between 1700 and 1735. By far the most satisfactory accounts are from the township of Atherton, chiefly known (often under the name of Chowbent) as the major centre of the nail-making industry in the North West.[113] Its poor accounts are impressive in their detail, and as the township was densely populated they also contain information on a large amount of expenditure and a significant number of paupers. Accounts are missing for the years 1715, 1720, 1725 and 1726, and the appearance of a workhouse by 1733 means that regular pensioners disappear from the

112   BALS, PKE/1, Kearsley Overseers' Accounts, 1707–59.
113   Tupling, 'Early Metal Trade', pp. 20–1; Timmins, *Made in Lancashire*, pp. 23–5.

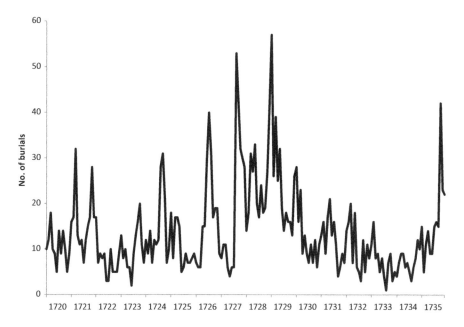

Figure 27: Monthly burials in Leigh parish, 1720–35

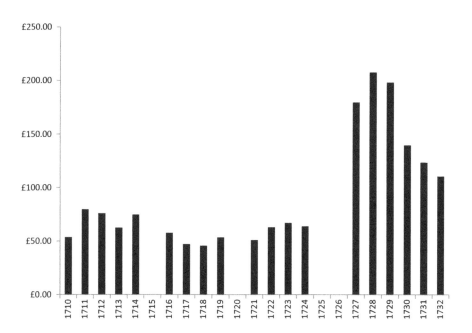

Figure 28: Poor expenditure in Atherton, 1710–32

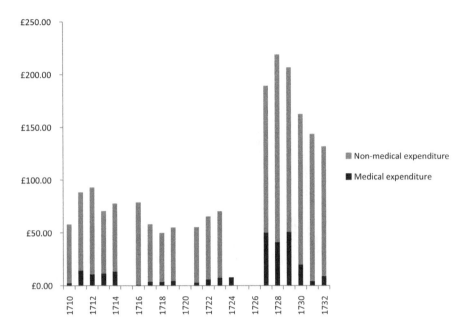

Figure 29: Explicitly medical expenditure in Atherton (i), 1710–32

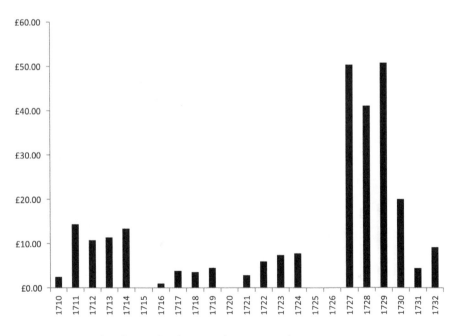

Figure 30: Explicitly medical expenditure in Atherton (ii), 1710–32

accounts from then onwards, but apart from this they provide excellent data.

The parish of Leigh, of which Atherton formed a part, suffered from an acute mortality crisis beginning in August 1727, but it escaped a major spike in burials later that year, in contrast to other parishes (Figure 27).[114] Its most severe period of mortality came in the winter of 1728/29, and although the monthly number of burials tailed off slightly thereafter, it remained high until the spring of 1730. The township accounts show a clear peak in the cost of relief (Figure 28). Between 1710 and 1724, a mean of nearly £70 was spent on doles to the poor per year. This rose to £205 between 1727 and 1729, before dropping to £146 in the three subsequent years. That the fall in dole expenditure after the crisis was not complete in the following years is significant, suggesting a lasting impact of the crisis in terms of broken family units and wiped-out savings. A similar story is told by the aggregate numbers of paupers receiving relief: this averaged sixty-nine between 1710 and 1723, rising to 112 during the crisis, though this fell back to seventy-four afterwards. As is to be expected, medical costs increased, too. It is clear that the years 1727 to 1729 (and to a lesser extent 1730) saw abnormally high expenditure on medical poor relief (Figures 29–30). Thus while an average of £6.87 was assigned to explicitly medical poor relief per year between 1710 and 1723, these costs hit a mean of £47.45 between 1727 and 1729.[115] They remained above trend at £20.01 in 1730 before dropping back down to £4.43 and £9.16 the following two years. This represents a mean of 10 per cent of annual dole expenditure going on medical care between 1710 and 1723, 23 per cent during the height of the crisis, 14 per cent in 1730, and then 5 per cent in 1731–32. The *number* of paupers receiving medical care also rose (Figure 31). An average of seventeen paupers received medical care paid for directly by the township between 1710 and 1723; between 1727 and 1729 this had risen to

114   *The Registers of Leigh Parish Church, 1701–1753*, ed. K. Taylor (LPRS, clv, Newport, 2002).

115   On some occasions, notably in later years, the Atherton overseers coupled different doles under one heading: thus Giles Marsh received £2 4s 3d in 1729/30 for 'sickness' and two years' rent in arrears, and we cannot tell what proportion of this dole was related specifically to Marsh's sickness. All such cases have been added to the medical expenses totals, but this means that the figures for the later years are slightly exaggerated. Fortunately, the amounts covered by such entries are not large: if we remove them from our analysis then the 1729/30 medical costs would be reduced from £50.83 to £44.28, and those of 1730/31 from £20.01 to £19.18. The difference for the rest of the period would be minuscule.

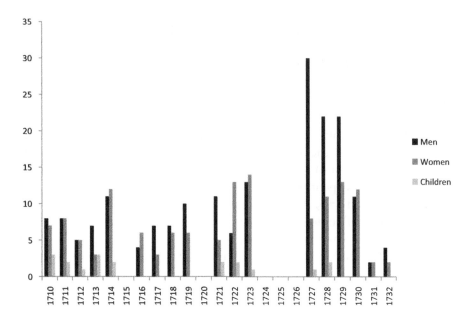

Figure 31: Paupers in receipt of medical relief, 1710–32

thirty-six, dropping back down to eleven again in the three years following. There is also an increase detectable in the proportion of paupers receiving direct medical aid, from 24 per cent in 1710–23 to 33 per cent in 1727–29, then down to 15 per cent in 1730–32, though this is admittedly less marked.

In addition, 1727 saw the first evidence of the regular employment of a single physician by the township. While individual doctors had been paid by the township to treat single paupers before (ten different doctors are mentioned between 1710 and 1732) the arrangement from 1727 to 1731 seems to have been different. Now, one doctor was employed to provide 'Physick to the Poore', and was expected to write up a bill at the end of the accounting year, the balance of which was then paid out of rates. The health crisis of the late 1720s seems to have encouraged Atherton's officers to rethink the administrative framework within which relief was provided: medical care was, to some degree, centralized.

The increase in the scale of direct medical care found in the Atherton overseers' accounts is just one facet of their story for the late 1720s. The crisis at the end of the decade saw a marked increase in the both the number of paupers and the average dole given to them (Tables 8–10). The mean adult-headed household dole rose from around £0.90 a year

Table 8: Paupers of Atherton, 1710–32

Period		1710–23 (mean p.a.)	1727–29 (mean p.a.)	1730–32 (mean p.a.)
Paupers	Total	832 (69)	333 (111)	158 (53)
	Male 'heads'	332 (27)	183 (61)	73 (24)
	Female 'heads'	406 (34)	108 (36)	59 (20)
	Child (groups)	93 (8)	41 (14)	26 (9)
Pensioners	Total	208 (17)	81 (27)	44 (15)
	Male 'heads'	67 (6)	30 (10)	11 (4)
	Female 'heads'	135 (11)	39 (13)	26 (9)
	Child	6 (1)	12 (4)	7 (2)

Table 9: Dole expenditure in Atherton, 1710–32

Period	1710–23	1727–29	1730–32
Total dole expenditure	£748.65 (£62.39 mean p.a.)	£585.30 (£195.10 mean p.a.)	£263.15 (£87.72 mean p.a.)
Mean dole per adult household	£0.90	£1.48	£1.44
Male to female ratio (no. of paupers)	0.8	1.7	1.2
Male to female (£ spent)	£0.85	£1.47	£0.87
Mean male dole	£0.92	£1.40	£1.21
Mean female dole	£0.88	£1.61	£1.72

Table 10: Atherton pensioners, 1710–32

Period	1710–23	1727–29	1730–32
Total regular expenditure (% of dole)	£434.12 (£36.18 p.a.) (58)	£265.37 (£88.46 p.a.) (45)	£133.20 (£44.40 p.a.) (51)
Total pension expenditure (% of dole)	£321.15 (£26.76) (43)	£161.92 (£53.97) (28)	£73.77 (£24.59) (28)
Mean pension per adult household	£1.53	£1.86	£1.60
Male to female ratio (no. of paupers)	0.5	0.8	0.4
Male to female (£ spent)	£0.60	£0.66	£0.37
Mean male pension	£1.73	£1.70	£1.44
Mean female pension	£1.44	£1.98	£1.67

before the crisis to £1.48, remaining high in the three ensuing years. There was an increase in the cost of irregular doles, including sickness relief, clothing costs, and trade tools. The township was effectively spending an extra £80.43 per year on irregular doles. There was a major increase in both the number of named male paupers (probably equating to heads of households) and in the total amount spent on them, though paradoxically the increase in the doles given to female paupers was greater than that for males. Indeed, looking at pensions, whilst those given to females rose from £1.44 in 1710–23 to £1.98 during the crisis, the male average actually *fell* (albeit very slightly) from £1.73 to £1.70. Meanwhile, the increase in the *number* of male pensioners was significant (6 per annum to 10), but that for women was much less so (11 to 13). Thus while the number of paupers (including male pensioners) increased, the female pensioner category, which was usually the backbone of early modern poor accounts, remained stable in number. Why this should be is hard to explain; presumably by this point a high proportion of marginal women were normally receiving relief anyway, giving less room for an increase. On the other hand, while far fewer marginal men received poor relief in normal years, this left plenty of scope for increase during crises. Overall, this suggests a repeat of the pattern experienced in 1674 Bolton: an increase in the number of male paupers reflecting the short-term poverty of many otherwise functioning nuclear households.

Conclusion

In contrast to the crisis of the 1670s, or the 1690s, or of 1709–10, that of 1727–30 *did* see a major mortality crisis in Lancashire. The decisive factor appears to have been the presence of autonomous epidemic disease. In each of the preceding crises the main problem was one of food shortage. In some parts of north-western Europe – in Scotland in 1674–75 and the 1690s, and in France in 1709–10, for example – these shortages led to deaths through famine. In north-west England, it seems likely that formal poor relief helped prevent mortality crises on these occasions, but in the crisis of the late 1720s the sheer virulence of the epidemics unleashed – possibly partly themselves touched off by food shortages in Ireland – proved too much.[116] In fact, although poor relief almost certainly took some of the edge off the 1720s crisis, food shortages and social dislocation – perhaps indicated by the very noticeable peak in Quarter Sessions cases dealing with settlement – can hardly have helped.[117] Famine deaths are usually caused most immediately by disease, spreading unusually far and wide thanks to the dislocation caused by food shortages. So it might be tempting to see 1727–30 as another English famine, a last gasp of the demographic Old Regime, thus challenging the broadly optimistic picture outlined above in which poor relief helped Lancashire escape famine by ensuring the poor could afford to eat. But this should be resisted. Commentators from the period referred to it as a 'sickly' time, and although they described it as 'scarce' and told of high prices, there is no evidence of widespread starvation, nor am I aware of any English commentators who described the crisis as famine. Given how well-documented the period was, and how clear the evidence of famine is for Ireland just over a decade later in 1740–42, this silence is deafening. Geographical evidence bolsters this argument: in Lancashire, southern and lowland parishes were hit hardest – in a famine we would expect the poorer upland and northern ones to be worst affected, whereas the south would import disease more quickly. Nationally, we find the relatively grain-rich county of Warwickshire badly affected, whereas Cumberland and Northumberland seem to have escaped.[118] Such things can never be wholly proven beyond reasonable doubt, but the evidence points very

---

116   J. Schellekens, 'Irish Famines and English Mortality in the Eighteenth Century', *Journal of Interdisciplinary History*, 27 (1996), 29–42.
117   LA, QSP/1153–403.
118   Wrigley and Schofield, *Population History*, p. 682.

strongly to the crisis of 1727–30 being one of epidemic disease – worsened by dearth, no doubt, but *not* a famine. The lesson for the Poor Law, then, becomes that whilst redistributive taxation could be a useful weapon against harvest crises and dearth, it could not prevent mortality crises riding on the back of virulent epidemics. It could ensure the poor were fed, it could not protect them from the spread of bacteria and viruses that no-one yet understood.

Conclusion: Worldly Crosses

We all, alas, are subject to misfortune.

Daniel Defoe (1729)[1]

In 1661, a group of petitioners from Failsworth appealed to Manchester Sessions for the relief of one of their neighbours, Elizabeth Chatterton. It had, they claimed, 'pleased almighty god *for reasons best known to himselfe*' to lay a 'heavy affliction' on her, which we learn from a previous petition was lameness.[2] It was the uncertainty of life that this statement represents, in which the visiting of personal misfortune was the unpredictable prerogative of Almighty God, which formed the key to 'deserving' poverty under the Old Poor Law. The year, too, is significant, for it was one of high prices. As was Elizabeth's widowhood: her capacity to engage in production was hampered, her costs of living raised, and her protection from a patriarchal labour market was lost. She was, in other words, unfortunate.

Many petitioners, indeed, wrote specifically of misfortune and providence. In a tiny petition, not more than five inches by three, and in a quivering hand, Silvester Laithwaite of Ormskirk had told justices in 1638 that he 'by misfortunat occasions is brought poore & lowe of meanes'.[3] Lawrence Charnley of Haighton, meanwhile, told JPs in 1686 that he had formerly been 'a man of an estaite', but 'through debts and severall of the inconveniences which haith light upon him through the providence of almighty God' he had been forced to sell it.[4] Thomas Townley of Thornley, too, claimed in 1697 to have been of an ancient family, but that he was reduced to want by 'providence'.[5] Thomas Mason of Lathom

---

1   Quoted in: Webb and Webb, *English Poor Law History, Part One*, p. 248.
2   LA, QSP/208/31; QSP/200/28. My italics.
3   LA, QSB/1/198/34.
4   LA, QSP/611/14.
5   LA, QSP/794/4.

had lived well, he said in 1702, but 'through some losses & misfortunes befalling him' he was 'reduced to very great poverty'.[6] And it is hard not to sympathize with John Troughton, a pauper of Arkholme who petitioned in 1689 that his wife had had 'a cancer in her brest' for four years. He had suffered, he said, 'many crosses and losses in this world'.[7]

This book has offered a detailed exploration of English 'deserving poverty'. The main causes of this poverty were the infirmities of old age, sickness, and nuclear household failure. Meanwhile, poverty resulting from trade depression, harvest failures, epidemics, or some combination of the three, while apparently of much lesser importance in the longer term, led to some massive spikes in the level of hardship, dragging many marginal households into poverty. In 1674–75 it was trade stoppage and harvest failure which set off a serious 'poverty crisis'; in 1727–30 these scourges were compounded by a virulent and mortal set of epidemics. While the Poor Law could keep people alive in times of shortage, it was largely powerless in the face of disease.

At each turn, the structure of society played a critical role in deter-mining the nature and severity of misfortune. Elizabeth Chatterton had originally been maintained by the charity of her neighbours, though she had no 'friends' locally: her descent into indigence was simultaneously hastened by her lack of nearby kin, and cushioned by the kindness of her neighbours. We cannot know for sure, but her living in the midst of the Manchester textile zone, with all the employment opportunities that brought, may concurrently have allowed her to earn money despite her lameness, but may also have left her more vulnerable to periodic economic crises, like that of 1658–62, when her petitions were written. On a more fundamental level, the unequal earning power between the sexes not only held back her economic potential from childhood, but also left her dramatically vulnerable when her husband died. Destitution was the end result of a confluence of interrelated social realities.

Official poor relief, of course, was a comparatively new addition to this world. Elizabeth Chatterton could probably remember a time when there was virtually no rate-funded provision for the destitute in Lancashire. But its development in the period allows us, I think, to end on an optimistic note. There is plenty of evidence of nitpicking, exclusion, and the vigilant protection of the ratepayers' interests, but official poor relief at least

6   LA, QSP/876/18.
7   LA, QSP/667/7.

provided some kind of safety net against the hardest conditions of social deprivation. The century or so after 1630, particularly once the maelstrom of the 1640s and 1650s was out of the way, saw an alleviation of economic tensions in English society, an easing of the fears about vagrancy, and the ultimate disappearance of famine from this kingdom if not (crucially) from elsewhere in the British Isles or Empire. All this against a background of rising market dependency and social polarization.[8] The reduction of population pressure and a general growth in prosperity were key reasons behind this social easing. But the entrenchment of the Poor Law was crucial too, for – by the end of our period – the provision of some social security against worldly misfortunes had become part of the fabric of English society.

---

8   Cf. S. Hindle, 'The Growth of Social Stability in Restoration England', *The European Legacy*, 5 (2000), 563–76; Walter and Schofield, 'Famine, Disease and Crisis Mortality', pp. 28–61; Wrightson, *Earthly Necessities*, pp. 227–330.

Bibliography

Manuscript and Archival Sources

Bolton Archives and Local Studies
PBO/1/1–2, Bolton Parish Records.
PKE/1, Kearsley Overseers' Accounts, 1707–59.

Cumbria Record Office, Barrow Branch
BD/HJ/90/Bundle 24/6, Bond, 1680.
BD/HJ/89/Bundle 10/2, Affidavit, 1681.

Cumbria Record Office, Carlisle Headquarters
D Lons/L1/1/24/26, Mary Preston to Lady Lowther, 22 October 1673.
D/NT/38, Bargain and Sale, 1679.

Cumbria Record Office, Kendal Branch
WD/Ry/Box 35/1, Lists of Poor Householders, 1685 and 1687.
WPR/62/W1, Troutbeck Overseers' Accounts, 1640–43.
WPR/83/7/3–5, Hawkshead Overseers' Accounts, 1690–1808.
WPR/83/7/6–8, Monk Coniston and Skelwith Overseers' Accounts, 1691–1808.

Lancashire Archives, Preston
Bury Township Overseers' Accounts, 1692–1760, microfilm copy.
DDCa/7/1/3, Cartmel Manorial Papers, 1658–1721.
DDCl/400, Steward's Accounts, 1707–29.
DDHu/53/36, Order of Lancaster Assizes Concerning Payments for the Relief of the Poor in Bolton, 1687.
DDKe, Kenyon of Peel, Family Papers.
DDX/1834/1, Duxbury Overseers' Account Book, 1653–1820.
PR/256, Croston Township Accounts, 1717–1855.
PR/264–5, Halsall Township Accounts, 1694–1885.

PR/499–500, Caton Township Accounts, 1714–95.
PR/872, Alston Churchwardens', Overseers' and Constables' Accounts, 1712–1817.
PR/2592/2, Bispham Town's Book, 1722–1808.
PR/2667, Nether Wyresdale Town Accounts Book, 1685–1837.
PR/2863/3/7, Padiham Overseers' Accounts and Papers, 1696–1829.
PR/2890/2/1, Accrington (New and Old) Parish Accounts, 1691–1800.
PR/3168/7/9, Tarleton Overseers' Accounts, 1708–67.
QSB/1/1–301, Quarter Sessions Recognizance Rolls, 1605–48.
QSJ/8/1/201–3, Sacrament Certificates, 20 July 1673.
QSO/2/1–100, Quarter Sessions Order Books, 1626–1731.
QSP/1–1629, Quarter Sessions Petitions, 1648–1750.
QSR/17–123, Quarter Sessions Roll, 1620–1729.
RCLn/10/7, Spiritual Will and Testament of Ann Houghton, 1699.
WRW, Archdeaconry of Richmond Probate Records.

Manchester Archives and Local Studies
L82/2/1, Goodshaw Overseers' Accounts, 1691–1741.
L160/2/1, Prestwich Churchwardens' and Overseers' Accounts, 1646–83.
M/10/7/2/1, Cheetham Overseers' Accounts, 1693–1791.
M/10/9/2/1, Chorlton-on-Medlock Overseers' Accounts, 1718–94.

The National Archives, London
SP16, State Papers Domestic, Charles I.
E179/250/11, Lancashire Hearth Tax Returns, Lady Day 1664.

Oldham Local Studies and Archives
UDCr/18, Crompton Poor, 1597.

Wigan Record Office, Leigh
TR/Ath/C/2/1–8, Atherton Overseers' Accounts, 1692–1751.
TR/Pe/C/1/1–37, Pennington Overseers Papers, 1699–1750.

Printed Primary Sources

Abstract of the Returns made by the Overseers of the Poor (London, 1777).
The Account Book of Clement Taylor of Finsthwaite, 1712–1753, ed. J. D. Martin (RSLC, cxxxv, Chester, 1997).

The Account Book of Richard Latham, 1724–1767, ed. L. Weatherill (RSEH, New Ser., xv, Oxford, 1990).

An Account of Several Work-houses for Employing and Maintaining the Poor, 1st edn (London, 1725).

An Account of Several Work-houses for Employing and Maintaining the Poor, 2nd edn (London, 1732).

Ady, T., *A Perfect Discovery of Witches* (London, 1661).

The Annals of Manchester: A Chronological Record from the Earliest Times to the End of 1885, ed. W. E. A. Axon (Manchester, 1886).

Annual Report of the Poor Law Commissioners for England and Wales, 13 vols (London, 1835–47).

Bacon, F., *The Essayes or Counsels, Civill and Morall, of Francis Lord Verulam, Viscount St Alban* (London, 1626).

Blundell, N., *The Great Diurnal of Nicholas Blundell of Little Crosby, Lancs. transcribed by Frank Tyrer*, ed. J. J. Bagley, 3 vols (RSLC, cx, cxii, cxiv, Chester, 1966–72).

Blundell, W., *A Cavalier's Notebook*, ed. T. E. Gibson (London, 1880).

Bristol Corporation of the Poor: Selected Records, 1696–1898, ed. E. E. Butcher (Bristol Record Society, iii, Bristol, 1932).

Burn, R., *The History of the Poor Laws: With Observations* (London, 1764).

Camden, W., *Britannia*, trans. P. Holland (London, 1610).

The Churchwardens' Accounts of Prescot, Lancashire, 1523–1607, ed. F. A. Bailey (RSLC, civ, Preston, 1953).

Defoe, D., *A Tour Through the Whole Island of Great Britain*, ed. G. D. H. Cole and D. C. Browning, 2 vols (London, 1962).

An Ease for Overseers of the Poore (Cambridge, 1601).

Essex Pauper Letters, 1731–1837, ed. T. Sokoll (RSEH, New Series, xxx, Oxford, 2001).

Fell, S., *The Household Account Book of Sarah Fell of Swarthmoor Hall*, ed. N. Penney (Cambridge, 1920).

Fleming, D., *Estate and Household Accounts of Sir Daniel Fleming of Rydal Hall, Westmorland, 1688–1701*, ed. B. Tyson (Cumberland and Westmorland Antiquarian and Archaeological Society Record Series, xiii, Kendal, 2001).

Gough, R., *The History of Myddle*, ed. D. Hey (Harmondsworth, 1981).

Harrold, E., *The Diary of Edmund Harrold, Wigmaker of Manchester, 1712–15*, ed. C. Horner (Manchester, 2008).

Hillary, W., *A Practical Essay on the Small-pox. To which is added, An*

Account of the Principal Variations of the Weather at Ripon, and the Concomitant Epidemical Diseases, From the Year 1726, to the End of the Year 1734, 2nd edn (London, 1740).

Historical Manuscripts Commission, *Fourteenth Report, Appendix, Part IV: The Manuscripts of Lord Kenyon* (London, 1894).

——, *Report on the Manuscripts of the Marquis of Lothian Preserved at Blickling Hall, Norfolk* (London, 1905).

Holt, J., *A General View of the Agriculture of the County of Lancashire* (London, 1795).

The House and Farm Accounts of the Shuttleworths of Gawthorpe Hall, ed. J. Harland, 4 vols (CS, Old Ser., xxxv, xli, xliii, xlvi, Manchester, 1856–58).

Josselin, R., *The Diary of Ralph Josselin, 1616–1683*, ed. A. Macfarlane (RSEH, New Ser., iii, London, 1976).

Lancashire Quarter Sessions Records, ed. J. Tait (CS, New Ser., lxxvii, Manchester, 1917).

Liverpool Town Books: Proceedings of Assemblies, Common Councils, Portmoot Courts, &c, 1550–1862, ed. J. A. Twemlow, 2 vols (Liverpool, 1918–35).

Lowe, R., *The Diary of Roger Lowe of Ashton-in-Makerfield, Lancashire, 1663–74*, ed. W. L. Sachse (London, 1938).

Martindale, A., *Life of Adam Martindale*, ed. R. Parkinson (CS, Old Ser., iv, Manchester, 1845).

Materials for an Account of the Provincial Synod of the County of Lancaster, 1646–1660, ed. W. A. Shaw (Manchester, 1890).

Narratives of the Poor in Eighteenth-Century England, Vol. I: Voices of the Poor: Poor Law Depositions and Letters, ed. S. King, T. Nutt and A. Tomkins (London, 2006).

Newcome, H., *The Autobiography of Henry Newcome, M.A.*, ed. Richard Parkinson, 2 vols (CS, Old Ser., xxvi, xxvii, Manchester, 1852).

The Norwich Census of the Poor, 1570, ed. J. F. Pound (Norfolk Record Society, xl, Norwich, 1971).

The Oldest Register Book of the Parish of Hawkshead, 1568–1704, ed. H. S. Cowper (London, 1897).

Orders and Directions, together with a commission for the better administration of justice, and more perfect information of His Majestie (London, 1631).

The Parish Registers of Garstang Church, 1660–1734, ed. H. Brierley and A. Sparke (LPRS, lxviii, Preston, 1932).

Parliamentary Papers, 1818, vol. 5, Report from Poor Law Committee.

Poor Relief in Elizabethan Ipswich, ed. J. Webb (Suffolk Records Society, ix, Ipswich, 1966).

Pope, F. R., 'The Accounts of the Constables and Overseers of Parr, 1688–1729', unpublished transcription, copy in Lancashire Archives (1971).

Poverty in Early Stuart Salisbury, ed. P. Slack (Wiltshire Record Society, xxxi, Devizes, 1975).

Prescot Churchwardens' Accounts, 1635–1663, ed. T. Steele (RSLC, cxxxvii, Stroud, 2002).

Proceedings in Parliament, 1626, ed. W. B. Bidwell and M. Jansson, 4 vols (London, 1991–96).

Proceedings of the Lancashire Justices of the Peace at the Sheriff's Table During Assize Week, ed. B. W. Quintrell (RSLC, cxxi, Chester, 1981).

The Registers of Leigh Parish Church, 1701–1753, ed. K. Taylor (LPRS, clv, Newport, 2002).

The Registers of the Parish Church of Deane: Burials, 1604–1750, ed. A. Sparke (LPRS, liv, Bolton, 1917).

The Registers of the Parish Church of Whittington in the County of Lancaster, 1538–1764, ed. F. Wrigley and T. H. Winder (LPRS, iii, Rochdale, 1899).

The Second Register Book of the Parish of Hawkshead in the Diocese of Carlisle and the County of Lancaster, 1705–1797, ed. K. Leonard and G. O. G. Leonard (Hawkshead, 1968).

Seventeenth-Century Economic Documents, ed. J. Thirsk and J. P. Cooper (Oxford, 1972).

Smith, A., *The Wealth of Nations*, new edn (New York, 2003).

'The State, Civil and Ecclesiastical, of the County of Lancaster, about the year 1590', in *Chetham Miscellanies vol. 5* (CS, Old Ser., xcvi, Manchester, 1875), pp. 1–13.

Stout, W., *The Autobiography of William Stout of Lancaster, 1665–1752*, ed. J. D. Marshall (CS, 3rd Ser., xiv, Manchester, 1967).

'T.H.', *A Ha! Christmas* (London, 1647).

The Township Booke of Halliwell, ed. A. Sparke (CS, New Ser., lxix, Manchester, 1910).

Trentham Parish Register, ed. S. W. Hutchinson (Stoke-on-Trent, 1906).

A True Representation of the Present Sad and Lamentable Condition of the County of Lancaster … (London, 1649).

Tusser, T., *Five Hundred Points of Good Husbandry*, 1614 edn (London, 1614).

West Riding Sessions Rolls, 1597/8–1642, ed. J. Lister, 2 vols (Yorkshire Archaeological Society Record Series, iii, liv, Leeds, 1888–1915).

Westmorland Hearth Tax: Michaelmas 1670 & Surveys 1674–5, ed. C. Phillips, C. Ferguson and A. Wareham (Cumberland and Westmorland Antiquarian and Archaeological Society, Extra Series, xix, London, 2008).

Wintringham, C., *Commentarius Nosologicus: a Treatise on the Study of Diseases: Embracing the Epidemic Diseases and Variations in Weather in the City of York and Neighbouring Places through Twenty Consecutive Years*, trans. E. Johnson (Pocklington, 1979).

Secondary Works

Adair, R., *Courtship, Illegitimacy and Marriage in Early Modern England* (Manchester, 1996).

Addy, J., 'Bishop Porteus' Visitation of the Diocese of Chester, 1778', *Northern History*, 13 (1977), 175–98.

——, 'Sin, Sex and Society in Seventeenth Century Lancashire', *Lancashire Local Historian*, 4 (1986), 8–19.

Anderson, B. L., 'The Attorney and the Early Capital Market in Lancashire', in *Liverpool and Merseyside: Essays in the Economic and Social History of the Port and its Hinterland*, ed. J. R. Harris (London, 1969), pp. 50–77.

Anderson, M., *Family Structure in Nineteenth Century Lancashire* (Cambridge, 1971).

Appleby, A. B., 'Diet in Sixteenth-century England: Sources, Problems, Possibilities', in *Health, Medicine and Mortality in the Sixteenth Century*, ed. C. Webster (Cambridge, 1979), pp. 97–116.

——, 'Disease or Famine? Mortality in Cumberland and Westmorland, 1580–1640', *EcHR*, 2nd Ser., 26 (1973), 403–32.

——, 'Epidemics and Famine in the Little Ice Age', *Journal of Interdisciplinary History*, 10 (1980), 643–63.

——, *Famine in Tudor and Stuart England* (Liverpool, 1978).

——, 'Grain Prices and Subsistence Crises in England and France, 1590–1740', *Journal of Economic History*, 39 (1979), 865–87.

Appleby, J. O., *Economic Thought and Ideology in Seventeenth-Century England* (Princeton, 1978).

Archer, I. W., 'The Charity of Early Modern Londoners', *TRHS*, 6th Series, 12 (2002), 223–44.

——, *The Pursuit of Stability: Social Relations in Elizabethan London* (Cambridge, 1991).

Arkell, T., 'Identifying Regional Variations from the Hearth Tax', *Local Historian*, 33 (2003), 148–74.

——, 'The Incidence of Poverty in England in the Later Seventeenth Century', *Social History*, 12 (1987), 23–47.

——, 'Multiplying Factors for Estimating Population Totals from the Hearth Tax', *LPS*, 28 (1982), 51–7.

Ascott, D. E., F. Lewis and M. Power, *Liverpool, 1660–1750: People, Prosperity and Power* (Liverpool, 2006).

Ashton, T. S., *Economic Fluctuations in England, 1700–1800* (Oxford, 1959).

Atkin, M., 'Some Settlement Patterns in Lancashire', in *Medieval Villages: a Review of Current Work*, ed. D. Hooke (Oxford, 1985).

Bailey, F. A., 'The Court Leet of Prescot', *THSLC*, 84 (1932), 63–85.

Bailey, J., '"Think wot a Mother must feel": Parenting in English Pauper Letters, c.1760–1834', *Family and Community History*, 13 (2010), 5–19.

——, *Unquiet Lives: Marriage and Marriage Breakdown in England, 1660–1800* (Cambridge, 2003).

Baker, J., I. Levitt and R. Pope (eds), *A Guide to the Lancashire Records: The Poor Law, 1750–1850* (Preston, 1996).

Barker, T. C. and J. R. Harris, *A Merseyside Town in the Industrial Revolution: St Helens, 1750–1900* (London, 1959).

Barr, N. A., *Economics of the Welfare State*, 4th edn (Oxford, 2004).

Barrett, S., 'Kinship, Poor Relief and the Welfare Process in Early Modern England' in *The Poor in England, 1700–1850: An Economy of Makeshifts*, ed. S. King and A. Tomkins (Manchester, 2003), pp. 199–227.

Beckett, J. V., 'The Decline of the Small Landowner in Eighteenth- and Nineteenth-century England: Some Regional Considerations', *AgHR*, 30 (1982), 97–111.

Beier, A. L., *Masterless Men: the Vagrancy Problem in England, 1560–1640* (London, 1985).

——, 'Poor Relief in Warwickshire, 1630–60', *PP*, 35 (1966), 77–100.

——, *The Problem of the Poor in Tudor and Early Stuart England* (London, 1983).

Beier, A. L. and R. Finlay (eds), *The Making of the Metropolis: London, 1500–1700* (London, 1986).

Ben-Amos, I. K., *The Culture of Giving: Informal Support and Gift-Exchange in Early Modern England* (Cambridge, 2008).

——, 'Gifts and Favors: Informal Support in Early Modern England', *Journal of Modern History*, 72 (2000), 295–338.

——, 'Women Apprentices in the Trade and Crafts of Early Modern Bristol', *Continuity and Change*, 6 (1991), 227–52.

Bennett, J. M., 'Conviviality and Charity in Medieval and Early Modern England', *PP*, 134 (1992), 19–41.

——, 'Medieval Women, Modern Women: Across the Great Divide', in *Culture and History, 1350–1600: Essays on English Communities, Identities and Writings*, ed. D. Aers (Hemel Hempstead, 1992), pp. 147–76.

Bennett, W., *The History of Burnley*, 4 vols (Burnley, 1946–51).

Berger, P., 'French Administration in the Famine of 1693', *European Studies Review*, 8 (1978), 101–27.

Bingham, R. K., *Kendal: A Social History* (Milnthorpe, 1995).

Birtles, S., 'Common Land, Poor Relief and Enclosure: the Use of Manorial Resources in Fulfilling Parish Obligations, 1601–1834', *PP*, 165 (1999), 74–106.

Blackwood, B. G., 'The Economic State of the Lancashire Gentry on the Eve of the Civil War', *Northern History*, 12 (1976), 53–83.

——, *The Lancashire Gentry and the Great Rebellion, 1640–60* (CS, 3rd Ser., xxv, Manchester, 1973).

——, 'Plebeian Catholics in Later Stuart Lancashire', *Northern History*, 25 (1989), 153–73.

Bond, M. F., 'Windsor's Experiment in Poor-relief, 1621–1829', *Berkshire Archaeological Journal*, 48 (1945), 31–42.

Botelho, L. A., 'Aged and Impotent: Parish Relief of the Aged Poor in Early Modern Suffolk', in *Charity, Self-interest and Welfare in the English Past*, ed. M. J. Daunton (London, 1996), pp. 91–111.

——, *Old Age and the English Poor Law, 1500–1700* (Woodbridge, 2004).

Bouch, C. M. L., 'Poor Law Documents of the Parish of Great Salkeld', *CW2*, 49 (1949), 142–7.

Bouch, C. M. L. and G. P. Jones, *A Short Economic and Social History of the Lake Counties, 1500–1830* (Manchester, 1961).

Boulton, J., 'Going on the Parish: the Parish Pension and its Meaning in the London Suburbs, 1640–1724', in *Chronicling Poverty: the Voices and Strategies of the English Poor, 1640–1840*, ed. T. Hitchcock, P. King and P. Sharpe (London, 1997), pp. 19–46.

——, '"It is extreme necessity that makes me do this": Some "Survival Strategies" of Pauper Households in London's West End during the Early Eighteenth Century', *International Review of Social History*, Supplement 8 (2000), 47–70.

——, *Neighbourhood and Society: A London Suburb in the Seventeenth Century* (Cambridge, 1987).

Bowden, P. J., 'Statistical Appendix', in *AHEW*, vol. 4, pp. 814–70.

——, 'Statistical Appendix', in *AHEW*, vol. 5, pp. 827–902.

——, *The Wool Trade in Tudor and Stuart England* (London, 1962).

Braddick, M. J. and J. Walter, 'Introduction. Grids of Power: Order, Hierarchy and Subordination in Early Modern Society', in *Negotiating Power in Early Modern Society: Order, Hierarchy and Subordination in Britain and Ireland*, ed. M. J. Braddick and J. Walter (Cambridge, 2001), pp. 1–42.

—— (eds), *Negotiating Power in Early Modern Society: Order, Hierarchy and Subordination in Britain and Ireland* (Cambridge, 2001).

Brailsford, H. N., *The Levellers and the English Revolution* (London, 1961).

Brigg, M., 'The Forest of Pendle in the Seventeenth Century, I', *THSLC*, 113 (1961), 65–96.

——, 'The Forest of Pendle in the Seventeenth Century, II', *THSLC*, 115 (1963), 65–90.

Broad, J., 'Housing the Rural Poor in Southern England, 1650–1850', *AgHR*, 48 (2000), 151–70.

——, 'Parish Economies of Welfare, 1650–1834', *Historical Journal*, 42 (1999), 985–1006.

——, 'The Smallholder and Cottager after Disafforestation: a Legacy of Poverty?', in *Bernwood: the Life and Afterlife of a Forest*, ed. J. Broad and R. W. Hoyle (Preston, 1997), pp. 90–107.

——, *Transforming English Rural Society: The Verneys and the Claydons, 1600–1820* (Cambridge, 2004).

Broad, J. and R. W. Hoyle (eds), *Bernwood: the Life and Afterlife of a Forest* (Preston, 1997).

Broadbridge, S. R., 'The Old Poor Law in the Parish of Stone', *North Staffordshire Journal of Field Studies*, 13 (1973), 11–25.

Brookes, C. C., *History of Steeple Aston and Middle Aston* (Shipston-on-Stour, 1929).

Brown, R. L., *The Parish Pauper and the Poor Law: The Poor Law in Welshpool* (Welshpool, 2002).

Browning, A., 'Historical Revisions, 52: The Stop of the Exchequer, 1672', *History*, New Ser., 14 (1929), 333–7.

Brundage, A., *The English Poor Laws, 1700–1930* (Basingstoke, 2002).

Brunskill, R. W., *Traditional Buildings of Cumbria: the County of the Lakes* (London, 2002).

Buckatzsch, E. J., 'The Geographical Distribution of Wealth in England, 1086–1843: an Experimental Survey of Certain Tax Assessments', *EcHR*, 2nd Ser., 3 (1950), 180–202.

Bull, S. and M. Seed, *Bloody Preston: The Battle of Preston, 1648* (Lancaster, 1998).

Burne, R. V. H., 'The Treatment of the Poor in the Eighteenth Century in Chester', *Journal of the Chester and North Wales Architectural, Archaeological and Historic Society*, 52 (1965), 33–48.

Butler, W., *The Customs and Tenant-right of the Northern Counties* (Millom, 1925).

Capp, B. S., *When Gossips Meet: Women, Family and Neighbourhood in Early Modern England* (Oxford, 2003).

Cassell, W. A., 'The Parish and the Poor in New Brentford, 1720–1834', *Transactions of the London and Middlesex Archaeological Society*, 23 (1972), 174–93.

Cavallo, S. and L. Warner, 'Introduction', in *Widowhood in Medieval and Early Modern Europe*, ed. S. Cavallo and L. Warner (Harlow, 1999), pp. 3–23.

—— (eds), *Widowhood in Medieval and Early Modern Europe* (Harlow, 1999).

Chalklin, C. W. and M. A. Havinden (eds), *Rural Change and Urban Growth: Essays in English Regional History in Honour of W. G. Hoskins* (London, 1974).

Chambers, J. D., *The Vale of Trent, 1670–1800: A Regional Study of Economic Change* (London, 1957).

Charlesworth, A. (ed.), *An Atlas of Rural Protest in Britain, 1548–1900* (London, 1983).

Charlesworth, L., *Welfare's Forgotten Past: A Socio-Legal History of the Poor Law* (Abingdon, 2010).

Chartres, J. A., 'The Marketing of Agricultural Produce', in *AHEW*, vol. 5, pp. 406–502.

Chaytor, M., 'Household and Kinship: Ryton in the Late Sixteenth and Early Seventeenth Centuries', *History Workshop Journal*, 10 (1980), 25–60.

Clark, E., 'Some Aspects of Social Security in Medieval England', *Journal of Family History*, 7 (1982), 307–20.

Clark, P., *The English Alehouse: A Social History, 1200–1830* (London, 1983).

——, 'Migration in England during the Late Seventeenth and Early Eighteenth Centuries', in *Migration and Society in Early Modern England*, ed. P. Clark and D. Souden (London, 1987), pp. 213–52.

Clark, P. and D. Souden (eds), *Migration and Society in Early Modern England* (London, 1987).

Clarkson, L. A., *Proto-Industrialization: The First Phase of Industrialization?* (Basingstoke, 1984).

Clarkson, L. A. and E. M. Crawford, *Feast and Famine: A History of Food and Nutrition in Ireland, 1500–1920* (Oxford, 2001).

Clemens, P. G. E., 'The Rise of Liverpool, 1665–1750', *EcHR*, 2nd Ser., 29 (1976), 211–25.

Cliffe, J. T., *The Yorkshire Gentry from the Reformation to the Civil War* (London, 1969).

Coats, A. W., 'Economic Thought and Poor Law Policy in the Eighteenth Century', *EcHR*, 2nd Ser., 13 (1961), 34–78.

——, 'The Relief of Poverty, Attitudes to Labour and Economic Change in England, 1660–1782', *International Review of Social History*, 21 (1978), 98–121.

Cockayne, E., *Hubbub: Filth, Noise and Stench in England, 1600–1770* (London, 2007).

Coleman, D. C., *The Economy of England, 1450–1740* (Oxford, 1977).

——, 'Proto-industrialisation: a Concept Too Many?', *EcHR*, 2nd Ser., 36 (1983), 435–48.

Collinson, P., 'Christian Socialism in Elizabethan Suffolk: Thomas Carew and his Caveat for Clothiers', in *Counties and Communities: Essays on East Anglian History, Presented to Hassell Smith*, ed. C. Rawcliffe, R. Virgoe and R. G. Wilson (Norwich, 1996), pp. 161–78.

——, 'Puritanism and the Poor', in *Pragmatic Utopias: Ideals and Communities, 1200–1630*, ed. R. Horrox and S. Rees-Jones (Cambridge, 2001), pp. 242–58.

Cooper, J. P., 'The Social Distribution of Land and Men in England, 1436–1700', in *EcHR*, 2nd Ser., 20 (1967), 419–40.

Cowper, H. S., *Hawkshead (the Northernmost Parish of Lancashire)* (London, 1899).

Creighton, C., *A History of Epidemics in Britain*, 2 vols (Cambridge, 1891–94).

Crosby, A., 'A Poor Diet for Poor People? Workhouse Food in Lancashire, 1750–1834', *Lancashire Local Historian*, 9 (1994), 20–8.

Cullen, K. J., *Famine in Scotland: the 'Ill Years' of the 1690s* (Edinburgh, 2010).

Cullen, K. J., C. A. Whatley and M. Young, 'King William's Ill Years: New Evidence on the Impact of Scarcity and Harvest Failure during the Crisis of the 1690s on Tayside', *Scottish Historical Review*, 85 (2006), 250–76.

Cunningham, H., 'The Employment and Unemployment of Children in England, c.1680–1851', *PP*, 126 (1990), 115–50.

Dalziel, N., 'Trade and Transition, 1690–1815', in *A History of Lancaster, 1193–1993*, ed. A. White, new edn (Edinburgh, 2001), pp. 117–72.

Daunton, M. J. (ed.), *Charity, Self-interest and Welfare in the English Past* (London, 1996).

——, 'Introduction', in *Charity, Self-interest and Welfare in the English Past*, ed. M. J. Daunton (London, 1996), pp. 1–22.

——, *Poverty and Progress: An Economic and Social History of Britain, 1700–1850* (Oxford, 1995).

Davies, C. S. L., 'Slavery and Protector Somerset: the Vagrancy Act of 1547', *EcHR*, 2nd Ser., 19 (1966), 533–49.

Davis, R., 'English Foreign Trade, 1660–1700', *EcHR*, 2nd Ser., 7 (1954), 150–66.

Dickson, D., 'In Search of the Old Irish Poor Law', in *Economy and Society in Scotland and Ireland, 1500–1939*, ed. R. Mitchison and P. Roebuck (Edinburgh, 1988), pp. 149–59.

Dobson, M. J., *Contours of Death and Disease in Early Modern England* (Cambridge, 1997).

Douglas, A. W., 'Cotton Textiles in England: the East India Company's Attempt to Exploit Developments in Fashion, 1660–1721', *Journal of British Studies*, 8 (1969), 28–43.

Duffy, C., *The Military Experience in the Age of Reason* (London, 1987).

Duncan, C. J. and S. Scott, 'The Mortality Crisis of 1623 in North-west England', *LPS*, 58 (1997), 14–25.

Dunn, R. M., 'The London Weavers' Riot of 1675', *Guildhall Studies in London History*, 1 (1973), 13–23.

Duxbury, A. H., 'The Decline of the Cumbrian Yeoman – Ravenstonedale: a Case Study', *CW2*, 94 (1994), 201–13.

Dyer, C., *Making a Living in the Middle Ages: the People of Britain, 850–1520* (London, 2002).

——, 'Poverty and its Relief in Late Medieval England', *PP*, 216 (2012), 41–78.

Eddy, J. A., 'The "Maunder Minimum": Sunspots and Climate in the Reign of Louis XIV', in *The General Crisis of the Seventeenth Century*, ed. G. Parker and L. M. Smith, 2nd edn (London, 1997), pp. 264–98.

Elder, M., *The Slave Trade and the Economic Development of Eighteenth-Century Lancaster* (Halifax, 1992).

Elton, G. R., 'Parliament', in *The Reign of Elizabeth I*, ed. C. Haigh (Basingstoke, 1984), pp. 79–100.

Emmison, F. G., 'Poor Relief Accounts of Two Rural Parishes in Bedfordshire, 1563–1598', *EcHR*, 3 (1931–32), 102–16.

——, 'The Relief of the Poor at Eaton Socon, 1706–1834', *Publications of the Bedfordshire Historical Record Society*, 15 (1933), 1–98.

Erickson, A. L., 'Property and Widowhood in England, 1660–1840', in *Widowhood in Medieval and Early Modern Europe*, ed. S. Cavallo and L. Warner (Harlow, 1999), pp. 145–63.

——, *Women and Property in Early Modern England* (London, 1993).

Evans, E. and J. V. Beckett, 'Cumberland, Westmorland, and Furness', in *AHEW*, vol. 5, pp. 3–29.

Evans, H. R., 'Poor-Law Administration at Ashburton from 1598 to 1612', *Devon and Cornwall Notes and Queries*, 25, no. 2 (1952), 41–7.

Everitt, A. M., 'Common Land', in *Rural England: An Illustrated History of the Landscape*, ed. J. Thirsk (Oxford, 2000), pp. 210–35

——, 'The Marketing of Agricultural Produce, 1500–1640', in *AHEW*, vol. 4, pp. 15–156.

——, 'Social Mobility in Early Modern England', *PP*, 33 (1966), 56–73.

Eversley, D. E. C., 'A Survey of Population in an Area of Worcestershire from 1660 to 1850 on the Basis of Parish Registers', in *Population in History: Essays in Historical Demography*, ed. D. V. Glass and D. E. C. Eversley (London, 1965), pp. 394–421.

Farnie, D. A. and D. J. Jeremy (eds), *The Fibre that Changed the World: the Cotton Industry in International Perspective, 1600–1990s* (Oxford, 2004).

Farrer, W. and J. Brownbill (eds), *The Victoria History of the County of Lancaster*, 8 vols (London, 1906–14).

Feldman, D., 'Migrants, Immigrants and Welfare from the Old Poor Law to the Welfare State', *TRHS*, 6th Ser., 13 (2003), 79–104.

Fessler, A., 'The Management of Lunacy in Seventeenth Century England. An Investigation of Quarter Sessions Records', *Proceedings of the Royal Society of Medicine*, 49 (1956), 901–7

——, 'The Official Attitude towards the Sick Poor in Seventeenth-century Lancashire', *THSLC*, 102 (1950), 85–113.

——, 'Skin Diseases in 17th and 18th Century Lancashire Local History Documents', *Bulletin of the History of Medicine*, 27 (1953), 414–19.

Fideler, P. A., *Social Welfare in Pre-Industrial England: The Old Poor Law Tradition* (Basingstoke, 2005).

Fildes, V., 'Maternal Feelings Reassessed: Child Abandonment and Neglect in London and Westminster, 1550–1800', in *Women as Mothers in Pre-industrial England: Essays in Memory of Dorothy McLaren*, ed. V. Fildes (London, 1990), pp. 139–78.

Fissell, M. E., *Patients, Power and the Poor in Eighteenth-Century Bristol* (Cambridge, 1991).

——, 'The "Sick and Drooping Poor" in Eighteenth-century Bristol and its Region', *Social History of Medicine*, 2 (1989), 35–58.

Fitzroy Jones, I., 'Aspects of Poor Law Administration, Seventeenth to Nineteenth Centuries, from Trull Overseers' Accounts', *Proceedings of the Somersetshire Archaeological and Natural History Society*, 95 (1950), 72–105.

Fletcher, A., *Gender, Sex and Subordination in England, 1500–1800* (London, 1995).

——, *Reform in the Provinces: The Government of Stuart England* (London, 1986).

Flinn, M., *Scottish Population History from the 17th Century to the 1930s* (Cambridge, 1977).

Forster, G. C. F., 'York in the 17th Century', in *The Victoria History of Yorkshire: the City of York*, ed. P. M. Tillot (London, 1961), pp. 160–206.

Forsyth, J., 'Jonathan Wilson (1693–1780): His Diary and Account Book', *CW2*, 98 (1998), 207–31.

Foster, C. F., *Capital and Innovation: How Britain Became the First Industrial Nation* (Northwich, 2004).

——, *Seven Households: Life in Cheshire and Lancashire, 1582–1774* (Northwich, 2002).

France, R. S., *Guide to the Lancashire Record Office*, 3rd edn (Preston, 1985).

——, 'A History of Plague in Lancashire', *THSLC*, 90 (1938), 1–175.

——, 'On Some Stanley Cadets in the Reign of Charles II', *THSLC*, 96 (1945), 78–81.

——, 'The Poor Brettarghs of Penketh', *THSLC*, 99 (1947), 89–93.

French, H. R., 'Accumulation and Aspirations among the "Parish Gentry": Economic Strategies and Social Identity in a Pennine family, 1650–1780', *THSLC*, 149 (1999), 19–49.

——, *The Middle Sort of People in Provincial England, 1600–1750* (Oxford, 2007).

——, 'Urban Common Rights, Enclosure and the Market: Clitheroe Town Moors, 1764–1802', *AgHR*, 51 (2003), 40–68.

Garnett, M. E., *The Dated Buildings of South Lonsdale* (Lancaster, 1994).

——, 'The Great Rebuilding and Economic Change in South Lonsdale, 1600–1730', *THSLC*, 137 (1987), 55–75.

Gibson, A. J. S. and T. C. Smout, *Prices, Food, and Wages in Scotland, 1550–1780* (Cambridge, 1995).

Glass, D. V. and D. E. C. Eversley (eds), *Population in History: Essays in Historical Demography* (London, 1965).

Goldie, M., 'The Unacknowledged Republic: Officeholding in Early Modern England', in *The Politics of the Excluded, 1500–1850*, ed. T. Harris (Basingstoke, 2001), pp. 153–94.

Goldstone, J. A., *Revolution and Rebellion in the Early Modern World* (Oxford, 1991).

Gooder, A., 'The Population Crisis of 1727–30 in Warwickshire', *Midland History*, 1 (1972), 1–22.

Goodman, P. H., 'Eighteenth Century Poor Law Administration in the Parish of Oswestry', *Transactions of the Shropshire Archaeological Society*, 56 (1960), 328–42.

Goose, N., 'The English Almshouse and the Mixed Economy of Welfare: Medieval to Modern', *Local Historian*, 40 (2010), 3–19.

——, 'The Rise and Decline of Philanthropy in Early Modern Colchester: the Unacceptable Face of Mercantilism?', *Social History*, 31 (2006), 469–87.

Goose, N. and H. Looijesteijn, 'Almshouses in England and the Dutch

Republic *circa* 1350–1800: a comparative perspective', *Journal of Social History*, 45 (2012), 1049–73.

Greenslade, M. W., 'Parish Government and Poor Relief', in M. V. Greenslade, *The Victoria History of the County of Staffordshire, Vol. XIV: Lichfield* (London, 1990), pp. 87–92.

Griffiths, P., A. Fox and S. Hindle (eds), *The Experience of Authority in Early Modern England* (Basingstoke, 1996).

Gritt, A. J., 'Making good land from bad: the drainage of west Lancashire, c.1650–1850', *Rural History*, 19 (2008), 1–27.

——, 'Mortality Crisis and Household Structure: An Analysis of Parish Registers and the Compton Census, Broughton, Lancashire, 1667–1676', *LPS*, 79 (2008), 38–65.

——, 'The Operation of Lifeleasehold in South-west Lancashire, 1649–97', *AgHR*, 53 (2005), 1–23.

——, 'The "Survival" of Service in the English Agricultural Labour Force: Lessons from Lancashire, c.1650–1851', *AgHR*, 50 (2002), 25–50.

Guscott, S. J., *Humphrey Chetham, 1580–1653: Fortune, Politics and Mercantile Culture in Seventeenth-Century England* (CS, 3rd Ser., xlv, Manchester, 2003).

Haigh, C., *Reformation and Resistance in Tudor Lancashire* (London, 1975).

Hajnal, J., 'European Marriage Patterns in Perspective', in *Population in History: Essays in Historical Demography*, ed. D. V. Glass and D. E. C. Eversley (London, 1965), pp. 101–43.

Hampson, E. M., *The Treatment of Poverty in Cambridgeshire, 1597–1834* (Cambridge, 1934).

Hanly, M., 'The Economy of Makeshifts and the Poor Law: a Game of Chance?', in *The Poor in England, 1700–1850: An Economy of Makeshifts*, ed. S. King and A. Tomkins (Manchester, 2003), pp. 76–99.

——, 'Women and the Poor Law: 1760–1830', *Lancashire Local Historian*, 15 (2002), 20–30.

Harris, J. R. (ed.), *Liverpool and Merseyside: Essays in the Economic and Social History of the Port and its Hinterland* (London, 1969).

——, 'Origins of the St Helens Glass Industry', *Northern History*, 3 (1968), 105–17.

Harris, M., '"Inky Blots and Rotten Parchment Bonds": London, Charity Briefs and the Guildhall Library', *Historical Research*, 66 (1993), 98–110.

Harris, T. (ed.), *The Politics of the Excluded, 1500–1850* (Basingstoke, 2001).

Hart, A., *The Textile Industry in Early Eighteenth Century Lancashire: the Region's Industry Before the Age of the Factory* (Saarbrücken, 2009).

Hartwell, C., M. Hyde and N. Pevsner, *Lancashire: Manchester and the South-East* (London, 2004).

Harvey, R., 'English Pre-Industrial Ballads on Poverty, 1500–1700', *The Historian*, 41 (1984), 539–61.

Hatcher, J., 'Understanding the Population History of England, 1450–1750', *PP*, 180 (2003), 83–130.

Hay, D., 'War, Dearth and Theft in the Eighteenth Century: the Record of the English Courts', *PP*, 95 (1982), 117–60.

Hayman, A., *Mersey and Irwell Navigation to Manchester Ship Canal, 1720–1887* (Manchester, 1981).

Heal, F., *Hospitality in Early Modern England* (Oxford, 1990).

Heal, F. and C. Holmes, *The Gentry in England and Wales, 1500–1700* (Basingstoke, 1994).

Healey, J., 'Agrarian Social Structure in the Central Lake District: the Fall of the "Mountain Republic"?', *Northern History*, 44, no. 2 (2007), 73–91.

——, 'The Development of Poor Relief in Lancashire, c.1598–1680', *Historical Journal*, 53 (2010), 551–72.

——, 'Land, Population, and Famine in the English Uplands: A Westmorland Case Study', *AgHR*, 59 (2011), 151–75.

——, 'Poverty, Deservingness and Popular Politics: the Contested Relief of Agnes Braithwaite, 1701–06', *THSLC*, 145 (2007), 131–56.

——, 'Poverty in an Industrializing Town: Deserving Hardship in Bolton, 1674–99', *Social History*, 35 (2010), 125–47.

——, 'Socially Selective Mortality during the Population Crisis of 1727–1730: Evidence from Lancashire', *LPS*, 81 (2008), 58–74.

——, '"The Tymes Being Soe Hard With Poore People": Poverty and the Economic Crisis of 1672–76 in Lancashire', *THSLC*, 162 (2013), 49–69.

Hey, D. G., *An English Rural Community: Myddle under the Tudors and Stuarts* (Leicester, 1974).

——, 'Moorlands', in *Rural England: An Illustrated History of the Landscape*, ed. J. Thirsk (Oxford, 2000), pp. 188–209.

——, 'Yorkshire and Lancashire', in *AHEW*, vol. 5, pp. 59–86.

Higham, M. C., 'The Organisation and Production of Textiles in North-west England in the Medieval Period, Including Woollen

Processing, but with Particular Reference to Linen', in *A History of Linen in the North West*, ed. E. Roberts (Lancaster, 1998), pp. 1–21.

Higham, N. J., *A Frontier Landscape: the North West in the Middle Ages* (Macclesfield, 2004).

Hill, C., *The Century of Revolution, 1603–1714* (Edinburgh, 1961).

——, 'The Poor and the People', in *The Collected Essays of Christopher Hill, Vol. III: People and Ideas in 17th Century England* (Brighton, 1986), pp. 247–83.

Hindle, S., *The Birthpangs of Welfare: Poor Relief and Parish Governance in Seventeenth-Century Warwickshire* (Dugdale Society Occasional Papers, xl, Stratford-upon-Avon, 2000).

——, 'Dearth and the English Revolution: the Harvest Crisis of 1647–50', *EcHR*, 2nd Ser., 61, Supplement 1 (2008), 64–98.

——, 'Dearth, Fasting and Alms: the Campaign for General Hospitality in Late Elizabethan England', *PP*, 172 (2001), 44–86.

——, 'Dependency, Shame and Belonging: Badging the Deserving Poor, c.1550–1750', *Cultural and Social History*, 1 (2004), 29–58.

——, 'Exclusion Crises: Poverty, Migration and Parochial Responsibility in English Rural Communities, c.1560–1660', *Rural History*, 7 (1996), 125–49.

——, 'Exhortation and Entitlement: Negotiating Inequality in English Rural Communities, 1550–1650', in *Negotiating Power in Early Modern Society: Order, Hierarchy and Subordination in Britain and Ireland*, ed. M. J. Braddick and J. Walter, pp. 102–22.

——, 'The Growth of Social Stability in Restoration England', *The European Legacy*, 5 (2000), 563–76.

——, '"Not by bread only"? Common Right, Parish Relief and Endowed Charity in a Forest Economy, c.1600–1800', in *The Poor in England, 1700–1850: An Economy of Makeshifts*, ed. S. King and A. Tomkins (Manchester, 2003), pp. 39–75.

——, *On the Parish? The Micro-Politics of Poor Relief in Rural England, c.1550–1750* (Oxford, 2004).

——, 'Persuasion and Protest in the Caddington Common Enclosure Dispute, 1635–1639', *PP*, 158 (1998), 37–78.

——, 'The Political Culture of the Middling Sort in English Rural Communities', in *The Politics of the Excluded, 1500–1850*, ed. T. Harris (Basingstoke, 2001), pp. 125–52.

——, 'Power, Poor Relief and Social Relations in Holland Fen, c.1600–1800', *Historical Journal*, 41 (1998), 67–98.

——, 'The Problem of Pauper Marriage in Seventeenth-Century England',
  TRHS, 6th Ser., 8 (1998), 71–89.

——, 'The Shaming of Margaret Knowsley: Gossip, Gender and the
  Experience of Authority in Early Modern England', *Continuity and
  Change*, 9 (1994), 391–419.

——, *The State and Social Change in Early Modern England, 1550–1640*
  (Basingstoke, 2000).

Hinton, F. H., 'Notes on the Administration of the Relief of the Poor of
  Lacock, 1583–1834', *Wiltshire Archaeological Magazine*, 49 (1940–42),
  pp. 166–218.

Hipkin, S., 'The Coastal Metropolitan Corn Trade in Later Seventeenth-
  century England', *EcHR*, 2nd Ser., 65 (2012), 220–55.

Hitchcock, T., *Down and Out in Eighteenth-Century London* (London,
  2004).

——, 'Paupers and Preachers: the SPCK and the Parochial Workhouse
  Movement', in *Stilling the Grumbling Hive: the Response to Social
  and Economic Problems in England, 1589–1750*, ed. L. Davison,
  T. Hitchcock, T. Keirn and R. B. Shoemaker (Stroud, 1992).

Hitchcock, T., P. King and P. Sharpe (eds), *Chronicling Poverty: the Voices
  and Strategies of the English Poor, 1640–1840* (London, 1997).

——, 'Introduction', in *Chronicling Poverty: the Voices and Strategies of
  the English Poor, 1640–1840*, ed. T. Hitchcock, P. King and P. Sharpe
  (London, 1997), pp. 1–18.

Holmes, C., *Why Was Charles I Executed?* (London, 2006).

Hopkirk, M., 'The Administration of Poor Relief, 1604–1832, Illustrated
  from the Parochial Records of Danbury', *Essex Review*, 58 (1949),
  113–21.

Hoppit, J., *Risk and Failure in English Business, 1700–1800* (Cambridge,
  1987).

Horden, P., 'Household Care and Informal Networks: Comparisons and
  Continuities from Antiquity to the Present', in *The Locus of Care:
  Families, Communities, Institutions and the Provision of Welfare since
  Antiquity*, ed. P. Horden and R. Smith (London, 1998), pp. 21–67.

Horsfield, J. K., 'The "Stop of the Exchequer" Revisited', *EcHR*, 2nd Ser.,
  35 (1982), 511–28.

Hoskins, W. G., 'Harvest Fluctuations and English Economic History,
  1480–1619', *AgHR*, 12 (1964), 28–46.

——, 'Harvest Fluctuations and English Economic History, 1620–1759',
  AgHR, 16 (1968), 15–31.

——, *The Midland Peasant: The Economic and Social History of a Leicestershire Village* (London, 1957).

Howson, W. G., 'Plague, Poverty and Population in Parts of North-west England, 1580–1720', *THSLC*, 112 (1960), 29–55.

Hoyle, R. W., 'An Ancient and Laudable Custom: the Definition and Development of Tenant Right in North-western England in the Sixteenth Century', *PP*, 116 (1987), 24–55.

——, 'Famine as Agricultural Catastrophe: the Crisis of 1622–4 in East Lancashire', *EcHR*, 2nd Ser., 63 (2010), 974–1002.

Hoyle, R. W. and H. R. French, 'The Land Market of a Pennine Manor: Slaidburn, 1650–1780', *Continuity and Change*, 14 (1999), 349–83.

Hoyle, R. W. and C. J. Spencer, 'The Slaidburn Poor Pasture: Changing Configurations of Popular Politics in the Eighteenth- and Early Nineteenth-Century Village', *Social History*, 31 (2006), 182–205.

Hudson, P., 'Proto-industrialisation: the Case of the West Riding Wool Textile Industry in the 18th and Early 19th Centuries', *History Workshop Journal*, 12 (1981), 34–61.

——, 'The Regional Perspective', in *Regions and Industries: a Perspective on the Industrial Revolution in Britain*, ed. P. Hudson (Cambridge, 1989), pp. 5–40.

—— (ed.), *Regions and Industries: a Perspective on the Industrial Revolution in Britain* (Cambridge, 1989).

Hudson, P. and King, S., 'Two Textile Townships, c.1660–1820: a Comparative Demographic Analysis', *EcHR*, 2nd Series, 53 (2000), 706–41.

Hufton, O., *The Poor of Eighteenth-Century France, 1750–1789* (Oxford, 1974).

Humphries, J., 'Enclosures, Common rights, and Women: the Proletarianisation of Families in the Late Eighteenth and Early Nineteenth Centuries', *Journal of Economic History*, 50 (1990), 17–42.

Humphries, J. and K. D. M. Snell, 'Introduction', in *Women, Work and Wages in England, 1600–1850*, ed. P. Lane, N. Raven and K. D. M. Snell (Woodbridge, 2004), pp. 1–14.

Hunt, D., *A History of Preston* (Preston, 1992)

Ingram, M. J., *Church Courts, Sex and Marriage in England, 1570–1640* (Cambridge, 1987).

——, 'Shame and Pain: Themes and Variations in Tudor Punishments', in *Penal Practice and Culture, 1500–1900: Punishing the English*, ed. S. Devereaux and P. Griffiths (Basingstoke, 2004), pp. 36–62.

Innes, J., 'The "Mixed Economy of Welfare" in Early Modern England: Assessments of the Options from Hale to Malthus (c.1683–1803)' in *Charity, Self-interest and Welfare in the English Past*, ed. M. J. Daunton (London, 1996), pp. 139–80.

——, 'Parliament and the Shaping of Eighteenth-Century English Social Policy', *TRHS*, 5th Series, 40 (1990), 63–92.

——, 'Prisons for the Poor: English Bridewells, 1555–1800', in *Labour, Law and Crime: An Historical Perspective*, ed. F. Snyder and D. Hay (London, 1987), pp. 42–122.

——, 'The State and the Poor: Eighteenth-century England in European Perspective', in *Rethinking Leviathan: the Eighteenth-Century State in Britain and Germany*, ed. J. Brewer and E. Hellmuth (Oxford, 1999), pp. 225–80.

James, M., *Social Problems and Policy during the Puritan Revolution, 1640–60* (London, 1930).

Johnson, P. A., 'Risk, Redistribution and Social Welfare in Britain from the Poor Law to Beveridge', in *Charity, Self-interest and Welfare in the English Past*, ed. M. J. Daunton (London, 1996), pp. 225–48.

Johnston, J. A., 'The Impact of the Epidemics of 1727–30 in South-west Worcestershire', *Medical History*, 15 (1971), 278–92.

——, 'The Parish Registers and Poor Law records of Powick, 1663–1841', *Transactions of the Worcestershire Archaeological Society*, 9 (1984), 55–66.

Jones, C., 'Some Recent Trends in the History of Charity', in *Charity, Self-interest and Welfare in the English Past*, ed. M. J. Daunton (London, 1996), pp. 51–63.

Jones, G. P., 'The Population of Broughton-in-Furness in the Eighteenth Century', *CW2*, 53 (1953), 136–48.

——, 'Some Population Problems Relating to Cumberland and Westmorland in the 18th Century', *CW2*, 58 (1959), 123–39.

Jones, P., *Making Ends Meet (Poor Relief in 18th Century Mangotsfield)* (Downend, 1998).

Jones, P. D., '"I cannot keep my place without being deascent": Pauper Letters, Parish Clothing and Pragmatism in the South of England, 1750–1830', *Rural History*, 20 (2009), 31–49.

Jordan, W. K., *Philanthropy in England 1480–1660: A Study of the Changing Pattern of English Social Aspirations* (London, 1959).

——, *The Social Institutions of Lancashire: A Study of the Changing*

Patterns of Aspirations in Lancashire, 1480–1660 (CS, 3rd Ser., xi, Manchester, 1962).

Jütte, R., *Poverty and Deviance in Early Modern Europe* (Cambridge, 1994).

Keibek, S. A. J. and L. Shaw-Taylor, 'Early Modern Rural By-employments: a Re-examination of the Probate Inventory Evidence', *AgHR*, 61 (2013), 244–81.

Kent, D. A., '"Gone for a soldier": Family Breakdown and the Demography of Desertion in a London Parish, 1750–91', *LPS*, 45 (1990), 27–42.

Kent, J. R., *The English Village Constable, 1580–1642: A Social and Administrative Study* (Oxford, 1986).

——, 'Population Mobility and Alms: Poor Migrants in the Midlands during the Early Seventeenth Century', *LPS*, 27 (1981), 35–51.

Kent, J. R. and S. King, 'Changing Patterns of Poor Relief in Some English Rural Parishes, *circa* 1650–1750', *Rural History*, 14 (2003), 119–56.

Kermode, J. I. and C. B. Phillips (eds), *Seventeenth-Century Lancashire: Essays Presented to J. J. Bagley* (Liverpool, 1983).

Kerridge, E., *Textile Manufactures in Early Modern England* (Manchester, 1985).

——, *Trade and Banking in Early Modern England* (Manchester, 1988).

Kidd, A. J., 'Touchet, Samuel (c.1705–1773)', in *Oxford Dictionary of National Biography* (Oxford, 2004).

King, P., 'Customary Rights and Women's Earnings: the Importance of Gleaning to the Rural Labouring Poor', *EcHR*, 2nd Ser., 44 (1991), 461–76.

——, 'Pauper Inventories and the Material Lives of the Poor in the Eighteenth and Early Nineteenth Centuries', in *Chronicling Poverty: the Voices and Strategies of the English Poor, 1640–1840*, ed. T. Hitchcock, P. King and P. Sharpe (London, 1997), pp. 155–91.

King, S., '"I fear you will think me too presumtuous in my demands but necessity has no law": Clothing in English Pauper Letters, 1800–1834', *International Review of Social History*, 54 (2009), 207–36.

——, '"It is impossible for our Vestry to judge his case into perfection from here": Managing the Distance Dimensions of Poor Relief, 1800–40', *Rural History*, 16 (2005), 161–89.

——, 'Locating and Characterizing Poor Households in Late-Seventeenth Century Bolton: Sources and Interpretations', *LPS*, 68 (2002), 42–62.

——, 'Making the Most of Opportunity: the Economy of Makeshifts in the Early Modern North', in *The Poor in England, 1700–1850: An*

Economy of Makeshifts, ed. S. King and A. Tomkins (Manchester, 2003), pp. 228–57.

——, '"Meer pennies for my baskitt will be enough": Women, Work and Welfare, 1770–1830', in *Women, Work and Wages in England, 1600–1850*, ed. P. Lane, N. Raven and K. D. M. Snell (Woodbridge, 2004), pp. 119–40.

——, 'Poor Relief and English Economic Development Reappraised', *EcHR*, 2nd Ser., 50 (1997), 360–8.

——, *Poverty and Welfare in England, 1700–1850: A Regional Perspective* (Manchester, 2000).

——, 'Reclothing the English poor, 1750–1840', *Textile History*, 33 (2002), 37–47.

——, 'Reconstructing Lives: the Poor, the Poor Law and Welfare in Calverley, 1650–1820', *Social History*, 22 (1997), 318–38.

King, S. and A. Tomkins (eds), *The Poor in England, 1700–1850: An Economy of Makeshifts* (Manchester, 2003).

King, W. J., 'Regulation of Alehouses in Stuart Lancashire: an Example of Discretionary Administration of the Law', *THSLC*, 129 (1980), 31–46.

Kondo, K., 'The Church and Politics in "Disaffected" Manchester, 1718–31', *Historical Research*, 80, no. 207 (2007), 100–23.

——, 'The Workhouse Issue at Manchester: Selected Documents, 1729–35', *Bulletin of the Faculty of Letters, Nagoya University*, 33 (1987), 1–96.

Kussmaul, A., *A General View of the Rural Economy of England, 1538–1840* (Cambridge, 1990).

——, *Servants in Husbandry in Early Modern England* (Cambridge, 1981).

Landau, N., 'The Laws of Settlement and the Surveillance of Immigration in Eighteenth-century Kent', *Continuity and Change*, 3 (1988), 391–420.

——, 'The Regulation of Immigration, Economic Structures and Definitions of the Poor in Eighteenth-century England', *Historical Journal*, 33 (1990), 541–72.

——, 'Who Was Subjected to the Laws of Settlement? Procedure under the Settlement Laws in Eighteenth-century England', *AgHR*, 43 (1995), 139–59.

Landers, J., *Death and the Metropolis: Studies in the Demographic History of London, 1670–1830* (Cambridge, 1993).

Landers, J. and A. Mouzas, 'Burial Seasonality and Causes of Death in London, 1670–1819', *Population Studies*, 42 (1988), 59–83.

Lane, P., N. Raven and K. D. M. Snell (eds), *Women, Work and Wages in England, 1600–1850* (Woodbridge, 2004).

Langelüddecke, H., '"Patchy and Spasmodic"?: The Response of Justices of the Peace to Charles I's Book of Orders', *English Historical Review*, 113 (1998), 1231–48.

——, '"The poorest and sympleste sorte of people"? The Selection of Parish Officers during the Personal Rule of Charles I', *Historical Research*, 80, no. 208 (2007), 225–60.

Langton, J., *Geographical Change and the Industrial Revolution: Coalmining in South West Lancashire, 1590–1799* (Cambridge, 1979).

Laslett, P., 'Family, Kinship and the Collectivity as Systems of Support in Pre-industrial Europe: a Consideration of the "Nuclear Hardship" Hypothesis', *Continuity and Change*, 3 (1988), 153–75.

——, *Family Life and Illicit Love in Earlier Generations: Essays in Historical Sociology* (Cambridge, 1977).

——, *The World We Have Lost* (London, 1965).

——, *The World We Have Lost – Further Explored* (London, 1983).

Lawson, P., 'Property Crime and Hard Times in England, 1559–1624', *Law and History Review*, 4 (1986), 95–127.

Lees, L. H., *The Solidarities of Strangers: the English Poor Laws and the People, 1700–1948* (Cambridge, 1998).

——, 'The Survival of the Unfit: Welfare Policies and Family Maintenance in Nineteenth-century London', in *The Uses of Charity: the Poor on Relief in the Nineteenth-Century Metropolis*, ed. P. Mathias (Philadelphia, 1990), pp. 68–91.

Leeuwen, M. H. D. van, 'The Logic of Charity: Poor Relief in Preindustrial Europe', *Journal of Interdisciplinary History*, 24 (1994), 589–613.

Lemire, B., *The Business of Everyday Life: Gender, Practice and Social Politics in England, c.1600–1900* (Manchester, 2005).

——, 'Consumerism in Pre-Industrial and Early Industrial England: the Trade in Secondhand Clothes', *Journal of British Studies*, 27 (1988), 1–24.

——, *Fashion's Favourite: the Cotton Trade and the Consumer in Britain, 1660–1800* (Oxford, 1991).

Leonard, E. M., *The Early History of English Poor Relief* (Cambridge, 1900).

Levene, A., 'The Origins of the Children of the London Foundling Hospital, 1741–1760', *Continuity and Change*, 18 (2003), 201–36.

Levine, D. and K. Wrightson, *The Making of an Industrial Society: Whickham, 1560–1765* (Oxford, 1991).

Li, M. H., *The Great Recoinage of 1696 to 1699* (London, 1963).

Lis, C. and H. Soly, 'Policing the Early Modern Proletariat, 1450–1850', in *Proletarianization and Family History*, ed. D. Levine (Orlando, 1984), pp. 163–228.

——, *Poverty and Capitalism in Pre-industrial Europe* (Brighton, 1979).

Livi-Bacci, M., *Population and Nutrition: An Essay on European Demographic History* (Cambridge, 1990).

Lloyd, S., '"Agents in their own concerns"? Charity and the Economy of Makeshifts in Eighteenth-century Britain', in *The Poor in England, 1700–1850: An Economy of Makeshifts*, ed. S. King and A. Tomkins (Manchester, 2003), pp. 100–36.

Lowe, N., *The Lancashire Textile Industry in the Sixteenth Century* (CS, 3rd Ser., xx, Manchester, 1972).

Lyle, M. A., 'Regionality in the Late Old Poor Law: the Treatment of Chargeable Bastards from Rural Queries', *AgHR*, 53 (2005), 141–57.

Machin, R., 'The Great Rebuilding: a Reassessment', *PP*, 77 (1977), 35–56.

McCord, N., *North East England: an Economic and Social History* (London, 1979).

McCord, N. and R. Thompson, *The Northern Counties from AD 1000* (London, 1998).

Macfarlane, A., *The Family Life of Ralph Josselin, a Seventeenth-century Clergyman: an Essay in Historical Anthropology* (Cambridge, 1970).

——, *Marriage and Love in England: Modes of Reproduction, 1300–1840* (Oxford, 1986).

——, 'The Myth of the Peasantry: Family and Economy in a Northern Parish', in *Land, Kinship and Life-cycle*, ed. R. M. Smith (Cambridge, 1984), pp. 333–49.

——, *The Origins of English Individualism: the Family, Property and Social Transition* (Oxford, 1978).

MacFarlane, S., 'Social Policy and the Poor in the Later Seventeenth Century', in *The Making of the Metropolis: London, 1500–1700*, ed. A. L. Beier and R. Finlay (London, 1986), pp. 252–77.

McIntosh, M. K., 'Local Responses to the Poor in Late Medieval and Tudor England', *Continuity and Change*, 3 (1988), 209–45.

——, *Poor Relief and Community in Hadleigh, Suffolk 1547–1600* (Hatfield, 2013).

———, 'Poor Relief in Elizabethan English Communities: an Analysis of Collectors' Accounts', *EcHR*, forthcoming.

———, *Poor Relief in England, 1350–1600* (Cambridge, 2012).

———, 'Poverty, Charity, and Coercion in Elizabethan England', *Journal of Interdisciplinary History*, 35 (2005), 457–79.

———, *Working Women in English Society, 1300–1620* (Cambridge, 2005).

McNabb, J., 'Ceremony versus Consent: Courtship, Illegitimacy, and Reputation in Northwest England, 1560–1610', *Sixteenth Century Journal*, 37 (2006), 59–81.

Manley, G., 'Central England Temperatures: Monthly Means, 1659 to 1973', *Quarterly Journal of the Royal Meteorological Society*, 100 (1974), 389–405.

Marshall, D., *The English Poor in the Eighteenth Century: A Study in Social and Administrative History* (London, 1926).

Marshall, J. D., 'Agrarian Wealth and Social Structure in Pre-industrial Cumbria', *EcHR*, 2nd Ser., 33 (1980), 503–21.

———, 'Communities, Societies, Regions and Local History: Perceptions of Locality in High and Low Furness', *Local Historian*, 26 (1996), 36–47.

———, 'The Domestic Economy of the Lakeland Yeoman, 1660–1749', *CW2*, 73 (1973), 190–219.

———, *Furness and the Industrial Revolution* (Barrow-in-Furness, 1958).

———, *Lancashire* (Newton Abbot, 1974).

———, *Old Lakeland: Some Cumbrian Social History* (Newton Abbot, 1971).

———, *The Old Poor Law, 1795–1834*, 2nd edn (Basingstoke, 1985).

———, 'Stages of Industrialisation in Cumbria', in *Regions and Industries: a Perspective on the Industrial Revolution in Britain*, ed. P. Hudson (Cambridge, 1989), pp. 132–55.

Martin, J. E., *Feudalism to Capitalism: Peasant and Landlord in English Agrarian Development* (London, 1983).

Mascuch, M., 'Social Mobility and Middling Self-Identity: the Ethos of British Autobiographers, 1600–1750', *Social History*, 20 (1995), 45–61.

Mathias, P., 'Adam's Burden: Diagnoses of Poverty in Post-medieval Europe and the Third World Now', *Tijdschrift voor Geschiedenis*, 89 (1976), 589–613.

———, *The First Industrial Nation: An Economic History of Britain, 1700–1914*, 2nd edn (London, 1983).

Medick, H., 'The Proto-industrial Family Economy', *Social History*, 3 (1976), 291–315.

Meldrum, T., *Domestic Service and Gender, 1660–1750: Life and Work in the London Household* (London, 2000).

Millward, R., 'The Cumbrian Town between 1600 and 1800', in *Rural Change and Urban Growth: Essays in English Regional History in Honour of W. G. Hoskins*, ed. C. W. Chalklin and M. A. Havinden (London, 1974), pp. 202–28.

——, *Lancashire: An Illustrated Essay on the History of the Landscape* (London, 1955).

Mitchison, R., *The Old Poor Law in Scotland: the Experience of Poverty, 1574–1845* (Edinburgh, 2000).

——, 'Who Were the Poor in Scotland, 1690–1830?', in *Economy and Society in Scotland and Ireland, 1500–1939*, ed. R. Mitchison and P. Roebuck (Edinburgh, 1988), pp. 140–8.

Mitchison, R. and P. Roebuck (eds), *Economy and Society in Scotland and Ireland, 1500–1939* (Edinburgh, 1988).

Moisa, M., 'Conviviality and Charity in Medieval and Early Modern England', *PP*, 154 (1997), 221–34.

Mourholme Local History Society, *How it Was: a North Lancashire Parish in the Seventeenth Century* (Carnforth, 1998).

Muldrew, C., *The Economy of Obligation: The Culture of Credit and Social Relations in Early Modern England* (London, 1998).

——, *Food, Energy and the Creation of Industriousness: Work and Material Culture in Agrarian England, 1550–1780* (Cambridge, 2011).

——, '"Th'ancient Distaff" and "Whirling Spindle": Measuring the Contribution of Spinning to Household Earnings and the National Economy in England, 1550–1770', *EcHR*, 2nd Ser., 65 (2012), 498–526.

Muldrew, C. and S. King, 'Cash, Wages and the Economy of Makeshifts in England, 1650–1800', in *Experiencing Wages: Social and Cultural Aspects of Wage Forms in Europe since 1500*, ed. P. Scholliers and L. D. Schwarz (Oxford, 2003), pp. 155–82.

Mullet, M., 'Reformation and Renewal, 1450–1690', in *A History of Lancaster, 1193–1993*, ed. A. White, new edn (Edinburgh, 2001), pp. 73–116.

Mullineux, C. E., *Pauper and Poorhouse: A Study of the Administration of the Poor Laws in a Lancashire Parish* (Pendlebury, 1966).

Neeson, J. M., *Commoners: Common Right, Enclosure and Social Change in England, 1700–1820* (Cambridge, 1993).

Nelson, I., 'Famine and Mortality Crises in Mid-Sussex, 1606–1640', *LPS*, 46 (1991), 39–49.

——, 'Providing for the Poor, 1600–1834', in *Wivelsfield: the History of a Wealden Parish*, ed. H. Warne (Wivelsfield, 1994), pp. 123–43.

Newman-Brown, W., 'The Receipt of Poor Relief and Family Situation: Aldenham, Hertfordshire, 1630–90', in *Land, Kinship and Life-cycle*, ed. R. M. Smith (Cambridge, 1984), pp. 405–22.

Nicholls, G., *A History of the English Poor Law*, 2 vols (London, 1904).

O'Hara, D., *Courtship and Constraint: Rethinking the Making of Marriage in Tudor England* (Manchester, 2000).

Oosterveen, K., 'Deaths by Suicide, Drowning and Misadventure in Hawkshead, 1620–1700', *LPS*, 4 (1970), 17–20.

——, 'Hawkshead (Lancs.) Mobility (Geographical and Occupational) as shown by the Reconstitution of the Parish from the Registers, 1585–1840', *LPS*, 12 (1974), 38–41.

Ottaway, S. R., *The Decline of Life: Old Age in Eighteenth-Century England* (Cambridge, 2004).

——, 'Providing for the Elderly in Eighteenth-Century England', *Continuity and Change*, 13 (1998), 391–418.

Outhwaite, R. B., 'Dearth and Government Intervention in English Grain Markets, 1590–1700', *EcHR*, 2nd Ser., 34 (1981), 389–406.

Overton, M., *Agricultural Revolution in England: the Transformation of the Agrarian Economy, 1500–1850* (Cambridge, 1996).

Oxley, G. W., 'The Permanent Poor in South-west Lancashire under the Old Poor Law', in *Liverpool and Merseyside: Essays in the Economic and Social History of the Port and its Hinterland*, ed. J. R. Harris (London, 1969), pp. 16–49.

——, *Poor Relief in England and Wales, 1601–1834* (Newton Abbot, 1974).

Palliser, D. M., 'Dearth and Disease in Staffordshire, 1540–1670', in *Rural Change and Urban Growth: Essays in English Regional History in Honour of W. G. Hoskins*, ed. C. W. Chalklin and M. A. Havinden (London, 1974), pp. 54–75.

——, 'Tawney's Century: Brave New World or Malthusian Trap?', *EcHR*, 2nd Ser., 35 (1982), 339–53.

Parker, G. and L. M. Smith (eds), *The General Crisis of the Seventeenth Century*, 2nd edn (London, 1997).

Parsons, M. A., 'Poor Relief in Troutbeck, 1640–1836', *CW2*, 95 (1995), 169–86.

Patriquin, L., *Agrarian Capitalism and Poor Relief in England, 1500–1860: Rethinking the Origins of the Welfare State* (Basingstoke, 2007).

Pearl, V., 'Puritans and Poor Relief: the London Workhouse, 1649–1660', in *Puritans and Revolutionaries: Essays in Seventeenth-Century History Presented to Christopher Hill*, ed. D. H. Pennington and K. Thomas (Oxford, 1978), pp. 206–32.

——, 'Social Policy in Early Modern London', in *History and Imagination: Essays in Honour of H. R. Trevor-Roper*, ed. H. Lloyd-Jones, V. Pearl and B. Worden (London, 1981), pp. 115–31.

Pearson, S., *Rural Houses of the Lancashire Pennines, 1560 to 1760* (London, 1985).

Pelling, M., *The Common Lot: Sickness, Medical Occupations and the Urban Poor in Early Modern England* (London, 1998).

——, 'Finding Widowers: Men without Women in English Towns before 1700', in *Widowhood in Medieval and Early Modern Europe*, ed. S. Cavallo and L. Warner (Harlow, 1999), pp. 37–54.

——, 'Old Age, Poverty, and Disability in Early Modern Norwich: Work, Remarriage, and other Expedients', in *Life, Death and the Elderly*, ed. M. Pelling and R. M. Smith (London, 1991), pp. 74–101.

Pelling, M. and R. M. Smith (eds), *Life, Death and the Elderly* (London, 1991).

Perkins, J., 'Deaths in Stuart Lancashire: Some New Interpretations', *Lancashire Local Historian*, 8 (1993), 18–32.

Peters, C., *Women in Early Modern Britain, 1450–1640* (Basingstoke, 2004).

Petford, A. J., 'The Process of Enclosure in Saddleworth, 1625–1834', *Transactions of the Lancashire and Cheshire Antiquarian Society*, 84 (1987), 78–117.

Pevsner, N., *Lancashire: The Rural North* (Harmondsworth, 1969).

Phillips, C. B. and J. H. Smith, *Lancashire and Cheshire from AD 1540* (London, 1994).

Pidcock, B., 'Domestic Textile Production in the Sixteenth and Seventeenth Centuries', in *Rural Industries of the Lune Valley*, ed. M. Winstanley (Lancaster, 2000), pp. 20–40.

——, 'The Spinners and Weavers of Swarthmoor Hall, Ulverston, in the Late 17th Century', CW2, 95 (1995), 153–67.

Pitman, J., 'Tradition and Exclusion: Parochial Officeholding in Early Modern England, a Case Study from North Norfolk, 1580–1640', *Rural History*, 15 (2004), 27–45.

Pollard, R. and N. Pevsner, *Lancashire: Liverpool and the South-West* (London, 2006).

Poole, A., 'Welfare Provision in Seventeenth-Century Kent: a Look at Biddenden and Neighbouring Parishes', *Archaeologia Cantiana*, 126 (2006), 257–77.

Poole, R., 'Lancashire Wakes Week', *History Today*, 34, no. 8 (1984), 22–9.

—— (ed.), *The Lancashire Witches: Histories and Stories* (Manchester, 2002).

Porter, J., 'A Forest in Transition: Bowland, 1500–1650', *THSLC*, 125 (1974), 40–60.

——, *The Making of the Central Pennines* (Ashbourne, 1980).

——, 'Waste Land Reclamation in the Sixteenth and Seventeenth Centuries: the Case of South-eastern Bowland, 1550–1630', *THSLC*, 127 (1977), 1–23.

Pound, J. F., 'An Elizabethan Census of the Poor: the Treatment of Vagrancy in Norwich, 1570–1580', *University of Birmingham Historical Journal*, 8 (1962), 135–51.

——, *Poverty and Vagrancy in Tudor England*, 2nd edn (London, 1986).

Pounds, N. J. F., 'John Huxham's Medical Diary: 1728–1752', *LPS*, 12 (1974), 34–7.

Power, M. J., 'The Social Topography of Restoration London', in *The Making of the Metropolis: London, 1500–1700*, ed. A. L. Beier and R. Finlay (London, 1986), pp. 199–223.

Price, F. D., 'A North Oxfordshire Parish and its Poor: Wigginton, 1730–1830', *Cake and Cockhorse*, 2 (1962), 1–6.

Prior, M., 'Women and the Urban Economy: Oxford, 1500–1800', in *Women in English Society, 1500–1800*, ed. M. Prior (London, 1985), pp. 93–117.

Quintrell, B. W., 'Government in Perspective: Lancashire and the Privy Council, 1570–1640', *THSLC*, 131 (1981), 35–62.

——, 'The Making of Charles I's Book of Orders', *English Historical Review*, 95, no. 376 (1980), 553–72.

Richardson, R. C., *Puritanism in North-West England: A Regional Study of the Diocese of Chester to 1642* (Manchester, 1972).

Rideout, E. H., 'Poor Law Administration in North Meols in the Eighteenth Century', *THSLC*, 81 (1930), 62–109.

Roberts, E. (ed.), *A History of Linen in the North West* (Lancaster, 1998).

Robinson, M., 'The Linen Industry in North Lancashire and Cumbria, 1660–1830', in *A History of Linen in the North West*, ed. E. Roberts (Lancaster, 1998), pp. 44–65.

Rogers, C. D., *The Lancashire Population Crisis of 1623* (Manchester, 1975).

Rogers, G., 'Custom and Common Right: Waste Land Enclosure and Social Change in West Lancashire', *AgHR*, 41 (1993), 137–54.

Rogers, J. E. T., *A History of Agriculture and Prices in England*, 7 vols (Oxford, 1866–1902).

Rollinson, W., *A History of Man in the Lake District* (London, 1967).

——, 'Schemes for the Reclamation of Land from the Sea in North Lancashire during the Eighteenth and Nineteenth Centuries', *THSLC*, 115 (1963), 133–45.

Romano, R., 'Between the Sixteenth and Seventeenth Centuries: the Economic Crisis of 1619–22', in *The General Crisis of the Seventeenth Century*, ed. G. Parker and L. M. Smith, 2nd edn (London, 1997), pp. 128–52.

Rose, M. B., 'Introduction: the Rise of the Cotton Industry in Lancashire to 1830', in *The Lancashire Cotton Industry: a History since 1700*, ed. M. B. Rose (Preston, 1996), pp. 1–28.

Ruggles, S., 'The Limitations of English Family Reconstitution: *English Population History from Family Reconstitution, 1580–1837*', *Continuity and Change*, 14 (1999), 105–30.

Rushton, N. S. and W. Sigle-Rushton, 'Monastic Poor Relief in Sixteenth-century England', *Journal of Interdisciplinary History*, 32 (2001), 193–217.

Rushton, P., 'Lunatics and Idiots: Mental Disorder, the Community and the Poor Law in North East England, 1600–1800', *Medical History*, 32 (1988), 34–50.

——, 'The Poor Law, the Parish and the Community in North-east England, 1600–1800', *Northern History*, 25 (1989), 135–52.

Salaman, R. N., *The History and Social Influence of the Potato* (Cambridge, 1949).

Schellekens, J., 'Irish Famines and English Mortality in the Eighteenth Century', *Journal of Interdisciplinary History*, 27 (1996), 29–42.

Schofield, P. R., 'The Social Economy of the Medieval Village in the Early Fourteenth Century', *EcHR*, 2nd Ser., 61, Supplement 1 (2008), 38–63.

Schofield, R. S., 'Family Structure, Demographic Behaviour and Economic growth', in *Famine, Disease and the Social Order*, ed. J. Walter and R. S. Schofield (Cambridge, 1989), pp. 279–304.

——, 'The Geographical Distribution of Wealth in England, 1334–1649', *EcHR*, 2nd Ser., 18 (1965), 483–510.

——, 'Perinatal Mortality in Hawkshead, Lancashire, 1581–1710', *LPS*, 4 (1970), 11–16.

Schwarz, S., 'Economic Change in North-east Lancashire, c.1660–1760', *THSLC*, 144 (1994), 47–93.

Scott, J. C., *Domination and the Arts of Resistance: Hidden Transcripts* (London, 1990).

——, *Weapons of the Weak: Everyday Forms of Peasant Resistance* (London, 1985).

Scott, S. H., *A Westmorland Village: the Story of the Old Homesteads and 'Statesman' Families of Troutbeck* (Westminster, 1904).

Shakeshaft, P., *The History of Freckleton* (Lancaster, 2001).

Shammas, C., 'Food Expenditures and Economic Well-being in Early Modern England', *Journal of Economic History*, 43 (1983), 89–100.

——, 'The World Women Knew: Women Workers in the North of England during the Late Seventeenth Century', in *The World of William Penn*, ed. R. S. Dunn and M. Maples-Dunn (Philadelphia, 1986), pp. 99–116.

Sharpe, J. A., *Early Modern England: A Social History, 1550–1760*, 2nd edn (London, 1997).

——, 'Social Strain and Social Dislocation', in *The Reign of Elizabeth I: Court and Culture in the Last Decade*, ed. J. Guy (Cambridge, 1995), pp. 192–211.

Sharpe, K. M., *The Personal Rule of Charles I* (London, 1992).

Sharpe, P., 'Literally Spinsters: A New Interpretation of Local Economy and Demography in Colyton in the Seventeenth and Eighteenth Centuries', *EcHR*, 2nd Ser., 44 (1991), 46–65.

——, 'Poor Children as Apprentices in Colyton, 1598–1830', *Continuity and Change*, 6 (1991), 253–70.

——, *Population and Society in an East Devon Parish: Reproducing Colyton, 1540–1840* (Exeter, 2002).

Shaw, R. C., 'The Town Fields of Lancashire', *THSLC*, 114 (1962), 23–36.

Shaw-Taylor, L., 'Labourers, Cows, Common Rights and Parliamentary Enclosure: the Evidence of Contemporary Comment, c.1760–1810', *PP*, 171 (2001), 95–126.

——, 'Parliamentary Enclosure and the Emergence of an English Agricultural Proletariat', *Journal of Economic History*, 61 (2001), 640–62.

——, 'The rise of agrarian capitalism and the decline of family farming in England', *EcHR*, 2nd Ser., 65 (2012), 26–60.

Shelley, R. J. A., 'Wigan and Liverpool Pewterers', *THSLC*, 97 (1947), 2–16.

Shepard, A., *Meanings of Manhood in Early Modern England* (Oxford, 2003).

——, 'Poverty, Labour and the Language of Social Description in Early Modern England', *PP*, 201 (2008), 51–95.

Shore, H., 'Crime, Criminal Networks and the Survival Strategies of the Poor in Early Eighteenth Century London', in *The Poor in England, 1700–1850: An Economy of Makeshifts*, ed. S. King and A. Tomkins (Manchester, 2003), pp. 137–65.

Singleton, F. J., 'The Influence of Geographical Factors on the Development of the Common Fields of Lancashire', *THSLC*, 115 (1963), 31–40.

Singleton, J., 'The Lancashire Cotton Industry, the Royal Navy, and the British Empire, c.1700–1960', in *The Fibre that Changed the World: the Cotton Industry in International Perspective, 1600–1990s*, ed. D. A. Farnie and D. J. Jeremy (Oxford, 2004), pp. 57–84.

Skinner, J., '"Crisis Mortality" in Buckinghamshire, 1600–1750', *LPS*, 28 (1982), 67–72.

Slack, P., 'Books of Orders: the Making of English Social Policy, 1577–1631', *TRHS*, 5th Ser., 30 (1980), 1–22.

——, *The English Poor Law, 1531–1782* (Basingstoke, 1990).

——, *From Reformation to Improvement: Public Welfare in Early-Modern England* (Oxford, 1999).

——, *The Impact of Plague in Tudor and Stuart England* (Oxford, 1985).

——, *Poverty and Policy in Tudor and Stuart England* (London, 1988).

——, 'Poverty and Politics in Salisbury, 1597–1666', in *Crisis and Order in English Towns, 1500–1700: Essays in Urban History*, ed. P. Clark and P. Slack (London, 1972), pp. 164–203.

——, 'Vagrants and Vagrancy in England, 1598–1664', *EcHR*, 2nd Ser., 27 (1974), 360–79.

Smail, J., *The Origins of Middle Class Culture: Halifax, Yorkshire, 1660–1780* (London, 1994).

Smith, R., 'The Relief of Urban Poverty outside the Poor Law, 1800–1850: a Study of Nottingham', *Midland History*, 11 (1974), 215–24.

Smith, R. M., 'Ageing and Well-being in Early-modern England: Pension Trends and Gender Preferences under the English Old Poor Law, c.1650–1800', in P. Johnson and P. Thane (eds), *Old Age from Antiquity to Post-Modernity* (London, 1998), pp. 64–95.

——, 'Charity, Self-interest and Welfare: Reflections from Demographic and Family History', in *Charity, Self-interest and Welfare in the English Past*, ed. M. J. Daunton (London, 1996), pp. 23–49.

—— (ed.), *Land, Kinship and Life-cycle* (Cambridge, 1984).

——, 'The Manorial Court and the Elderly Tenant in Late Medieval England', in *Life, Death and the Elderly*, ed. M. Pelling and R. M. Smith (London, 1991), pp. 36–61.

——, 'Some Issues Concerning Families and their Property in Rural England, 1250–1800', in R. M. Smith (ed.), *Land, Kinship and Life-cycle* (Cambridge, 1984), pp. 1–86.

——, 'The Structured Dependency of the Elderly as a Recent Development: some Sceptical Historical Thoughts', *Ageing and Society*, 4 (1984), 409–28.

Snell, K. D. M., *Annals of the Labouring Poor: Social Change and Agrarian England, 1660–1900* (Cambridge, 1985).

——, 'Belonging and Community: Understandings of "Home" and "Friends" among the English Poor, 1750–1850', *EcHR*, 2nd Ser., 65 (2012), 1–25.

——, *Parish and Belonging: Community, Identity and Welfare in England and Wales, 1700–1950* (Cambridge, 2006).

——, 'Pauper Settlement and the Right to Poor Relief in England and Wales', *Continuity and Change*, 6 (1991), 375–415.

Sokoll, T., 'Old Age in Poverty: the Record of Essex Pauper Letters, 1780–1834', in *Chronicling Poverty: the Voices and Strategies of the English Poor, 1640–1840*, ed. T. Hitchcock, P. King and P. Sharpe (London, 1997), pp. 127–54.

Solar, P. M., 'Poor Relief and English Economic Development before the Industrial Revolution', *EcHR*, 2nd Ser., 48 (1995), 1–22.

——, 'Poor Relief and English Economic Development: a Renewed Plea for Comparative History', *EcHR*, 2nd Ser., 50 (1997), 369–74.

Song, B. K., 'Agrarian Policies on Pauper Settlement and Migration, Oxfordshire, 1750–1834', *Continuity and Change*, 13 (1998), 363–89.

Souden, D., '"East, west – home's best"? Regional Patterns in Migration in Early Modern England', in *Migration and Society in Early Modern England*, ed. P. Clark and D. Souden (London, 1987), pp. 292–332.

Speake, R., 'The Historical Demography of Warton Parish before 1801', *THSLC*, 122 (1970), 43–65.

Spufford, M., *Contrasting Communities: English Villagers in the 16th and 17th Centuries* (London, 1974).

——, 'Eccleshall, Staffordshire: a Bishop's Estate of Dairymen, Dairy

Wives and the Poor', in *Rural England: An Illustrated History of the Landscape*, ed. J. Thirsk (Oxford, 2000), pp. 290–306.

——, 'The Scope of Local History, and the Potential of the Hearth Tax Returns', *Local Historian*, 30 (2000), 202–21.

Stanley, P. E., *The House of Stanley: The History of an English Family from the 12th Century* (Edinburgh, 1998).

Stapleton, B., 'Inherited Poverty and Life-cycle Poverty: Odiham, Hampshire, 1650–1850', *Social History*, 18 (1993), 339–55.

Stewart-Brown, R., *Notes on Childwall* (Liverpool, 1914).

Stobart, J. C., *The First Industrial Region: North-west England, c.1700–60* (Manchester, 2004).

Stone, D. J., 'Consumption of Field Crops in Late Medieval England', in *Food in Medieval England: Diet and Nutrition*, ed. C. M. Woolgar, D. Serjeantson and T. Waldon (Oxford, 2006), pp. 11–26.

Stone, L., *The Crisis of the Aristocracy, 1558–1641* (London, 1965).

——, *The Family, Sex and Marriage in England, 1500–1800* (London, 1977).

——, 'Social Mobility in England, 1500–1700', *PP*, 33 (1966), 16–55.

Stringer, A., 'Depth and Diversity in Parochial Healthcare: Northamptonshire, 1750–1830', *Family and Community History*, 9 (2006), 43–54.

Styles, J., 'Embezzlement, Industry and the Law in England, 1500–1800', in *Manufacture in Town and Country before the Factory*, ed. M. Berg, P. Hudson and M. Sonenscher (Cambridge, 1983), pp. 173–205.

Supple, B. E., *Commercial Crisis and Change in England, 1600–1642* (Cambridge, 1959).

——, 'Insurance in British History', in *The Historian and the Business of Insurance*, ed. O. M. Westall (Manchester, 1984), pp. 1–8.

Swain, J. T., 'Capital Formation by Clothiers in North-east Lancashire, c.1550–1640', *Northern History*, 33 (1997), 54–72.

——, *Industry before the Industrial Revolution: North-east Lancashire, c.1500–1640* (CS, 3rd Ser., xxxii, Manchester, 1986).

——, 'The Lancashire Witch Trials of 1612 and 1634 and the Economics of Witchcraft', *Northern History*, 30 (1994), 64–85.

Swanson, S. G., 'The Medieval Foundations of John Locke's Theory of Natural Rights: Rights of Subsistence and the Principle of Extreme Necessity', *History of Political Thought*, 18 (1997), 399–459.

Tadmor, N., 'The Concept of the Household Family in Eighteenth-Century England', *PP*, 151 (1996), 111–40.

——, 'Early Modern English Kinship in the Long Run: Reflections on Continuity and Change', *Continuity and Change*, 25 (2010), 15–48.

——, *Family and Friends in Eighteenth-Century England: Household, Kinship and Patronage* (Cambridge, 2000).

Tate, W. E., *The Parish Chest*, 3rd edn (Cambridge, 1969).

Tawney, R. H., *Religion and the Rise of Capitalism: An Historical Study* (London, 1926).

Taylor, J. S., 'A Different Kind of Speenhamland: Nonresident Relief in the Industrial Revolution', *Journal of British Studies*, 30 (1991), 183–208.

——, 'The Impact of Pauper Settlement, 1691–1834', *PP*, 73 (1976), 42–74.

——, 'Voices in the Crowd: the Kirkby Lonsdale Township Letters, 1809–36', in *Chronicling Poverty: the Voices and Strategies of the English Poor, 1640–1840*, ed. T. Hitchcock, P. King and P. Sharpe (London, 1997), pp. 109–26.

Taylor, P., 'Quarter Sessions in Lancashire in the Middle of the Eighteenth Century: the Court in Session and its Records', *THSLC*, 139 (1989), 63–82.

Thane, P., 'Old People and their Families in the English Past', in *Charity, Self-interest and Welfare in the English Past*, ed. M. J. Daunton (London, 1996), pp. 113–38.

Thirsk, J. (ed.), *The Agrarian History of England and Wales, Vol. IV: 1500–1640* (Cambridge, 1967).

—— (ed.), *The Agrarian History of England and Wales, Vol. V: 1640–1750* (Cambridge, 1984–85).

——, 'The Crown as projector on its own estates, from Elizabeth I to Charles I', in *The Estates of the English Crown, 1558–1640*, ed. R. W. Hoyle (Cambridge, 1992), pp. 297–352.

——, *The Rural Economy of England: Collected Essays* (London, 1984).

—— (ed.), *Rural England: An Illustrated History of the Landscape* (Oxford, 2000).

Thomas, K., *Religion and the Decline of Magic: Studies in Popular Beliefs in Sixteenth and Seventeenth Century England* (London, 1971).

Thompson, T. W., *Wordsworth's Hawkshead*, ed. R. Woof (Oxford, 1970).

Thomson, D., 'Welfare and the Historians', in *The World We Have Gained: Histories of Population and Social Structure*, ed. L. Bonfield, R. M. Smith and K. Wrightson (Oxford, 1986), pp. 355–78.

Timmins, J. G., *Made in Lancashire: A History of Regional Industrialisation* (Manchester, 1998).

Tomkins, A., *The Experience of Urban Poverty, 1723–82: Parish, Charity and Credit* (Manchester, 2006).

——, 'Pawnbroking and the Survival Strategies of the Urban Poor in 1770s York', in *The Poor in England, 1700–1850: An Economy of Makeshifts*, ed. S. King and A. Tomkins (Manchester, 2003), pp. 166–98.

Tomkins, A. and S. King, 'Introduction', in *The Poor in England, 1700–1850: An Economy of Makeshifts*, ed. S. King and A. Tomkins (Manchester, 2003), pp. 1–38.

Tupling, G. H., 'The Early Metal Trade and the Beginnings of Engineering in Lancashire', *Transactions of the Lancashire and Cheshire Antiquarian Society*, 61 (1951), 1–34.

——, *The Economic History of Rossendale* (CS, New Ser., lxxxvi, Manchester, 1927).

Tyrer, F., 'The Common Fields of Little Crosby', *THSLC*, 114 (1962), 37–48.

Underdown, D., *Fire From Heaven: Life in an English Town in the Seventeenth Century* (London, 1992).

Vaux, H., 'The Poor of Otham and Nearby Parishes: the Coxheath Poor House', *Archaeologia Cantiana*, 126 (2006), 49–70.

Vries, J. de, 'The Industrial Revolution and the Industrious Revolution', *Journal of Economic History*, 54 (1994), 249–70.

Wadsworth, A. P. and J. De Lacy Mann, *The Cotton Trade and Industrial Lancashire, 1600–1780* (Manchester, 1931).

Wales, T., 'Poverty, Poor Relief and the Life-cycle: Some Evidence from Seventeenth-Century Norfolk', in *Land, Kinship and Life-cycle*, ed. R. M. Smith (Cambridge, 1984), pp. 351–404.

Walker, G., *Crime, Gender, and the Social Order in Early Modern England* (Cambridge, 2003).

Walter, J., 'The Social Economy of Dearth in Early Modern England', in *Famine, Disease and the Social Order*, ed. J. Walter and R. S. Schofield (Cambridge, 1989), pp. 75–128.

Walter, J. and R. S. Schofield, 'Famine, Disease and Crisis Mortality in Early Modern Society', in *Famine, Disease and the Social Order*, ed. J. Walter and R. S. Schofield (Cambridge, 1989), pp. 1–73.

—— (eds), *Famine, Disease and the Social Order* (Cambridge, 1989).

Walter, J. and K. Wrightson, 'Dearth and the Social Order in Early Modern England', *PP*, 71 (1976), 22–42.

Walton, J. K., *Lancashire: a Social History, 1558–1939* (Manchester, 1987).

——, 'Proto-industrialization and the First Industrial Revolution: the

Case of Lancashire', in *Regions and Industries: a Perspective on the Industrial Revolution in Britain*, ed. P. Hudson (Cambridge, 1989), pp. 41–68.

Walton, J. R., 'Some Cumbrian Pauper Narratives, 1770–1830', *CW2*, 99 (1999), 237–49.

Watson, C., 'The Early Administration of the Old Poor Law in Leyland Hundred, Lancashire: the Importance of the Township', *Local Historian*, 40 (2010), 266–80.

Watts, S. J., 'Tenant Right in Early Seventeenth-century Northumberland', *Northern History*, 6 (1971), 64–87.

Webb, B. and S. Webb, *English Local Government, Vol. VII: English Poor Law History, Part One: The Old Poor Law* (London, 1927).

Webb, N. C., 'Poverty and the Poor Law in Formby, 1701–1900', *Lancashire Local Historian*, 9 (1994), 12–19.

White, A. (ed.), *A History of Lancaster, 1193–1993*, new edn (Edinburgh, 2001).

——, *Pele Towers of the Morecambe Bay Area: A Survey* (Lancaster, 1972).

Whyte, I. D., *Migration and Society in Britain, 1500–1830* (Basingstoke, 2000).

——, 'Proto-industrialisation in Scotland', in *Regions and Industries: a Perspective on the Industrial Revolution in Britain*, ed. P. Hudson (Cambridge, 1989), pp. 228–51.

——, *Transforming Fell and Valley: Landscape and Parliamentary Enclosure in North West England* (Lancaster, 2003).

Whyte, I. D. and K. A. Whyte, 'Debt and Credit, Poverty and Prosperity in a Seventeenth-century Scottish Rural Community', in *Economy and Society in Scotland and Ireland, 1500–1939*, ed. R. Mitchison and P. Roebuck (Edinburgh, 1988), pp. 70–80.

Wilkinson, D. J., 'Performance and Motivation amongst the Justices of the Peace in Early Stuart Lancashire', *THSLC*, 138 (1989), 35–65.

Willan, T. S., *Elizabethan Manchester* (CS, 3rd Ser., xxvii, Manchester, 1980).

——, 'Manchester Clothiers in the Early Seventeenth Century', *Textile History*, 10 (1979), 175–83.

——, 'Plague in Perspective: the Case of Manchester in 1605', *THSLC*, 132 (1983), 29–40.

Williams, M., '"Our poore people in tumults arose": Living in Poverty in Earls Colne, Essex, 1560–1640', *Rural History*, 13 (2002), 123–43.

Williams, S. A., 'Malthus, Marriage and Poor Law Allowances Revisited: a Bedfordshire Case Study, 1770–1834', *AgHR*, 52 (2004), 56–82.

——, *Poverty, Gender and Life-cycle under the English Poor Law* (Woodbridge, 2011).

Wilson, C., 'Poverty and Philanthropy in Early Modern England', in *Aspects of Poverty in Early Modern Europe*, ed. T. Riis (Florence, 1981), pp. 253–79.

Winchester, A. J. L., 'Field, Wood and Forest – Landscapes of Medieval Lancashire', in *Lancashire Local Studies in Honour of Diana Winterbotham*, ed. A. Crosby (Preston, 1993), pp. 7–28.

——, *The Harvest of the Hills: Rural Life in Northern England and the Scottish Borders, 1400–1700* (Edinburgh, 2000).

——, *Landscape and Society in Medieval Cumbria* (Edinburgh, 1987).

——, 'Responses to the 1623 Famine in Two Lancashire Manors', *LPS*, 36 (1986), 47–8.

Winterbotham, D., '"Sackclothes and fustyans and such like com'odyties". Early Linen Manufacture in the Manchester region', in *A History of Linen in the North West*, ed. E. Roberts (Lancaster, 1998), pp. 22–43.

Wood, A. C., *A History of the Levant Company* (Oxford, 1935).

Wood, C. J., *The Duke's Cut: The Bridgewater Canal* (Stroud, 2002).

Woodward, D., 'The Determination of Wage Rates in the Early Modern North of England', *EcHR*, 2nd Ser., 47 (1994), 22–43.

——, *Men at Work: Labourers and Building Craftsmen in the Towns of Northern England, 1450–1750* (Cambridge, 1995).

——, 'Straw, Bracken and the Wicklow Whale: the Exploitation of Natural Resources in England since 1500', *PP*, 159 (1998), 43–76.

Woodward, N., 'Crisis Mortality in a Welsh Market Town: Carmarthen, 1675–1799', *Welsh History Review*, 22 (2005), 432–62.

Wordie, J. R., 'The Chronology of English Enclosure, 1500–1914', *EcHR*, 2nd Ser., 36 (1983), 483–505.

Wrightson, K., 'Alehouses, Order and Reformation in Rural England, 1590–1660', in *Popular Culture and Class Conflict, 1590–1914: Explorations in the History of Labour and Leisure*, ed. E. Yeo and S. Yeo (Brighton, 1981), pp. 1–27.

——, 'Aspects of Social Differentiation in Rural England, c.1580–1660', *Journal of Peasant Studies*, 5 (1977), 33–47.

——, *Earthly Necessities: Economic Lives in Early Modern Britain* (London, 2000).

——, 'The Enclosure of English Social History', *Rural History*, 1 (1990), 73–81.

——, *English Society, 1580–1680* (London, 1982).

——, 'Estates, Degrees and Sorts: Changing Perceptions of Society in Tudor and Stuart England', in *Language, History and Class*, ed. P. J. Corfield (Oxford, 1991), pp. 30–52.

——, 'The Politics of the Parish in Early Modern England', in *The Experience of Authority in Early Modern England*, ed. P. Griffiths, A. Fox and S. Hindle (Basingstoke, 1996), pp. 10–46.

——, 'Two Concepts of Order: Justices, Constables and Jurymen in Seventeenth-century England', in *An Ungovernable People? The English and their Law in the Seventeenth and Eighteenth Centuries*, ed. J. Brewer and J. Styles (London, 1980), pp. 21–46.

Wrightson, K. and D. Levine, *Poverty and Piety in and English Village: Terling, 1525–1700*, 2nd edn (Oxford, 1995).

Wrigley, E. A., *Continuity, Chance and Change: the Character of the Industrial Revolution in England* (Cambridge, 1988).

——, 'The Divergence of England: the Growth of the English Economy in the Seventeenth and Eighteenth Centuries', *TRHS*, 6th Ser., 10 (2000), 117–41.

Wrigley, E. A. and R. S. Davies (eds), *English Population History from Family Reconstitution, 1580–1837* (Cambridge, 1997).

Wrigley, E. A. and R. S. Schofield, *The Population History of England, 1541–1871: A Reconstruction* (London, 1981).

Youd, G., 'The Common Fields of Lancashire', *THSLC*, 113 (1961), 1–41.

Unpublished Papers and Theses

Edwards, E. M., 'Crisis in Lancashire: A Survey of the 1720s Demographic Crisis' (Univ. of Central Lancashire MA thesis, 2009).

Hudson, G. L., 'Ex-servicemen, War Widows and the English County Pension Scheme, 1593–1679' (Univ. of Oxford DPhil thesis, 1995).

King, W. J., 'Prosecution of Illegal Behavior in Seventeenth-century England, with Emphasis on Lancashire' (Univ. of Michigan PhD thesis, 1977).

Langelüddecke, H. A., 'Secular Policy Enforcement during the Personal Rule of Charles I: the Administrative Work of Parish Officers in the 1630s' (Univ. of Oxford DPhil thesis, 1995).

Oxley, G. W., 'The Old Poor Law in West Derby Hundred, 1601–1837' (Univ. of Liverpool PhD thesis, 1966).

Toft, B. H., 'Widowhood in a Market Town: Abingdon, 1540–1720' (Univ. of Oxford DPhil thesis, 1983).

Tyrer, F., 'The Poor Law in the Seventeenth and Early Eighteenth Centuries, with Case-histories in Crosby and District in the County of Lancashire', unpublished volume, Lancashire Archives (1956).

Wilkinson, D. J., 'The Justices of the Peace and their Work in Lancashire, 1603–1642' (Univ. of Oxford M.Litt. thesis, 1982).

Wrightson, K., 'The Puritan Reformation of Manners, with special reference to the Counties of Lancashire and Essex' (Cambridge Univ. PhD thesis, 1974).

Index

Note: page numbers in *italics* refer to figures; 'n' = note

abiding houses   7, 9
accidents   182–3
accommodation
   inadequate   101–2
   outbuildings and barns as   145, 155–6
   provided by neighbours   151, 156, 159
   See also cottages; houses
Adamson, Edward   156
Adlington   119
Ady, Thomas   161
Agrarian History of England and Wales,
   The (*AHEW*)   213, 225, 226, 227
agriculture   30, 31, 33, 41–5
   accidents   183
   effect of population growth on   40
   employment   52–3, 206, 207
   floods   208–9
   as part of dual economy   52
   social structure   124
   See also harvests
ague   127, 200, 201, 241
Albin, Margaret   196
Aldenham (Hertfordshire)   191
Aldred, James   140
alehouses   220
ale-selling   138
Alkrington   69, 221, 230
Alleains, Elizabeth   182
Allithwaite   65
Almond, Jane   161
almshouses   5, 172
Aloftus, Simon   175
Alston-with-Hothersall   209
Amounderness Hundred   32, 39, 53,
   59–60, 76
Anglezarke. *See* Bolton-le-Moors
anthropology   23, 24

appeals   10, 14, 87, 89–95, 97, 102, 104,
   106–9, 167
   timing of   206–7, 218
   See also petitions; Quarter Sessions
Appleby, A. B.   218(n21), 227, 228–9
apprentices
   archives of indentures   82
   child   8, 13, 62, 63–4, 64, 135, 152, 224
   unreliable   188
Ardwick   151, 160, 238
Arkell, Tom   114
Arkholme   105, 256
Ashton   148
Ashton, John   183
Ashton, Nicholas   209
Ashton-in-Makerfield   46, 129, 183, 220
Ashton-under-Lyne   57, 80–1, 156, 202,
   222
Ashworth, Jane   236
Aspull, Adam   119
Assheton, John   135
Assizes   56, 61, 77
Astley, Elizabeth   104
Astley, Martha   103
Astley, Thomas   100
Astney, John   65
Atherton   246–52
   doles   249, 250, 251, 252
   employment of physician   250
   female paupers   192
   and Leigh parish burials   247, 249
   marriage subsidized by parish   202
   medical care costs (1710–32)   246–7,
      248, 249–50, 250
   nail-making   46
   nicknames   84
   out-relief   140
   pensioners   174, 252, 252

poor relief expenditure (1710–32)   246,
    247, 249, 250, 251, 252
runaway wife   198–9
types of paupers (1710–32)   251
workhouse   81
Atherton, Humphrey   209
Atkinson, Elizabeth   238
Atkinson, Henry, Junior   159
Aughton, Thomas   176
Aynsdale   157
Aynsworth, Anne   130
Ayre, William   120

Bacon, Francis   201
badges, pauper   11, 80
Bailey, Joanne   197, 201
Bank, William and Abraham   1–2, 3
Banks, Thomas (Bolton fustian-weaver)
    140–1, 238
Banks, Thomas (of Poulton-le-Sands)
    121
Bannister, Margaret   148
barley   30, 42, 43
    as cheap foodstuff   45, 144
    prices   216, 242, 243
    prohibition of malting (1648)   220
Barlow, Jane   119
Bashforth, Elizabeth   210
Bateson, John   210
Baxendale, Ellen   154
Bedfordshire   115, 202(n171)
begging   94, 152, 161–5, 171
    in Civil War   68
    considered shameful   163–4
    effect of compulsory rates on   160–1
    licences   109, 166, 167, 207
    linked with times of dearth   216, 220,
        225
    neighbours' attitudes to   165
    prevented by age and sickness   176
    statutes against   8, 161
    toleration of   60–1
    workhouses as means of preventing
        80
Beier, A. L.   16
Bell, Thomas   123
Ben-Amos, Ilana Krausman   150
bequests
    educational   36
    to the poor   158, 166, 167
Berry, Elizabeth   135

Berry, John and Margaret   119–20
Bickerstaffe   100–1, 129
    Stanley family   123–4
Biddenden (Kent)   191
billeting
    of the poor   60–1, 64
    of soldiers   210, 220
Billinge   145
birth rates   38
Bispham   60, 92
Blackburn   104
    textile industry   33, 47, 48, 231
Blackburn Hundred   32, 39, 76, 88
    child apprentices   64
    report to the Privy Council   62
Blackley   137, 164, 221
Blackrod   105, 133, 184, 236
Blackwood, B. G.   51, 53, 124–5
Blakeley, Roger   107
blindness
    1601 statute on   13
    as common complaint   181
    individual cases   67, 91, 119, 120, 144,
        147, 183, 201
    linked with old age   175
    taken advantage of   188
Blundell, Nicholas   43, 240–1, 242
Blundell, William   161–3, 225
Bolton
    1674 crisis   224–5, 227, 231–4
    censuses of the poor   14, 86–7, 90,
        136–7, 171, 173, 180–1, 203, 231,
        232, 234
    characteristics of pauper households
        (1674)   232, 233, 234
    employment of children   203
    failure of nuclear households   190
    household size   151
    implementation of poor relief   58–9,
        68
    increase in male paupers (1674)   252
    migration from   142
    old age   174, 178
    percentage of households by
        circumstance (1674–99)   232, 234
    petition of overseers (1674)   224, 225,
        227, 231–2
    petitioners from   140–1, 205, 238
    poor relief expenditure (1674–99)   231
    population   40
    provision of accommodation   156

Puritanism 36
Quarter Sessions (1679) 171
refusal of poor relief 91
sickness 180, 182
textile industry and fustian trade 33,
47, 135, 136, 140–1, 231
Bolton Holmes 30
Bolton-le-Moors 73, 74, 75, 87, 135,
224–5
Bolton-le-Sands 30, 31
Books of Orders 61–2
Booth, Robert (of Denton) 195
Booth, Robert (of Manchester) 236
Bordman, Alice 154
Bostock, Jane 182
Botelho, Lynn 174, 178
Bovell, Elizabeth 99
Bowden, Peter 225
Bowker, Margaret (of Manchester) 222
Bowker, Margaret (of Moston) 120–1,
160
Bowyer, Deborah 97–8
Bozer, Ellen 100
Bradell, Nicholas 132
Bradley, Anne, husband of 141–2
Bradshaw 121, 171, 209
Bradshaw, Sir Roger 138
Braithwaite, Agnes
journey from Hawkshead to Lancaster
29–31, 92
parish officers petition against relief
for 105
petitions by 82, 97, 132, 144, 176
stoppage of allowance and debt 144
Brand, Edward, and wife 197
brass industry 46
Bray, Elizabeth 122
Bray, Nicholas 121–2
Brearely, Cuthbert 167
Breightmet 97, 143
Bretherton, Margaret 204
Brettargh family 123
Bridge, Frances 156
Bridge, Francis (of Chorley) 180
Bridge, Francis (of Dedwenclough) 151–2
Bridge, Jane 177
Bridge, Thomas 59
Brindle 92
Brine, Matthew 59
Bristol 16, 44, 149
Broadbank, Richard 95

Brookes, Elizabeth 144
Broughton 100, 124, 184, 200
Broughton-in-Amounderness 121, 129,
183, 234–5
Broughton-in-Cartmel 65
Browne, Anna 195
Browne, James 105, 203
Browne, Richard 163
Buckley, Mary 193
burials
Colne (1670–79) 235
East Lancashire (1668–79) 228, 229
Leigh parish (1720–35) 247, 249
peak in (1727–30) 239, 240, 241, 242,
244, 245
Burne, Robert 176
Burnley 47, 71, 72, 80
Burrow, Agnes 138–9
Burrow, John 175
Bury
administrative divisions 73
child apprenticeships 135
implementation of poor relief 59, 61
orphans 153
petitioners from 119, 142, 176, 236
poor relief expenditure (1697–99) 236,
237
poor relief expenditure (1692–1713)
237
poor relief expenditure (late 1720s)
245, 246
population 40
sub-parochial dispute 75
textile industry 33, 48
Bury, Andrew 150
Bury, Humphrey 120
Bury, Widow 174
Butler, Priscilla 99, 121
Butler, Robert 239
Butterworth, Edmund 224
Byrom, Bryan 146
Byrom, Edward 208
Byrom, Sarah 91
Byrom family 123

'calico acts' (1700 and 1721) 47–8
Callon, Margaret 129
Cambridge Group for the History of
Population and Social Structure 24,
25, 53
Cambridgeshire 16, 141, 201

Camden, William   29
cancer   98, 129, 185, 256
Canfield, Jane   139
Capp, Bernard   199, 200–1
carding   134, 193
Cartmel   59, 81
    billeting   60–1, 64
Case, Elizabeth   66–7
Castleton   99, 151, 224
Catholicism   36, 53, 122, 163
    Recusants   105, 157, 167
Caton   105
cattle   42, 133, 144, 149, 238
Cawson, John (aged complainant about
    rent)   204–5
Cawson, John (of Quernmore)   107
censuses of the poor   13, 174
    Bolton   14, 86–7, 90, 136–7, 171, 173,
        180–1, 203, 231, 232, 234
    Norwich   180, 191
    Salisbury   180
Chadderton   90, 155, 200, 208
Chaigley   99, 221
Chamney, Katherine   195
chantries   5
character, good   104
charity
    and begging   164–5
    Christmas and   165
    Church and   70, 166–7
    as custom   156–7
    effect of compulsory rates on   160–1
    of elites   154–5, 161–3
    at festivities   157
    formal   165–7
    medieval   5
    national appeal for (1649)   220
    of neighbours   94, 100, 120, 127,
        152–61, 176, 177, 256
    petitioners' appeals for   103
    as practical assistance   177
    provision of accommodation   155–6,
        159
Charles I, Personal Rule   59–66, 164
Charles II   74, 75, 187. See also
    Restoration
Charles, Thomas   187
Charlesworth, Lorie   18–19, 102–3
Charnley, Lawrence   118–19, 255
Chatterton, Elizabeth   255, 256
Cheetham   91, 174, 192, 246

Cheshire   53, 57, 72
Chester   9
Chetham, Humphrey   47, 51
Chetham family   154
Chew, Edmund   100
chickens   132–3
children
    abandoned   152
    apprenticeships   8, 13, 62, 63–4, 64,
        135, 152, 224
    cases of hardship   92–3, 98, 99–100,
        119, 125, 129, 153–4, 156, 184–5,
        189, 198–200, 202–3, 204
    as cause of poverty   24, 25, 26, 191
    dispersal of families   151
    economic contribution of   203–4
    employment of   21, 134, 203–4
    illegitimate   37, 95, 202
    marriage of   37
    orphaned   146, 153, 203
    rearing considered as women's work
        200–1
    settlement on   202
Childwall   59
Chipping   104, 122
Chorley   122, 180, 183
Chorlton, Adam, and wife   202
Chow, Mary   119
Chowbent. See Atherton
Christmas   165
Church
    censured for neglect of poor   58
    charity   166–7
    collections   70, 167
    local weakness encourages
        nonconformity   36–7
church briefs   166, 172, 207
churchwardens
    accounts   55, 67, 86, 167
    administration of funeral doles   159
    cases referred back to   94
    Civil War and   68
    discretion of   13
    investigations by   90–1
    meeting of   9
Civil War   66–8
    breakdown of poor relief system   217
    economic impact   217–18, 220
    effect on Royalist gentry   125
    enlistment   197–8
    former soldiers   98

loss of goods 99, 196
 mortality 40
 poor relief reactivated after 215
 Shireburn family and 122
 Stanley family and 50
civility 119
civitas, mandatory 12
Claife 76, 123
Clark, George 157
Claughton 73–4, 100
Clayton, Hugh 59
clergy 36, 76, 117, 123
Clitheroe 71, 135
cloth. *See* textile industry
clothes, second-hand 146
Clough, Richard 155
Cloughe, George and John 188
clover 43
coalmining 31, 33, 45, 51, 52, *117*, 183
Colchester (Essex) 166
collectors for the poor 6, 8–9
collectors of the rates 9
Collinge, Mary 101
Colne 71
 burials (1670–79) 235
 household size 151
 textile industry 47
Colyton (Devon) 192
common land 131–2
common law entitlement 18–19, 102–3
Comsell, John 122
Coniston Water 35, 50
Cooke, Thomas. *See* Rothmell, Thomas
corn. *See* grain
cost-cutting 144–6
cottagers 40, 53, 130, 132
cottages 118, 129, 130
 leasehold 194
Cottom, Henry 104
cotton industry 33, 47, 48, 49
 depressions 222, 224, 227–8
 post-1697 boom 231
 See also fustian industry
Cowper, Robert (of Broughton) 184–5
Cowper, Robert (of Nether Burrow) 118,
 175
Cowper, William 98
Cowperthwaite, Hugh 84
Cratfield (Suffolk) 178
credit 143–4, 197

crime 167–8, 171, 209, 211
crises 212–54
 1630–70 215–24, 256
 1674–75 224–35, 256
 1680–1715 234–9
 1727–30 79, 240–54, 256
 late 1740s 79
 chronology 213–15
 Malthusian 38, 40, 41
 See also dearth; mortality crises
Crompton 120, 201
 census of the poor 56
Crompton, Sarah 135
Crookall, Ellen 91
Crooke, Margaret 97
Croser, Margaret 152
Croston 68, 76, 104
Crumpsall 101, 184
Cudworth, Elizabeth 131
Culcheth 164
Cumberland 89, 104, 106, 174, 218, 228,
 253
Cundliffe, Christopher 143
Cunning Northerne Begger, The 162
custom 103, 156–7, 168

Dalton 81, 98, 135, 145, 204
Dandy, Elizabeth 181
Davenport, Joanna and Ann 151
Davis, Ralph 225, 227
Davison, Grace 89
Dawson, John (of Blackley) 164, 221
Dawson, John (of Hornby) 138
Deane 58, 72, 76, 77–8, 135
 peak in burials 241
dearth
 1594–97 212
 1629–31 216–17
 1636–38 65, 215–17
 1647–50 40, 68, 132, 164, 218–21
 1657–63 223
 1674–75 70, 224–34
 1728 242
 1730 80
 Books of Orders and 61
 and crime 168
 Henry Newcombe on 212
 'social economy' of 215
 See also crises; famine
Debdell, Isabel 159

debt   126, 143–4
    absconded husbands and   195–6
    individual cases   2, 118, 119, 125, 132,
        153, 155, 185, 195–6, 205, 208, 235
Defoe, Daniel   33–4, 114, 115, 134, 255
demography, historical   24. *See also*
    population
Denny, Agnes   156
deserving poor   5, 13, 25–6, 95, 255, 256
Dickenson, William   119
Dickinson, Samuel   165, 186
diocesan population returns   39
disease. *See* epidemics; sickness
disputes
    land   209
    with neighbours   210–11
    property   118(n17)
    sub-parochial   73–6, 87
Dissenters   37, 167
Dobson, Thomas   185
Dodds, John   132
Dods, Anne   161
doles   13, 62, 70, 77, 84, 109
    Atherton   249, 250, 251, 252
    Bolton   233, 234
    elites' provision of   165
    funeral   70, 157–9
    Lonsdale Hundred   63
    for multiple hardships   173–4
    Prescot   67
    Prestwich   70
    and sickness   180
domestic economy, concept of   22
Dorchester (Dorset)   177
Dorset   178
Downholland   68, 102, 163
Draper, Henry   98, 145
Drinkwater, Robert   142
drunkenness   105, 106
Dutch Wars   222, 224, 227
Duxbury   68(n71), 86
Dyer, Christopher   115

Ease for Overseers of the Poore, An   4, 9,
    134, 160
East Hoathly (Sussex)   116
Easter
    parish meetings   83
    Quarter Sessions   206, 207
Eaton, Jean   93, 142
Eccles   68, 76, 97, 175

Eccleston   59, 72, 104, 149, 159
economy, Lancashire   14, 33–4, 37–8,
    40–1, 54
economy, national   172, 204–7
    1670s   225
    1690s   235–6
    1720s   242
economy of makeshifts   20, 21–2, 128,
    132, 156, 177. *See also* 'making shift'
education   35–6, 125, 166, 205
elites
    charity of   154–5, 161–3
    as paupers   121–5, 126
embezzlement, industrial   168
employment   133–9
    agricultural   52–3, 206, 207
    ale-selling   138
    child   21, 134, 203–4
    coalminers   45, 52, 117
    effect of Civil War on   217–18
    Elizabethan provision for   13
    and gender   190
    industrial   134, 206–7
    labourers   35, 114, 117
    migration   139–42
    at Morecambe Bay   30
    odd jobs   137–8
    old age and   134
    service   117, 138–9, 151, 154, 182, 186
    in textile industry   31, 117, 134–6,
        192–3, 207, 256
    unwillingness to work   105, 225
    women and   21, 22, 193, 199–200
    work shortages   217, 227, 236, 238
    workhouses as spur to   80–1
    See also occupations; unemployment;
        wages
enclosure   43
endowments   165–6
English, Anthony   97
entrepreneurs   51
environmental risks   207–11
epidemics   41, 228, 235, 239
    1727–30   240–1, 245, 253–4, 256
    See also sickness
Epiphany, Quarter Sessions   206
Erleham, Jane   203
Essex   115–16, 178. *See also* Colchester
Esthwaite Waterside   1
Ettiforth, James   132
Europe   4, 5, 180, 189–90, 253

Euxton   97, 205
Euxton, William   210
excise   138
Exclusion Crisis   235

Failsworth   255
families
    breakdown   26, 85, 94, 173
    budgeting   21–2
    effect of Civil War on   218
    large   202–4
    nuclear hardship   24–5
    reconstituting life histories of   85
    See also children; households, nuclear;
        kin
famine
    in 1623   30, 38, 40, 60, 61, 228, 245
    disappearance of   38–9, 257
    Ireland   239, 253
    and mortality rates   40
    not evidenced in 1727–30 crisis   253
    report of (1649)   219, 220
    Scotland   41, 231, 235, 253
    See also dearth
Farnworth   77–8, 151
Farnworth, Robert   186
Fawcett, Alice   138
Fazakerley   103, 177
Fell, Sarah   44, 158, 161, 165, 167, 226
festivals   157
Fideler, Paul   18, 115
    on two strands of welfare history   12
Fieldhouse alias Punder, Jane   164
Fiennes, Celia   33
fire   207–8
Fish, Susan   151
Fish, Widow   208
Fisher, Christopher   174
Fissell, Mary   149
Fitton, Thomas   161
Fleming, Sir Daniel   154–5, 158, 161, 165
Fletcher, Ellis   156
Fletcher alias Jovill, John   176
Flitcroft, Elizabeth   160
floods   208–9
food
    imported   44
    prices   144–5, 165, 207, 213, 214, 216,
        218, 223, 228–9, 231, 235, 236, 238,
        239, 241–2, 245–6
    rioting   239

shortages   40, 239, 253
staples   44–5
See also grain; potatoes
Formby   157
Foster, Thomas   100
Foster, William   180
France   6, 21, 141, 253
France, Edward   184
France, Reginald Sharpe   123
Freeman, Esther   147
'friends', use of term   152–3
Friscoe, James   100
fuel, collecting   131, 132, 176
funeral doles   70, 157–9
Furness
    agriculture   42, 45
    begging   60
    billeting   60–1, 64
    charity as custom   157
    clergy   36
    funeral doles   158
    industry   50
    landscape   34–5
    population   41
    tenant right   43
    workhouses   81
fustian industry   47–8, 52, 135, 136,
    140–1, 193, 207
    depressions   222, 224, 227, 238
Fylde, the   33, 34, 43

Garner, Isabel   120
Garstang   72, 156, 239
Garths, Jane   100
Gaskell, Alice   89
Gaskell, Elizabeth   195
Gawthorpe Hall. See Shuttleworth family
gender ratios
    of Atherton pensioners   252
    and households   190, 192–3
    of Lonsdale pensioners   63
    See also women
gentry   51, 117, 117–18, 124–5, 126
Gerrard, Ellin   176
Gerrard, Thomas   2–3
Gill, Margery   205
Gille, William   182
gleaning   131, 168
Gleast, Lettice   147
Golborne   102, 140–1, 204

goods
    loss of 99, 196
    provision of 84
    selling 142–3, 146
    stocks of 7, 8, 57, 224
Goodson, Elizabeth 97
Goose, Nigel 166
Gorton 163, 182
Gough, Richard 11, 157
grain
    cheap 144–5
    exported 44
    imported 44, 242
    licences 220
    prices 214, 216, 225, 226, 226–7, 228,
        238, 239, 242, 243
    shortages 218, 220, 228, 242
    See also barley; harvests; oats; wheat
Grasmere 151, 158
Grayson, Thomas 188
Graystock, Ellen 188
Great Bolton 74, 75
Great Harwood 41
Great Recoinage 235–6
Green, Cornelius and Mary 31
Greene, Thomas 183–4
Gritt, Andy 52–3

habitation orders 108, 224
Haigh 138, 154, 199
Haighton 118, 238, 255
hair, selling 143
Halifax, George Savile, Marquis of,
    'Oeconomy of the House' 200
Hall, Abraham 184
Halliwell 83–4, 246
Halsall 246
Halsall, Isabel 166–7
Halworth, Margaret 144
Hamer, Mary 186
hamlets 71, 73, 76, 77
Hampson, Edward 97
Hampson, Ethel 16
Hardman, Isabel 181
Hardmans, James 153
hardship
    'deserving' 172, 173–4
    multiple 173–4
    single 173
Hargreaves, John 119
Harmson, Anne 137

Harrison, Mary 140
Harrison, Richard 185
Harrison, Ruth 239
Harrold, Edmund 200
Hart, James 200
harvests
    poor 41, 204, 223, 225, 226–7, 231,
        235, 238, 239, 240, 242, 256
    post-1651 improvement 221–2
    as temporary employment 206
Haslam, Alice 173–4
Haslingden 189, 195
Haslome, William 143
Hatton, Sarah 100
Hawkshead
    aged paupers 174, 175
    attempt to tax whole parish 76
    Bank family 1–2
    billeting 65
    common fells 30, 132, 175–6
    female paupers 192
    as first port of call for petitioners 90
    former overseer as petitioner 84
    lodging and burial of beggar 156
    marriage of John Holme 155
    medical care costs in 1720s 246
    Nicholson family 123
    poor relief costs in 1720s 245
    textile industry 50
    See also Braithwaite, Agnes
Haworth, Oliver 203–4
Heal, Felicity 156
Heald, Dorothy. *See* Nuttall, Dorothy
Healey, Mary 99
Heap, Elizabeth (of Downholland) 102
Heap, Elizabeth (of Ormskirk) 140
Hearth Tax
    exemption 114
    returns 35, 39, 52, 88, 228
Heaton 69, 72, 165, 186, 230
Heaton, Elizabeth 101
Heaton, John 144
Heaton Fallowfield 69
Hedenham (Norfolk) 177
Heigham, Thomas 99
hemp 134
Hesketh (beggar) 163
Hesketh, Bridget 196
Hesketh, Henry 105
Hey, Isabel (of Dalton) 204
Hey, Isabel (of Westhoughton) 153

Higginson, Anthony   102, 137–8
Hill, John   224
Hill, Mary   182
Hilton, Henry   142
Hilton, Richard   120
Hilton, Thomas, and wife   203
Hindle, Steve   10, 68, 93, 97, 202, 212,
    215, 220
    on Cumberland   89, 104, 106, 174
    On the Parish   23–4, 89
Hindley   119, 154, 236
Hindley, William   181, 183
Hindley family   123
historiography   15–26
    bottom-up approach   20–6
    legalistic approach   18–19
    local studies   17–18
    top-down approach   15–20
Hitchcock, Tim   23
Hodgson, Richard   99
Hodgson, Widdowe   63
Hoghton, Lady   160
Holker   65
Holland, Thomas   208
Holland family   125
Holme, Edward   164
Holme, John   154–5
Holt, Alice   186
Holt, Ralph   97
Holte, Gabriell   90
Hoole, Elizabeth   99
Hoole, William   204
Hopwood, Rebecca   238
Hornby   138, 146–7
Hornby, Alice   89
Horneby, Alexander   63
Horner, George   100
horses   183, 208, 241
hospitals, medieval   5
Houghton, Ann   167
Houghton, Frances   210
Houghton, William and John   149
household economy
    children's contribution to   203–4
    effect of sickness   181
    male attitudes to housework and child-
        rearing   200–1
    women's contribution to   199–201
households, nuclear   24–5, 189–204
    breakdown/failure   25, 172, 173, 190

circumstances in Bolton (1674–99)
    232, 232, 233
    females as head of   137, 192–3
    size   150–1, 202–3
    See also families
houses
    rents   70, 77
    repairs   208
    See also cottages
houses of correction   60, 80, 95, 98
Howard, John   200
Howorth, Alice and John   141
Howsman, Anne   177
Hoyle, James   92–3
Huddleston, Elizabeth   184
Hudson, James   227
Hufton, Olwen   21, 141
Hulton, William, family of   122
humanism   5
Humphries, Jane   133
Hunt, Thomas   99
husbandmen   35, 92, 99, 117, 124, 126,
    156
husbands
    deserted   190, 191, 198–9
    made to face obligations   202
    runaway   11, 101, 102, 119, 122, 123,
        150, 151–2, 190, 191, 194–8, 198, 205
Huttons, Lawrence   156

Ightenhill   58–9, 72
illegitimacy   37, 95, 202
impotent poor   5, 8, 13, 19, 58, 62, 68, 179
imprisonment   191, 198, 209
Ince   99, 100, 199
industrialization   37–8, 168
industry   33–4, 45–50
    depressions   222, 224–5, 227–9
    employment   134
    and kin networks   150
    See also metalworking; textile industry
Ingham, Robert   98
Ingram, Martin   197
Innes, Joanna   16–17
Inskip-with-Sowerby   182
insurance
    commercial   207
    social   172
Interregnum   16, 138
Ipswich (Suffolk)   191

Ireland
    emigration to   195, 210
    famine   239, 253
    food shortages   253
    loss of lands in   210
    paupers from   150
    payments to widow in   140
    potatoes   33
    and textile industry   47, 48
    wars   210, 235
Irish Cattle Act (1667)   42

Jordan, W. K.   10, 36, 165–6
Josselin, Ralph   113, 220
Jovill, John. *See* Fletcher, John
justices of the peace (JPs)
    Bolton   58–9
    discretion by   13
    divisional meetings   61–2
    documentation   82
    gentry as   51
    Petty Sessions   91–2, 225
    report on poor relief practices (1683)
        76–7
    returns to Privy Council   61–3
    Sheriff's Table   56, 75
    statutory obligations   6–7, 9–10, 11, 66
    See also Quarter Sessions
Jütte, R.   181

Kearsley   77–8, 135, 143, 186
    poor relief expenditure (late 1720s)
        245, 246
Keckwick, Alice   119, 205
Kellet, Jane   133
Kellett, John   200
Kennison, Mary   163–4
Kent, Joan   11, 17
Kenyon, Roger   76
Kew, Jennet   163
kin
    cruelty   160
    extent of   150
    legal obligations   147, 148
    support of   146–52, 153
    See also families
Kindsley, John   154
King, Peter   23, 115–16
King, Steve   11, 17, 24, 87, 149, 150, 192,
    178, 180
King's Bench   77

King's Evil   181, 186–7
Kirkall, James   227
Kirkby, James   68
Kirkby Ireleth   65
Kirkham   62–3, 80, 91, 209
'Knatchbull's Act' (1723)   80
Knipe, Elizabeth   90
Knott, Nicholas   187–8
Knowles, Alice   95
Knowles, Edmund   182

Laborer, William   205
labourers   35, 114, 117
Lacock (Wiltshire)   11
Laithwaite, Silvester   255
lameness   13, 173, 175, 181
    individual cases   70, 99, 101, 103, 135,
        142, 143, 148, 149, 152, 155, 176,
        184–5, 186, 199, 255
Lancashire
    border conflict   35, 107, 210
    climate   34
    economy   14, 33–4, 37–8, 40–1, 54
    Hundred boundaries   32
    landscape/topography   29–33, 34–5, 54
    literacy and education   35–6
    medieval poverty   35
    northern   29–31, 34, 42, 44, 50, 85,
        206–7, 224
    regional variety   34
    religion   36–7
    social structure   50–3
    southern   31–3, 34, 45, 50, 88, 192–3,
        206–7
    See also agriculture; industry;
        population; trade
Lancaster
    commerce   31
    gender ratio   192
    implementation of poor relief   67–8,
        72
    journey to   29–31
    peaks in petitions   221, 223–4
    petitioners from   177, 195
    Quarter Sessions   87, 88, 105, 134,
        156, 165, 192, 207, 221
    size of parish   71
    workhouse   80–1
Lancaster, Duchy of   51
Lancaster, John   63

land
  access to   129–33
  alienation of   130–1
  common   131–2
  disputes   209
  loss of   210
  tenures   43–4
landholding, reorganization of   130
landlords
  bad   119, 205
  property reverts to   130, 194
landowners
  nobility as   50–1
  and tenants' rights   43–4
language (of petitions)   98–104, 177
Laslett, Peter   24–5, 225
Latham, Robert   92
Lathom   90, 105, 203, 255–6
Lathome, Peter   59
Law, Ellen   148
lawsuits, cost of   122, 209
Lea, Alice   154
Leach, Ralph   100
Leathwaite, Humphrey   141, 157
Leech, Elizabeth   156
Leech, Robert   156
Lees, Lynn Hollen   22
legal rights, concept of   18–19, 97, 102–3
Leigh   148, 187, 193
  burials (1720–35)   247, 249
Leigh, Alice   185
Leigh, Anne   201
Leigh, John (of Crompton)   201
Leigh, John (of Walton-le-Dale)   208–9
Leighe, John   59
Leonard, E. M.   16
letters, pauper   96
Lewthwaite, Alexander   102
Leyland   210, 238
Leyland Hundred   32
  cattle-rearing   42
  effects of dearth   216
  literacy   35
  poor relief   62, 76
  population   39
  prosecutions for theft   168
  Quarter Sessions order   75
life-cycle poverty   21, 24–5
linen   33, 47–8, 50, 134, 135
literacy   35–6
Little Crosby   43, 195, 211

Little Hilton   2–3
Liverpool
  charity school   80
  growth   33, 38, 46–7
  house of correction   60
  immigrant petition   93, 142
  industry   46
  poor relief   57
  port   33, 46–7
  workhouse   81
Livesey   99, 141
Livesey, James   148–9
livestock   132–3
  death or loss of   207, 208
  See also cattle; sheep
Lomas, Jane   205
Lomax, John (of Bolton)   91
Lomax, John (of Bradshaw)   121, 171,
    209
London
  appeal for charity from   220
  debtors flee to   195, 196
  financial market   228
  Manchester's challenge to   49
  medical treatment   187
  plague   224
  St Martin's parish   174
  Tudor   5
Longton, Abraham   154
Longworth, Anne   156
Lonsdale Hundred   32
  female pensioners   192
  list of pensioners (1638)   63
  poor relief   64–5, 76
  population   39
looms, new technology   49
Low, Mary   236
Lowe, Edmund   77
Lowe, Roger   55, 98–9
Lowther, Lady   227
Lucas, Edward   152
Lytham   60
  farm stewards' accounts   242, 243

McIntosh, Marjorie   7, 8–9, 10, 18, 56, 58
Maddison, Lawrence   103
Makater, William   177
'making shift'   127–8, 133, 141, 172. See
    also economy of makeshifts
malnutrition   240
Malthusian crisis   38, 40, 41

Manchester
    charitable families   154
    doctor   187
    economy and trade   33–4, 38
    funeral dole   157
    gender ratio   192
    house of correction   80
    opposition to workhouse scheme   81,
        135–6
    peaks in petitions   222, 229
    petitioners from   101, 102, 120, 122,
        137, 144, 155, 181, 182, 187, 188,
        196, 210, 222, 224, 236
    poor relief drive   61
    population growth   39, 48–9
    Puritanism   36
    Quarter Sessions   87–8, 95, 124, 135,
        138, 142, 151–2, 165, 192, 195–6,
        207, 209, 238
    size of parish   71
    textile industry   47–9, 231, 256
Manchester, William   217
Manchester Act (1736)   48
manorial courts   72–3, 164
    records   55
manors, land use   132
marginality   25–6, 52, 53, 113–14, 126,
    228
    of industrial workers   134
marriage
    child   37
    economic advantages   201
    local practices   35, 37
    parishes' attitudes to   202
    remarriage   151
    volatility of   196–7
    women's role in   200–1
Marsh, Giles   249(n114)
Marsh, John   159
Marshall, Dorothy   16
Martan, Margary   149
Martindale, Adam   157–8
Mascuch, Michael   115
Mason, Thomas   255–6
Mawdesley   103, 133
Mawdesley, James   186
medical care   84
    costs of   180, 183–4, 185–8, 246–50
Melling   59, 72, 73–4, 89, 210
Melling-in-Lonsdale   75
men, single   191

mental illness   181–2, 185, 187, 188
Mercer, Ann   186
Mersey and Irwell navigation   47
metalworking   33, 45–6, 51, 52, 117, 246
Michaelmas, Quarter Sessions   206
micro-politics   21, 22–4
Middleton   59, 150, 153
middling sort   113, 114–16, 117, 118–21,
    124, 128
Midgley, Samuel   120
migration   139–42
    seasonal   141
Miles, Martha   208
mineral-working   45, 88, 183, 193
'misfortune', references to   255–6
Mollineaux, Rachel   150
Molyneux, James   121
Molyneux family   51
monasteries   5
Monk Coniston   84, 155
Moone, Alice   153–4
Morecambe Bay   29, 30, 34
Morecroft, James   211
Morecroft, Thomas   187
Moreton, Thomas   199
Morres, Hugh   156
mortality crises   40, 223–4
    1727–30   240–54, 256
    decline in   38, 41
    Scotland   41
mortality rates   38, 40, 41. See also burials
Moston   120–1, 131, 143, 160
Muldrew, Craig   22, 115, 136, 144, 197
Myddle (Shropshire)   11

nail-making   46, 52, 246
Nailor, Thomas   127
names
    clustering   85
    cross-referencing   85
    nicknames   83–4
neighbours
    bad   105–6
    borrowing from   143, 144
    charity of   94, 100, 120, 127, 152–61,
        176, 177, 256
    credit from   128
    disputes with   210–11
    endorsement by   93, 107–8
    exploitation by   188

petitioners consider themselves as
  'good'   119–20, 126
reactions to begging   164–5
residing with   151, 156, 159
uncharitable   160
violent   209, 211
working for   137
Nether Burrow   118, 175
New Accrington, poor relief expenditure
  (late 1720s)   245
New Social History   20–1
Newchurch-in-Rossendale   208, 239
Newcome, Henry   212
Newman-Brown, W.   24, 114–15, 191–2
Nichols, John   175
Nicholson, Henry, and wife   76, 123
Nicholson, Richard   138
Nicholson, William   201
nobility   50–1, 123–4
Noblet, George   129
Noblett, James   103
nonconformity   36–7
Norfolk   24, 63, 177, 190–1. *See also*
  Norwich
Norres, Henry   156
North Lonsdale
  billeting   60–1, 64–5
  petitions   66, 88
North Walsham (Norfolk)   63
Northumberland   71, 191, 253
Norwich   5, 180, 190, 191
'nuclear hardship'   24–5. *See also*
  households, nuclear
Nuttall, Christopher   184
Nuttall, Dorothy   209

oats   42, 44, 45
  prices   216, 226, 227, 242, 243
occupations   117, 117–18, 136
  household poverty by (Bolton)   136,
    137
  See also employment
Ogden, Elizabeth   196
O'Hara, Diane   197
old age   19, 24, 25, 26, 62, 94, 124, 131,
  174–9
  almshouses   172
  as aspect of multiple hardship   173–4
  defining   178–9
  and employment   134
  importance of two incomes   201

individual cases   2, 29, 63, 103, 129,
    130, 142, 147, 150, 153, 154, 204–5,
    209, 210, 236
  mentioned in reports to the Privy
    Council   62
  not an automatic condition for relief
    178
  possessions as insurance against   143
  practical assistance   177
  questionable claims   175
  sickness linked with   175, 179–80,
    240–1
Oldham   48, 160, 227
Oldham, John   143
Oldham, William   175
Orders and Directions (1631)   61–2
Ormskirk
  market dispute   211
  permitted begging   60
  petitioners from   100, 140, 175, 176,
    201, 255
  poor relief   72
  Quarter Sessions   87, 88, 97, 124, 125,
    145, 165, 193, 207
  timing of petitions   216
Orrell, Anne   181
Ottaway, Susan   22(n63), 174, 177–8
out-relief   140
Over Kellet   138, 187
overseers of the poor   8, 9, 11, 12, 13, 59,
  62, 73
  accounts   17, 55, 56, 68–70, 78, 82,
    83–6, 140, 167, 198–9
  allegations and complaints against
    97–8, 101–2
  attendance at Quarter Sessions   108
  Bolton (in 1674 crisis)   224, 225, 227
  books of the poor   83
  cases referred back to   94–5
  during Civil War   67, 68
  as first port of call for petitioners   90
  investigations by   90–1
  look to Quarter Sessions for guidance
    89–90
  recalcitrant   215
  refusals by   91, 92, 171
Owen, Margaret   196
Owsey, Henry   102
Oxley, George   16

Padiham   72, 202

parishes 71–7
 Easter meetings 83
 petitions opposing poor relief 105–6
 size 25, 71, 73, 76
 statutory obligations 8, 9, 11–12
 subdivisions and disputes 71–6
 See also overseers of the poor; registers,
  parish
Parkinson, Thomas 209
Parliament 6, 8, 11
 returns made to 56, 78
Partington, Elizabeth 101–2
pawning 143–4
peat, collecting 131, 132, 176
pele towers 29, 35
Pelling, M. 180–1, 191
Pemberton 97, 181, 209
Pemberton, Alice 133
Pemberton, Elizabeth 154
Pendle 72
Pendle Forest, copyholders 42
Pendlebury, Adam 185
Pendlebury, Alice 211
Pendleton, William 184
Penketh, Rebecca 196
Pennines 33, 34, 42, 53
Pennington 159, 180
Pennington, John 199
Pennington family 146
Penny, Deborah 175
pensions 65, 70, 77, 81
 military 109
Percivall, John 144, 188
petitions 82, 87–96
 archive 14, 67, 88–9
 complaints against overseers 97–8,
  101–2
 correlation with times of crisis 213,
  214, 215, 216, 221, 222, 223, 229,
  230, 236, 237
 decline in volume 92
 descriptions of reasons for 94
 endorsements 94, 107–8
 as evidence of difficult years 96
 as evidence of 'economy of makeshifts'
  128
 as evidence of migration 140
 by former contributors to poor relief
  120–1, 126, 172
 'group' 159

language and descriptions of
  deprivation 98–104, 177
 occupations mentioned in *117*, 117–18
 opposing poor relief 105, 129
 outcomes 94–5
 peaks at times of dearth 218, 253
 at Petty Sessions 91–2
 politics of 97–109
 quality of information 96, 109
 quantification of 95–6
 refusals 91, 95
 regional distribution 87–8
 reliability 106–9
 seasonal distribution 205, 206, 206–7
 self-written 93
 size of sample 109
 social mobility in 116–26
 townships and 73
 written by neighbours or scribes 93–4,
  96, 103
 See also Quarter Sessions
petty constables 67(n62), 73, 209
Petty Sessions 91–2, 225
pewter 46
physicians 187–8, 250
pigs 132
Pilkington 119, 203
Pilkington, Elizabeth 92
Pilkington, Martha and James 195–6
pillage 210
plague 38–9, 40, 224
Platt, Mary 68
Pleasington 130, 148–9, 152, 238
poor, the
 as active agents 20–1
 deserving 5, 13, 25–6, 95, 255, 256
 formerly well-off 115–16, 117–26, 255
 identifying 21, 113
 impotent 5, 8, 13, 19, 58, 62, 68, 179
 'labouring' 114
 undeserving 5, 95
poor boxes 166
Poor Law
 compulsory rates 6–7
 costs 10–11, 79–80, 81
 discretionary interpretation by officers
  13, 19
 as effective safety net 256–7
 increased dependence during
  depressions 225
 issue of settlement 11

marriage prevention cases 202
micro-politics of 21, 22–4
as only one part of domestic economy
20, 22
seventeenth century as turning point
12
as system of social insurance 172
treated as common-law right 18–19
Tudor 4–12, 56–9
uniqueness as national system 4, 6
Poor Law statutes, Georgian
1722 90
1723 80
Poor Law statutes, Stuart
1626 11
1662 8, 11, 19, 71, 74, 75, 77, 87, 224
1685 71, 77
1692 8, 11, 90
1697 80
Poor Law statutes, Tudor 6–10, 56, 57
ambiguity 7, 9
implementation process 10
1572 6–7, 9–10
1598 (39 Elizabeth I) 7–8, 9–10, 12,
58, 66, 71, 83, 212
1601 (43 Elizabeth I) 8, 9, 10, 12, 13,
59, 66, 68, 71, 75, 83, 132, 147, 161,
224
poor relief
1630s as turning point in adoption of
216–17
composite of expenditure in townships
78, 79
establishment of rate-funded relief 66,
81
expenditure (1647–81) 230
expenditure (1670s) 235
expenditure (1710–39) 244
expenditure (Bolton, 1674–99) 231
expenditure (Bury, 1692–1713) 236,
237
high expenditure (1727–30) 245, 246,
247, 249, 250
improvements in circumstances 106
increased spending on (1674–75) 229
increases and reductions in payments to
individuals 77–9
needs-based 172, 173
only paid to small subset of 'poor'
114
redistributive nature of 172

residuality 172, 178
social implications 113–16
types of 77
popular culture 37
population
estimates 39, 78
growth 4–5, 38–41, 78, 133
mortality rates 38, 40, 41
studies 24
Poslingford (Suffolk) 178
potatoes 33, 43, 44–5, 145, 242
prices 243
pottery 46
Poulton 60, 72
Poulton-le-Fylde 62–3, 210
Poulton-le-Sands 121, 210
poverty
causes 171–2, 179
as concept with multiple meanings
114
fear of 114–15
pregnancy 181, 183
abandonment during 151–2, 196
Presbyterianism 36–7
Prescot
churchwardens' accounts 67, 86
dispute 108
funeral doles 157–8
implementation of poor relief 57, 59,
66–7, 72, 89
industry 46
petitioner from 208
Prestbury (Cheshire) 72
Preston
agrarian economy and 33
gender ratio 192
industry 46
peak in petitions (1669) 223–4
petitioners from 188, 204
plague 38(n29)
poor institutions 80
population 39–40
Quarter Sessions 87, 88, 94, 98, 118,
121, 141, 165, 189, 192, 195, 207
school 80, 152
Prestwich
church collections 167
female paupers 192
overseers' accounts 68, 69–70, 86
overseers' investigations 90
petitioner from 160

poor relief cases   173–4
poor relief expenditure (1647–81)   229,
    230, 235
prices
    cheap food   144–5
    cotton   222
    grain   214, 216, 225, 226, 226–7,
        228–9, 238, 239, 242, 243
    high   165, 207, 213, 216, 218, 223,
        225–7, 228, 231, 235, 236–7, 238,
        239, 241–2, 246, 255
    inflation   4–5, 145, 204
    wool   225
Priest Hutton   102, 137–9
Privy Council
    clampdowns on begging   164
    important role of   65
    receives report on dearth   215
    returns made to   56, 61–3, 73
probate records   143
professional occupations   117–18, 124
proletarianization   22, 52–3
property
    damage to   210
    disputes   118(n17)
    women's rights   194–5
Protestantism   36–7
Protestation Oaths   53
'providence', references to   255
Puddletown (Dorset)   178
Punder, Jane. See Fieldhouse, Jane
Puritanism   36–7, 66
putting-out system   49–50

Quakers   37, 167
Quarter Sessions
    appeals process and guidance role   87,
        89–91, 92, 97, 102, 104, 106–9, 167
    awards licences to beg   166
    during civil war   66, 68, 217
    four sittings   87–8
    orders parish meetings   75
    overseers' attendance at   108
    personal attendance at   92–3, 108
    records   55–6, 58, 59, 61, 67, 72, 94
    referrals back to local officers   94–5
    spurious claims to   225
    timing of appeals   206–7, 218
    See also petitions; and under Lancaster;
        Manchester; Ormskirk; Preston;
        Wigan

Radcliffe, Ellen   164
Radcliffe, Samuel   121
Rainford   77, 95, 120, 123–4, 188
rates, poor   66, 70, 81, 160–1
rates-in-aid   73–7, 87
Recusants   105, 157, 167
Red Bank   30, 31
Redditch Heaton   230
registers, parish   6, 10, 38, 85, 139, 156,
    175, 228
    of burials   242
religion   36–7, 104, 105. See also
    Catholicism; Church
Renshall, John   183
Renshaw, Elizabeth   181
rents
    house   70, 77
    market   44, 194
    rises   204–5
    in time of dearth   227
Restoration, the   37, 50, 74. See also
    Charles II
Ribble valley   43
Ribchester   132, 164
Rigby, Anne   175
Rigby, Mary   99
rights
    petitioners' concept of   18–19, 97,
        101–3
    tenants'   43–4
    women's   194–5
rivers   34
Roberts, Alice   100
Robinson, Hugh   103
Robinson, James   175
Robinson, John   236
Robinson, Robert   236
Rochdale
    child apprentices   64
    church charity   167
    implementation of poor relief   59, 62,
        90
    petitioners from   93, 99, 121, 184
    textile industry   33, 48
Roe, Mary   101
Rogers, J. E. T.   225
Roscoe, James   238
Roscow, Adam   236
Rosse, Anne   102
Rossendale
    complaint against overseers   98

employment of children   203–4
expansion   41
industry   48
Rothmell, Thomas   137
Rothwell, Elizabeth   100–1
Rothwell, William   238
Roylands, James   222
Ruggles, Steven   85
Rumworth   77–8, 159
    Petty Sessions   91–2
rural communities   5–6, 7, 114–15, 124,
    126
Rydal   155, 158
Rydeing, John   160
Ryding, John   195
Rydings, Grace   153
Rylough, John   131
Rymer, Nicholas   238
Rymyngton, Elizabeth   59

Sagar, Thomas   209
St Michael's on Wyre   122
St Peter's Bywell (Northumberland)   191
Salesbury, Margaret   99
Salford
    and dearth   218–20
    petitioners from   89, 95, 99, 143, 147,
        152
    poor relief   211
Salford Hundred   32
    high number of 'economic' petitions
        207
    industrial depression   222
    literacy   35
    prosecutions for theft   167–8
Salisbury   180, 190, 191
Salisbury, Margaret   221
Samlesbury   142, 161
Sandholme, John   182
Sandiforth, John   236
Satterthwaite   76, 123
Scarisbrick   164, 182, 187
Scofield, R. S.   240
Scoles, Robert   222
Scolfield, Jane   142
Scorer, Edward   148, 187
Scotforth   67, 163
Scotland
    border conflict   35, 107, 210
    dearth   218
    famine   41, 231, 235, 253

mortality crises   41
price rises   226
wars in   102, 147, 151
Scott, James C.   23, 24
scribes   93, 96, 98, 103, 107
Sedden, Ellen   159
Sedden, George   143
Seddon, Roger   205
Seed, Jane   164
Seedall, Oliver   185
Seeds, Anne   105
self-sufficiency   129–46
servants   35, 117, 138–9, 151, 154, 182, 186
Sessions Rolls   94
settlement, laws of   141
settlement certificate   140
settlement examinations   96
Shackley, James   205
Shammas, Carole   145
Sharpe, James   212
Sharpe, Pamela   23
Sharples   57, 58, 156
Sharples, Henry   99
Sharples, Robert   103
Shaw, Evan   160
Shaw, Jane   103
sheep   42, 208
Shelmerdine, James   160–1, 165, 238
Shepard, Alex   179
Shepard, John   101
Sheriff's Table   56, 75
Shireburn, Alexander   122
Shireburn family   122, 123
Shuttleworth   73
Shuttleworth family, accounts   57, 58, 72
sickness   25, 26, 84, 85, 127, 142, 179–89
    accidents   182–3
    as aspect of multiple hardship   173–4
    failures of treatment   187–8
    help from neighbours   157
    linked with old age   175, 179–80,
        240–1
    linked with poverty   189
    medical care costs   180, 183–4, 185–8,
        246–50
    mental illness   181–2, 185, 187, 188
    physicians   187–8, 250
    types of   181
    See also ague; blindness; cancer;
        epidemics; King's Evil; lameness;
        plague

Silverdale   138, 152, 209
Simpson, Alice   134–5, 175
Simpson, John   138, 199–200
Singleton, John   183
Singleton, Robert   121
Singleton, Thomas   201
Skelmersdale   142, 208
Skerton   31, 134, 175, 185
Slack, Paul   6, 8, 9, 10, 11, 19–20, 23, 180, 190
Slyne   31
smallwares   47, 49
Smalshaw family   100
Smethurst, Robert   153
Smith, Adam   139
Smith, Jane   108
Smith, Richard   24, 149, 174, 178
Smith, William   101
Snell, Keith   116
social differentiation   113–16
social justice   101–2
social mobility, downward   115–16, 117–26
societas, voluntary   12
soldiers   *117*
   Civil War   98, 217–18
   enlistment   147, 197–8, *198*, 205
   former   98, 103, 122
   pressed   137, 198, 210
   quartering   210, 220
   runaway husbands as   102, 191, 196, 197
   and Scottish wars   147, 151
Somerset   61
sources, documentary   55–6, 82–7
   cross-referencing   85
   See also censuses of the poor; overseers of the poor, accounts; petitions
Speake, Mary   104
spinning   22, 52, 134–5, 136, 193
   child labour   203
'spinster', use of term   191(n105)
Standish   62, 72, 127, 166
Standish, Ralph   104
Stanley, Isabel   123–4
Stanley, Ursula   124
Stanley family
   Bickerstaffe branch   123–4
   Earls of Derby   50–1
starvation   40, 218
statutes

against begging   8, 161
   See also Poor Law statutes
stocks of goods   7, 8, 57, 224
Stop of the Exchequer (1672)   227–8
Stout, William   31, 44, 80, 135, 145, 241–2
Stretford   181, 183
subtenants   40, 130
Sudell, Edmund   147
Sudell, Edward   186
Suffolk   178. *See also* Ipswich
Sumner, Huskell   104
survival strategies   127–68
   dependence on others   146–68
   self-sufficiency   129–46
Swarthmoor Hall, grain prices   226, 226–7
Swift, Elizabeth   195

tabling fees   77
Tarleton   76, 156, 181, 239
Tarleton, Jane   153, 186
Tattershall, Esther   93
Tattershall, Richard   239
taxation   10, 62, 109, 231, 246
   disputes   74–5
   redistributive   61, 254
Taylor, Isabel   189, 195
Taylor, James Stephen   139–40
Taylor, John   100, 155
Taylor, Thomas   207–8
Taylor, Widow   102
tenants' rights   43–4
Terling (Essex)   178
textile industry   47–50
   depressions   222, 224–5, 238
   employment   31, *117*, 134–6, 192–3, 207, 256
   entrepreneurs   51
   exports   225
   innovations   49
   trade   33, 47, 49
   women's wages   193
   workers   52, 54
   See also cotton industry; linen; spinning; weaving; woollens
theft   167–8, 171, 209, 211
Thompson, Jennet   209
Thomson, Martha   211
Thornton, Margaret   138
Thornton, Thomas   129
Thorp, John   236

Thorpe, John 208
Thropp, Hugh 211
Ticole, William 149
Tilling, Anne 174
Tomlinson, Richard 234–5
Tompson, John 239
Tonge 69, 120, 203, 230
Tonge, John 120
Topping, Henry 129
Tottington 59, 72–3, 133, 140, 186, 192
Touchet, Thomas 51
Towers, William 67
Townley, Thomas 255
townships 8, 25, 51, 68–70, 71–7, 78, 85, 224
distribution of petitions 88
as first port of call for petitioners 90
high poor relief costs in late 1720s 245, 246
and labour migration 139–40
look to Quarter Sessions for guidance 89
role and disputes 73–7, 87
shortage of records 86
trade
agricultural 44
depression 68, 75
impact of political uncertainties 217
slumps 220, 221, 222, 224, 225, 227–8, 238, 239, 256
textile 33, 47, 49
Troughton, John 256
True Representation of the Present Sad and Lamentable Condition of the County of Lancaster 219, 220
Tudor era 4–12, 50, 56–9. *See also* Poor Law statutes, Tudor
Tunstall 163
turf, digging for 176
Turner, Thomas 116
turnips 43
Tusser, Thomas 143
Twiston 104, 119
Tyldesley 101–2, 107
Tyldesley, Richard 2–3
Tyldesley-cum-Shakerly 103, 105–6

Underdown, David 177
unemployment 95, 172, 201, 204, 205–7, 227, 236
Upholland 89, 98, 177, 238

urbanization 39, 130

vagrancy 8, 257
Vagrancy Act (1547) 8
Valentine, Ellen 119
Vaux, Anne 201
vestryman 13, 215
vills 71, 76

wages 41, 114, 133–9
low 177, 221, 222
women's 193
wakes 37
Wales, Tim 24, 63, 177, 190–1
Walker, Elizabeth 196
Walker, John 130
Walmsley family 51
Walsh, Hugh 199
Walton-le-Dale 160, 175, 196, 200, 208–9
Ward, William 221
Waring, Thomas 222
Warrington
ban on begging 164
industry 46
petition 98
population 39, 40
workhouse 80–1
wars 100, 197–8, 238
Dutch 222, 224, 227
effect on trade 225, 227
Irish 210, 235
Scottish 102, 147, 151
See also Civil War
Warton-in-Lonsdale 75–6, 103
Warwickshire 16, 114, 253
Waterhouse, Isabel 235
Watson, Jane 204
Wayman, Dorothy 105
weather. *See* winters
weaving 31, 33, 52, 136
new looms 49
Webb, Beatrice and Sidney 15
Webster, Thomas 119
West Derby 119, 205
West Derby Hundred 32
cattle-rearing 42
dearth 218
industry 45
literacy 35
population growth 39, 41

prosecutions for theft   168
Quarter Sessions order   75
Westhead, William   90
Westhoughton   153, 200, 222
Westmorland   35, 53, 71–2, 151, 158, 218,
    228
wetlands   34
Whalley
    funeral doles   158–9
    pauper apprentices   64
    poor relief   58–9
    population growth   41
    size of parish   71
    townships   71, 72
wheat   45, 144
    prices   216, 226, 227, 228, 243
Wheelton   148, 187
Whitaker, Ann   98
Whitchurch (Oxfordshire)   178
Whittaker, James   133
Whittingham   101, 144, 185, 196, 236
Whittingham family   123
Whittington   139
Whitworth   167
widowers   190, 191–2, 194, 199–201
widows   173, 190–2, 194
    individual cases   63, 98, 99, 100, 101,
        102, 108, 142, 144, 148, 156, 181,
        193, 204, 208, 209, 211, 255, 256
    See also Braithwaite, Agnes
widow's portion   194
Wigan
    church charity   167
    gender ratio   192
    industry and trade   33, 46
    petitioners from   121
    poor relief   72
    population   39–40
    potato market   145
    Quarter Sessions   87, 88, 108, 129,
        140, 149, 165, 188, 192, 207
    report of famine in   220
    timing of petitions   216
Wilding, Lawrence, and family   125
Wilkinson, Richard   200
Wilkinson, William   105–6
Willasie, Margaret   91
Willasy, Robert   189
Williams, Samantha   24, 115
Williamson, Hannah   187
Wilson, Edward   179

Wilson, Ellin   103
Wilson, Oliver   175
Winchester   164
Winchester, Angus   132
Windermere   29, 35, 151
Windle   81, 146, 208
Winstanley, Hugh   65
Winstanley, William   94
winters   99, 135, 176, 192, 206–7, 208,
    226–7
Winwick   68, 72
witch crazes   37
wives
    abandoned   11, 101, 102, 119, 122,
        123, 150, 151–2, 190, 191, 194–8,
        198, 205
    battered   147
    relief given to   84
    runaway   190, 191, 198–9
Wolfenden, Anne   155–6
women
    effect of Civil War on   218
    friendly society   167
    as heads of households   137, 192–3
    life expectancy   193–4
    literacy   35
    property rights   194–5
    and service   151
    single   190, 191, 193–4
    single mothers   204
    and spinning   22, 134–5, 136, 137
    wages   193
    work   21, 22, 192–3, 199–200
    See also gender ratios; widows; wives
Wood, Thomasine   149–50
wood gathering   131, 132
Woodcock, James   187
Woodhouse, Ellen   100
Woodplumpton   91, 100, 161, 176
woollens   33, 48, 49–50, 134, 135, 193,
    207, 217
    depressions   225, 238
Woorall, John   142, 143–4
work. See employment
workhouses   11–12, 57, 80–1, 115
    Manchester opposition to   81, 135–6
Worrall, Elizabeth   152
Worrall, John   208
Worsley   185, 187
Worsley, John   99–100
Worsley, Robert   57

Worsley family   154
worsted fabrics   48
Wrightson, Keith   23, 52, 113–14, 138,
    157, 167, 217
Wrigley, E. A.   240
Wynwicke   167

Yeamans, Rachel   158
yeomen   1–2, 35, 117, 119, 120, 126, 156
Yorkshire   5, 51, 53, 245
    West Riding   9, 33, 71, 140, 149
Younghusband, James   120
Youngs, John   199

Printed and bound by CPI Group (UK) Ltd, Croydon, CR0 4YY

13/04/2025

14656514-0005